ANYONE FOR TENNIS?

*In memory of John Parsons, the well-respected, and much-missed,
doyen of lawn tennis writers*

ANYONE FOR TENNIS?

The Telegraph

Book of

Wimbledon

edited by Martin Smith

First published in Great Britain
2010 by Aurum Press Ltd
7 Greenland Street, London NW1 0ND
www.aurumpress.co.uk

Photographs: p vi, Fred Perry, 29 June 1936, courtesy of Hudson/
Topical Press Agency/Getty Images; p xxii-1, the Renshaw brothers, 1883,
courtesy of Hulton Archive/Getty Images;
p 26-7, Suzanne Lenglen, 1926, courtesy of Central Press/
Hulton Archive/Getty Images; p 82-3, Rod Laver,
5 July 1961, courtesy of Central Press/Getty Images; p 132-3, Björn Borg,
8 July 1976, courtesy of Popperfoto/Getty Images; p 180-1,
Martina Navratilova during the 1987 Women's Singles semi-final,
courtesy of Allsport UK/Allsport/Getty Images; p 252-3, Pete Sampras,
1 July 1993, courtesy of Getty Images; p 326-7, Roger Federer victorious,
5 July 2009, courtesy of Simon Bruty/Sports Illustrated/Getty Images.

A catalogue record for this book is available from the British Library.

ISBN 978 1 84513 543 0

1 3 5 7 9 10 8 6 4 2
2007 2009 2011 2010 2008

Typeset in Spectrum by Saxon Graphics, Derby
Printed by MPG Books, Bodmin, Cornwall

CONTENTS

INTRODUCTION

As the roof slid over Centre Court, the old traditionalist could only put down his umbrella, shrug his shoulders and content himself that at least Wimbledon was still played on grass, as lawn tennis was intended to be. It was Wimbledon's Marmite moment: the Championships indoors, at night, under lights; you either loved it or hated it. Whichever side of the net you fell, 29 June 2009 was the day the 132-year-old Wimbledon Championships changed for ever. Progress was 40–0 up and serving for the match. As the popular modern idiom has it: Get over it.

Green tarpaulin and efficient court-coverers notwithstanding, there is no arguing that rain is the curse of 'tennis in an English summer garden', as Wimbledon markets itself. More significantly, it is also the curse of Wimbledon's paymasters, the broadcasters at home and abroad, who want nothing less than fresh, live action to fill their schedules. It matters not a jot that Wimbledon has always caught up with itself in the end, bar a day or two, and, besides, haven't some of its more memorable finales been played out on third Mondays (the Ivanisevic–Rafter final in 2001, for example, or McEnroe's swansong in the doubles a decade earlier)? No, the television companies are paying for the privilege and theirs is the tune to which sporting bodies like Wimbledon must dance. Hence the £80 million spent on the retractable roof, closing at a rate of eight inches a second, to provide continual play.

So there we were, past bedtime, a week or so after Midsummer's Day, waiting for Andy Murray to put us – and the Swiss No. 2 Stanislas Wawrinka – out of our collective misery and reach the quarter-finals of the men's singles. Maybe 'misery' is the wrong word for a five-set epic that turned out to be the most dramatic match in the 123rd edition of the Wimbledon Championships. As a piece of theatre, the first full match under the roof had everything to keep 12.6 million viewers glued to the BBC's coverage, not to mention the 15,000 spectators sweating inside the floodlit glasshouse. Suddenly SW19 had become the noisy, pumped-up, rowdy Flushing Meadows during one of the US Open's evening sessions; or maybe the All-England Club had been gatecrashed by stragglers from an AC/DC concert. It was all a bit unnerving. After all, wasn't Wimbledon meant to be a summer garden party, played on grass and accompanied by sun, strawberries and the cream of society? Why had it suddenly become an indoor tournament, played as darkness consumed south-west London and finishing at a time, in newspaper terms, when football 'rewrites' would normally be dropping into sports-desk in-boxes?

It had been at 4.47 that June afternoon that the roof finally enclosed Wimbledon's showcase court. Rain had fallen for the first time during the 2009 Championships, holding off as long as the second Monday for a change, and Ian Ritchie, chief executive of the All-England Club, was itching to try out the new technology. 'We've been waiting for it for so long,' he was quoted as saying. 'It's the first time ever at Wimbledon somebody's [been] waiting for rain.' Of course, it was Sod's Law that the rain had actually stopped by the time the cover was firmly in place. By then history was past the point of no return. Within half an hour play was able to resume in the interrupted ladies' singles match between Dinara Safina, the world No. 1, and former champion Amelie Mauresmo. Once Safina had completed the formalities of her three-set win, it was decided to press ahead with the scheduled order of play, keep the roof in place and allow Murray and Wawrinka to play out their fourth-round match, regardless of how long it took.

As their evening schedule was ripped to shreds, the BBC must have wondered whether the brave new world they were experimenting with wasn't a tad inconvenient. When Murray allowed Wawrinka back into the match at two sets all, it looked as if the momentum was with the Swiss and we were about to go to bed depressed by another great British sporting disaster. But there was drama still to come before we hit the sack. Not least when Wawrinka levelled in the final set after being 3–0 down, and a nation's heart rate climbed alarmingly, before Murray finished the match with a flourish and a whipped forehand down the line. It was 10.38p.m., the latest Wimbledon finish by a long chalk. It may only be a benchmark for the future.

The Daily Telegraph, of course, debated the pros and cons of a night-time Wimbledon as if it were a matter of national importance – which in a way it was, particularly as *EastEnders* had been shunted to BBC2 – and both sides of the argument put forward then are recorded further on in this book. Murray had his own opinions: the hothouse flower complained about the humidity under the dome, likening it to a bath. However, to the millions watching, he seemed to enjoy sharing his bath-time with us.

It was the only time the roof was required during a remarkably dry Championships. Murray would go on to breeze past Juan Carlos Ferrero in the quarter-finals, but would fall short of becoming the first British man since Bunny Austin, in 1938, to reach the final, let alone win it, as Fred Perry had done for the third successive time as long ago as 1936.

———

Finding a successor to Fred Perry has become something of a Holy Grail for British tennis. Indeed, 2009 also marked the 100th anniversary of Britain's last pre-Perry success in the gentlemen's single-handed championship, as it was then known. That was when Arthur Gore, at forty-one Wimbledon's oldest champion, won for the third time in the days of the challenge-round system when the reigning champion had only to beat the winner of the all-comers' competition to retain his title. Gore, incidentally, was a notable Wimbledon character: his total of thirty appearances in the tournament between 1888 and 1922 is another record.

However, even before Perry's first success, in 1934, there were noises being made about the quarter-of-a-century gap since Britain's previous win; the *Telegraph*'s correspondent noted as an aside in 1919 that, incredibly, it was ten years since a Briton had triumphed. Since Perry's last triumph, the decibels have been going up every year as we approach three-quarters of a century without British fingerprints on the silver-gilt cup with its pineapple-topped lid. Andy Murray, in 2009, joined fellow post-war Brits Mike Sangster, Roger Taylor and Tim Henman in reaching the semi-finals but going no further. Henman managed it four times (1998, 1999, 2001 and 2002). His best chance came in 2001 when he was leading Goran Ivanisevic two sets to one (having won the third set 6–0) and leading 4–1 in the fourth, when rain forced the match into a third day. If ever a roof over Centre Court would have been welcomed, even by the most trenchant Luddite, it was that long weekend. Even Ivanisevic admitted that he must have a 'friend upstairs', the rainmaker, who halted Henman's momentum in its tracks and gave the wild-card entry a helpful shove towards his one and only Wimbledon title.

Now Murray is the latest racket-wielder to be burdened with the expectations of an impatient nation. Of Perry's would-be successors, he appears to have the best credentials: he has shown he can take on the world's greats and frequently beat the likes of Roger Federer and Rafael Nadal on different surfaces, if not yet on grass. The first hurdle is winning a semi-final, the second is making the most of the opportunity when he is left standing on the second Sunday of the tournament.

In the interests of equality, it ought to be mentioned that Britain's women have been slightly more successful than the men over the same period. Dorothy Round, Perry's erstwhile two-times doubles-winning partner, won her second singles title in 1937, and was emulated in 1961 by Angela Mortimer, by Ann Jones eight years later, and by Virginia Wade, in 1977, at the Centenary Championships. There is, sadly, no British woman likely to hold aloft the Venus Rosewater Dish in the foreseeable future.

It wasn't always so. British players dominated the first thirty years of Wimbledon. Not surprising really: we invented lawn tennis and it took the Americans, Australians and French a few years to catch up. But once they did, that was it for us.

Though there were forerunners of the game performed for Elizabeth I, and something vaguely recognisable was played in France, it was not until the Victorians adapted 'real tennis' to the great outdoors that the game we know today started to appear. The proliferation of croquet pitches on the well-rolled, moss-free, shrubless lawns of Victorian country houses were ideal when leisured society sought something a little more energetic than chasing balls through hoops. Major Walter Clopton Wingfield is credited with starting the game – indeed his bust at the headquarters of the Lawn Tennis Association is inscribed 'Inventor of Lawn Tennis'. He called it 'Sphairistike', borrowed from the ancient Greek for 'playing ball', though quickly abandoned because it proved almost unpronounceable, and unveiled his patented game at a Christmas party at a country house at Nantclwyd, North Wales, in 1873. Whether he was the true inventor of the game is debatable, but he certainly acted as the catalyst; within two years the Marylebone

Cricket Club had issued an embryonic set of rules. Lawn tennis was first played at the All-England Croquet Club in Wimbledon that year, and two years later the first Lawn Tennis Championship was held. It really did take off that quickly, and its popularity grew so steadily that the first United States Championship was held in 1881. (The other tournaments that complete the modern-day Grand Slam were not far behind, either: the French held their inaugural championship in 1891, and the Australians in 1905.)

Twenty-two players entered the first Wimbledon in 1877, competing for the title of gentlemen's single-handed champion and a trophy valued at twenty-five guineas, presented by the *Field* magazine. Spencer Gore, a rackets player and an old Harrovian, was the first champion, beating William Marshall in straight sets. The final had to be postponed from its scheduled date — and for a further four days due to the inevitable rain — because it clashed with the Eton versus Harrow cricket match, one of the annual events that made up the London summer social season, though soon to be joined and eventually usurped by Wimbledon. At the time, though, *The Daily Telegraph* had not spotted the Lawn Tennis Championship on the calendar, ignoring the first tournament completely, though it did provide extensive coverage of the Wimbledon Rifle Meeting — incidentally, you wonder if the tennis was interrupted by the bangs from the range as it would later be inconvenienced by the belching of the steam trains arriving at the adjoining station. The schools cricket match received two and a half columns of broadsheet *Telegraph* space — the equivalent of about 1,500 words of tightly set text (nowadays it is likely to have just the score printed in 6-point type in the results section).

If the *Telegraph* had sent a correspondent to the Worple Road tennis courts they would have noticed Gore had perfected the art of volleying against opponents who were mainly converted real tennis players who hit the ball obligingly high over the net. Because service dominated so many games at the first Wimbledon, the service line was moved four feet closer to the net the following year as the newfangled game continued to be refined. Frank Hadow had evidently paid attention to Gore's modus operandi because, in the challenge round of 1878, he simply lobbed the ball over his opponent's head and tired him out. By then, *The Daily Telegraph* had caught up with the growing interest in the game and, apart from day one, carried daily coverage, reproduced in full on the following pages. However, you would have required a magnifying glass to spot the brief items, under the capped headline 'Lawn Tennis Championship', at the bottom of a page dominated, in sporting terms, by horse racing, cricket and the aforementioned rifle shooting. Interest was increasing, though: while there were two hundred spectators at the first final, there were 3,500 packed into Worple Road in 1885. The Renshaw brothers, William and Ernest, who dominated the 1880s, were responsible for popularising the game to the extent that a railway halt had to be built close to the All-England Club grounds to transport enthusiasts from the City. The Renshaws' hard, flat hitting, plus a penchant for volleying and smashing, brought a different dimension to the genteel country-house pastime. Indeed William, the younger twin by fifteen minutes, perfected what became known as the 'Renshaw Rush', an early form of serve-and-volley that has since dominated the sport, and which earned him the nomenclature the 'father of lawn tennis'. Mind you, off the court, the feel of a vicarage tea party was still evident: 'strawberries and cream' has become a clichéd shorthand for the refined atmosphere at Wimbledon. It is not a new phenomenon: as Renshaw Junior was preparing to win the first of seven titles in 1881, the *Telegraph* reported that the refreshment pavilion had emptied as the players entered the court, 'for strawberries and cream and even ices ... had no charms for the enthusiastic multitude once the rivals were ordered to be ready'. The ices, though, could barely have melted by the time the multitude returned to the pavilion: Renshaw's demolition of the Rev. John Hartley was so devastating that the incumbent champion won just two games in what still remains one of Wimbledon's most comprehensive defeats.

The Renshaw brothers met in three finals, Ernie forever in his brother's shadow, and the unfortunate Herbert Lawford, a beaten finalist five times, and champion only once, must have wished he had been born in another era. His record, though, of six Wimbledon final appearances is the equal of Rod Laver, Jimmy Connors, Björn Borg and Pete Sampras, and one more than John McEnroe, to put it in a modern context; besides, the distinctive figure in hooped jersey and cap, white knickerbockers and black socks, is credited with introducing topspin to tennis thanks to the unorthodox 'Lawford forehand'. His role as the male equivalent of a perennial bridesmaid was handed on to Frank Riseley and Arthur Gore, who were the unwitting fall guys when the Doherty brothers, Lawrence and Reginald ('H.L.' and 'R.F.'), took over the Renshaws' mantle. The new kids on the block had been encouraged by their father to take up tennis for health reasons, as both suffered from respiratory problems. They took to the game with relish, and won every singles title between 1897 and 1906, bar the morsel they allowed Gore when he beat Reggie in 1901, as well as emulating the

Renshaws with a similar succession of 'four-handed', or doubles, championships, which had been introduced in 1884.

Wimbledon also opened its doors to embrace women in 1884, though it would not be until 2007 that they were considered equal to the men, at least in terms of prize money. It would be through the women's game that the first chink in Britain's domination of Wimbledon would appear, though before that happened we could sit back and wave our Union Flags. As a precursor to the Williams sisters' regular meetings in the finals of the early twenty-first century, the first ladies' singles final was contested by nineteen-year-old vicar's daughter Maud Watson and her sister, Lillian, seven years her senior. The younger girl, in her white corset and petticoats, would win the first two titles before losing, in 1886, to Blanche Bingley (later Mrs G.W. Hillyard). Miss Bingley, a six-times winner, would still be playing in finals into the new century, by which time she had married Commander George Hillyard, a naval officer, county cricketer with Middlesex and Leicestershire, and, later, gold medallist at the 1908 London Olympics in the men's doubles with R.F. Doherty. Commander Hillyard later became secretary of the renamed All-England Lawn Tennis and Croquet Club and director of the Championships. Miss Bingley, however, had to play second fiddle for five of the seven finals between 1887 and 1893 – she was beaten on each occasion while Lottie Dod reigned supreme – though her appearance in thirteen finals is a Wimbledon record, as is the fourteen-year time span between her first and last titles. Her nemesis, Miss Dod, the 'Little Wonder', was only fifteen years and ten months, still the youngest Wimbledon champion, when she beat Miss Bingley for the first time. In their five meetings Miss Dod only conceded one set, but after winning in 1893 she lost interest in tennis, and went on to excel at golf, hockey, skating and archery.

However, the exploits of Miss Dod and Mrs Hillyard would be eclipsed in the pre-First World War years by Dorothea Douglass (later Mrs Lambert Chambers), who won seven titles between 1903 and 1914, a record only surpassed by Martina Navratilova (nine wins) and Helen Wills Moody (eight), and equalled by Steffi Graf. She was even sufficiently fit, in her late thirties, to defend her title in the first championship after the Great War, and held two match points against the twenty-year-old French girl Suzanne Lenglen before losing a match of forty-four games. Mlle Lenglen would win six of the first seven finals after the war before falling out with Wimbledon officials in 1926 when she unknowingly kept Queen Mary waiting in the Royal Box before a match, for which she was mercilessly criticised, and promptly turned professional in a fit of pique. Ted Tinling, the tennis fashion guru, writes lovingly, within these pages, of Mlle Lenglen, whom he had known when he was a doting boy. Like the Dohertys, 'Suzanne' had turned to tennis to overcome girlhood breathing difficulties. With her daring and flamboyant outfits – her dress revealed unimagined flesh at a time when everyone else's body was covered from tip to toe – she brought glamour and interest to women's tennis and became the original female sports star. Mlle Lenglen was, however, the second non-British woman to hold the Wimbledon title. The first was May Sutton, who had been born in Plymouth, but moved to California at the age of six, and played under the American flag. She was already United States champion when she arrived at Wimbledon in 1905, shocking the natives by rolling up her sleeves and baring her elbows, as well as wearing a skirt that showed her ankles. She also beat the British heroine, Miss Douglass, against whom she would also contest the following two finals, losing and then regaining the title. In fact, 1907 was the first *annus horribilis* for British tennis at Wimbledon. In a vision of the future, the men's title also went out of the country as the Australian Norman Brookes, the first men's overseas finalist two years earlier, returned to mark the end of the Doherty era when beating Arthur Gore in the final. Brendan Gallagher celebrated the centenary of Sir Norman's victory with a fitting tribute, included in this book. Though Gore would win in Brookes's absence in 1908 and 1909, the Australian would return and triumph in 1914. Only Fred Perry, in 1934, 1935 and 1936, would thereafter manage to keep the title in Britain. The floodgates open, the foreign invasion turned into an unstoppable torrent.

Lawn tennis correspondent of *The Daily Telegraph* is more a vocation than a job; the incumbents can only be prised away from their life's calling by premature death or retirement. Until Mark Hodgkinson was appointed in 2005, the *Telegraph* had employed just four lawn tennis correspondents in the ninety-five years since A. Wallis Myers became the first in 1909. Myers reigned like a sermonising headmaster, an enlightened despot, for more than thirty years until his death, aged sixty, just before the last pre-war Wimbledon. John Olliff, a former Davis Cup player, took over once hostilities were concluded, but died mid-Wimbledon 1951 – coincidentally, fifty-eight years to the day before the roof closed over Andy Murray – at the young age of forty-two. Lance Tingay's subsequent twenty-nine years' service, bridging the age of 'open' tennis, was only curtailed by retirement, though he continued to contribute occasional articles into his seventies. John Parsons replaced Tingay in January 1981 and was still covering a tournament, the Nasdaq-100 Open in Miami, just before he died in April 2004, aged sixty-six. Their obituaries underline the standing and authority each brought to the position; Myers was even the subject of a glowing, posthumous leader article. Between them they had seen every Wimbledon from the late nineteenth century.

The 'A' in Wallis Myers stood for Arthur. Not that you would have known, until, like Inspector Morse, his first name became public knowledge after his death. His was one of the first bylines to appear in the *Telegraph*, whose journalists had hitherto been cloaked in anonymity. As an active player, who had partnered some of the top players of the day at doubles, he could spot and analyse weaknesses from his courtside vantage point. His reports were long and thorough, full of the ball-by-ball commentary which was necessary in the days before television and radio. He was also a historian who recognised his role as a chronicler of the game. He predicted this tome, nearly ninety years ago, when he signed off his last report from Wimbledon's original home in Worple Road with meticulous detail of Mlle Lenglen's winning shot in the ladies' doubles, 'in case some future historian may search for the closing stroke on a court of so many burning memories'.

When he took on the newly created position in 1909, it was at the end of the era of British supremacy at their own tournament. Improved transport and the alacrity with which the game was taken up around the world were to blame. Myers would often sprinkle his later reports with comparisons to the players of his youth, the Renshaws, the Dohertys, as well as the New Zealander Anthony Wilding, who won for four years in succession before losing to Norman Brookes in the last final before the Great War. Wilding lost his life in the French trenches the following year, leaving hypothetical how many more Wimbledon titles he might have won. The women, meanwhile, did not travel so well, and Myers was able to report on all-British finals until Wimbledon closed down for four years, during which time Myers served in the Ministry of Information (as Olliff would in the Second World War).

When Wimbledon resumed, the world order had changed. Australia, in the shape of Gerald Patterson, and America, with Bill Tilden and Bill Johnston, underlined that by sharing the immediate post-war titles, though it was players from just across the Channel who reigned for much of the 1920s.

With the move to larger premises in Church Road in 1922, the challenge round was abandoned – holders had to fight their way through what used to be the all-comers' rounds like everyone else. It did not stop Mlle Lenglen, though. She may well have won every singles title between 1919 and 1925 had she not had to withdraw, suffering from jaundice, after winning her quarter-final in 1924. France's loss was Britain's gain as Kitty McKane, later Mrs Godfree, quelled the up-and-coming Helen Wills, and then won again after Mlle Lenglen had flounced out and turned professional. The Tricolore, though, flew unopposed for six successive gentlemen's championships. It was the era of the 'Four Musketeers' – though Jacques Brugnon, the elder of the quartet, never progressed beyond the quarter-finals on his own, he was a four-times Wimbledon doubles champion – and five of the six singles finals between 1924 and 1929 were all-French affairs. Jean Borotra, René Lacoste and Henri Cochet each won the title twice, swapping it between themselves like the heroes in Alexander Dumas's novels. They were like characters from another world: Borotra, 'the Bounding Basque' with his matinee idol looks, ever-so-French debonair manner, topped off with his trademark blue beret; Lacoste, 'the Crocodile', the youngest, the most pugnacious, the student of tactics; and Cochet, the 'Ballboy of Lyon' after his childhood calling, probably the most gifted, cool and nonchalant, a magician with the racket. It was a time like no other: a sense of fun and excitement between the wars. However, though Yvon Petra would win the first men's singles after the Second World War, France's record dipped below Britain's in terms of Wimbledon wins, and it was not until 2006 that Amelie Mauresmo finally emulated Mlle Lenglen.

Though the Americans, through Tilden, Sidney Wood, Ellsworth Vines, Don Budge, Bobby Riggs, Mrs Moody, Helen Jacobs and Alice Marble, would wrap up most of the pre-1939 titles, Myers was able to report on significant British successes. Dorothy Round became the first player to take a set from Mrs Moody in her eight successful finals, and would go on to win two singles titles herself, as well as partnering Fred Perry to two mixed doubles. Myers was not perhaps as lavish in his praise for Perry's three successive singles wins between 1934 and 1936, but then Perry did not fit neatly into the public-school-dominated society of the time; maybe if Myers had known they would be Britain's last men's success to date he might have been more fulsome. When Perry completed his hat-trick, Myers dedicated most of his article to Gottfried Von Cramm's debilitating injury, which restricted the German to two games. Von Cramm, beaten by Perry the previous year, and again by Budge the following year, gallantly played on so he did not spoil Perry's success, but what was Perry supposed to do? Perry's Davis Cup team-mate, Bunny Austin, beaten comfortably by Vines in 1932, fared little better than Von Cramm in 1938 when he became the last Briton to appear in a men's singles final. It was also Myers's last final as he died shortly before the start of the 1939 tournament.

John Olliff arrived at the *Telegraph* with an impressive pedigree as a player. He had beaten Fred Perry in the British Hard Court Championships in 1931, and twice partnered Perry to the doubles title there. He had also joined Von Cramm to win the London Grass Court doubles at Queen's in 1939, and two days before his death in 1951 had watched Von Cramm return to Wimbledon, where he lost courageously to Jaroslav Drobny. Apart from Petra's win for France, Olliff's brief tenure coincided with total dominance in the singles for America. He showed a scholarly knowledge of the game, and continued Myers's historical perspective.

Lance Tingay, taking over in 1951, would report on some of the biggest changes, the biggest stories, in Wimbledon's history. The advent of professionalism was already well advanced during the 1920s and 1930s, but it was the promptings of 1947 champion Jack Kramer which accelerated its eventual takeover. Tingay was concluding many of his end-of-Championship commentaries, particularly in the early 1960s, with the expectation that this would be the last amateur-only Wimbledon. However, the professionals had to wait until 1968 to be admitted, and Rod Laver — whom the great commentator Dan Maskell picked out as the best player he ever saw in a Sunday magazine article reprinted here — was only then able to resume a run of titles interrupted six years earlier, when he had turned pro. It was the era of the Australians, initiated by Frank Sedgman in 1952, and continued by Lew Hoad, Ashley Cooper, Neale Fraser, Laver, Roy Emerson and John Newcombe before the well dried up in 1971 — Pat Cash's victory in 1987 and Lleyton Hewitt's triumph in 2002 providing lone splashes. America maintained their run in the women's singles, principally through Louise Brough, Maureen Connolly and Althea Gibson, the first black champion, and later with Billie-Jean King and Chris Evert.

Where Myers and Olliff would cover Wimbledon alone, Tingay found himself accompanied by summer refugees from the football circuit, like Roger Malone and Bob Oxby, as sports coverage in general, and Wimbledon in particular, expanded in the 1960s. The birth of the *Sunday Telegraph* at the beginning of the decade meant seven-day publishing, and Henry Raven arrived to add a lighter touch to the *Telegraph*'s tennis coverage. Lew Hoad, twice Wimbledon champion, was signed up for several Championships to provide his analysis, particularly of the women's singles finals, which in the late 1960s were still held on the second Saturday. In more recent times, the *Sunday Telegraph* was fortunate enough to employ that consummate analyst, John McEnroe, who was never slow in coming forward with his views on what ailed the modern game. Over the years the daily paper has used the services of former players like Fred Perry, Chris Evert, Billie-Jean King, Michael Stich, Pam Shriver and, recently, Boris Becker, to complement its own writers.

Unlike Olliff before him, or Parsons after, Tingay was able to report some success for British players. Angela Mortimer ended twenty-four years without home triumph in the women's singles by winning the all-British contest against Christine Truman in 1961, followed by Ann Jones's fightback to beat Mrs King in 1969 and Virginia Wade's victory over Betty Stove eight years later. He also had to report the boycott of the 1973 Championships by eighty-one members of the Association of Tennis Professionals following the suspension of Nikki Pilic by the Yugoslav tennis authorities for refusing to play in a Davis Cup tie. From his reports, Tingay evidently had a soft spot for the Australian Evonne Goolagong, winner in 1971, and it must have been sweet that his last women's final, in 1980, should be won by the now married Mrs Cawley. He departed SW19 just as Björn Borg secured his fifth consecutive men's singles title, a record for the modern Championships, subsequently equalled in 2007 by Roger Federer.

John Parsons succeeded Tingay in 1981 and would remain there for nearly a quarter of a century during which the women's game was dominated by Martina Navratilova, Steffi Graf and the Williams sisters, while McEnroe, Becker and seven-times champion Pete Sampras would mop up the majority of the men's titles between them.

Like Tingay, J.P. found himself joined by an increasing cast of colleagues. From sports correspondent Roger Heywood in the early 1980s, covering the latest misdemeanour by McEnroe, to features writers Michael Calvin, Lewine Mair and Ian Ridley, to an accreditation list that would grow to more than a dozen by 2009, and include along the way Sue Mott, Paul Hayward, Andrew Baker, Giles Smith, William Johnson, Martin Johnson, Claire Middleton and Kaz Mochlinski. The *Sunday Telegraph*, too, have sent their own team, led at various times by Ronald Atkin, David Miller, Neil Harman and Clive White. A daily diary, later retitled Court & Social, was introduced in the early 1990s and compiled initially by Lewine Mair (LM when examples appear later in this book), who handed over to Sarah Edworthy (SE) and, for 2004, to correspondent-in-waiting Mark Hodgkinson (MH).

Hodgkinson has been fortunate to preside over the Roger Federer–Rafael Nadal era. Federer has won six of the last seven men's titles, and played Nadal in three of them. Their meeting in 2008, spanning sixty-two games, and won by Nadal, his only success on grass, was one of the greatest matches seen in Wimbledon's long history. A repeat in 2010 would not be unwelcome – unless Murray chooses this year to carry off the Grail.

Wimbledon is more than just a lawn tennis tournament, though, albeit the most important and the one everyone wants to win. While tennis is the centrepiece, its *raison d'être*, it is also a corporate event, an integral part of the sporting social scene that takes in Henley and Ascot. Strawberries and cream are the perfect metaphor for a fortnight of overindulgence. It is a time when tennis doesn't just stay on the sports pages; every section of the newspaper has its own take on Wimbledon. The fashion department will use it to parade the latest leisure wear, or unveil what the players will be wearing; food and drink will offer tips on what to include in your Wimbledon hamper; property will preview what's available from the local estate agents and the type of accommodation being rented by the better-off players; travel will suggest mini-breaks centred on Wimbledon, or showcase trips to the other Grand Slam tournaments; gardening will offer tips on how your lawn could look like Centre Court; one of the regular columnists, like Michael Parkinson, Taki, Russell Davies, Boris Johnson or Oliver Pritchett, will take their own slant on the Championships; even Sebastian Faulks, when he was on the staff before becoming one of this country's most celebrated modern novelists, provided an anecdote-filled tour of Wimbledon. Pictures and reports will appear on the front page of the news section, and the diary sections, from Peterborough to Spy and Mandrake, will include little snippets from Wimbledon. There is probably no other event that unites the newspaper in this way. Why, even that redoubtable editor Max Hastings, whose sporting interests did not extend far from hunting, shooting and fishing, always issued strict instructions that the Wimbledon draw must be set out clearly, accurately and with room for followers to fill in the scores, and that the presses be stopped to get that day's order of play into the paper as quickly as possible. Mrs Hastings, you see, was a Wimbledon devotee.

This book does not purport to be a complete or comprehensive history of Wimbledon; rather it is a compendium of the best, varied and notable bits of *Telegraph* coverage over the last century and a third. Some of the reports have necessarily been edited to remove the more routine details of long-forgotten forehands, backhands and rallies. Otherwise the selected articles are largely as the writers filed them, often up against deadlines, in cramped conditions and with rain trickling down their necks. It is not all glamour.

Anyway, you've seen the newspaper, now read the book.

––––––––––––

This book would not have been possible without the help of a number of people. Consequently, my thanks must go to Caroline Buckland, Head of Books and Entertainment, for commissioning this book, and ensuring its smooth progression, and to Aurum – in particular my hard-working editors Graham Coster, Sam Harrison and Barbara Phelan – for publishing it; to the always helpful Gavin Fuller, Lorraine Goodspeed and the rest of the staff in the *Telegraph* library for facilitating the research, and making visits to Victoria a source of enjoyment again; to my trusted former colleague Andrew Baker for his steadying influence, guidance and excellent advice, as always; to the writers, the men and women who for two weeks every year are fortunate enough to be sent out to grass – in the nicest possible sense; and, not least, the many members of the production team who performed the original editing, and wrote the headlines, when the copy first arrived in Fleet Street, South Quay, Canary Wharf or Victoria. They have my admiration and appreciation.

MARTIN SMITH
March 2010

CHAPTER ONE
THE EARLY YEARS
(1878–1914)

LAWN TENNIS CHAMPIONSHIP

The second annual contest for the Lawn Tennis Championship commenced on Monday last, at 4p.m., on the lawns of the All-England Croquet and Lawn Tennis Club, Wimbledon. The matches are open to all-comers, bona fide amateurs. The winner of the all-comers' will have to play the present champion, Mr Spencer Gore, for the Championship and Challenge Cup. The competition attracted 23 entries, the entrance being fixed at £1 1s. Some of the matches on Monday were very close, and a great deal of first-class play was shown by nearly all the competitors.

Yesterday, in the second round, Mr Erskine (walkover), his adversary being absent; Mr Porter beat Hon G. Montgomerie; Mr Hamilton beat Hon. S. Montgomerie; Mr Brackenbury beat Mr C.G. Heathcote; Mr P.F. Hadow beat Mr A.S. Tabor; Mr Brown beat Mr Dalby, Mr Lawford beat Captain Grimston; Mr Myers beat Mr A.A. Hadow; Mr Seymour (a bye). The third round will be played this day (Wednesday) at 4p.m.

LAWN TENNIS CHAMPIONSHIP

Yesterday the third ties were played of the matches on the ground of the All-England Club, Wimbledon. The scores were as follows: Mr L. Erskine beat Mr F.W. Porter three sets to one; Mr C.G. Hamilton beat Mr E.B. Brackenbury three sets to love, Mr Brackenbury being rather lame from an injury to his leg at cricket; Mr P.F. Hadow beat Mr A.C. Brown three sets to love; and Mr R.F. Lawford beat Mr E.R. Seymour three sets to one; Mr A.T. Myers (a bye). All the five players now left in must either save their stake or win a prize. The fourth round will be played this day at 4p.m.

LAWN TENNIS CHAMPIONSHIP

Yesterday the fourth round of this competition was played on the grounds of the All-England Club, at Wimbledon. The match between Mr L. Erskine and Mr C.G. Hamilton attracted a very large gallery, and elicited a fine display of lawn tennis throughout. Each won two sets, and in the conquering one each was five games, and Mr Erskine only won the odd game by the advantage stroke. The match between Mr P.F. Hadow and Mr A.T. Myers was less keenly contested, Mr Hadow winning three sets to love; Mr Lawford a bye. The three left in will take the three prizes. The matches are postponed over the Eton and Harrow Match, and will be resumed on the club ground on Monday, at 4p.m.

16 JULY 1878

LAWN TENNIS CHAMPIONSHIP

The fifth round was played yesterday on the grounds of the All-England Club, Wimbledon. The score was: Mr L. Erskine beat Mr R.F. Lawford by three sets to love, the first by six games to three, the second by six games to one, and the third by six games to three. Mr P.F. Hadow (a bye). Today Mr Erskine will play Mr Hadow in the final of the all-comers' for the Gold Prize at 4p.m.

17 JULY 1878

LAWN TENNIS CHAMPIONSHIP

The final round of the all-comers' was played yesterday on the ground of the All-England Club, Wimbledon. Messrs L. Erskine and P.F. Hadow, the last two left in, had to contend for the Gold Prize, the match being the best of five sets.

In the first the players were game and game, until 'three all' was called, when Mr Hadow went to the front with two games running. Mr Erskine landed the next game, and then Mr Hadow won two consecutive games and the set; one set love. The second set Mr Hadow won two games, then Mr Erskine two. Mr Hadow secured the three following, and Mr Erskine followed with two to his score. Mr Hadow then added the tenth game to his, and won the set by six games to four. Two sets love. In the third set Mr Erskine led off with two games, and Mr Hadow followed suit with two. The next game fell to Mr Erskine, when Mr Hadow scored three running. Mr Erskine got the ninth game, and Mr Hadow the tenth, thus winning the third set again by six games to four, and the match.

Mr Hadow consequently wins the all-comers' Gold Prize, value 19 guineas, and Mr Erskine takes the Silver Prize, value nine guineas. Mr R.F. Lawford has the third prize, value four guineas. There will be no play today, but on Thursday Mr Hadow will have to contend with Mr Spencer Gore for the Championship and the silver Challenge Cup, value 25 guineas, at 4p.m.

LAWN TENNIS CHAMPIONSHIP

Yesterday several hundred spectators assembled on the grounds of the All-England Club, Wimbledon, to witness the match between Mr P.F. Hadow (winner of the Gold Prize, 1878) and Mr Spencer Gore (champion, 1877), for the Lawn Tennis Championship, and silver Challenge Cup, value 25 guineas.

In the first set Mr Gore won the first game by four strokes to one. Mr Hadow then won four running, the first a love game, the others by four strokes to two, four to one, and advantage (twice). Mr Gore won the next four games, by advantage (three times), four strokes to two, four strokes to one, and advantage (once). An advantage set was now played. Mr Hadow won the first game after deuce had been reached twice, and the second, a love game. Seven games to five, one set to love, Mr Hadow wins. The second set was won by Mr Hadow easily by six games to one. The one game Mr Gore secured (the second) was by four strokes to two. The others were scored to Mr Hadow as follows: four strokes to two (three times), advantage and game (twice), and a love game. In the third set Mr Hadow won the first game by four strokes to one. Mr Gore won the next two by four strokes to two each. The fourth game was very close, deuce being reached three times, when Mr Hadow won. Mr Gore won the fifth, after deuce had been called twice. Then Mr Hadow secured a game by four strokes to two, and Mr Gore the two following, by four strokes to one each. Mr Hadow won the next two, by four strokes to two each, and another advantage set had to be played. Each won three short games – games all being called three times. Next Mr Hadow won, first a love game, making him advantage game, and then ensued a very long game, deuce being called four times. Mr Hadow finally won advantage and game. Three sets to love and the match.

Mr Hadow consequently becomes lawn tennis champion for 1878 and holds the silver Challenge Cup until next July.

LAWN TENNIS

The final round of the open Championship was played on the grounds of the All-England Club at Wimbledon yesterday. The weather being fine, a very large number of spectators assembled to witness the proceedings. The players were Mr J.T. Hartley and Mr V. St. Leger, the Irish champion. The contest was very keenly fought throughout, and it was the general opinion of those present that this was one of the best matches of the season. Mr St. Leger, however, did not display his usual form. In the end Mr Hartley won by three sets to love, the scores of the different sets being: Number one, six games against two; number two, six games against four; number three, six games against two. The play of the competitors was frequently applauded. On the conclusion of the Championship contest, a members' handicap, which had to be postponed from the previous day on account of the rain, was run through.

16 JULY 1880

LAWN TENNIS

Great interest has throughout been seen in the Lawn Tennis Championship contest which for some days past has been in progress at the grounds of the All-England Club at Wimbledon. Much greater excitement, however, was manifested yesterday when the winner of the gold medal (Mr H.F. Lawford) and the champion of England for 1879 (Mr J.T. Hartley) played for the Championship honours. Both men may be said to stand at the top of the tree in the lawn tennis world. Mr Lawford recently won the Prince's Club Cup, and played brilliantly throughout the week in the Wimbledon gathering, while Mr J.T. Hartley won at the All-England Grounds last year, and beat the Irish champion, Mr St. Leger. An extraordinarily large attendance honoured the players yesterday, and the two prettily decorated grandstands erected for the occasion were well filled. The weather, though not fine, was at least dry, and the wind favourable for the competition. Four sets were played. The first was won by Hartley, six games to three, and the second by the same player. Mr Lawford won the third; but Mr Hartley, again playing brilliantly, won the last, and thus came out the winner by three sets to one. He therefore retains the Championship for another year. He has thus won the Championship Cup two years, and should he retain his skill sufficiently to carry it off next year it will become his property.

14 JULY 1881

LAWN TENNIS CHAMPIONSHIP

'Youth will be served,' and what will henceforth be known as the 'Renshaw smashes' yesterday took the Challenge Cup and the title of champion from the accomplished player who for two years has held the proud position of premier lawn tennis player of England. The week's play has led up to this event with marvellous consistency. The previous contests had left three prominent players in the field besides the then champion, Mr J.T. Hartley – namely, Mr W. Renshaw, Mr Lawford, and Mr Richardson – and, considering the previous meetings of the gentlemen who were now to fight for the Championship, the issue seemed very doubtful. Mr Renshaw had won the Irish Challenge Cup in 1880, but had failed to show in the last heats of that year in the All-England Club ground, when Mr Lawford had beaten all competitors till he was in turn vanquished by the redoubtable Hartley. But since then Renshaw had made himself renowned, not only by his extraordinary service, but also by his volleying. He came, too, with a prestige from Prince's Ground which it was not easy to overlook, and in the matches he had played in the past week had shown himself so superior to all the combatants to whom he was opposed that there were not a few who believed he must eventually win the Championship. On the other hand, Richardson had in 1880 shown himself a powerful player, and was found in the matches already played during this tournament to have improved particularly in the swiftness of his service. There remained, therefore, much doubt among the unprejudiced, and the great question still was which of the three aspirants to the Championship would beat his rivals, and whether he in turn would have any chance with the renowned holder of the Cup. Monday saw the first of the struggles, Richardson drawing a bye, and Lawford and Renshaw entering the court against each other. At first the play seemed very even, Lawford's service being more certain, though not always so effective as that of Renshaw, while his all-round play was pronounced extremely good. Indeed, the first set went so much in Lawford's favour that he won six games to one, and the general opinion was that his opponent was overmatched. The second set still left the issue doubtful, for though Renshaw was successful, it was only by six games to three. And so the contest went on till the fifth set, when, after a tremendous fight, Renshaw was declared the winner. It was then seen that both in point of service, return, and volleying his play was extraordinary, and that his chances of gaining the Championship were growing. Next day (Tuesday) saw Richardson on the ground in presence of a vast number of spectators, who had assembled to witness the contest for the Gold Prize. The battle was, however, very one-sided, for, in less than an hour, Mr Renshaw had won by three sets to love, and now was left to compete with the champion.

Yesterday afternoon found the lawn tennis ground at Wimbledon thronged with a large and fashionable assemblage, for the young player who had thus brilliantly fought his way to the front rank, and Mr Hartley, who, for two successive years, had proved invincible, were to decide the question of Championship, and it was generally felt that the contest must be a sharp one. If Hartley could but win the cup once more it was permanently his, and there were not wanting many to assert their belief that, notwithstanding all that Renshaw had done, he would be quite unable to beat the conqueror of the best men of the last two years. Renshaw's friends were, however, hopeful, descrying, as they did, in the Irish champion power of movement, quickness of eye, and resource such as they had not noticed in any lawn tennis player before. The refreshment pavilion consequently emptied directly it was known that the umpire had ascended the stand, for strawberries and cream and even ices, notwithstanding that the heat of the sun was almost intolerable, had no charms for the enthusiastic multitude when once the rivals were ordered to be ready. Then it was whispered for the first time that Hartley was not in good form, and that he had been unwell for some few days previous to the match. It was soon apparent that something was the matter, for, although Renshaw had the worst court to play in and the sun full in his eyes, the champion was wholly unable to do anything with his service or to meet his volleying. The rallies never exceeded at the opening of the game more than three or four volleys, Renshaw winning every one, till at last a love set stood to his credit, and ends were changed. With the sun against him, it was not to be expected that Hartley would make any better show. A game was, however, placed to his credit, but Renshaw rapidly ran up six, one after another, and thus secured the second set. Then came the final struggle, for, of course, on the third set hung everything. With ends changed once more, the players took up their positions, and Renshaw, without more ado, won a couple of games immediately. Hartley now for a moment pulled himself together, and playing, for the first time during the afternoon, with considerable skill, won a game; but his success ceased here. In the next game he ran ahead at first, but was quickly caught up, and an exciting struggle ensued, in which, though advantage was called four times, Renshaw continued to hold his own, eventually winning. Five games to one shortly afterwards were called for the Irish champion, and then, serving four balls with a rapidity that absolutely astonished all onlookers, Renshaw carried off the game, set, match, championship, and cup. It is needless to say that the cheers which greeted this achievement were tremendous, and the announcement that an extra game to fill up the time — for the Championship match had only lasted about three-quarters of an hour — would be played between Richardson and Lawford created but little excitement. The interest in the meeting had died away with the great victory of Mr Renshaw.

It is evident now that in the new champion the lovers of lawn tennis have a singularly powerful player. His service is not always effective, for the reason that he seems often unable to deliver the swift balls upon which he puts a large amount of 'cut' without touching the nets, but his under twist service is almost beyond the power of return, and when he sends in a fast ball it is generally so near the line as to perplex the quickest player. Mr Hartley was from first to last unable to deal with either style of service, and failed continually. But the strong point with Renshaw is his volleying. He scarcely allows a single ball to pass him. Now and then of course he moves on, but, as a rule, he catches all that come, and either sends them at a terrific pace over the net, or, failing that, into it. He is famous, however, for what are called 'his smashes', running up to the net, catching the ball as it falls in the air, and then sending it down into his opponent's court at a pace which defies any attempt to return it. It was not long ago determined that volleying may not be allowed [before the ball has passed] over the net, and it is noticeable that Renshaw never errs in regard to this, but he is at the net invariably, and volleys the ball back upon his opponent over and over again, increasing the force every time, till he absolutely beats him out of the court. As a rule, it may be said that Renshaw's success is due more to straightforward, hard play, a wonderfully quick eye and strong wrist, and the power to move over the court with such rapidity as to meet the best efforts of any competitor. In the opinion of good judges of the game such a player as the Cheltonian has not before been seen in a lawn tennis court. This year the men who met each other in the tournament were all round in much better form than on any previous occasion, if Hartley be excepted, and Renshaw has proved himself so immeasurably superior to any of them that he may fairly be regarded as a really phenomenal player.

16 JULY 1884

LAWN TENNIS CHAMPIONSHIP

Once again W. Renshaw has given unmistakeable proof of his superiority over all other players in this now popular game, as yesterday he defeated

H.F. Lawford, who on Monday scored such a brilliant victory over C.W. Grinstead, of the West Middlesex LTC, in the final of the all-comers' prize.

Fortunately the weather was fine, and at the time fixed for play to commence there would be fully 2,500 visitors on the pretty ground of the All-England Club at Wimbledon. Mr Lawford, in addition to winning the all-comers' prize on Monday, holds the championship of Ireland, and from the fine form he displayed in defeating Mr Grinstead on that occasion, his chance of adding the English title to his other victories was by no means considered impossible by his friends. Still Renshaw's splendid play during the season, and his previous successes, caused him to be made a strong favourite, and the result fully justified the confidence expressed in his ability to retain the title he had held for the past three years.

When the players entered the courts the wind blew from the west, with rather more force than was desirable, and the shifting rays of the sun were something in favour of the occupant of the western court. Being successful in the toss, the Irish champion selected this position, and Renshaw gave him the service. This did not benefit Lawford, as Renshaw scarcely ever let him have a look in for the first set, as he placed six games in succession to his credit, and thus scored a love set in the short space of 11 minutes.

The second set was more evenly contested, but again the champion exhibited the better play, as he won six games to four, after 25 minutes' sharp work. In the third, and what proved to be the last set, Lawford played exceedingly well, although on several occasions he was 'faulted' for serving with one foot off the ground. After 16 games had been contested in 34 minutes, Renshaw won the third set by nine games to seven, and the Championship by three sets to love, this making his fourth successive victory. Mr Alfred Schuit officiated as umpire, and Mr W. Jones was referee. At the base-lines Messrs J.R. Dwight and W. Lovegrove umpired. Much enthusiasm was manifested during the match, and Mr Renshaw was warmly congratulated on the termination.

17 JULY 1884

THE LADIES' CHAMPIONSHIP AND FOUR-HANDED MATCHES

There was a very good attendance yesterday at the All-England Lawn Tennis Club Grounds, Wimbledon, when the above events were commenced, and a good deal of interest attached to the four-handed match, wherein the two American players, Messrs Dwight and Sears, had to meet Mr J.T. Hartley, the ex-champion, and Mr R.T. Richardson. The visitors were successful, and both played in excellent form. In the ladies' Championship, Miss Maud Watson showed a decided superiority over the other contestants, and in all probability will secure the prize, unless some of those left in develop unexpected form. The weather was fine, and the courts in good order, and there was not so much wind as yesterday.

21 JULY 1884

THE LADIES' CHAMPIONSHIP

A numerous and fashionable company assembled at the grounds of the All-England Tennis Club, Wimbledon, last Saturday, when the finals of the ladies' Championship and four-handed matches were decided. Weather of a charming description prevailed, and, although the destination of the prize in both events was tolerably certain, considerable interest was evinced in the play. Miss Maud Watson was left in with Miss Watson in the final of the ladies' single, and, after some very good play, defeated her by two sets to one. The four-handed Championship rested between the Brothers Renshaw and Lewis and Williams, and the former were successful by three sets to one.

14 JULY 1886

LAWN TENNIS CHAMPIONSHIP

About 3,000 spectators were present yesterday afternoon at the All-England Lawn Tennis Club enclosure at Wimbledon to witness the competition for the Championship between W. Renshaw (the holder of the title) and H.F. Lawford. The weather was of the finest, and what little wind there was did not interfere with play to any extent. Lawford, winning the toss, served the ball from the station end of the court soon after four, but in the first set could not win a single game, which was called six to love in favour of Renshaw. The loser played much better in the next, and made amends by taking the second set by seven games to five, but Renshaw afforded very little opportunity for scoring after this, as he took the third and fourth sets by six games to three and six to four respectively, and thus won the match by three sets to one (6–0, 5–7, 6–3, 6–4).

LAWN TENNIS CHAMPIONSHIPS

Although the gloomy state of the weather on Saturday afternoon was against the play, still the precautions taken by the executive left nothing to be desired, and when the large company arrived at the enclosure at Wimbledon, they found that the games could be played without much discomfort. Miss Bingley very unexpectedly defeated Miss Maud Watson, the holder of the ladies' Championship, and the Brothers Renshaw had plenty to do in disposing of C.E. Farrer and A.J. Stanley. Mr S.A.E. Hickson was umpire.

Ladies Championship: Miss Bingley beat Miss M. Watson (holder) by two sets to one (6–3, 6–3). Gentlemen's four-handed Championship: W. and E. Renshaw beat C.E. Farrer and A.J. Stanley by three sets to one (6–3, 6–3, 4–6, 7–5).

LAWN TENNIS CHAMPIONSHIP MEETING

Play was continued on the All-England Lawn Tennis Ground, at Wimbledon, yesterday afternoon, with the meeting of Miss L. Dod and Miss B. Bingley (holder) for the ladies' Championship and the 50 guineas Challenge Cup. As was generally anticipated, the result was in favour of the first-named, who, after some good play in the first set, eventually won easily. Miss Dod is only 16 years of age, and, as she bids fair to improve still further, the young lady will probably uphold the title for some time to come. In the four-handed Championship match the Hon. P.B. Lyon and H.W. Wilberforce beat J.H. Crispe and Barrett-Smith very easily, the winners also securing the 60 guineas Challenge Cup held by E. and W. Renshaw. This was on account of the latter having, unfortunately, sprained the sinews of his right arm, which will also incapacitate him from defending his right to the single-handed Championship.

LAWN TENNIS CHAMPIONSHIP

The final heat in the Lawn Tennis Championship meeting was played on the All-England Lawn Tennis Ground, Wimbledon, yesterday, when there was a large attendance. Usually it has been the rule for the winner of the last game to meet the holder of the Championship and play for that title and the Challenge Cup, but this was rendered unnecessary on the present occasion, W. Renshaw resigning, owing to an injured arm. H.F. Lawford and E. Renshaw, who came together for the final heat, therefore competed for the Championship in addition to the 30 guineas prize. The play was not of such high class as is usually the case, although it was close all through, and, in the end, Lawford won by three sets to two, taking the second by six games to three, the fourth and fifth by six games to four. Renshaw won the first by six to one, and the third by six to three.

9 JULY 1889

LAWN TENNIS CHAMPIONSHIPS

Considerable interest centred on yesterday afternoon's proceedings at the All-England enclosure at Wimbledon, and there must have been nearly 2,000 spectators in attendance. By defeating H.S. Barlow in the final round of the open singles on Saturday, W. Renshaw was called on to play his brother Ernest, the holder of the title of champion and the 100-guinea Challenge Cup. The game was very evenly contested until towards the close, when W. Renshaw, who displayed all his old brilliant form, won the match with a score of three sets to one (6–4, 6–1, 3–6, 6–0). The time of the match was one hour five minutes 40 seconds. W. Renshaw had previous to the present occasion held the title six years in succession.

8 JULY 1890

THE LAWN TENNIS CHAMPIONSHIP

With the exception of a shower or two the weather was favourable for the decision of the Championship at Wimbledon yesterday. Some brilliant play was witnessed by the very large company. The match was between W.J. Hamilton, of the Fitzwilliam Club, Dublin, the winner of the gentlemen's open singles, and W. Renshaw, the holder of the title and Challenge Cup. At first it looked as though the holder would still retain his title, but after having two sets to one in his favour, the contest soon assumed a different aspect, as Hamilton brought play to two sets all, and followed it up by winning the deciding set.

19 JULY 1893

LAWN TENNIS CHAMPIONSHIP

Considerable interest was taken in the proceedings at the Wimbledon courts yesterday as Mrs Hillyard, having been successful in the all-comers' contest for the ladies' Championship, had to meet Miss Dod, the holder, for the title and possession of the Challenge Cup, value 50 guineas. When play commenced there was a large and distinguished company present, including a good proportion of ladies. Play of a sound, and at times brilliant character was witnessed in the course of the three sets, but although Mrs Hillyard scored to start with, she was unable to sustain the effort, and Miss Dod upheld her reputation by winning the second set very easily, and the third after a fairly interesting encounter, thus holding the Championship for the third year in succession, in addition to 1887 and 1888. The weather was fine and bright during the decision of the ladies' match, but in the final tie of the gentlemen's all-comers' double Championship it was very dull and a storm appeared imminent. Fortunately, however, although a little rain fell, it did not amount to much, but the light was not good. The competitors were J. Pim and F.O. Stoker v W. and H. Baddeley, and the result was a victory for the Irish pair, who defeated the brothers by three sets to two, some of the form displayed being of a brilliant description. Today the winners meet E. Lewis and H.S. Barlow, the holders.

1 JULY 1897

LAWN TENNIS CHAMPIONSHIPS

The Championship round of the gentlemen's singles was the principal attraction on the card, and it was not surprising to find a very large company present at Wimbledon yesterday afternoon. R.F. Doherty, who had won the competition right out, had yesterday to meet the holder of the title, H.S. Mahony, to decide who should hold possession of the Challenge Cup for the year. The first-named was the more fancied of the pair, and in the result he scored a rather easy victory over the holder, winning by three sets to love, taking the first by 6–4, the second 6–4, and the third by 6–3. The winner played in excellent form, but Mahony lacked his usual dash.

ALL-ENGLAND CHAMPIONSHIPS

In the presence of a large crowd, the Championship rounds in the gentlemen's and ladies' singles, which had been postponed from the previous day, were decided yesterday at Wimbledon. In the former, R.F. Doherty, champion for the past three years, had as an opponent S.H. Smith, of Stroud, the Northern Counties champion. The latter did well at the start, but then Doherty altogether outplayed the challenger, and eventually won the title for the fourth year in succession by three sets to one. In the ladies' event, Mrs Hillyard and Miss C. Cooper, who have now contested the Championship round for a number of years, were opposed to each other, Mrs Hillyard being the champion of last year. A splendid match was seen, Mrs Hillyard retaining her title after a hard struggle.

GENTLEMEN'S SINGLES CHAMPIONSHIP

R.F. Doherty, All England (holder), beat S.H. Smith, Stroud (challenger) by three sets to one (6–8, 6–3, 6–1, 6–2). The first set provided a very keen struggle indeed. Smith won the first two games, but then Doherty played brilliantly, and keeping his man hard at work caused the game to be called four all. He then took a lead, but the challenger improved, and winning the next four out of five took a splendid set. But this time Doherty had taken the measure of his opponent, and, notwithstanding the fact that Smith took the first two games in the second set, and at one time led by three to one, he was given no further chance, as the holder, by splendid play, took five games in succession and pulled the set out of the fire. The third was very one-sided, as, after being called one game all, Doherty went away with a succession of five and won the set in the easiest manner. At the start of the fourth Smith made an effort, as, after Doherty had secured an advantage of two, he caused it to be called two all. Doherty, however, won the next four, this giving him the set and the Championship.

LADIES' SINGLES CHAMPIONSHIP

Mrs Hillyard, All England (holder), beat Miss C. Cooper, Surbiton (challenger), by two sets to one (4–6, 6–4, 6–4). In the first set Mrs Hillyard showed best form at the start, but then Miss Cooper took the last four games, and won the set. In the second, Miss Cooper went away with a long lead, but Mrs Hillyard then came out with some brilliant service, and, taking four games, won the set, the players now being level. In the last and deciding set Miss Cooper led by three to one at the end of the fourth game, but once again Mrs Hillyard played up in remarkably fine form, and caused the match to be called four all. The holder then took the next two games, and thus won the set and the match.

4 JULY 1901

LAWN TENNIS CHAMPIONSHIPS

It was expected that the postponement of Tuesday would affect the attendance at Wimbledon, but it was more than up to the average of the last three days. The excitement was very great when the pairs went into the court, and it became more so when it was seen that the Americans [Dwight Davis and H. Ward] secured the opening set. This, however, was equalised by the Messrs Doherty [R.F. and H.L.] taking the next set, in which they only lost two games, and the third also after nine games had been played. Then came a set in which each pair in turn gained alternate games; when, however, seven games had been called the English pair won one of the Americans' service games, and Mr H.L. Doherty also winning his service game, gave the English pair the set by nine games to seven, and the match by three sets to one amid tremendous and prolonged cheering.

Mrs Sterry defeated the holder, Mrs Hillyard, for the Championship, and Mr H.L. Doherty, with Mrs Sterry as his partner, had no difficulty in carrying off the ladies' and gentlemen's doubles.

2 JULY 1903

ALL-ENGLAND CHAMPIONSHIPS

Although there was only one match to be played to bring this highly successful meeting to a conclusion, the courts at the All-England Club's ground at Wimbledon were crowded with spectators. The weather was again delightful, and the courts, in spite of the wear and tear they have received during the last eight days, were in superb condition. The match which had to be decided was one of the most important of the whole meeting. Last year, it will be remembered, F.L. Riseley and S.H. Smith wrested the title of doubles champions of England from the brothers R.F. and H.L. Doherty. By all-round superiority over all their opponents this season the Dohertys had once more won their way into the Championship round, and the two Gloucestershire players were called upon to meet the opponents whom they so narrowly defeated last year. This time, however, the Dohertys were strong favourites. As it turned out, one player on each side was not at his best, Smith not showing his real form for the champions, and R.F. Doherty for the challengers was much inferior to the player he used to be in his singles Championship days. So it turned out that H.L. Doherty was able to devote his attention mainly to his opponent in the challenge round of the singles, and outplayed him.

In the opening game of the first set Smith and Riseley flattered their supporters, but the Dohertys secured the second and third games. A ding-dong set was witnessed throughout, the holders again taking the lead at the first game. After this, however, the Dohertys, playing with great brilliancy, placed themselves ahead, and won the set by six games to four. There was another good fight in the second set, but the holders lost several good chances by bad service on the part of Smith, who made a couple of double-faults. This handicapped them to some extent, and H.L. Doherty, playing in confident and forceful style, put the issue beyond doubt by winning the last three games in succession, and after being one game down, won the set by six to four. The Dohertys went away with the lead in the third and what proved to be the last set. They won the first two games, but the holders were not yet done with. Smith was seen to more advantage, and winning three games in succession the Gloucester men again took the lead. It was, however, a forlorn hope, and showing much the better form towards the close the Dohertys won the set at 6–4, and the match and Championship at three sets to love.

It had been a rather disappointing game, but there was naturally a good deal of applause, and the famous brothers were warmly congratulated on regaining the laurels they lost last year. That there is a better combination is hardly possible, unless it be that Riseley could take the place of the elder Doherty.

WINNERS FOR THE LAST TEN YEARS

1894 – W. Baddeley and H. Baddeley
1895 – W. Baddeley and H. Baddeley

1896 – W. Baddeley and H. Baddeley
1897 – R.F. Doherty and H.L. Doherty
1898 – R.F. Doherty and H.L. Doherty
1899 – R.F. Doherty and H.L. Doherty
1900 – R.F. Doherty and H.L. Doherty
1901 – R.F. Doherty and H.L. Doherty
1902 – S.H. Smith and F.L. Riseley
1903 – R.F. Doherty and H.L. Doherty

4 JULY 1904

ALL-ENGLAND CHAMPIONSHIPS

This competition was continued in very fine weather and before a tremendous crowd, on the All-England Club grounds, yesterday, the principal attraction being the tie for the gentlemen's Championship singles, between H.L. Doherty (holder) and F.L. Riseley (challenger). The first set Mr Doherty secured very easily, only losing one game; the second he also won, after Mr Riseley had taken a decided lead. Both the second and third sets were advantage, and were won by the holder of the title, 12 games being played in the second, and 14 in the third set. The scores 6–1, 7–5, 8–6.

10 JULY 1905

THE CHAMPIONSHIPS

It is barely possible that Saturday's lawn tennis can be beaten as an event in the history of the game. Before the Championship began the gates of the All-England Club had to be closed; not another person could be packed into the Centre Court at Wimbledon; every inch had two inches of humanity crammed inside. In the little space within the four stands not a breath of breeze arrived, yet the spectators forgot the heat in the play.

In one sense the play in the ladies' final was disappointing, for Miss Douglass was never once on her game. How far the injured wrist was responsible it is impossible to say. In practice the holder of 1903 and 1904 has been playing magnificently; on the other hand, the wrist is needed as an explanation because Miss Douglass is the most consistent of players. It was a surprise that Miss Sutton won in two straight sets, but not a surprise on the play. Miss Douglass never looked like winning. She could not find her length or her accuracy. Her drives had only the ghost of their proper force, and the pace told on her more than it ought. Nothing of this detracts from the sincere congratulations which everyone offers to the American lady champion – now the English lady champion also. She has lost not one set in the Championships or the Northerns, and has played with pluck, judgment, and tremendous energy throughout.

After Miss Douglass had won the first game, Miss Sutton took the next five. Then Miss Douglass made two more, and lost the set 3–6. The second set went 6–4 to Miss Sutton. No one thinks she deserved less to win, because they would like to see the match replayed with Miss Douglass in form. Miss Douglass, out of form, put up a hard, plucky game. Perhaps at Brighton or Eastbourne, if Miss Sutton stays so long, we may see another match, with another result.

In the Championship England took a vicarious revenge. Brookes was at the form of his grand game. Until the last few games he was everything he has been. Following up each shot to the net he was brilliant and clever. H.L. Doherty was better still. The perfect ease of his accuracy and pass was never more noticeable. He passed Brookes – over, to right, to left – dealt beautifully with the difficult service, and played at the ground in wonderful style. Those low volleys were all in order; everything was in order. Norman Brookes has done well, and shown that Australian tennis is everything but the very best. H.L. Doherty has done everything we have learned to expect, and goes on unbeaten for another year. His patience is one of the pillars of his game. Able to kill, he is content to wait; to give rope time after time with every encouragement to suicide. Sooner or later Doherty's opponents grow tired, and bang! the mistake is made convenient to a degree that makes it inevitable.

5 JULY 1907

MR BROOKES BECOMES CHAMPION
Our Special Correspondent

In yesterday's two singles an English crowd experienced the pleasure of hope without expectation, and the blessing of those who expect little. Miss Sutton was altogether too good for Miss Wilson. She was at her best, and at her best her pace and variety of stroke can hardly be beaten. Yet for a long time Miss C.M. Wilson held her. From 2–5 she caught up to 4–5, after being within a point of losing, and though the score was less even in the second set hardly a game was not closely fought, hardly a point was won without a struggle.

Particularly in the beginning of the first set, and the end of the second, Miss Wilson came up to the net with great effect. She missed very few of those net shots, and, following up with judgment, killed on occasion with neatness and vigour. Indeed, her style has rarely been seen to better advantage, for all the time she was changing her strokes, her length, and her position. Her most unfortunate shots were her short ones, both volleys and off the ground. If they had gone over the net they would have been invaluable, but in almost every case they found the tape instead.

At the opening of the second set Miss Sutton was hitting her hardest. The pace was great, and for a time Miss Wilson was forced to a defensive game – tactics which sent Miss Sutton to 5–1. In the seventh game Miss Wilson again tried hard to get to the net. After being 0–40 down in her service, within an ace of loss, she pulled up finely, and when her advantage had been called for the fifth time, won the game. This, however, was her last, and Miss Sutton took the match at 6–4, 6–2.

Perhaps the most conspicuous excellence of the winner's style lies in her treatment of crises. She may be within a point of winning; she may be, as she was in the first set, within a point of letting her opponent make it five all, or even win. But she will go for her shot all the more. She is never so brilliant as when she is just balanced on an edge, on whichever side she may appear to be falling. Throughout the afternoon the wind down the court made the committee-box end much the better.

The final of the all-comers' singles, bearing with it the Championship, has now gone out of England for the first time since its inception by the All-England Club in 1877. We have held it for 30 years, and it has never been in better hands than it is today. At the close of the match Mr Norman Brookes was heartily cheered for a victory well deserved. A strong favourite from the first, he has won his seven rounds by hard and, above all, clever play. In the seven rounds he has won 21 and lost four sets – two to Mr Wilding and two to Mr Behr. Every player and spectator will congratulate the new champion with sincerity. He takes the cup a long way off, but it is a distance which he and his Australian friends have helped to lessen in our minds.

No one who has ever seen Mr Gore play will imagine that he was not game from beginning to end. But it is idle to pretend that he was not completely outplayed. After three all in the first set he never got level with his opponent. And though the match was all over in 38 minutes, it was plain that the pace told. The match should have been weight for age, save that it is difficult as one watches to remember that Mr Gore needs any such allowance. In the first set Mr Gore was all over the court, and he gained the net constantly and smashed with fine judgment. But afterwards he was kept back. The second and third sets went in just the same way. In each Mr Brookes took four games to love; in each Mr Gore made two games upon the end. Usually no kind of break in the service upsets Mr Gore in the least, but yesterday he failed several times to get his racket fairly on to the ball. In all the match he won one only of Mr Brookes's services – the sixth game of the last set.

5 JULY 1909

CHAMPIONSHIP CHALLENGE ROUND

VICTORY OF THE HOLDER

Our Special Correspondent

When M.J.G. Ritchie, challenging A.W. Gore for the Championship at Wimbledon on Saturday, led by two sets to love and two games to love, there could not have been a man in the crowd, over 3,000 strong, who did not consider the match fought and won. That opinion, I have reason to know, was shared at the time by both players. Such a commanding lead held by a man who showed no sign of physical distress over an opponent who was obviously searching for a second wind foreshadowed an early and conclusive triumph. Gore had stated that he would never play through the Championship again; an unsuccessful defence of the title on this occasion was to be his last public appearance in singles. Now, as the result of what took place after he had reached a position apparently hopeless, the veteran will be seen again in the challenge round next year – the oldest lawn tennis champion, born before the game was invented.

Ritchie was undoubtedly the favoured candidate before the match began. His defeat of Gore on the covered courts at Queen's Club in the spring by three sets to love, his form throughout the Championship culminating in his victory over Roper Barrett, his superior powers of endurance, and the holder's performances in practice, had indicated the assumption of the title by a new figure. The well-known tonic effect which the environment of the Centre Court has on Gore's game – he has broken many hearts and records on its surface – was certainly a point in his favour, but his exhibition in the first two sets rather gave a fallacious aspect to this advantage. His lapses were not aberrations of the moment incidental to every long encounter, a netted drive or a loose ball here and there; they were wholesale and continuous, and reflected a man who was right off his game. Probably the explanation for his erratic display in the first half of the match was due to a preconcerted notion that to win at all he must win quickly. Knowing his physical resources to be inferior to his adversary's, he adopted a forward policy, to give him a straight-set victory. Thus he went into court too eager to snatch winning aces by hurricane drives, but, failing to strike his true form, to get into either his strokes or his stride, he became anxious and distraught, and went from bad to worse. The result was that Ritchie had only to pursue a steady game, chiefly of a defensive character, to forge ahead. So long as his opponent continued to beat himself no unusual exertion on his part was required. From a spectacular viewpoint, the match, of course, suffered in consequence, and for a Championship round the standard was admittedly much below the average. There came, however, one period in the first set where Gore, having converted 0–3 into 4–3, had an excellent chance to draw first blood. Ritchie, who was serving, presented him with two double-faults, and he stood at 0–40. The subsequent loss of this game to the holder was a serious concession; it meant, practically speaking, the loss of the set.

The one-sided character of the contest at the beginning of the second set may be judged from the fact that in it Ritchie won his 12th successive ace, and Gore only secured a solitary game. The poor length of the holder's drives, shrewd lobbing by Ritchie whenever his opponent advanced to the net, and the former's machine-like accuracy from the baseline, contributed to this result, barren of a single deuce game. Then came Ritchie's tragic miscalculation. Lulled into a sense of security, with the prize seemingly within his immediate grasp, he began to rest on his oars. The aggressive note in his game was modulated, and gradually died away. Even then the fatal consequence of this slackness was not realised. Gore was still faulty in his aim. The burst of vigour which he commanded had the look of a desperate effort to lessen the measure of his defeat rather than a bid for victory. His title being as good as gone, he wanted only to save his reputation — that was the impression. Ritchie must also have taken this view, for he made no effort to save the third set; indeed, he deliberately threw away the last two games. His idea, evidently, was to recover his ascendancy and chase a tired man to destruction in the fourth set. But Gore did not oblige him by quietly capitulating, consoled with his one set. On the contrary, he took on a new lease of life, hit with greater freedom and a lower trajectory, found that favourite spot of his in the backhand corner, and assumed the aggressive for the first time. There was a fierce struggle for the sixth and seventh games, both of which crucial bouts the holder won, and then 'two sets all' was called. Could Gore last out and achieve a memorable triumph? Was Ritchie so morally affected by the turn events had taken as to be incapable of a final rally? The holder won the first two games, the second after deuce: the challenger, his last desperate spurt, as it proved, replied by taking the next two. Then there was only one man left to fight. Conscious of approaching triumph, the holder played in these last four games, two of which he won to love, in his best and breeziest style. For the second successive year the man whose heart was said to be weak had won the Championship after a five-set struggle.

I append the scores in this remarkable match, which lasted one hour and a half. It will be observed that the holder won 13 more aces than the challenger.

FIRST SET

Gore...	2	3	1	4	4	4	4	4	2	4	0	3	4	0 − 39 ... 6
Ritchie...	4	5	4	1	2	0	2	6	4	2	4	5	2	4 − 45 ... 8

SECOND SET

Gore...	0	1	4	2	2	2	1 − 12 ... 1
Ritchie...	4	4	0	4	4	4	4 − 24 ... 6

THIRD SET

Gore...	3	0	4	4	6	4	4	4 − 29 ... 6
Ritchie...	5	5	1	1	4	1	2	0 − 19 ... 2

FOURTH SET

Gore...	4	2	4	5	3	5	6	4 − 33 ... 6
Ritchie...	1	4	1	3	5	3	4	1 − 22 ... 2

FIFTH SET

Gore...	4	5	2	1	4	4	4	4 − 28 ... 6
Ritchie...	2	3	4	4	0	0	2	2 − 17 ... 2

MR WILDING BEATEN IN THREE SETS

CHALLENGE ROUND SURPRISE

A. Wallis Myers
WIMBLEDON, Saturday

Mr Norman Brookes, whom one may term the Australian Achilles – brave, impatient of command, and relentless – achieved a memorable triumph at Wimbledon today. In a challenge round of only 70 minutes, before 6,000 spectators, who had anticipated an exactly opposite result, he beat Mr Wilding, the holder of the title, by three sets to love, and regained the Championship which, on his last visit to England, he had held seven years ago.

Though a New Zealander by birth – his father was a well-known West of England sportsman before he migrated to Christchurch – Mr Wilding was almost a home-bred champion, who had learned wisdom from the lips and his strokes from the hand of former English champions. Hence by nine people out of ten he was regarded as the custodian of something more personal than his own prestige; he was the last English bulwark, against which it was hoped the Australian invader would hurl himself in vain.

In justice to the holder I think it may be said that he was at some disadvantage in not 'playing through'. It is the champion's prerogative to be spared the stress and strain of the eliminating competition, but the relief is not so valuable as it looks. Indeed, I believe the embarrassed start of Mr Wilding – which gave his opponent the first four games almost without a struggle – was due appreciably to the fact that he was playing his first singles match on the Centre Court for 12 months. He had enjoyed many practice games on it, of course, but these always took place in the morning, with the sun at a different angle, and without the disturbing music of crowds.

As soon as I saw Wilding serve and Brookes return in the first game, the feeling came that the match would develop on unexpected lines. In the first case the ball was hit without purpose and without confidence; in the second, every shot seemed to carry the authority of decision. And when the challenger had taken his own service game from 30, had won Wilding's from 0–30, and had then crossed to the bad side, with the sun in his eyes, and secured the fourth game from 15, one did not see how the holder could save the first set. However, he nearly drew level at four all. Wilding's stout heart (he has been a passenger in an aeroplane which had engine trouble in mid-air) was coming to his rescue; he was beginning to see through the glare; and, like one of the King's cream-coloured ponies that draws the Coronation coach, was getting his ears accustomed to the buzz around him. Here are the figures of the first set:

FIRST SET

Brookes	4	4	5	4	3	2	2	5	2	5 – 36 … 6
Wilding	2	2	3	1	5	4	4	3	4	3 – 31 … 4

The Australian's methods up to now, and, indeed, all through the match, were similar in design and results to those employed by Mr Beals Wright, also a left-hander, in the final of 1910, when the American also encountered Mr Wilding. That is to say, he attacked from start to finish, and attacked at close range, where the subtlety of his volleying could be best exploited, and where its demoralising influence on his opponent's game could be best exercised.

The second set went with the service up to 4–4, the holder having the lead at 1–0, 2–1, 3–2, and 4–3. He was 40–15 in the ninth game, but then Brookes hit two fine forehand drives off the service – drives which led up, after a few exchanges, to his favourite winning volley, a forehand slice. Once level, he did not let the game go. Wilding braced from 0–40 to deuce in the next game, but the effort was not sustained.

The third set was noteworthy for the Australian's fine play at the back of the court. Pausing a little, he let Wilding come to the net and gain a 2–0 lead. Brookes won the third and fourth games from 15, and led 4–3, but the champion averted a 5–3 by courageous driving, and himself went ahead at 5–4. It was in the next three games that Brookes played so well when away from the net which was his base. He answered Wilding's hardest forehand drives with shots just as severe and more intelligently placed. Deuce was called once in the tenth game – Brookes had one lucky net-cord – but Wilding was never in a stroke of the set. He saved match point twice in the 12th game, once with a cool-headed volley. On the other occasion Brookes volleyed a foot out down the line. The third time was the last time – a drop which the champion could not reach. The strokes in the second and third sets are appended:

SECOND SET

Brookes	1	4	4	4	1	4	3	4	7	5 – 37 … 6
Wilding	4	0	2	6	4	2	5	2	5	3 – 33 … 4

THIRD SET

Brookes	2	1	4	4	2	4	4	3	5	5	4	7	— 45 ... 7
Wilding	5	4	1	1	4	0	2	5	7	3	2	5	— 39 ... 5

Mr Brookes was warmly applauded by the crowd. Outside the courts jubilant Australians gathered, and Champagne flowed in his honour. But because, in the racecourse sense, the favourite was beaten, the majority of the onlookers were singularly quiet. They could not quite make head or tail of it all. They forgot that men are not machines, and that lawn tennis is a game in which psychology plays a leading part. I hazard the belief that every time the ball left Mr Brookes's racket, held by his hand, it carried with it to his opponent a current of the Australian personality. Every winning volley increased the voltage of this current.

The other matches included a challenge round of the ladies' singles. In an excellent contest, Mrs Larcombe just failed to win a set against Mrs Chambers. She rallied from 2–5 to 5–5 in the first, and led 4–3 in the second, and the difference in the aggregate of strokes was only ten; but the holder's cross drives, demanding an excursion on the part of her opponent, had slightly more accuracy and depth than those of Mrs Larcombe. Mrs Chambers also had an advantage in service which she employed in the critical games. By winning the title for the seventh time, Mrs Chambers eclipses Mrs Hillyard's record.

CHAPTER TWO
BETWEEN THE WARS
(1919–39)

MLLE LENGLEN'S VICTORY

KING AND QUEEN PRESENT

Our Special Correspondent

WIMBLEDON, Saturday

The greatest ladies' challenge round in the history of lawn tennis! After 20 years' experience of the game in many countries and amid many vicissitudes, the historian has need for circumspection, but one may safely declare that the match between Mrs Lambert Chambers and Mlle Lenglen on the Centre Court today has never been equalled in the high quality of its play, the sustained uncertainty of its issue, and the tense excitement of its finish. The circumstances surrounding this contest were unique; so were the attendant attributes. On the one hand was a British player who had won the blue riband of the lawn on seven occasions, and had not been beaten at Wimbledon for 11 years – a lady who, if she had retained her title today, would have retired from singles with a record superior to that of Willie Renshaw on the men's side; on the other a young French girl, born in the devastated province of Picardy, who had brought her racket across the Channel for the first time, and who was playing on a surface and before a crowd foreign to her nature, and perhaps inimical to her training.

Small wonder that a contest between these two to decide the world's Championship should have expressed the culminating interest in a Championship meeting already remarkable for its popular appeal and its cosmopolitan competition; nor that the relatively small resources of the All-England ground – almost a miniature arena beside the giant stadium at Forest Hills, New York – should have been strained to the uttermost; nor that, when the vast throng discovered to their great delight that the King and Queen, paying a surprise visit with their daughter, shared the intense enthusiasm of their subjects, the occasion was felt to be altogether unprecedented.

The advent of the Royal party had wisely, in view of the crowded ground, been kept a secret by the executive. His Majesty had let it be known to Commander Hillyard, RN, (with whom he served as a middy on the *Britannia*) that he desired no ceremony; that he came in a private capacity, as a former president of the All-England Club. It is well known, too, that Princess Mary is a player of considerable promise, and has witnessed matches at Queen's Club. Motoring down from London after the victory march of London troops, the distinguished visitors arrived shortly after three o'clock, during the progress of a doubles in which two Australians, a New Zealander, and an Englishman were participating. Their appearance in the committee box (of which Lord Curzon, Admiral Beatty, and Mr Hughes were also occupants during the afternoon) was met with a burst of cheering from nearly 10,000 throats, the match being 'held up' while the ovation lasted. The King, who was in civilian dress, raised his brown bowler hat repeatedly in response, while the Queen (wearing cornflower blue) and Princess Mary (in a white coat and skirt with a torque in blue) smiled their acknowledgements with obvious pleasure. No spectators in the vast throng watched the ladies' match with keener zest or closer attention. During its tense stages, when the issue hung on a single stroke, the King and the Princess by his side did not attempt to conceal their excitement. His Majesty, who had removed his hat, leaned eagerly forward in his seat, applauding heartily at the end of every long rally – impartially, it goes without saying. That he enjoyed the experience and was amazed at the skill and endurance of both ladies was evidenced not only by what he said afterwards, but by his exclamations during the contest. When they left, after a stay of over an hour and a half, the King, Queen and the Princess – escorted to their motor by Mr H. Wilson Fox, MP (president of the club), and Commander Hillyard – were given another popular reception. I may add that at the conclusion of the match his Majesty expressed a desire to congratulate both the winner and the loser on their splendid and courageous fight. A message was sent to the dressing-room, to which the exhausted rivals had repaired, but it was understood neither was then in a condition to reappear – and after what both had gone through one is not in the least surprised.

Level in score though the players were at one set all, the odds at that point seemed to favour the English defender. She appeared to be less distressed physically than her opponent – Mlle Lenglen had to send for brandy at the interval, and she asked a linesman to vacate his seat so that she might rest for a period rather beyond the normal – and the champion's game was so well under control and so free from lapse that English hopes were raised. These were dashed, however, when the challenger, drawing fresh vitality from some hidden springs, went to 4–1 in the final set. She had been a little lucky – a net-cord in the fourth and a double-fault in the fifth game – but the vigour and resourcefulness of her play were undeniable. Most of the games had gone to deuce. The sixth game, however, Mrs Chambers won to love, her service gaining an unexpected speed. A spectator called out in the seventh game, Mlle Lenglen sacrificed a critical point, and 4–3 was called. Fine passing shots, pulled out on the run, brought the champion to 4–4; there was nothing in the match. A love game to Mrs Chambers against her opponent's service looked to be a winning lead; the challenger, nothing daunted, replied with a love game. Five all!

The crowd were now worked up to a pitch of the tensest excitement, and the umpire had to call for silence during the rallies. You could almost have heard a pin drop on the turf while the ball was speeding backwards and forwards during the next rally, while 10,000 pairs of eyes were glued on the players. A long deuce game, and Mlle Lenglen drove out; 6–5 to Mrs Chambers. She went to 40–15 in the next game – twice within an ace of the match. It seemed morally certain she would be receiving the congratulations of her friends a moment later. Mlle Lenglen had come to the net on a deep drive; the champion's return from a cross volley appeared to be going out of reach. The French racket went out desperately, the ball hit the wood and went over – a lucky and misshapen stop volley. Another gruelling volley, won by the French girl, brought her to deuce; once more they were level. From that dread moment she moved forward steadily to victory. She was 7–6 from 15, and 8–7 from a service now inspired. The 16th game she took to love, and the long tension was over. The scores were 10–8, 4–6, 9–7.

As soon as she was sure of her Championship, won under such desperate conditions, Mlle Lenglen swept off her soft white hat and rushed forward, with streaming locks, to shake hands with her opponent. It was her great moment of triumph, and she may be pardoned exultation. Kissed on the court by one of her countrymen, she was overwhelmed by her parents when she emerged, pressed on all sides, through the corridor. I have witnessed M. Lenglen's devotion for several years – it is sometimes embarrassing to tournament executives – but his joy on this occasion was ecstatic. The deliverance of France's lost provinces did not produce stronger emotion than the deliverance of Suzanne from what looked like certain defeat. I heard nothing but praise for Mrs Chambers's splendid and heroic defence. On the whole, I think she had a little the worst of the luck; but on a day when both ladies were so obviously at the top of their form, luck must come in somewhere.

8 JULY 1919

PATTERSON WINS SINGLES

THREE-SET VICTORY

Our Special Correspondent
WIMBLEDON, Monday

The sands of Wimbledon have almost run out. Today, on its third Monday, another young champion came into his own at the expense of an old. Gerald Patterson defeated Norman Brookes in the challenge round of the singles Championship by three sets to love, and one's instant conviction that a new generation of players had come in with the war's close was confirmed. The theory that a man over 40 possesses the quickness of eye or limb to compass the modern attacking game was always physiologically unsound. It survived in this country because our older men, stoical in adversity and supremely steady in defence, could exploit their strategy at the expense of temperamental deficiencies or unmatured volleying skill. Patterson might exchange his ground strokes with several English players and be a sounder model for youth to imitate, but his service, complementary volleying, and lobbing proved enough in themselves to win the Championship, and these weapons, coolly directed by an unruffled mind, suggest that the qualities of youth and athletic fitness will henceforward dominate the game.

That the holder had shed much of his pace of foot and ball since his victory over Wilding in 1914 could escape no discerning eye. He had shown this decline in doubles since his arrival; his form in practice singles did not inspire his supporters with any great confidence. Today he was clearly outpaced and outfooted. He won only two of his opponent's service games throughout the match, and these with difficulty. He frequently mistimed volleys and tossed out of court; at least four times he missed simple shots with the court open before him. This was not Championship form, and did not deserve to win; it was not the form of 1907, still less was it the form of 1914. In short, the great career of Norman Brookes on the courts – and perhaps no career has been more notable, for it synchronised with the tremendous advance in attack – must now be regarded retrospectively. His mantle was passed today to a fellow-townsman. Melbourne produced the first successful invader of Wimbledon. It has now furnished another, who, in taking the title, has deposed the first. It comes rather as a shock to realise that no Englishman has won the Championship for ten years.

2 JULY 1920

THE LADY CHAMPION

MLLE LENGLEN RETAINS TITLE

A. Wallis Myers CBE

Mlle Suzanne Lenglen is still the lady champion. A year ago, when she first entered the lists at Wimbledon, she played Mrs Lambert Chambers, the holder, a match of 40 games – a struggle so keen and level that none saw the end until the final stroke. The champion was then within a point – twice within a point, to be accurate – of saving her title, and, who shall say, of retiring with it after a great career. This year, to everyone's keen delight, Mrs Chambers re-entered the all-comers', in which she had last competed seven years ago, and showed her undecaying talent by winning it, losing only one set on the way. Thus she exchanged shoes with Mlle Lenglen – hers were those of the challenger, the French girl, many years her junior, wore those of the holder. A vast throng gathered in a dun light, threatening rain, to see this great return battle. It was more than France against England. It was a debate, with the whole of the lawn tennis world listening, to settle an issue that, by the score, had been adjourned 12 months ago.

Last year 40 momentous games! This year, only 15, and only four of them, the first four, waged between equal parties. At 5–2 Mrs Chambers won another game; that was her last; the holder took the second set to love and the match with perfect ease and confidence. Was Mrs Chambers herself? She certainly did not give her friends that impression, for her driving had neither its sting nor its length of Wednesday, and she seemed to get worse as the match developed. I can only assume something ailed her, and that she was not able to exert the physical effort requisite for a strenuous match of this kind. Had the challenger been quite fit, she must have made a better fight; I do not think she could have won on the form which Mlle Lenglen displayed yesterday. Every stroke included in the lawn tennis repertoire (if we exclude the Tildenian slam) was exploited by the French girl with delightful ease and elegance. She did not once falter, and when she had put the first set behind her, conscious of its moral support, the variety of her play and her confidence both, Gallic fashion, increased. Poor as her rival became in the last few games, accommodating the holder by the short length of her returns and the short arc of her lobs, there remained the impression that the all-court game of Mlle Lenglen, supported by great agility and the cutest sense of anticipation, were proof against the best driving. So far as strategy went, the champion seemed, I thought, to vary her method of last year. She nursed the corners of her opponent's court in turn, four shots to one corner and the fifth (say) to the other, and then a similar attack on the other corner. This driving was always conducted with an eye on the net and an advance in its direction for a volleying coup. Of course, as the pace of her opponent's returns slackened, as they did in the second set, Mlle Lenglen came up more frequently, and rarely without success. In her last service game she illustrated her complete abandon by winning two aces outright.

So, at the age of 21, Mlle Lenglen is champion for a second year. Her mother and father were delighted witnesses of her new triumph, and (exercising the same privilege which he claimed last year, as a champion who had partnered her as a little girl), M. Max Decugis kissed her on the Centre Court before the public gaze when the match was over.

5 JULY 1920

DEFEAT OF PATTERSON

DISAPPOINTING DISPLAY

A. Wallis Myers CBE

The Championships are over, and in the American lawn tennis calendar 3 July will be coloured almost as brightly as 4 July in the national calendar. When McLoughlin played Wilding in the challenge round on 4 July 1913, patriotic visitors from the States were so sure of victory that each brought a little flag to Wimbledon ready to unfurl it on the Centre Court as soon as the citadel had been stormed. The confidence of our cousins was rudely shaken on that occasion, and on Saturday, seven years later, American hopes were more subdued, though, if the truth be known, their foundations were stronger; for the holder in 1920 had not been tested like the holder in 1913. Patterson was the first post-war champion; he had been crowned after a world convulsion the nervous shock of which had been experienced at first hand by himself and his chief rivals; form had not had time to re-classify; last year was not normal. I ventured to throw out this warning in *The Daily Telegraph* on the eve of the Championships and at the same time to express the belief that the type of game pursued by this year's American team would probably re-establish the supremacy of the all-court game over that of the serving and volleying specialists. In other words, I thought we might get back, through Johnston or Williams or Tilden, to that complete lawn tennis first practised by Renshaw and subsequently developed under modern conditions by Pim, the Dohertys, and by Wilding.

One of the earliest arrivals before the gates of the All-England Club was a lady who had seen Lawford beat Ernest Renshaw in '87. As she posted herself on a camp-stool before seven o'clock in the morning her vigil might have made Irving envious. By half-past ten the camp was firmly pitched, an hour later the queue at the railway entrance stretched nearly to Wimbledon Station, and at half-past 12, when the gates were open, there was material for capital films.

William Tilden deprived Patterson of his Championship by three sets to one, and the score of 2–6, 6–3, 6–2, 6–4 in the American's favour represents not unfairly the measure of his victory. But the figures do not convey and cannot convey the amazingly poor quality of the first two sets, the chances that went unaccepted by both men, the exposure of Patterson's backhand weakness, and the confident, triumphant way in which Tilden handled the Australian's service in the latter portion of the match. Excitement there was; speculation before the match had been too rife to prevent that; and none could fail to be moved by the endeavour of America to create a much-desired and long-sought precedent at Wimbledon nor by the fact that a Melbourne youth had travelled across the world to thwart it. But few if any challenge rounds at Wimbledon (I can only recall the Wilding and Barrett tie in 1911) have been so devoid of high-class rallies, have yielded such an amazing crop of technical blunders or made one so thankful, in the interests of stroke production (however much one may deplore the defeat of an Empire envoy) that Tilden won.

The new champion, like Patterson the year before, doubtless benefited by playing through. He had imbibed the atmosphere of the Centre Court in singles and doubles for a fortnight; his knee strained when playing Shimidzu, stood the strain of Saturday's contest well (incidentally he had consulted Wilding's former doctor); he imagined, and rightly, that his toughest opponent had been Kingscote, and he faced the match with Patterson conscious that he had outmanoeuvred Brookes, a much sounder general, in America. Nevertheless, Tilden, confident as he was, did not play his best game in the challenge round. If he had played a week earlier as he had played on Saturday, Kingscote would have beaten him, and by now possibly have been champion in his place. Nor was Patterson at his best. But the reason for that was Tilden.

4 JULY 1921

TILDEN KEEPS HIS TITLE

STRANGE CHALLENGE ROUND

A. Wallis Myers, CBE

Mr Tilden remains lawn tennis champion. He was twice within a stroke of losing his title at Wimbledon on Saturday in the challenge round, but kept it, and that is doubtless all which will concern his fervent countrymen. Within a fortnight America has won the polo cup and the golf, boxing, and lawn tennis Championships, the first and last amateur contests, the other two open to professionals. It is a quadruple feat which European sportsmen, mindful of America's resources and of her enterprise and 'push', mindful, too, of the longer suspension of their own sports occasioned by the war, will both acclaim and understand. America had just enough war to brace her manhood and stimulate her self-esteem; we and France and Belgium had so much war that even now, nearly three years after its close, we do not realise adequately the reserves that it swept away, the enormous void that only slowly, and with great patience, can be filled up.

Saturday's climax to a fortnight's play brought, appropriately enough, another packed house to the Centre Court. Siege was laid to the gates of the All-England Club as early as six in the morning; the paper wrappings of an invading army, pioneers on the path of patience, choked the wheels of patrons who, lunching more normally in town, drove down in motors to their numbered seats. Princess Mary, paying her third visit, arrived early, and stayed to the very end – cheered as she departed, having expressed to Commander Hillyard her great pleasure, augmented by her knowledge of the game, in coming to Wimbledon. Her brother, the Duke of York, is, by the way, to perform himself this week in the Air Force Service doubles at Queen's Club.

In the crowd every variety of the King's subjects, at home and abroad, and the citizens of other lands, were represented. The great majority were zealous students of lawn tennis and familiar with the rites which time has made traditional at Wimbledon. A percentage was there for the first time. This was evident by the activities of plain-clothes detectives and the personal losses sustained by guileless spectators. It was also revealed when play was in progress and when some of Mr Tilden's best drop shots drew a derogatory cry, almost suggesting that the champion was 'hitting below the belt'. As a fact, in slicing the ball into a region where it was irrecoverable, he was hitting 'over the belt' in two senses. It was, of course, a perfectly legitimate move, and his opponent, to the detriment of his own concentration, audibly expressed his indignation with the silly interruptions.

Mr Tilden told me afterwards that he found Saturday's crowd a little different in temperament – I gathered a little less decorous and generous – than the crowds of last year. I reminded him of two things, and I fancy he agreed with their relevance. The first was the introduction, as a result of the game's deepening vogue, of that element into the gallery which knows nothing of technique, and regards the match merely from the film or domestic drama point of view. Secondly, that his own reputation was so high and so firmly established that the crowd would naturally rally to the Jack who seemed to be killing the Giant, and that their feelings might justifiably be carried away, and even seem to his recently convalescent mind almost riotous when, by the youthful slayer's own faulty tactics or the giant's convulsive strength, exhibited at the wrong moment for the crowd's sympathetic interest, yet obviously at the right moment for his own personal interests, the 'monster' did not fall. I might also have added that continuous sunshine and drought, coming to a country which is trained to expect neither, provokes undue excitability. The phenomenon may even affect players, not to the extent that they ignore or violate sporting instincts, with which the vast majority are endowed, but in a subconscious manner which causes them to lose their proper perspective, and even their sense of dignity.

Under the stress and strain of Saturday's conditions the two contestants between them produced a match (perhaps the last challenge round on the famous Centre Court) which had periods of acute unreality; interludes when neither player appeared to be mentally at war with the other, when the suggestion almost of some concerted arrangement was put forward quite seriously in the stands. If one thought this last theory worthy of examination – it seemed to gain support from the fact that Norton wittingly sacrificed both the second and third sets from losing positions, and even went so far as to emphasise his squandermania by netting the last balls of the third set, while the ballboys were still in court – it was ruled out entirely by the tense and 'all out' character of the final set. I have been the weary onlooker of five-set matches between professionals on Continental courts, in which it was obvious that the two men had arranged, probably in the interests of the gallery, to go the full contest, and also agreed, in the interests of business, that the home professional should win the final set. But such collusion is unthinkable when amateurs meet. Neither the Renshaws nor the Dohertys (though the brothers occasionally played a friendly set or two) would meet each other in public tournaments lest this tradition, impossible to break, should by any example of theirs be imperilled. Tilden and Norton have been like brothers during the Championship (the American was one of Norton's main supporters in the latter's progress through the all-comers'), and I think it quite likely that, admiring the champion as much as he does, the 'boy' did not 'see enough red' to press home his earlier advantage on an 'enemy' obviously below form by his recent illness.

Nothing else on Saturday mattered very much. It is true two new doubles champions were enthroned, both of English birth, and one of them a late convert to the virtues of lawn tennis, a Triple Blue at Cambridge. Lycett and Woosnam did not lose a set to the Lowes, though the brothers, never relaxing their efforts, led 5–4 in the third set. The winners were in the advantageous position of hitting from a pedestal. The other two doubles champions kept their titles. Mlle Lenglen and Miss Ryan beat Mrs Beamish and Mrs Peacock, almost as easily as Lycett and Miss Ryan beat Woosnam and Miss Howkins.

It was left for Mlle Lenglen to hit the last ball at a Championship meeting which may be the last on the present ground. It was a smash severe enough to knock the racket out of Mrs Peacock's hand. I add that incident to Centre Court annals, in case some future historian may search for the closing stroke on a court of so many burning memories.

26 JUNE 1922

NEW WIMBLEDON TODAY

CHAMPIONSHIP PROSPECTS

A. Wallis Myers, CBE

Forty-five years ago 200 enthusiasts gathered round a croquet lawn in Wimbledon to watch the first organised match of a new ball game. It was called lawn tennis, deriving its name from the tennis disciple who invented it a few years earlier, and its support from the players of tennis and rackets. Most of them met in leisure, they were anxious to pursue some form of their original pastime in the open air, and on their own private lawns. There was a code of laws in 1877, drawn up by a select committee of the All-England Croquet Club, but the code differed materially from an earlier code made at Lord's by the MCC, and its authors must have pondered whether the 22 competitors, to say nothing of the world outside Wimbledon, would accept it. Not only did the first Championship produce a worthy champion, Mr

Spencer Gore, an Old Harrovian; it initiated a cult which before very long, despite vicissitudes of fortune, bravely faced by the faithful, was destined to become the most cosmopolitan game in the world, a game which now numbers more votaries than any ball game ever invented.

Today, in the presence of the King, a former president and the present patron of the All-England Club, a new landmark in the history of lawn tennis will be open to the public gaze. It has been called the New Wimbledon, and answers that title in the spaciousness of its accommodation and their approaches, in the freshness of its Cumberland turf, and the newness of its benches. But it is really the Old Wimbledon transplanted to a new and richer soil. Its traditional roots have been preserved, many of its beloved attributes have been kept intact; its milieu despite evolutionary changes, will remain the same. I can well believe that some of the old habitués (fervent members of the camp-stool and sandwich brigade) will feel lost and lonely on their first visit, but their homesickness will be assuaged by their great personal comfort and by the satisfaction that their own loyalty in the past has justified an extension, which permits many thousands more to share their pleasure.

Not every great player could give of his best on the old Centre Court. Tilden could do it in 1920 because his vivid imagination was inspired by the ghosts of other great players who hovered round that ancient rectangle of turf; the Dohertys could do it because the old Centre Court was almost the birthplace of their fame. But many overseas players, and some from our own shires as well, found the place too confined, its heat too oppressive, the excited crowds, pent up on level ground, too contiguous. Especially were the big drivers affected, men like S.H. Smith, Parke, and W.M. Johnson. (Their perspective of a court is a little different to that of the volleyer; they go into the 'country' more, and neither their confidence nor their strokes were as firm on the old Centre Court as on other match courts.) The committee of the All-England Club really had no option. Ever since the Championships were revived after the war (and even at the Wimbledons of McLoughlin, Wilding and Brookes before the war) the demand for seats had exceeded – painfully exceeded – the supply. The pint bottle into which a quart had to be poured was revolting; it threatened to break. So did the tram couplings which drew thousands along the congested Worple Road, and the serenity of the quiet householders who had their side-roads invaded by a riot of motorcars.

This year's Championships will be decided on a new plan as well as on a new plane. There will be no challenge rounds, nothing between the winners of the all-comers' and the throne. This change of routine, if conforming with modern ideas, throws a much heavier responsibility on the draw. One man may come in the Championship door over a path strewn with pitfalls, his body strained and his nerves inflamed by many an ugly climb; his rival, challenging his entry, may be comparatively fresh after a passage smooth and carefree. In an entry of 128 under the present system there are bound to be soft segments and even unspeculative quarters, and the committee will probably find, after a year or two of the present anomalous plan (having regard to the disparity of talent competing) that they must either cut down the candidates to those of real Championship mettle or adopt the new American method of 'seeding the draw' – that is to say, making the first three rounds, in effect, a qualifying competition for 16 selected players. This device is not really favouring the few at the expense of the many; it is helping the many by making it as sure as possible that the ultimate champion shall have had a full test and be worthy to lead his fellows.

Today's programme on the Centre Court, having regard to the protagonists engaged at Wimbledon, is not a thrilling one. Precedent is broken in introducing ladies' singles and men's doubles on the first day. If the idea is to give the greatest variety on an auspicious occasion the public would doubtless have preferred to see more of the overseas players, whose advent has made the New Wimbledon possible. But the public, once the King has declared the new Centre Court open, are likely to go in search of their own favourites: and they will find some engaged on side courts during the afternoon. To an Englishman will be given the privilege of serving the first ball – a fitting selection on a day when England's pioneer work is to be recognised. But a more discerning master of ceremonies, it seems to me, would have taken special care that the leading representatives of the nations which have made lawn tennis what it is – the universal game – and Wimbledon what it rightly claims to be – the headquarters of this catholic pastime – should have followed England into the chief arena.

27 JUNE 1922

NEW WIMBLEDON OPENED

THE KING'S VISIT

A. Wallis Myers, CBE

Through a falling barometer and leaden, dripping skies, Fate was unkind to the New Wimbledon on its opening day. But Fate might have been harsher.

The rain ceased just long enough for the King to sound the tocsin for the removal of the covers from the new Centre Court, and for their Majesties, in the presence of thousands of interested onlookers, to witness the first match on a beautiful strip of new Cumberland turf. To say that the weather spoiled the opening act would not be true; no disciple of a game which has encircled the globe, bringing to headquarters the cream of the world's talent, could fail to have his pulses quickened and his memory searched by this dignified, yet simple, prelude. But the Championships themselves – the competition which had drawn the public as well as the King and Queen to the modern Wimbledon – were held up. There was no play except on the Centre Court, and only about an hour and a half all told of that – in all six sets.

Punctual as ever, the Royal patron of the All-England Club and the Queen arrived at the Royal entrance by motorcar at the scheduled time. They were received by Mr H.W.W. Wilberforce (president of the club), Commander G.W. Hillyard, RN, Mr G.A. Carnlia, and other members of the Committee of Management. Proceeding at once to the Royal Box, the King and Queen were cheered by the large throng rising from the thousands of seats round the Championship court, while the band rendered the National Anthem. Their Majesties, with Commander Hillyard by their side, gazed out on a huge mantle of green canvas, its water-full creases suggesting in the still-falling rain that no player's foot would tread the turf beneath that afternoon.

But this foreboding was not fulfilled. After Captain Stanley Peach, F.R.I.B.A., had been presented to the King, the architect of the new ground had the privilege of conducting the Royal visitors over its chief features. The former President of the premier club was, I am informed, deeply impressed by all he saw. He made special inquiries about the workmen who had built the grandstand – in record time, by the way – and when told that the job had been completed without the slightest friction of any kind – the most harmonious job since the war, indeed – he expressed the highest satisfaction. The King also inquired about the comforts and arrangements for the general public, and since these were inordinately tested yesterday, considering the rain and the unfamiliarity of the spectators with the plan of the ground, personal evidence was offered to his Majesty of their value – a value which will obviously be enhanced on a fine day.

Shortly before half-past three the King and Queen returned to the Royal Box. By this time the rain had ceased. The moment had come for unveiling the new Centre Court. The uniformed staff were at their posts, each man, smart and alert, holding an edge of the giant tarpaulin. The King stepped to the corner of his box, and struck a gong three times. It was the signal for 'covers off'. Neatly and mechanically, each man drilled to his task, the mantle was rolled back. In less than a couple of minutes there was disclosed in the King's view and to the public's a perfectly dry lawn that looked in the distance like a green carpet of handsome pile. In a twinkling the posts were put in their sockets, the net adjusted, and the court, with its umpire and linesmen, ready for play – a swift and admirably engineered metamorphosis warmly cheered by the crowd.

The two English competitors, Major Kingscote and L.A. Godfree, came out, and the latter spun his racket round. Kingscote lost the toss, and Godfree elected to serve; it was an honour no man, and least of all a young player, could hesitate about choosing. Well, Godfree, so far from showing any nervousness, delivered a fast ball which, if it did not beat his opponent outright, brought a netted return. As quick as lightning the server dashed to the net and commandeered the ball. He put it safely away in his coat pocket by the umpire's stand – a memento, with one green patch on his virgin whiteness, that its owner will doubtless treasure for the rest of his life.

The first single was not a close one; it was not even a very good one, but it revealed Kingscote in good fettle, quick on the ball, quick in stowing it away, adroit in the third set, which he won to love, in lobbing over Godfree's head. As one had anticipated, the surface was on the slow side not only in its influence on the ball's flight, but slow to the passage of feet in pursuit. A few days of hot sunshine (if we get them) will harden it, but the new Centre Court – this year at any rate – can never be the hard, high-bounding plane, so suitable for the Continentals, that the old Centre Court was last year and in other years (though not all); the marvel really is that, having regard to its birth last December, it is as good as it is. For this miracle we must thank Commander Hillyard. The tributes he received yesterday from the King and the public were fully deserved.

7 JULY 1923

LADIES' FINAL AT WIMBLEDON

'SUZANNE' STILL CHAMPION

A. Wallis Myers CBE

Suzanne is still champion! Losing only two games in each of the two sets in yesterday's final, the French girl came serenely through her challenge from

Miss McKane. She had swept through the tests at Wimbledon for the fifth successive year. And in this five years' reign, playing over 50 sets, she has only lost one – to Mrs Lambert Chambers in the challenge round of 1919, her first year. Verily, a remarkable record, and one that justifies the exclusive class in which she, and she alone, has been in the process.

The stage was set worthily for a great match. Commander Hillyard took the 'chair', as he always does in a Lenglen final; the lines were judged by well-known players, Johnston, Campbell, and Roper Barrett among them. The vast amphitheatre was again thronged with an expectant crowd, those exposed to the burning sun qualifying for the American appellation of 'fans'. And the heat required any artifice to relieve its rigours. Miss McKane followed a new fashion (introduced by Mrs Satterthwaite on the Riviera) of tying a handkerchief round her neck. Suzanne wore her lucky bracelet.

The heat undoubtedly had its influence on the play. It must have lightened the balls appreciably, and this caused many of Miss McKane's best drives to fly over their legal boundary; and since the English girl's only real chance lay in deep driving covered by an advance to the net – since a defence so well-equipped and so steadfastly maintained could only be shaken, if it was to be shaken at all, by persistent attack – Miss McKane would assuredly have preferred a cooler day. Nor, if the sun had been veiled, would she have missed the volleying coups, some of them so appetising, created by her own ground strokes. A chorus of 'Oh's!' went up when Miss McKane muffed an easy smash in the second game of the second set – Suzanne had renounced the rally, sure of its fate. But it was not so easy to volley in yesterday's burning afternoon glare. Perhaps this is one reason why, sensing the efficiency of more restrained methods, the champion rarely, if ever, went to the net.

There was no lack of confidence in Miss McKane's strokes. Rather did it seem to me that she had too much confidence in their tactical value, and did not change her system of play as and when its impression on Suzanne's game was found to be comparatively negligible. Thus, when the first game, in which she was 'vantage thrice, had shown a firm control (no certain attribute at any time in a Centre Court which contains Suzanne), it occurred to me that Miss McKane might have abandoned the sounding return to her opponent's backhand – she usually got in this quarter better than she gave – and have resolutely gone out for a winner on the other wing. But she preferred to wait for the error, which never came. Only on length that was much shorter did she attempt the forcing drive with its advance to volley. The success of these shots – the suspicion of stress which they seemed to implement on her adversary – appeared to invite their repetition. I dare say, having regard to Suzanne's swift mobility, they would have involved the disappointment of a clean pass on several occasions; but their mere exploitation would have forced the champion to abandon her purely defensive attitude, which seems to give her almost a fixed base. The conclusion I came to was that Miss McKane had the strokes to exert a much sterner pressure; she did not employ them enough in vigour or variety, and so Suzanne, finding that no threat by surprise would materialise, enjoyed a permanent security.

Losing the first game, which she might have won, Miss McKane forfeited the next four without any such probability. She was inaccurate; she beat herself; openings came, but were not accepted; the champion's steadiness was sufficient. Then, to prove her humanity, or perhaps to relieve the monotony, Mlle Lenglen hit three balls in succession out of court. Her opponent took a love game. Miss McKane also won the next game; she employed her cross forehand well on some mid-court returns and made one crisp, decisive volley. But the champion's lapses were only temporary. She won the eighth and set game without serious strain, and hit a harder ball in the first game of the second set. The increased pace put into these strokes confirmed the impression that Suzanne, despite the heat, had ample reserve stamina. A double-fault cost the champion the second game; she won the third on her opponent's errors, and the long fourth by keeping cool after Miss McKane, having achieved a fine sequence of volleys to win a point, was visibly reacting. Two really bad shots on her backhand – down the line as service returns – gave Miss McKane the fifth, and, as it proved, her last, game. The rest of the match was scarcely stimulating. Suzanne had no need to strike an aggressive note; the errors of her opponent in reply to her defensive shots were sufficient to carry her out. Miss McKane was 'vantage twice in the last game; no higher did British hopes rise.

5 JULY 1924

THRILLING FINAL AT WIMBLEDON

MISS MCKANE'S VICTORY

QUEEN A SPECTATOR

A. Wallis Myers, CBE

American Independence Day, the anniversary of McLoughlin's great bid for the singles Championship against Tony Wilding, and the stage set for another Californian quest – this time on the ladies' singles Championship. All the attributes of a great occasion were there. The sun was shining, the Centre Court was packed as it had never been packed before this year, the Queen (and with her the Duke and Duchess of York) was in the Royal Box. Commander Hillyard was in his accustomed place (for the final) on the umpire's chair; the lines were held by distinguished players. All that the day demanded was a great match. This desideratum, at first denied, was supplied. At the end of an hour and a quarter's play Miss McKane had beaten Miss Helen Wills by two sets to one, each set having yielded ten games.

But what an agony of suspense and fluctuation before the Championship point was scored! What a match for both ladies to dream about! What a brilliant break of all-court play which carried the American champion three times within a stroke of 5–1 in the second set – a lead, which had it been secured, must almost inevitably have given her the British Championship as well! What a wonderful recovery of Miss McKane, who, when all seemed lost, captured six games in succession and tipped the scales in her favour! Finally, what a thrilling final set, with every stroke of crucial value, with neither player 'rattled', yet straining every nerve for victory, with Miss Wills twice needing only a point for a 4–2 lead, and with Miss McKane determined she should not get it, with each country dead level at four all, and with England drawing on a deeper experience, just winning in the end.

Let me emphasise that the play, except in an early phase, when Miss Wills lost 12 successive points, was of a remarkably high standard. I doubt whether any Lenglen match at Wimbledon (except the first in 1919) has provided rallies so keenly contested or strokes of such resource, variety and skill. Helen Wills was as near her American best as I have ever seen her; she redeemed every estimate of her stroke equipment, speed and accuracy formed on the other side; save in her judgment on two or three occasions, when she returned balls that were going out of court, she revealed all the qualities of a champion. She flouted the notion that she could not move quickly over the court; she confounded those who imagined that her form in the international match was her true form, just as much as those who believed, after her earlier Championship matches at Wimbledon, that she could not hit a hard ball to the right place. If you ask why, with all these virtues, and with the commanding lead which they brought her, she did not win, the answer must be that Miss McKane's volleys in the last set, especially towards its close, were more incisive than her own. When the coup-searching came to its crisis, when each player had been moved from a winning position into a losing position by the enterprise of the other, when the good lob had been recovered or the low cross drive countered, when the advance for the kill was finally undertaken and the opportunity to make it was offered, it was Miss McKane who, with her longer experience of net play, stowed away the ball to a spot from which it never returned. Miss Wills made beautiful volleys, more polished in their lustre, some of them were, than the volleys of Miss McKane. I recollect one deep smash in the third set which McLoughlin could not have bettered. But the tendency was there – and it had a material effect on the last set – to chop the volley rather than to hit it with a plain-faced racket, as Miss McKane hits it.

The new lady champion, a native of London, is the first English title-holder since 1914. The reign of France was broken, perhaps only temporarily, by the retirement of Mlle Lenglen after five years' regality. Suzanne had won the hard-court Championship of the world in Paris before the war, when she was a child of 13. Miss Kathleen McKane did not come to fame until after the war, and she differs fundamentally from the French girl in that she had no coach to fashion either her strokes or her tactics. She is a self-made player, and an example and inspiration to all girls who, whatever their opportunity for practice, can push their way to the front by individual effort. She was one of many zealous, athletic English girls, adept at golf and badminton (of which she is the present champion), riding horse and sleigh with equal relish, who threw themselves as eagerly into war work as into peace play. I remember seeing her first play in 1919 at Chiswick Park, a pretty, merry volleyer, with a long vaulting stride, a natural hitter if there ever was one. She did not wear, and has never worn, the solemn mien of some players of her sex, and doubtless it has been this air of joyous abandon, index of an unaffected nature, which has made her so popular with crowds wherever she has played.

4 JULY 1925

'SUZANNE'S' TRIUMPH IN THE LADIES' CHAMPIONSHIP

A. Wallis Myers CBE

The first spoils were gathered at Wimbledon yesterday. Mlle Lenglen won the ladies' singles Championship for the sixth time – and with the loss of only five games in as many matches. When the quality of the opposing field is considered – and her adversaries have included Miss Ryan, Mrs Beamish,

Miss McKane, and Miss Fry — the average loss of only one game in all her Championship rounds is sufficient proof that the title is in its proper place. But for her attack of jaundice last spring, 'Suzanne' would not have had any break in her Championship career. She is now champion once more. The re-entry of the queen into her realm was one long processional triumph.

She was not at her best in the final yesterday. Conceivably her strength had been unduly taxed by the desperate mixed doubles she had to fight — and, with her own racket, win — the night before. But she beat Miss Fry 6–2, 6–0, and there was never the least doubt about her victory. The match was more arresting by the personalities engaged than the quality of the tennis. For thousands of people yesterday Friday was spelt Fryday. They came from all parts of the country — some from Stone, the Staffordshire home of the British competitor — to support and applaud a contest without precedent in the history of the game — a challenge from a girl of 19, new to the Centre Court as she was comparatively new to lawn tennis fame. Miss Joan Fry is not yet an artist at the game, but she possesses that quality which makes a direct appeal to the masses — the courage to beard a lioness in its den. She had the pluck as she had the patience, she had the physical reserves as she had the sound temperament, to run in hot pursuit of every ball, to return most of those within her reach, and prolong many a rally beyond its normal 'Suzanne' length. This was all the crowd wanted, and she did not disappoint them.

As an exhibition of women's modern tennis the match technically fell considerably below two of the other singles in which Mlle Lenglen has been engaged. Yet it had its thrills, and even its speculations. For even champions of the brightest hue have been known to shed some of their lustre when the need to keep it burnished is not insistent. 'Suzanne' was quiet and methodical rather than brilliant yesterday, and in this relatively subdued mood she came to her sixth Championship. Had she not linked arms with her victim as both left the court smiling, the public might have felt that their measure of 'incidents' had been too short.

Mlle Lenglen scored 31 points more than Miss Fry, and one may truthfully say that, though the French girl's play was not as impeccable as usual, British determination deserved every one of the 21 won against her. Here is the stroke summary:

FIRST SET

Mlle Lenglen	4	4	4	4	2	4	1	4	= 27 – 6
Miss Fry	1	1	2	0	4	1	4	0	= 13 – 2

SECOND SET

Mlle Lenglen	4	5	4	4	4	4 = 25 − 6
Miss Fry	1	3	1	2	1	0 = 8 − 0

Miss Fry's two games, the fifth and the seventh, were won from 30 and 15 respectively. I cannot recall that their owner did anything more remarkable in these two games than in any of the others. The natural 'swing-over' of her forehand drive was to Mlle Lenglen's backhand – the point of greatest resistance. Hence we had the spectacle of prolonged rallies, as we did in the Mallory match of two years ago, in which Mlle Lenglen allowed herself to be attacked in the sure knowledge that her defence was sound enough, any volleying complement being absent, to safeguard her interests. Now and then she essayed an attacking shot of her own, and was probably surprised to find that it did not yield an ace – so ubiquitous was Miss Fry: but in the main she used the palm of the hand and not the cane.

5 JULY 1926
BRITISH VICTORIES AT WIMBLEDON'S CLOSE
MRS GODFREE CHAMPION
A. Wallis Myers, CBE

Wimbledon's feverish fortnight closed on Saturday with two stirring British victories. The ladies' singles Championship was won by Mrs Godfree, and the mixed doubles Championship by Mrs Godfree and her husband. These successes, cheered by a swollen crowd mindful of the fact that invading legions had swept the board last year, made England equal with France in the distribution of the spoils. Each was credited with two titles, America claiming the remaining fifth.

In the matter of public patronage and interest the Jubilee meeting has reflected the expanding popularity of a pastime which now has no frontiers. Every day, and not one day more than another, brought its eager, capacity-filling crowds; had there been finer play no more people could have seen it. The new Wimbledon, treble the size of the old, has more than vindicated its creation; like its predecessor, it has already proved too small for its population. Those who have gone down to its sea in cars or trains have found its turbulent swell increasingly difficult to breast, and now that champions are paid as much attention off the court as on it the management are finding that the 'peep-holes' are all too small for the admiring gaze. Wimbledon, like Lord's, has no outfield which between the innings can be used as a parade ground; yet I am sure that these seething gangways and impassable roads do not give an adventurous thrill to the crowd.

Writing on Friday morning, I had ventured to say in estimating the chances in the ladies' singles final: 'The last Mrs Godfree is always the best. This is her chance.' Not until the decisive stage of the final set, in which Mlle de Alvarez held a winning lead of 3–1, and appeared to have bridled the brilliancy which had gained her the second set, did Mrs Godfree display the quality of a real champion, and, by matching the strokes of her opponent with others that were more intelligently co-ordinated for the finishing coup, earn her tactical triumph. It may be said of the Spanish girl that she was the greater stroke-player, and of Mrs Godfree that she was the greater match-player. The same was true of Alonso, another Spanish competitor of great fluency, after his defeat by Norton in the all-comers' final of 1921.

Mrs Godfree, ever keeping the score in mind, had won her final against Miss Wills in 1924 because she possessed the faculty for imposing the greater pressure just when its advent was least suspected, and when its moral value was of the highest. Mr Roper Barrett cultivated this power, and with it beat many a fine stroke-player. Mrs Godfree, though not such a deep student of tactics as Mr Barrett, has learned the secret and the efficacy of his plan; experience gave her the 1924 Championship as it gave her the 1926.

Another important factor which helped her to win on Saturday was her greater mobility. Some years ago the youngest and one of the greatest lady champions Wimbledon ever had, Miss Lottie Dod, gave this advice to her would-be imitators: 'Ladies should learn to run, and run their hardest, too, not merely stride. They would find (if they tried) that many a ball, seemingly out of reach, could be returned with ease; but, instead of running hard, they go a few steps and exclaim, "Oh! I can't", and stop.' This may be elementary advice; either because she could not or would not follow it, Mlle de Alvarez lost the abstract advantages of her superior speed of drive. It was as if she had prescribed the length of the rally in her own mind and its extension by the skill and ardour of her opponent was an eventuality she had not considered. It was not over-confidence; it was a lack of confidence in the resisting powers of Mrs Godfree.

The match went in alternating cycles; blocks of games were carried by independent waves, and it was just the uncertainty as to when these waves would come and what weight of points they could lift which made the match of entrancing interest from start to finish. Lenglen love sets may be very satisfying to the winner; they do not feed the competitive instinct of the crowd. Wimbledon loves its gamble. So it was intrigued when Mlle de Alvarez, gaining control after a very loose start, took the fourth and fifth games after Mrs Godfree had captured the first three.

But excitement did not really mount to the regions of ecstasy, to the rapture of delight that arrests the whole mind, until the Spanish invader had won the second set and made a climax possible. She had drawn on level terms and was to advance beyond them because the restrained and some-what monotonous game which Mrs Godfree was purposely pursuing had outlived its own value. The more phlegmatic British temperament had thought to extract excesses from the exuberant Latin by a policy of sheer stone-walling. But 'wait and see' is a foreign policy to a player whose maxim is 'hit and forward'. Trenched warfare fretted Mrs Godfree; she wanted to go over the top. The time for the offensive, however, had not yet arrived; it was most desirable to invite adventure by the enemy, to exhaust his reserves, to throw in the weight of surprise later. So, while Mrs Godfree was making lapses at the back of the court, Mlle de Alvarez was making beautiful winners from any part of it. The Spanish backhand down the line was a stroke of perfect symmetry and timing.

But sometimes it went out of court by a ball's breadth; as these narrow errors multiplied, so Mrs Godfree invited more and wider ones by volleying a tiring opponent. After her lead of 3–1 in the final set, Mlle de Alvarez did not win another game. She had been within a stroke of 4–1, serving a double-fault in the game but removing its impression by play of sterling insistence. The sixth and squaring game was won by the English pistol instead of by the long-range gun, and after losing her lead it was seen that Mlle de Alvarez had lost her retrieving power also. She might have won the ninth game, in which she was 40–15, had she possessed her former serenity and her former physical strength.

Even one recovery (her capture of the second set after losing the first) had been a novelty for the Spanish mind; her experience and her tempera-ment did not permit her to make another. The match, let me add, was admirably umpired by Commander G.W. Hillyard; it was 'lined' by a corps of distinguished players. The crowd showered their plaudits on the winner, and did not forget to express their appreciation of the loser's beautiful strokes. It may be that the invader was conscious that the home player had more sympathy among the onlookers; if it were so, she made no sign.

The Godfrees won the mixed doubles against Kinsey and Miss Browne. The last-named was willing enough to go in; it is her natural instinct to do so. Kinsey preferred the region of the service line. He was thus playing with the fire of the Godfrees' rackets and the flames consumed him. Mrs Godfree had no need in the match to restrain her ardour for tactical reasons; she hit hard and straight all the time. Needless to say, both she and her partner used the check volley in front of Kinsey. The score in the second British triumph was 6–3, 6–4.

7 JULY 1930

TILDEN CHAMPION AGAIN

TOO CLEVER FOR ALLISON

A. Wallis Myers

The King and Queen were at Wimbledon on Saturday to see W.T. Tilden, the American champion, defeat his youthful compatriot, Wilmer Allison, in the final of the men's singles Championship. The final was of first-rate quality and full of good measure for the public, though it lacked the tension and desperate bellicosity of a blood duel. Allison is a fine and advancing player, thoroughly modern in his dash and vehemence, but he is not yet quite of Tilden's class. To say that Tilden, in beating him, has never played better in his life – and I saw this assertion in print – is, of course, ridiculous. Allison's challenge, searching though it was, had nothing like the perpetual threat of Borotra's, nor was it conducted with the same piercing weapons. In the middle 1920s, when Tilden was in his prime, I saw him in his own country for several years in sequence face and hold at bay attacks from W.M. Johnston, which made their matches essentially more exciting and more strenuous than Saturday's encounter.

Against Johnston, Tilden, except on rare occasions, did not use the heavy slice which now reminds us that, because of its power-saving attribute, he is no longer a young man. He hit hard at and through his man all the time. Against Allison he opened with the old flat-driving, dynamic blows of sheer velocity, and with them, conceding Allison only three of his own service games, won the first set. Thus, with something in hand, he could afford, while fortifying himself against reprisal, to go slower. By reducing the pace of his ground shots he also reduced the margin of error; at the same time, by a more graduated and varied length, he made Allison do most of the running, draining his physical power of resistance for any later stage.

The energy which Tilden saved by these tactics – and they stretched the second set into 16 games – was reserved for his service, which, after the first game or two, was consistently fast and withering. When its power had ceased to govern the issue – when the end was almost in sight – Allison broke through it twice, but the feat was too late to matter. When the result was still in the balance Allison had no reply to Tilden's service. In six consecutive service games in the second set Tilden lost only two points. He won four love games and two from 15-each. Imagine the cruel efficiency of such a battering ram, its inexorable decision!

4 JULY 1932

ELLSWORTH VINES THE GREATEST YOUNG TENNIS PLAYER OF ALL TIME

H.W. AUSTIN OVERWHELMED IN THREE SETS

A. Wallis Myers

Wimbledon is over and America rules the lawn. As conclusively as Mrs Moody won the women's Championship the day before, Ellsworth Vines, also of California, won the men's on Saturday. He beat H.W. Austin in the final 6–4, 6–2, 6–0. Vines, the third American champion in succession, equalled the record of Tilden and Patterson by capturing the title on his first visit to England. He beat the record of H.L. Doherty, Tilden, Johnston, Lacoste, and Cochet by winning both the American and British Championships under the age of 21. That feat alone makes Vines the greatest young player of all time.

Saturday's setting was impressively complete. The King and Queen were there. Just as their Majesties patronised the first Anglo-French women's final in 1919 – the equal and exciting struggle between Mrs Lambert Chambers and Mlle Lenglen – so, 13 years later, they revealed their sustained interest in international lawn tennis by coming to see the first Anglo-American men's final. The Royal visitors, as they were escorted into the committee box by Sir Herbert Wilberforce and Commander Hillyard just before Vines and Austin came in, received a loyal ovation from 'a capacity crowd'.

Every inch of space in the big amphitheatre girding the court was occupied. Even the roller had its camping spectators. Hundreds had queued up overnight and had slept and breakfasted before the gates. Most of these patient investors were tennis 'fans'; a few were tennis financiers and sold their position in the line to the highest bidder. Ring seats purchased for a few shillings were exchanged for as many pounds. It was a great day, and fine weather and perfect organisation attended it.

But if Vines played wonderful tennis, it was not a wonderful match. It was a one-sided contest. Austin did not put up the fight which was expected. He was not, as we had hoped, the David for the Goliath. Vines was strong, menacing and ruthless – but not at first. He was, indeed, palpably nervous at the start, as if his youth and the occasion were not quite compatible. At this initial stage Vines was not the giant who had annihilated Crawford. His service was sluggish, the cannonball was shy. He was netting his drives; he was not bending down as he usually does to watch the barrel discharge of its shot, his cap-protected eye level with the gun.

Austin did not take advantage of this unsteady Vines. He might and should have won the opening set. I thought of H.L. Doherty and Norman Brookes 27 years earlier. The Australian had slain a line of Englishmen with his withering service – bolts more unfamiliar than, and as sinister as, those of Vines. Doherty accepted the challenge of the service and had Brookes in difficulties before he could develop his attack. He surprised him into more errors and won.

Austin had begun with a double-fault and lost the first game. That was a little disquieting, but he was confident enough in the second game, and broke through the American's service. He led 2–1 and 3–2, holding his own; the errors were coming from Vines; the battle, if anything, was going favourably for England. In the sixth game Vines served two aces – his first of the match – but he discounted their value by missing a volley and taking a ball that was sailing out. He was lucky, on strokes and tactics still indefinite, to level the score. Austin then lost his service to love. He served weakly, but his errors came after Vines had returned the ball. He did not exert the pressure which his opponent's unsteadiness demanded; he allowed the giant to find himself; he almost seemed to be sensing trouble before trouble came. Strong and resolute strokes were rare.

Vines bent to adjust his shoes as he crossed over, rising to increase his service speed. He went to 5–3 from 15. He was 'letting out' on his delivery; the ball was bounding off chalk; Austin was yielding to it. But he was not demoralised. Vines was still vulnerable in the deep corner, and Austin won the long ninth game. This time, on the cross-over, the American changed a broken shoelace for a sound one. The delay was disturbing to Austin, whose control had improved. He had no reply to three fast services in the tenth game. I could not help recalling Johnston's robust retorts to Tilden's cannonballs.

No man's knowledge can go beyond his experience. I found many observers of Saturday's final speaking as if the service of Vines was some novel and uncanny weapon impossible to counter and impossible to reproduce. The history of American and even French lawn tennis confounds that theory. At the beginning of the century Dwight Davis (who was present on Saturday) was serving nearly as fast as Vines, and finding players in his own country ready with a reply. R.N. Williams defeated M.E. McLoughlin in the final of the American Championship of 1914 by standing in and taking the Californian's thunderbolts on the rise; so did both Wilding and Parke at Wimbledon in 1913. Lacoste had an answer to Tilden's service, both in America and France, and passed on the recipe to Cochet. Vincent Richards, whose ground strokes bore no comparison to Austin's, could hold Tilden even in his prime by parrying his service. Patterson's service was a lethal instrument in England, but I saw Johnston win eight games against it in succession at Forest Hills in 1924. I also witnessed Borotra handle it unflinchingly and victoriously in a Davis Cup match on the same ground in 1925. The truth is that false values of the game have, through ignorance, obtained currency in this country. The lessons of history have been neglected.

Vines won the Championship – his winning shot, by the way, was an untouchable service stroke – by unadulterated lawn tennis. A wise and prudent general, he reserved his best display for the last two rounds. He did not play as well against Austin as against Crawford, but that was because Austin did not tax him as much.

8 JULY 1933

JACK CRAWFORD BEATS ELLSWORTH VINES IN GREAT WIMBLEDON FINAL

TITLE RETURNS TO EMPIRE AFTER EPIC MATCH

THRILLING STRUGGLE IN FIFTH SET: TWO PLAYERS OF GENIUS

A. Wallis Myers

Jack Crawford has made history for Australia and Wimbledon, bringing glory to both; and Ellsworth Vines helped to provide the epoch. The final in which Vines, the American holder, was beaten by the Australian champion after five sets (4–6, 11–9, 6–2, 2–6, 6–4) yielded one of the finest matches in the 53-year story of the Championships.

My own experience of Wimbledon finals only goes back 34 years. Mr S.A.E. Hickson, who was referee at the first and who witnessed his 53rd consecutive final yesterday, had no hesitation in affirming that for sustained quality of play, mutual attack on the service and the tense excitement of the last phase, the two-hour contest which Crawford and Vines waged was Wimbledon's greatest match.

The mind passes back in swift retrospect. Renshaw and Lawford had historic fights in the 1880s – genius against virility and confidence. Pim and Baddeley had several finals in which the science of the game was worthily revealed. The Dohertys showed us elegance of stroke play, but their finals in the main merely advertised their supremacy. A great Australian, Norman Brookes, who predicted that Crawford would one day come into his own, had his famous challenge with 'H.L.' in 1905. I took a hue; it was a match to remember, but it had no climax, and only went to three sets. Wilding and Roper Barrett had a match for speculation six years later; the latter retired in a heat wave at two sets all. Wilding's defending match against McLoughlin, another Californian giant, in 1913 had a family resemblance to yesterday's contest; it did not go beyond three sets. Neither the Cochet–Tilden match of 1927, nor the Cochet–Borotra match of 1930, memorable for their fluctuations, were finals. Lacoste played long finals against his countrymen and one great match against Tilden that was not a final.

Wimbledon, in truth, has rarely ended with a 'five-setter'. There have only been ten five-set finals in the history of the meeting. Yesterday's, for superlative play, refined co-ordination of strokes and tactics, continuous speed in service and the fighting vigour of both men at the finish, must rank first.

It was an ideal day for play. Breezes were stirring even under an almost cloudless sky, but the walls of the giant stadium destroyed their force, and only occasionally was the ball deflected by a current. I detected a few empty seats; they were those of the photographers who had gone out momentarily to reload. Everybody who could buy or cajole a seat was there, and every living champion of the past seemed to be in the members' stand. Australians were there in force. The most excited was Mrs Crawford, mixed doubles champion of Australia, with her husband – Vines was one of their opponents in the final. I am told she fainted after Jack had won his title. Mrs Norman Bayles, a well-known Australian hostess, was by her side to restore her. She was able to congratulate Jack through the dressing-room window.

She had told me in Paris, her love for Wimbledon being what it is, that she would sooner her husband won the singles Championship than that Australia should win the Davis Cup. His play yesterday almost deserved the double triumph.

As the new champion and the old left the court they were saluted by more applause; as they passed under the archway which led to the dressing-room both were still as self-possessed as if the match was about to begin. Australians flocked round their hero; many Americans added their congratulations. The match could have had no more sporting finish; and, of course, Jack Crawford has not an enemy in the world.

10 JULY 1933

MRS MOODY LOSES FIRST SET FOR SIX YEARS

LINE INCIDENT MARS MEMORABLE DUEL WITH MISS ROUND

A. Wallis Myers

Wimbledon is over, and its spoils have gone round the world. England has bettered her record of last year. In 1932 she had finalists in two of the major events. That achievement was repeated, but Miss Round came much nearer to bearing off a singles title on Saturday than Austin had done a year ago. Miss Round might have beaten Mrs Moody if she had enjoyed as much hardening match experience in recent weeks as, say, Miss Seriven. She had the strokes, mobility and will-power; her footwork all the time was superior to the champion's. The moral advantage was hers had she only divined it. But when the fruits of her tillage and patient tending were ripe she failed to gather them. Her tactics in the final set were, in fact, self-destroying. Mrs Moody, although less athletic, brought home the harvest first.

The setting was perfect for the final day. Keeping tradition, the King and Queen came down to grace the Royal Box. They followed the matches with unfading zest. Beside them, as keenly intent, was King Feisal, who doffed his black cap as he entered. Irak, too, has tennis courts; its King, like that of Sweden, may be a pioneer. In the front row, too, were Princess Arthur of Connaught and the Earl of Athlone, and Princess Ingrid of Sweden, who will no doubt describe to King Gustav [the] struggles in which some of his former tournament partners were engaged. The start of the women's final was delayed a quarter of an hour; the Royal cars were speeding from the palace. There was a sprinkling of rain in the interval; the only shower, if such it can be called, of the meeting. The tarpaulin crew came out, but sunshine drove them back again.

From 2.30 to 3.50p.m. Berkeley, California, battled against Dudley, Worcestershire. Nearly four years divided the ages of Mrs Moody, the holder, and Miss Round, her challenger – the exact period of Mrs Moody's supremacy. Commander Hillyard was not in the umpire's chair as usual; his presence was required in the Royal Box. Sir Herbert Wilberforce, the All-England Club chairman, was an absentee through illness. Another precedent was broken when players of international rank, with the exception of Mr Roper Barrett, were not placed on the lines. The deputies had done efficient work during the meeting; one hesitates to point the moral. But if Commander Hillyard and his team of first-class players had been on court the unfortunate episode at the end of the second set, which snapped the thread of a great struggle, making its reweaving extremely difficult, would probably not have occurred.

Competitors and crowd were alike disturbed. When thousands have their gaze fixed on every stroke in a Centre Court struggle, fierce and fluctuating as this one was, the minds of player and onlooker work in unison. A great wave of sympathy, as well as expectation, was always passing out; the ordeal of two girls was transmitted to the human walls that encircled them. Mass psychology, like fire and water, is a disintegrated force; it cannot be resisted. Crawford and Vines, without pause or impediment, were sparring on level terms and without a mental break of any kind for five sets; Mrs Moody and Miss Round had this experience for only one set and 13 games.

Before the contretemps the match ran a course so level that, excluding the holder's reputation, its end seemed unforetellable. Mrs Moody's service was not stronger than Miss Round's; it yielded, in fact, twice as many double-faults. Neither service pierced its opponent's guard, but the English length was better than the American; there was greater sting. Probably Mrs Moody had planned beforehand to win by sound defence; she duly won the first set 6–4.

In the second set, with Miss Round ahead 7–6, the champion fought back to be 15–40 on Miss Round's service. At 30–40, with every heart beating fast in the vast arena, came the episode to which reference has been made. Miss Round drove a ball hard towards the baseline. Mrs Moody was hot in pursuit. The ball appeared to cross the line by at least two inches. Mrs Moody checked her run, expecting to hear the linesman call. He gave no sign, meaning that the ball was good. The central umpire, taking his cue from Mrs Moody's action – she had arrested her stroke – called 7–7. He held to this decision when, in looking round at the linesman for corroboration, he saw the latter's arm shoot out. Here was the misunderstanding. The linesman was indicating that in his opinion the ball had touched the line at which his hand was pointing. The crowd was naturally depressed, and a section of it was articulate. Miss Round came to the net, asking that the point should be awarded to her opponent. She knew, and Mrs Moody knew, that the ball was out. The hiatus, coming when it did, upset morale. Nor did it appear to the crowd or to two exhausted girls less incidental when the service linesman, realising what had happened, walked to the umpire's chair to explain. Nobody felt happy when the scoreboard signalled deuce. The players thought the score was wrong, although it was legally right; the crowd considered the American had lost a critical stroke.

The next two points, which Miss Round won to give her the set at 8–6, were played in the atmosphere of tragedy. Miss Round lost the full volume of applause which, under normal circumstances, would have greeted her capture of the first set which – either as Miss Wills or as Mrs Moody – the champion had sacrificed at Wimbledon since 1927. The crucial breath of competition had gone out of the game; the moves seemed to be almost perfunctory. Miss Round's first mistake was to hit out wildly; her second to come up on balls that allowed Mrs Moody to lob for relief, her third to use the drop shot at the slightest provocation. Thus most of the rallies were shortened when it should have been Miss Round's fixed ambition to lengthen them. Steadier play on her part in the final set might have exhausted and thereby subdued the champion. Mrs Moody was allowed to have a minimum of running in a set where a little more might have turned the tide. After 2–2 Miss Round might have been 3–2 had she not fallen in running for a sideline shot. Her racket slipped from her hand, a ballboy advanced. She recovered it quickly, but not in time. A double-fault helped Mrs Moody to 4–2, and when 5–2 was signalled on the board you felt the end was near. Miss Round's pluck delayed it. The champion had driven out of court at match ball; Miss Round came to 'vantage with a good smash and won the game. But in the ninth she could only garner one point, and a match memorable for a splendid fight for two sets, yet losing some of its savour in the third, was over.

Two smiling girls running to the net with hands outstretched was a pleasing picture. As they left the court the crowd gave them a rich salute. For an hour and 30 minutes they had battled almost on level terms. The gulf between the champion and her rivals had been narrowed if not bridged.

TENNIS TITLE HOME AFTER 25 YEARS

PERRY HOLDER OF TRIPLE CROWN

CRAWFORD BEATEN IN STRAIGHT SETS

A. Wallis Myers

'From wandering on a foreign strand', the Lawn Tennis Championship has come back to England, its native place, after 25 years. Yesterday, at Wimbledon, before an expectant throng, hoping, but not quite sure until the end, F.J. Perry defeated J.H. Crawford, the holder, in the final, and became the first home-grown champion since 1909. The score was 6–3, 6–0, 7–5. Thus Perry became the holder of a notable triple crown. He is the champion of Wimbledon, Australia and America.

The result was epoch-making; the actual match was not an epic fight. It was, indeed, a hollow victory, only saved from becoming a debacle by the Australian's plucky but fruitless effort to turn the tide in the third set. Of Perry's fitness to hold the title by virtue of his play and resolution it gave open proof; as a spectacle and in relation to some much greater matches that had gone before this week it was almost an anti-climax.

For if the Perry enthroned yesterday was a better Perry than Wimbledon had ever seen – remorselessly accurate on the drive, very competent on the service, and brilliant on the few occasions when he ventured to the net – Crawford was certainly not the vibrant, resourceful, and calculating player who beat Vines in a classic match last year. He only gave glimpses of the champion; for the rest he was like a man living under the shadow of defeat, his weapons blunted, his eye out of focus, and his enterprise gone.

The new champion is a native of Stockport. He is a Middlesex club player converted into a champion by his own volatile, sanguine character, by the confidence of his father, and by the facilities for 'first ten' practice and experience all over the world provided by a discerning governing body. As he was moving steadily but surely to his goal yesterday – an excitement he could hardly suppress only serving to increase the force of his inflexible pressure – my mind reverted back 25 years to the challenge round at the old Wimbledon, when A.W. Gore, the last English champion, won the title for the third time. I have a vivid recollection of that encounter, because it produced one of the most surprising recoveries in the history of the Championship. M.J.C. Ritchie was two sets up on the reigning champion, and held a winning lead in the third. The holder – we did not think of him as a veteran in those days, although he was 41 – was gasping for breath. His passing seemed imminent, and probably Ritchie shared the opinion of the crowd. Gore's sound heart and the strength of his forehand drive turned the match completely round: he looked as if he could have played another set at the finish.

There was no similar denouement about yesterday's final – only a temporary interruption to Perry's progress in the third set. Before Crawford's belated stand came after the challenger had created a new record for any men's Wimbledon final. He had won 12 games in succession – nominally two love sets. Such a break against a man of Crawford's class and experience suggests a brand of play unprecedented in its mastery and precision. And such it was, even if allowance be made for Crawford's inadequate resistance and his extraordinary lack of initiative. The Australian had opened with a 3–1 lead. He had won the first two games with a rousing service, and had broken through Perry's service after a long dispute. Perry was 0–40, caught up, and then served a double-fault. This lapse on Perry's part seemed to unlock the floodgates which the Englishman, anxious to be cool and calm, had closed. You could see the gleam of battle in his eye; he was energised for a forward movement; he had taken off the gloves. On and on he went from this stage. Now the set at 6–3, next a love set, then the first game in the third set – a dozen games in a row. There was only one deuce game in the sequence, and very few rallies which did not reveal Perry as the master of his fate.

I confess that Crawford's tactics perplexed me. He seemed all the time to be playing into Perry's hands. His backhand returns were nearly all across the court, very rarely down the line. By this almost stereotyped play, with never a threat of a volleying sortie, he polished up Perry's backhand so that it became brighter than Crawford's own. It may be that Crawford was cramped by Perry's low trajectory and beautiful length; he had to take the line of least resistance. But desperate straits call for desperate remedies. Crawford seemed almost resigned to going down in his own way, Perry imposing his will all the time.

In the third set there was a change, but Crawford only once forced a lead. Perry allowed no serious decline; it was irrational for complete dominance to last for three sets. Each man won his service up to 4–4; at last the crowd were applauding an issue really joined. There was, indeed, a great shout of sympathy when Crawford, now coming in, showed the magic of his cross volleys. After he had won the ninth game, leading for the first time – Perry had served only his second double-fault of the match to give him game point – the holder raised the waning hopes of his supporters. They thought of Crawford's great recovery against Shields; they could see that their man was not physically exhausted.

Perry's play in the next three games was worthy of the champion he was soon to be. He got a point from a double-fault, but played the succeeding rallies with marvellous control, piloting Crawford from side to side until he got the opening for a sterling winner. He was tested overhead and found secure. He held his service gallantly in the 11th game, despite a double-fault. He then saw Crawford go to 40–0: his best service was back again. Perry was undismayed. Errors were forced from a baulked opponent; four points were taken in a row. The crucial Championship point had arrived. The end was like a damp squib exploding.

There was to be no final rally, no breathless suspense, no deafening clamour as Perry made the winning shot. Crawford was foot-faulted at match point for putting his toe on the line on his first service; on his second, doubtless depressed at this unlucky stroke of fortune, he served a double. It was a brave linesman who inflicted the penalty at this deathbed stage. The effect was to catch the gallery in a state of suspended animation. They almost caught their breath in sympathy before they gave the winner his well-merited ovation.

7 JULY 1934

PERRY'S LEAP OF TRIUMPH

A Special Representative

Fred Perry must have been the most excited man in England at four o'clock yesterday afternoon, the time his memorable match with Crawford concluded. He ran to the net, went over it with a flying leap, and almost hugged Crawford in his fervour. Afterwards he told me that he did not want to see another tennis ball for a week, and that he was going away for a short rest from the game. He did, in fact, disappear from the ground, to the disappointment of many 'fans' who wanted to shake his hand, or get his autograph, or whatever else fanship could think of. I asked his father if professionalism was the next step for the champion, but he only laughed. 'There is nothing of that sort in the offing,' he replied.

Sixteen thousand spectators saw the match, which was over in 70 minutes. Among them were many distinguished visitors, including Prince and Princess Arthur of Connaught, several foreign Ambassadors, and Sir Samuel Hoare, president of the Lawn Tennis Association. The demeanour of the crowd was almost perfect. Only once or twice had the umpire to call 'Quiet, please!' Cheering was reserved for the conclusion of games; during them the only sounds to be heard among that great assembly were the tap of the ball on the racket and the voice of the umpire.

But at the end of the match all the pent-up feeling broke loose, and the victor was rapturously cheered all the way out of the court. Obviously the match left no rancour between the contestants. As they disappeared into the dressing-room they shook hands again, and passed out of sight with Crawford's arm resting affectionately on Perry's shoulder.

7 JULY 1934

CHAMPION'S CAREER

A Special Correspondent

Frederick John Perry, the new champion, is the son of Mr S.J. Perry, formerly Labour and Co-operative MP for Kettering. He is 25 years of age, and his rise in the tennis world has been meteoric. Down to 1930 he was self-taught. In that year he won the singles Championship of Argentina, and the Lawn Tennis Association sent him to Maskell, the All-England coach, for instruction.

He began his tennis with the Brentham Club at Ealing. Later he went to the Herga Club and the Chiswick Park Club. In 1929 he won the world table tennis championship at Budapest, and the strokes with which he revolutionised that game he brought with him into first-class tennis.

He was chosen for Great Britain in the Davis Cup for 1931, and again in the two following years. In 1933 he won the decisive match against Merlin in the challenge round of the Davis Cup. He has also won the American Championship singles at Forest Hills and the Australian singles and (with G.P. Hughes) doubles Championships at Melbourne.

9 JULY 1934

GREAT FINAL IN THE WOMEN'S SINGLES

KING AND QUEEN SEE MISS ROUND DEFEAT MISS JACOBS

A. Wallis Myers

When Wimbledon ended on Saturday, with the King and Queen present, both the singles titles were in England's keeping; the gulf of 25 years had been doubly bridged. Miss Dorothy Round, of Dudley, who will be 25 next Friday – like Perry, born in the year of England's last double victory – defeated Miss Helen Jacobs, champion of America, by two sets to one (6–2, 5–7, 6–3). The achievement called for signal recognition, and the King and Queen, breaking precedent on a unique occasion, rose from their seats in the committee box and, moving to the entrance where the two new champions were waiting, offered their warm congratulations.

His Majesty, looking extremely well with a straw hat circled with the Guards riband; the Queen was in cream-coloured lace. One reflected on the change of fashion which time had brought – both on the court and off. The King, as Prince of Wales, had paid his first visit to Wimbledon – it had been the old ground, of course – in 1907. Then he came in frock coat and silk hat. He then saw the first invading champion, Miss May Sutton, of California, triumph for a second time. Miss Sutton wore a white skirt only removed from her shoes by four inches.

On Saturday, Miss Jacobs, another invader from the Pacific Coast, and Miss Round, her conqueror, came into court like bronzed Grecian maidens. The American was in shorts, with a coatee of navy blue; the English girl had a divided skirt, removing a yellow jumper to show the neat, man-like polo shirt. And the attributes of a battle-royal between two girls, who live 6,000 miles apart, were there. Yet they were sweetened by some homely touches. By a happy accident the sound of wedding bells from a distant church, mingling with the greeting, could be heard in the stands as the two players entered.

The heavy roller had groomed a perfect court and had then returned to its secluded corner to become the traditional coign of vantage for the groundstaff's wives. Lawn tennis had started as a family game; one liked the link of origin preserved. And in the stands to see the latest recruit to their hue were the past women champions – a total number which, I believe, even the Jubilee year of 1926 did not eclipse. I give their names, indicating in brackets the first or only year of their Championship: Mrs Hillyard (1886), Miss L. Dod (1887), Mrs Sterry (1895), Mrs Lambert Chambers (1902), Mrs Geen (1909), Mrs Larcombe (1912), Mlle Lenglen (1919), Mrs Godfree (1924), Mrs Moody (1927), Frl Aussem (1931). Only four past champions were absent – Miss Watson, the first of all, Miss Rice, Mrs Bundy and the late Miss Muriel Robb.

Apart from the annals of the game, Miss Round's victory, like that of Perry's the day before, had one outstanding virtue. It vindicated the value of pure stroke play; in defence and attack she upheld the best textbooks. Mrs Moody has a model service and a model drive; her volleying lacked the finish of a mistress. Suzanne was a perfect stroke-maker, the embodiment of poise; in her later years, so true was her back-court side, she only gave glimpses of the volleyer's art. Miss Round on Saturday was the complete player on view; there was scarcely a stroke in the game she did not exploit and in the correct way. She needed this full equipment to succeed, for in the challenge which Miss Jacobs offered every corner of her cupboard, so to speak, was searched.

In a survey of their relative strokes one saw the reasons for Miss Round's success. The American had a first service which, until its pace declined by physical reaction, was as powerful as Miss Round's. Her second service, however, was checked by the sheet behind it; it rose to give the receiver an inviting ball to drive. Later the factor was to tell – and to tell decisively. Where driving was concerned, especially in its relation to the volleying coup, Miss Round was intrinsically superior. On both wings she could get length and pace, the fundamental essentials, by a style at once sound and free from strain. The drives of Miss Jacobs by comparison were almost laboured. Her mainstay was a forehand chop, and she plied it with much pressure and industry. Her reserves were plain drives on both wings, but she only used them with confidence when she was not pinned back by the depth and 'fade-away' of the English attack.

This difference in driving equipment, suggesting the limitations of Miss Jacobs as a baseliner under intensive pressure, had a direct influence on the volleying excursions to which both resorted. When Miss Round came to the net it was behind a genuine forcing shot which only a complete driver, however fleet-footed, could handle with poise. When Miss Jacobs advanced it often had to be, for want of anything better, behind an under-cut return. Miss Round was, therefore, doubly favoured. She had time, because of the ball's slower pace, to get into position and to swing; she had the stroke in her bag to clinch the rally.

It may be asked why the player with the richer and more reliable strokes at her command did not win with a wider margin – why Miss Jacobs won the second set and was level at three all in the third. Could there be this disparity if the match wavered in the balance almost to the end? Strokes and the manner of making them do not always govern match play. Every wave must have its break before the next arrives; every artist with the racket seems to have a mental relaxation. Besides, it was a gruelling hot day; beakers of water at the side could not raise the drooping arm or prevent an unlucky phase. The American is a grim, persistent fighter; no one knew better the moral uncertainties which a third set crisis contains. Miss Jacobs was never beaten until the last shot was fired.

The match – admirably umpired, by the way, with only two or three rare decisions that looked doubtful – lasted one hour and ten minutes. Miss Jacobs had won the toss and naturally elected to serve. There was some rather tentative tennis, each searching for a touch, and Miss Jacobs won the first game on her opponent's errors. The English girl served her only double-fault of the match in the next game. Miss Jacobs served rather stiffly, and lost it. Miss Round revealed her tactics in the next two games – deep and run-provoking drives – and won them both to lead 3–1. It was a splendid start, and Miss Jacobs looked worried by the firmness of the attack. A beautiful drop shot – one thought of last year's drops that faded against Mrs Moody – carried Miss Round to 4–2, and then she won both the long seventh and eighth games after a great tussle, that proved that she held the key to victory. A fine cross-court drive gave Miss Round the set at 6–2.

The American must now have realised that patience and perseverance were not enough; she must save time and position by using the uncut drive. She opened the service in the second set confidently, but Miss Round had played herself in and met the increased pressure. She won the first game. New balls caused Miss Round to over-drive in the next; a service ace was discounted. Miss Jacobs won her service to love, but so did Miss Round; they were level at 2–2. Then Miss Jacobs came back to win from 15; again Miss Round squared with a love game. She was pressing the American remorselessly on her backhand; it was forced to yield. But this fine effort brought its reaction, and in the next two games, giving Miss Jacobs a 5–3 lead, she became uncertain for the first time. Miss Round recovered well in the ninth game, taking the last point with a beautiful toss. And in the tenth (when Mr Roper Barrett, the linesman, was unsighted, and a service had to be replayed) she levelled again at 5–5. Was Miss Round going straight out now? Miss Jacobs threw in all she had, including some top-spin drives which seemed to unsteady her opponent. The American served an express to reach 6–5, and won the 12th game from 15 with Miss Round driving out.

The crucial third set opened with Miss Round breaking through the opposing service from 30, and then losing her own to love. She pressed too hard for winners in the next game and lost that, too. Then her fine, fade-away drive and full repertoire of strokes began to tell again. She held her service for 30, and got another break to lead 3–2. But when Miss Jacobs had taken the sixth game to level the score you wondered whether staunchness after all might not get the better of style. Two long and tortuous games followed – Miss Jacobs picked up from 15–40 to deuce in the first. Both were claimed by Miss

Round. You knew that her heart was in the right place, and would remain there. The ninth, and victory, game was taken from 30. Miss Jacobs saved one match ball with a gallant advance which ended in a clean smash; only a great fighter could have made that kind of kill. Her effort to deuce the score failed; serene and confident, Miss Round made the winning stroke.

A tumultuous shout went up when the deed was done, the gallery of 16,000 rising to its feet. It was Miss Jacobs, the loser, who button-holed Miss Round and gently led her to the camera ordeal. They left the court together, but, such was her sympathy in the moment of triumph, one saw that Miss Round was smiling through a veil of tears.

6 JULY 1935

PERRY BEATS GERMAN IN THREE SETS

CHAMPION'S SPEED TOO MUCH FOR VON CRAMM

A. Wallis Myers

F.J. Perry is still champion, and the title which he regained for England last year remains at home. In a match of super-speed, lasting 80 minutes and bristling with gorgeous shots, the holder resisted the German challenge of Baron G. Von Cramm without losing a set. His score was 6–2, 6–4, 6–4. Wimbledon has yielded many closer and more fluctuating finals in the past. There have been matches in which net play has taken a more conspicuous part. But for the sustained pace of the ground shots, for refined, accurate driving, and for the thrusting power with which both men fought – Perry always a little quicker about the court than his rival – I cannot remember any contest quite like it. Tilden and Johnston in their heyday used to whip the ball with dazzling pace from the baseline, and the first would carry his pugnacity into the service. But they were neither as light-footed nor as quick in extracting the ball from the losing position as the champion and his challenger yesterday. They had caught the spirit of the time, which is speed.

Before I describe a contest which will certainly go down in history as a great final – great because of the quality of the play and the attacking character of nearly every shot – one may play a tribute of unstinted praise to the winner. Perry is not only the first 'playing through' champion to keep his title; he properly reserved for the last round, when the opposition was strongest, his soundest and most concentrated display. What a remarkable and romantic career Perry has had – the first 'people's champion' we may call him.

A native of Stockport, Lancashire, he has just turned 26 – two months older than Von Cramm. At Wallasey Grammar School and at Ealing County School he showed an aptitude for ball games, but it was not until he spent a family holiday at Eastbourne, and, as a boy of 15, watched the tournament in Devonshire Park, that his ambition to become a champion was fired. A year later he turned up at the Middlesex Junior Championship with a racket that had two strings missing, and reached the final. Then he competed in the junior Championship at Wimbledon, where his old racket collapsed in the middle of a game. But, as his father said afterwards, he came home like the proverbial dog with two tails, for he had hung up his clothes in the pavilion of the All-England Club in the locker used by René Lacoste, the reigning champion.

How Perry went to Budapest and became the first non-Hungarian competitor to win the world's table tennis championship; how he brought the quick-firing methods of the table tennis table, with the ball struck on the rise, to the tennis lawn, and came within a stroke of beating Austin at Queen's Club; how, given the opportunity to travel by his father and the Lawn Tennis Association, he subsequently won every important title open to competitors abroad, taking the crown at Wimbledon last year – that is only a bare outline of his upward flight.

His physical fitness is more a matter of instinct than rigorous training. He never touches alcohol, but is a moderate pipe-smoker. He does not like practice games; he can never be quite serious at them. Keenly competitive on the court, he is the easiest fellow to get on with off it. Incidentally, he can make a very neat after-dinner speech – and I've heard him tell an amusing story in more than one country.

It was a perfect day for a perfect final and the hunt for places was as zestful as ever. Queues had formed outside the gates when I was leaving the ground last night; enthusiasts flew over from the Continent; even the roller was covered with humanity. Both men had been training their eye on an outside court before the match, but the German did not betray the fact. He opened nervously, serving only one firm ball, and Perry drew early blood by winning the first two games. The champion was in complete touch from the start and the wristband which he wore could not have meant a weak arm – so manfully was he hitting all round the court.

Von Cramm won the third game, finding a target for his service and coming up behind it. By now his confidence and aim were back, and the crowd were treated to a sequence of glistening rallies, the ball often raising chalk, each man showing the boldest enterprise. The fifth game was a match in miniature. Von Cramm was serving and looked to have his grasp on it several times. He did not come to the net, as one thought he might have done, but he was producing the finest and deepest drives on both wings – searching the court, in fact, for some weakness. He found none. Perry was just too quick and too efficient for him. Shots that would have been winners against any other player became losers because the task of creating them could not be continuous against Perry's superb counter.

The first set, lasting 20 minutes, was Perry's at 6–2. He had conceded the German two of his own service games, serving himself with consistent fire and no suspicion of a double-fault. Von Cramm opened the second set with his service – slow back like a golfer, the ball struck with perfect timing – earning points. It was his first clean-cut game and Perry's reply to it was almost arrogant – a net attack that quickly levelled the score. They raced neck and neck for the next four games, both maintaining a fine length and speed, both recovering winners from the fringes of the court. Then the German's service lost some of its balance; he mistimed a couple of relatively easy ground shots; Perry had broken through.

Could the German get back this seemingly crucial game? He did so by a sudden net attack – one of the few games in which he used the volley as a scoring shot. But he did not maintain his high standard in the ninth game; Perry broke through his service from 15. He was just a second too quick for the incoming volleyer; the retort was too emphatic! Leading 5–4, you could see the gleam of battle in Perry's eye. He lost the first two points in the tenth game, but served too well not to carry the next four.

By normal reckoning the third set should have seen the pace reduced. But here were two super-athletes, well stocked with stamina; they moved just as rapidly, struck just as hard. It was an anxious set for both men – for Von Cramm because its loss meant the end of his endeavour; for Perry because he could see that his opponent had not yet been mastered. The German's unyielding mood was reflected in the first game. He served three splendid aces. Moving in with surer judgment, he also took the third from 0–40 down. But his service returns lacked precision; he lapsed at this stage over many. The fourth and fifth games were long and tortuous, but Perry's insistent defiance carried them both. He reached 4–2 with victory on the horizon. He could afford to sacrifice the seventh game, in which the German again served well; for the eighth was the Englishman's from 15. He led 5–3.

In the ninth game Von Cramm deserved his tumultuous applause. He had led 40–15 and then thrown his chance away. Perry got to 'vantage and match ball. Cool and calculating, the German came through this crisis. A brilliant service clinched the game. But the end was only delayed. Valiantly Von Cramm scored the first two points in the fateful tenth game. It was a tense moment. The German advanced behind two forcing shots to Perry's forehand; each time there was a gorgeous pass and the score was level. Another match ball came. The champion forced the pace; Von Cramm drove three inches out of court. The match was over. It had been won, as I have said, by super-speed. Perry was faster over the court than his opponent, more audacious, more consistent, never breaking down over the crucial coup. I have never seen a quicker mover.

As Perry left the club, Mlle Suzanne Lenglen, the former women's champion, kissed him on the cheek and said: 'You played some marvellous shots, Fred.' Afterwards Mlle Lenglen told me that she would not hope ever to see lawn tennis better played. Perry told me that he had enjoyed every minute of the match, but had been kept so hard at it that he did not know whether he was playing well or badly. Baron Von Cramm, a splendid sportsman, said that Perry was too good for him. He added that Perry's length and accuracy defeated him today, as on the rubble courts in Paris. 'I cannot beat him,' he said – 'it is doubtful if I ever shall while he keeps in his present form.'

4 JULY 1936

PERRY'S THIRD CHAMPIONSHIP

VON CRAMM INJURED AFTER FIRST GAME

A. Wallis Myers

Wimbledon's chief prize, King George's Cup and the men's singles Championship, remains in British custody, and F.J. Perry is the holder for the third successive year. But this record for the New Wimbledon, though redounding to the credit of the maker, was achieved without the customary ovation from a 15,000 gallery, without the customary struggle, and with Baron Von Cramm, after the opening set, physically out of action and unable to run. It was a disappointing finish to a final that promised so much. Fate has been unkind to many Wimbledon competitors this year. The victims of muscular strain have been many.

Austin stretched his 'riding muscle' in the French Championship a month ago and had to retire before a prospective match with Von Cramm. Wilmer Allison, the American champion, arrived in England from New

York suffering from the same accident. Gene Mako, Budge's partner in the doubles, tore a muscle in his chest and had to retire from Wimbledon. Zappa, the cheery Argentine, slipped and dislocated his arm. Borotra went into hospital on Thursday night, having torn a leg ligament, which was 'patched up' for the Frenchman to play in the doubles yesterday.

Finally, a cruel stroke of fortune, one of the best-trained athletes, the German champion, entered the Wimbledon ward, already full up. Von Cramm's injury – a torn muscle in the thigh – came in the second game, when he was serving. Von Cramm then realised, as he told me afterwards, that something had 'gone'. The perfect adversary, anxious to give Perry the full fruits of victory, he concealed his handicap as long as was humanly possible. 'I did not appreciate how serious it was,' he said, 'until movement, no doubt aggravating my complaint, I found that I could not run for the wide drive nor turn on my hips in my usual way.'

The huge expectant crowd, gathered for the match of the meeting between two great players, were at first mystified. They saw the keyed-up, rampant Perry serving like a demon and hitting winners on the drive and volley. But the German respondent, though he gave no outward sign to the gallery of any impediment or pain, and though he answered a friendly inquiry by Perry as they crossed over after the first set with a smiling assurance that nothing was wrong, was, for all practical purposes, out of the hunt.

The match, in short, was over after that first long game, with its three net-cords and its two double-faults – a fierce, fluctuating game, conducted at high tension, and a joyous game since it seemed to presage many more of equal intensity to come. To describe it in detail is but to tell the tale of an inevitable end. Von Cramm won the second game of the first set and the first game of the second set, in which Perry helped him by a double-fault. The others were all gathered by the champion with a margin widening as the effects of Von Cramm's ailment became more apparent and his inability to chase the ball more paralysing.

One's sympathy went out to both men – to the German for an accident not only ruining his chance yesterday, but probably imperilling Germany's chance in the Davis Cup; and to the champion for the unfulfilment of an ambition to defeat a sound opponent at the decisive stage of his defence. I was reminded, when I saw the courtly, chivalrous manner in which the German champion concealed his mortification from the crowd, that Perry's demeanour had been the same at Forest Hills last September when, in his match against Allison, he had fallen and sustained a painful internal injury.

Not a sign of petulance or dismay to the vast and eager American crowd when, an obviously wounded man, he continued to the end. These great players are great gentlemen, too.

Seeking a cause for this glut of casualties this year one is inclined to find it, first in the increasing nervous strain of modern lawn tennis – one big match after another in an atmosphere of public tension – and, secondly, in the weather changes of the present week that have made mobility on a damp surface more hazardous and more stressful on the bodily system. I offer respectfully a suggestion to the committee of management that they might lessen the physical demands on the players by divorcing the doubles from the singles. The plan is adopted in America to, I believe, the benefit of the standard of play, and it might, I think, be considered here without impairing the spectacular qualities of Wimbledon or preventing a fort-night's feast of attractive matches.

Perry owes his three Championships to his own skill and ardour, but I doubt whether he would have gained them if he had exposed himself to the diversion and extra physical strain of doubles matches interposed between his singles. It is significant that Von Cramm – quite normally, of course, for he entered for the two events, like many others – was required by the exigencies of the programmes to play a long and exacting doubles match against Allison and Van Ryn on the evening before he met Austin in the singles. After he had beaten Austin and on the same day there was another set in the same doubles contest waiting for him.

22 JUNE 1937

WIMBLEDON PLAY TELEVISED

SUCCESS OF NEW METHOD

A Television Correspondent

Television history was made yesterday when the play from the Centre Court at Wimbledon was successfully televised for more than 25 minutes in the afternoon programme. It was the first time that a great international outdoor event had been televised by wireless from the scene of its happen-ing, to Alexandra Palace, without an intervening land cable. It was, as an announcer said, 'a great achievement'.

Televiewers first saw the match in which H.W. Austin beat G.T. Rogers, and could observe every movement of the players. Even the marks of the passage of the lawn-mower over the grass were distinctly visible. There were also scenes of spectators in the stands, and their faces could be seen clearly. The television picture was accompanied by a commentary by Mr F.H. Grisewood. Later the match in which Jack Crawford, the Australian player, unexpectedly beat Roderick Menzel (Czechoslovakia) was televised.

5 JULY 1937
MISS ROUND REGAINS WOMEN'S TITLE AFTER EXCITING DUEL
A. Wallis Myers

Wimbledon is over, its prizes won and lost. It has been America's Wimbledon, yet the victory of Miss Dorothy Round, on Saturday, by which she regained the women's singles Championship, after the closest final against Mlle Jedrzejowska, champion of Poland, proves that talent and tenacity can still prevail in the home of lawn tennis. Miss Round had not given herself much of a thought this year, nor had the popular publicists. Perhaps this is why, moving in 'the unpierced shade', and seeded No. 7 in the official list, though she was No. 3 in the world's 'First Ten', her mind was less diverted and her chance, by sound judges of her game and character, deemed the stronger. She had not gone great guns this year. Señorita Lazana had beaten her at Bournemouth and Brighton, Miss McOstrich at Melbury. She had got her own back on the Chilean champion at Birmingham, but she came to Wimbledon without any blare of trumpets. Yet, if relative values count at all, the player who had defeated the holder conclusively in their Wightman Cup match at Wimbledon a year ago, and, on the same court, had confirmed this verdict at the Wimbledon just over, was at least a likely champion; and when her passage to the final without a 'vantage set in her five rounds was recorded, she herself might justly think her big chance had come again.

But Miss Round did not play in the final on Saturday – save in sections – with the confidence or consistency of earlier engagements. For this decline there were reasons. The day was sultry; hot pockets of air, influencing the ball's flight, had invaded the Centre Court; the top-spin attack of her opponent, who had been beaten in three successive tournaments in England, was encountered for the first time.

I believe that Miss Round's strokes and heart – for the latter was sorely needed in the third-set crisis – alone among those in competition at

Wimbledon this year, could have survived the sterling, fast-footed challenge which the Polish champion offered in the last round. And the champion of 1934 needed the psychological influences, which her own rival's excitable temperament created, to win through from 2–4 down. Miss Round's return from weakness to strength came exactly at the right moment. It was a match between conflicting reactions and, if on that account not of uniform good quality, it made it evenly balanced until the very end.

Greeting the loser in the whirl of Wimbledon after the match, I tended congratulations on her plucky fight. She was not thinking of the result. 'Oh, I am so excited,' she said. 'I am going to America for the first time.' The project had only just been fixed. I wondered silently whether the great tidings had not, after five weeks of disciplined schooling for the big event, subconsciously provoked her crucial double-faults in the final.

Now for the match in brief review. It was, as customary, well umpired and lined. Admiral Bruton was in the chair. There were no 'not-up' incidents, though the chasing up and down the court and across it was as strenuous and as keen as in any match this year. After a long first game, which the Pole might have won but for Miss Round's vigilance and speed of foot, Mlle Jedrzejowska showed that her service, fired on the centre-line chalk, might be a fruitful scorer. She took this game from 15 and went on to capture the next from 30, the gallery almost gasping in surprise when they found that a linesman had the temerity to foot-fault a woman ex-champion in her second service game. These service lapses, unprovoked by the opponent yet indicating natural strain, were to be a feature of the contest. The Pole served two double-faults when within a stroke of 3–1. Their advent seemed to turn the tide in the whole set.

Miss Round won five successive games, breaking through the service three times. She was directing her attack, as one thought she might, almost exclusively on the Jedrzejowska backhand, varying the length and strength as much as possible so as to unbalance the stance for the reply. It was unrelenting pressure and it prevailed. The Polish backhand, though its toughness under assault was often illustrated and though it could produce a winning coup – some of the drop shots which sprung from it were beautifully played – was not produced in the same way as Miss Round's. That meant that since the head of the racket was dropping and the follow-through not as full, the margin for error was greater. Miss Round has the perfect grip and makes the perfect stroke, and the anatomical strain is the less on that account.

The first set of eight games took 20 minutes; its successor had the same score and occupied the same time. Only Mlle Jedrzejowska won it. She started well by breaking the English service, helped by a net-cord. The loss of her own game from 30, aided by a double-fault, did not disturb her. She began to press into play what I have called before the 'Warsaw whiz-bang', the piercing, dipping forehand drive which is her own speciality and which few who meet it can resist.

Miss Round was creating the opening for this thunderbolt by the shorter length which time and the heat had brought to her own strokes; nor was she returning the service, even the guileless balls, with her former confidence. She was, in short, reacting ominously, while the other girl was in full cry. Three of the Pole's games were taken from 15; two service aces helped to win the fourth game, and even a great rally, one of the best of the match, could not save the eighth. Unless Miss Round could reimpose her pressure on the less dependable Polish backhand, using the volley for glancing strokes, her cause now looked doubtful. And it appeared really black after the first six games of the final set.

There were double-faults and net-cords, all the elements of tension to cause surprise; but Mlle Jedrzejowska, racing to and fro, and pulling out some splendid shots at the end of her run, arrived at 4—2 with a particularly well-played drop shot. It was now or never for Miss Round. She had to reassert her strokes and win. She did so. A service ace, one of her very few, helped to gather the seventh game; the eighth was captured to love because the Pole was, for the first time, title-conscious. When her rival, once behind, had caught and passed the leader, coming to 5—4 from 15, it looked as if the end were near. The last stroke of the game was a forehand bang that struck the green boundary before it struck the court.

Yet some 'happy, genial influence coming one knows not how or where' enabled Mlle Jedrzejowska to win the tenth and squaring game. She was a little lucky. A net-cord gave her a precious point; Miss Round fell in striving to save another. But there was no wavering, or even wonderful end. The next two games came to their calm pursuer with the loss of only one point. An erratic service return showed a loss of a once sure control; a double-fault from Poland influenced the fate of the last game. It had been an hour's exciting struggle, and both girls deserved the crowd's salute and a presentation to the two Princesses in the Royal Box. But the lapses in the match were too many to make it a great final.

BUDGE STILL WIMBLEDON CHAMPION

AUSTIN WINS ONLY FOUR GAMES IN HOPELESS FIGHT

A. Wallis Myers

The Wimbledon crown still rests on the red head of Donald Budge. Yesterday, defending his title before Queen Mary and a packed crowd of 15,000, the Californian defeated H.W. Austin in the final with the loss of only four games. The score was 6–1, 6–0, 6–3, and although these figures – a total of conceded games fewer than in any previous round – scarcely reflected the spirited struggle, which lasted nearly an hour, they pay a signal tribute to the champion's superior play.

Budge was, indeed, the king of the court, majestic in his power, unfaltering in his aim and pace, supreme in every department of the game. Last year, in picking up Perry's mantle, he lost one set in seven matches; this year, as befits an ennobled defender, he lost none. He won 129 games against the 40 collected by his seven challengers. Last year he won 128 games and lost 58. These are impressive figures and proclaim his relation to the field.

I was invited by several people yesterday to express an opinion about Budge's place in the hierarchy of champions. The Wimbledon closing today cannot answer that question. The class of opposition was not searching enough for a conclusive test. Budge was in an isolated class; only an accident could prevent his victory. Budge has set the hallmark on his fame. He is the first American holder to play through successfully at Wimbledon; he is the only player ever to hold the four major titles of the world at the same time. Those are honours enough without considering Budge's relation to Tilden, Lacoste, Vines, Perry and Borotra. I can only say that the present champion's task at Wimbledon this year had none of the testing severity and the mental and physical strain which faced Tilden when he 'played through' the American Championship six years in succession.

Dark clouds were gathering ominously when Queen Mary arrived at the Royal Box to see the finish of the women's doubles semi-final. Then all was clear for the big event of the day. At 3.10 Budge served out a game of five deuces – a level enough prelude. Three minutes later he had lost a love game with erratic strokes. Austin was swimming serenely in calm waters. Then the Californian waves reached him and his battle for life began. It proved to be a hopeless fight, and at 3.50, after 40 minutes' play, he had lost 14 games in succession and Budge was his complete master.

But he was never demoralised or incapable of reply. Indeed, his own control and mobility extracted the best from Budge, and the crowd would never have witnessed such a scintillating display from the champion – the best he has given to Wimbledon this year – if his opponent had not kindled the spark of genius by supplying the opposite role. At long last Austin's efforts to stem the sequence of games were rewarded. He won the fourth game in the third set, breaking through Budge's service to do it. The next game was his, too; he clinched it with a beautiful and daring half-volley. Then Budge's service intervened and 4–2 was called. Austin's last shots were not yet fired, and he made it 4–3. Then came a shower of rain and a 15-minute halt. Could the *coup de grâce* be arrested by some miraculous change?

Budge quickly supplied the answer, for when play was resumed he only lost one point in the next two games. To explain why the American secured his decisive break of 14 games it is only necessary to say that his speed of drive and the finishing force of his volleys commanded nearly all the rallies that really mattered. Austin played much better than he did against Vines in his last final of 1932. Then he did not make a match of it; this time he did. Budge said afterwards that he thought Austin was below his best form. I do not agree. The challenger played quite as well as he did against Henkel, but in yesterday's encounter he did not have the time or the room to make winning shots. Budge dictated the pace and the tactics, and when Budge's long arm shot out at short range – and what a telescopic reach he had – the English drive that might have mastered Henkel was cut off in its prime. The murder was complete.

4 JULY 1938

ALL WIMBLEDON TITLES FOR AMERICA

MRS MOODY'S RECORD FEAT IN WOMEN'S CHAMPIONSHIP

MISS JACOBS STRUGGLES THROUGH FINAL WITH STRAINED TENDON

A. Wallis Myers

It was America's Wimbledon. In 1930 the invading players from the States won four Championships and shared a fifth with Australia. This year they carried away all five. Three, as last year, were captured by Donald Budge, who, giant that he is, maintained his unbeaten record and only sacrificed one set in repeating a triple triumph. To Mrs Moody the Wimbledon which closed on Saturday brought a unique honour. By defeating Miss Helen

Jacobs in the final she claimed the women's singles for the eighth time, eclipsing the record established by Mrs Lambert Chambers, who was champion seven times.

The story of Mrs Moody's career at Wimbledon is worth its epitome. In 1924, when she first came over at the age of 18, she reached the final with conspicuous ease and appeared to have the title in her grasp when she led Miss McKane 6–4, 4–1. A lack of match-play experience and the courage of the English girl thwarted her. In 1926, the year of her famous contest with Mlle Lenglen at Cannes, Miss Wills had been forced to retire from the French Championships in Paris, a victim of appendicitis. Recovering from her operation, she came to Wimbledon as a spectator, but in 1927 she began her Championship reign, losing a set to Miss G. Sterry in the first round, but defeating Señorita de Alvarez in the final after a most exhilarating display.

She competed in 1928, 1929, 1930 (when she appeared as Mrs Moody) and 1932 without losing a set. The next year she was harried by Miss Dorothy Round in the final, but survived with the loss of the middle set. Returning after two years' absence, she was nearly beaten in the fourth round by a courageous Czech girl, Mlle Cepkova, who won the first set and had a point for a 4–1 lead in the second; and in the subsequent final, after an hour and 40 minutes' breathless play, she was within a stroke of losing the Championship to Miss Jacobs. Since she first competed at Wimbledon 14 years ago, Mrs Moody has won 111 sets and lost only six – four to English players, one to Mlle Cepkova and one to Miss Jacobs. In that period she has collected 22 love sets. Her total number of games won is 701; she has lost 263.

She came to her last final on Saturday before a stadium packed to its utmost limits, a crowd, many of whom had queued up outside the ground overnight and who waited, eagerly and expectantly, for this fourth Centre Court final between two of the keenest rivals the game has known. At the head of this concentrating gallery was Queen Mary, who arrived in the committee box just before the start of the final, and who had been present with King George V at Mlle Lenglen's first Championship final 19 years earlier. Her Majesty remained at Wimbledon for nearly four hours, coming back after the rain had interrupted play during the doubles to see the giant tarpaulin in mechanical action shedding its containing water. Queen Mary gave a gracious bow to every finalist, and during one of the intervals she conversed with W.T. Tilden, who was presented to her by Sir Louis Greig, the All-England Club chairman.

The Helens might come from the same Californian town – their families, indeed, actually occupied the same house in turn – have gone to the same college and graduated in tennis at the same club; but this neighbourly propinquity only added to ambitious zest and made competition all the stronger. And the incentive on the day was absorbing. If Helen I triumphed, she would claim a record reign. If Helen II succeeded, she would, as an unseeded player – 'the forgotten woman', so to speak – have come through the most talented field ever assembled at Wimbledon, including her famous rival from her home town.

But history repeated itself, and Mrs Moody prevailed again. Her score was 6–4, 6–0, but the figures, standing alone, do not tell the story of Miss Jacobs's defiant fight in the first set; nor of Mrs Moody's tranquil resistance, founded on a superiority of stroke technique; nor of the untimely accident to Miss Jacobs which rendered her almost *hors de combat* and suddenly changed the contest from a speculative and exciting struggle into a rapidly deflating encounter which could have only one ending. Miss Jacobs was forced to withdraw her resistance after straining her Achilles tendon in the ninth game of the first set. She had her right ankle tightly bound up when she came into court, having damaged it in her hectic struggle against Miss Marble two days earlier. Osteopathic treatment had seemingly put her right, but the plan of campaign which the ex-champion had rehearsed involved an intensive attack and rampant volleys, some of which the crowd applauded in the first half of the match, that only absolutely sound limbs could achieve.

After Miss Jacobs, down 2–4, had squared the issue by that kind of concentrated mental and physical effort which she alone can furnish, Mrs Moody appearing to falter before her challenge, she came within a stroke, after more grim rallies, of taking the lead at 5–4. Breathlessly she arrived at the net to intercept a passing shot down her forehand line. In stretching out for the coup – I doubted whether she could make it, since her opponent's thrust was splendidly directed – she pulled the bandaged tendon again. It was obvious from her face and from the fact that she rested for a moment on the umpire's chair, as they crossed over after the ninth game, that tragedy had come again to the Centre Court and that Miss Jacobs was through.

In the tenth game Mrs Moody calmly pursued her course without heed of passing events. She served four balls and her adversary, broken beyond repair, was beaten by all of them. This love game, the first 'soft' game of the match, gave her the first set. She won the second set with the loss of only three points, two in the first game and one in the fifth – an irrecoverable backhand drive by Miss Jacobs, made off her sound leg. But the match was really over, and Miss Jacobs, ignoring a request from Mrs Wightman, who came down to the court to suggest her retirement, merely played out time as best she could. Everyone was disappointed, for a battle-royal had been called off by intervening Fate; yet the true perspective of these playing-field accidents ought to be preserved.

Mrs Moody was criticised by many onlookers – and probably the public reception of her Championship record was cooler in consequence – for her apparent indifference to her adversary's affliction. She offered no sympathy on court. That is her way, and by this mental detachment and complete abstraction in the game itself she has come to her fame and to her record. When Von Cramm was incapacitated by a muscular injury two years ago, rendering his resistance to Perry only nominal, the British champion had to fight on under circumstances equally uninspiring. Perry more than once conveyed his sympathy to his crippled opponent. But Mrs Moody has not got Perry's nature; that fact is reflected in her staid and stoical play.

That good sport should be interrupted by an accident of the chase was unfortunate, alike to players and public, but women in full cry on a tennis court under modern conditions, the speed of the game having increased, must always be liable to physical mishap, and there is no call to make a great song about it. Instead we may congratulate both competitors – Mrs Moody on achieving her record eighth victory, in spite of Mrs Sperling's stubborn and all but successful fight in the semi-final, and Miss Jacobs for refusing 'to quit' and for giving Mrs Moody the satisfaction, denied to Miss Jacobs herself in New York five years earlier, of a finished match.

17 JUNE 1939

OBITUARY: ARTHUR WALLIS MYERS

DAILY TELEGRAPH LAWN TENNIS CORRESPONDENT
GREATEST CRITIC OF THE GAME

Mr Arthur Wallis Myers, who has often been described as the foremost lawn tennis critic in the world, died yesterday at the age of 60. He had been Lawn Tennis Correspondent of *The Daily Telegraph* for the past 31 years.

His knowledge of his subject was encyclopaedic, and with his skill as a vivid writer he combined the authoritative knowledge of one who for many years was a leading player. He could remember almost every big game played at all important meetings over a very long period; and in addition to being a friend of all the famous players of his time, was able with extraordinary skill to analyse their style. Particularly fascinating were his comparisons of technique, his estimates of capability, and his study of psychological aspects. His annual rankings in *The Daily Telegraph* of the ten leading players was quoted all over the world.

In 1924 he founded the International Lawn Tennis Club of Great Britain, of which he was subsequently elected chairman and vice-president, and he had the satisfaction of seeing many countries establish organisations in affiliation with it. Wallis Myers believed that lawn tennis was a wonderful medium for the promotion of international good feeling. He wanted to see 'the reconciling racket displace the severing sword'. In his belief hands across the net might also mean hands across the world.

But apart from the many tennis championships he won as a player, and the work he did as a captain of British teams sent to Europe, to South Africa in 1910–11 and 1933–34, and to India in 1930–31, he was above all a journalist. In that capacity he began work on the now defunct *Westminster Gazette,* and there were two striking examples of his keenness as a news-gatherer. Both concerned the coronation of King Edward VII. Calling at a silversmith's shop about some engraving he was having done in 1902, he received an apology for non-completion of the work because of urgent attention to a Royal order. Wallis Myers noticed an unfinished medal bearing the date of the coronation! He lost no time publishing the secret.

But many weeks later he had an even greater 'scoop', for while making inquiries on another subject he heard a distinguished civil servant say: 'What a calamity this is.' Out of that remark and the despondency he thought he had detected just before at Buckingham Palace, came his conclusion and subsequent report to his office of the sensational news that the coronation had been postponed.

Wallis Myers, in addition to being founder and editor of *The Lawn Tennis Almanack,* had been for more than 20 years the lawn tennis editor of *The Field.* A widely travelled man and a close student of affairs, he wrote many books. His principal works included *The Complete Lawn Tennis Player, Lawn Tennis at Home and Abroad, The Story of the Davis Cup, Fifty Years of Lawn Tennis* and *Principles and Practice of Lawn Tennis.*

His own successes on the court were very numerous. They date back to 1909, when he won the doubles and mixed doubles championships of the Riviera. In the same year, with S.N. Doust as his partner, he carried off the

Monte Carlo doubles. In subsequent years before the Great War he gained many successes in the South of France in doubles and mixed doubles. To a striking extent he continued his playing successes after the war, for at widely scattered meetings across the Channel and in many parts of England he went on to repeat his doubles and mixed doubles triumphs. Frequently he shared these honours with famous players, who included A.F. Wilding, A.R.F. Kingscote, F.R.L. Crawford and W.M. Johnston.

During the Great War he was attached to the Department of Information, and in addition to evolving some very effective ideas was sent on two special missions to Italy. He received the CBE in 1920, and in 1932 was made a Chevalier of the Legion of Honour. Mr Wallis Myers was a son of the Rev. J.B. Myers and was born at Kettering. Educated at Watford and The Leys, Cambridge, he married in 1900 Lilian Agnes, daughter of Captain Gentry, of Maldon, and she survives him, with one son and four daughters.

17 JUNE 1939
LEADER: A SERVANT OF SPORT

By the death of Mr Arthur Wallis Myers, *The Daily Telegraph* has been deprived of a contributor valued for more than 30 years. In youth, and even past middle-age, a fine lawn tennis player, particularly in doubles matches, Mr Myers had also established himself for a generation as an outstanding and always genial critic of court tactics. His powers of organisation in the game were tested not only as the captain of British teams abroad but often behind the scenes.

Though a man of varied interests, fortified by wartime service in the Ministry of Information and by wide travel, it is as a servant of sport that he has left a name. His death will be felt as a loss by leaders of lawn tennis throughout the world and in a special sense by *The Daily Telegraph* and its readers.

8 JULY 1939
R.L. RIGGS TRIUMPHS AT WIMBLEDON
E.T. COOKE DEFEATED IN FIVE-SET FINAL
Our Special Representative

Robert L. Riggs, of America, yesterday joined the select band of those who have conquered Wimbledon at the first attempt. He beat his compatriot,

E.T. Cooke, by 2–6, 8–6, 3–6, 6–3, 6–2 in the final of the men's singles. C.L. Patterson, W.T. Tilden and Ellsworth Vines are the only other players who have done it. Riggs, therefore, joins high company – but how vastly different his methods from those of the redoubtable hitters with whom his name is now linked.

And what a strange sight to see empty benches and walking-room on the terraces on a Wimbledon Finals day! Hundreds of the open stand seats – available only at the turnstiles – for which the midnight queues once formed, were unsold. And after two sets the vast arena half-emptied and the tea marquee filled. Presumably after a long reign of speed champions, who smote and smashed their way to titles in the grand spectacular manner, the quieter and more studious art of Riggs is poor 'box office'. Indeed, I heard one man who can remember Wimbledon in its pre-war setting, describe this Riggs–Cooke final as an anachronism.

If that is true, and the Renshaws, the Baddeleys, and the Dohertys match their wits as Riggs matched his against the speed and force which Cooke attempted to impose, the game itself will not suffer by a retrogressive step. The athletic prowess of a Borotra and the controlled hitting of a Johnston or a Vines are not given to all of us, and if a few club players were made to realise, watching Riggs, that science can still achieve much on the tennis court, their enjoyment of the game will increase.

Primarily, though, Riggs is to be praised for the fact that he won when below his best form. The effort to raise his game to its highest level was at times obvious. The strokes did not flow with the same spontaneity and sparkle as they had against Puncec, for example, but his will and determination were rigid, and even when everything appeared to be going against him he never lost sight of the ultimate goal. There were many rallies that, frankly, were boring, long backhand exchanges that cried out for a stroke of enterprise. But there were many just as enthralling, and the fluctuations of the score should have been enough to keep interest alive.

CHAPTER THREE
LAST OF THE
AMATEURS
(1946–67)

32 NATIONS AT WIMBLEDON REOPENING TODAY

John Olliff

The reopening of the Lawn Tennis Championship at the All-England Club, Wimbledon, today after six years of war provides the most tangible and poignant symbol of peace for all lawn tennis followers. Thirty-two nations of widely differing colours and creeds are here to contend for the highest honours in the game. Never before have the players from overseas been so keen to get here and never has their enthusiasm reached such a pitch. Many of them have had to overcome great difficulties in making the journey.

Never before have countries shown themselves to be such ardent lovers of the game as they have now by raising public subscriptions to meet their players' expenses in order that their country might be represented at Wimbledon. An example of this enthusiasm is the case of Miss Jadwiga Jedzrejowska, who arrived by air from Warsaw via Berlin just in time for the Championships. She has had little practice, and on arrival possessed no tennis clothes or shoes. She did not touch a racket during the whole of the war and her experiences in Poland do not bear repetition. She is thinner and obviously wearied and worn by her country's sufferings. Her obvious joy at being back once again at Wimbledon is shared by all the competitors from European countries ravaged by the Nazis.

If it is in some ways an austerity Wimbledon this year, it will not be in the quality of play. This was proved by the London grass-court championships at Queen's Club last week. I do not believe it is possible for two women to play much better tennis than Miss Pauline Betz and Miss Margaret Osborne played in the final of the women's singles. That it was a dress rehearsal for the Wimbledon final I have little doubt. Gerald Patterson, the great Australian player who won the first Wimbledon singles Championship after the last war, declared after seeing this match that Lenglen did not play better tennis when she beat Mrs Lambert Chambers to win her first Wimbledon Championship.

KRAMER TRIUMPHS EASILY AT WIMBLEDON

John Olliff

WIMBLEDON, Friday

Jack Kramer, of America, became the new tennis champion when he beat Tom Brown, also of America, in the final of the men's singles today, 6–1, 6–3, 6–2. His Majesty the King presented the cup to the winner, and both finalists were also congratulated by the Queen and Princess Margaret.

The final was a disappointment because Brown appeared overawed by his opponent's reputation and he was unable to provide a criterion by which to judge the new champion. Kramer did all that was required of him, and I have no doubt that if Brown had been in better form Kramer would have raised his game. It is idle to compare him with champions of the past because he has won his laurels in lean times, and there is really no player to test him. Great champions do not produce their best when it is unnecessary, and it is certain that Kramer was not at his best, the number of errors being remarkably high for a Wimbledon final. Brown's forehand was wildly erratic. He was jerking his body backwards and away from the ball, and his stroke was missing its mark by yards.

Kramer's brilliant play against Palls in the semi-final impressed many former champions, and one of them went so far as to say: 'I am not sure that he is not the best player I have ever seen.' He is a great champion and he should not be judged by his easy but unimpressive victory in the final.

THE MAGIC OF WIMBLEDON

John Olliff

'What mighty contests rise from trivial things!' – Pope

Eighty years ago Mr J.W. Walsh, the editor of *The Field,* and a few enthusiastic friends bought a small plot of ground in Worple Road, Wimbledon, and started a croquet club. On Monday, for two weeks, that 'trivial' little club, now the All-England Lawn Tennis and Croquet Club (removed to Church Road to give it elbow room in 1922) will be the scene of 'mighty contests' ·between the champions of over 30 nations from all over the world.

In the final of the first Championship in 1877 Mr Spencer Gore, a court tennis player, beat Mr W.C. Marshall, a rackets players, 6–1, 6–2, 6–4, before an enthusiastic crowd of 200 spectators. The match was due to be played on 16 July, but had to be postponed until 19 July as the two finalists insisted on watching the Eton and Harrow cricket match at Lord's.

Since those romantic days the name of Wimbledon has gathered such magic that the Championships have survived three wars, and the ever-increasing accommodation for spectators has become totally inadequate. Thousands of followers of the game who applied for seats in February will not see a ball struck on the Centre Court unless they are prepared to stand for hours in a queue with the prospect of being wedged like sardines in the standing enclosure if they fail to get one of the limited number of unreserved seats.

Men and women have been made world-famous at this great theatre of lawn tennis. Just as the incomparable Sarah Bernhardt thrilled the world from across the footlights at the Comédie-Française, Anna Pavlova raised ballet to the level of the other great arts at the St Petersburg Mariinsky Theatre, and Covent Garden made the immortal Patti, so Wimbledon made, and later ruined, its greatest artist, Suzanne Lenglen.

The Renshaws, the Dohertys, Brookes, Wilding, Lenglen, Wills, Lacoste, Cochet, Borotra, Vines, Budge, Perry, Kramer and the rest down to the present day are names which have been made by what was once in the dim past a little suburban croquet club which prohibited its members from playing in their shirt sleeves when ladies were present.

When I am not in the Press Box, or the Television Box, at Wimbledon during the next fortnight, I shall be in the members' stand listening to something which never bores me. There one finds the few remaining men and women who played with the great champions of the past. Mr J.G. Ritchie, F.L. Riseley, George Greville, Mrs Sterry, Mrs Lambert Chambers will all be there to compare the 1950 champions from personal experience with those of over fifty years ago. 'Yes, a fine stroke,' one hears them say, 'but Lenglen would never have given her the chance to play it.' 'Laurie Doherty would have killed that one stone dead', and so it goes on, an argument which can never be proved one way or the other.

But one can take a line through the intermediate players. As late as 1924 Brookes made his famous 'comeback' and beat F.T. Hunter, a Wimbledon finalist and Tilden's doubles partner. Mrs L.A. Godfree, who was beaten 6–0, 6–0 by Lenglen, subsequently won the Championship twice. In 1925 the standard was not appreciably lower than it is today and yet Suzanne Lenglen won the ladies' singles Championship with the loss of five games, a record which I think will never be beaten. It is interesting to record the scores of her last three matches in the Championship that year. In the quarter-final she beat Mrs Beamish 6–0, 6–0, in the semi-final she beat Miss K. McKane (Mrs Godfree) 6–0, 6–0, and in the final she beat Miss Joan Fry 6–2, 6–0.

That was during the great French era of 1924–29 when Lacoste, Cochet, Borotra and Brugnon, 'the Four Musketeers', swept all before them. It is curious how France produced all those great players at the same time and has now slipped back again to be a second-rate lawn tennis nation. The same has happened to Great Britain. Since the glorious era in the middle 1930s when Fred Perry, Bunny Austin and Dorothy Round were at the top of the tree, we have not produced a single outstanding player. The United States and Australia now provide all the leading players at Wimbledon with the exceptions of J. Drobny, the former Czechoslovakian, and E.W. Sturgess, of South Africa, and the curious part about it is that neither of these players can win a major championship.

The technique of lawn tennis is undoubtedly going through a period of transition. Everything is now sacrificed to greater power of stroke. More players appear every year who use the two-handed stroke on one wing or the other. The maximum power of stroke has now been achieved in this unorthodox way by G.E. Brown, of Australia, who would undoubtedly win the Championship if he could perfect his control of this murderous stroke. This change is also reflected in the forehand drive volley which has replaced the old short swing volley. This stroke has been perfected by O.W. Sidwell, of Australia, and is now used by nearly all the leading volleyers because of its far greater power.

The women's game has been revolutionised as far as technique is concerned by the Americans, who aim at playing as powerful and aggressive volleying games as men. That is why it is useless for our women to practise baseline driving for hours on end when the only answer to a complete volleyer is a volleying campaign. This was clearly borne out by Mrs B.E. Hilton (now Mrs Harrison), who nearly beat Miss L. Brough, the Wimbledon champion, and was the only British woman who attempted to play these Americans at their own game in the recent Wightman Cup debacle.

Britain is going through a lean period, but it is not the first time, and I am confident that we have some young material which will form the nucleus of a renaissance. It took 12 years for Britain to get back on the lawn tennis map after the First World War, and it looks like taking the same time after the Second. We have two outstandingly promising players in John Horn and Miss Susan Partridge. To them I say: 'Get into the fight against the toughest opposition you can find as often as you can.' There has been too much waiting for the big occasion and then not being prepared for the violence of the encounter.

Wimbledon is waiting for a new British champion, and, if Horn and Miss Partridge have the spirit I think they have, their names will be written in gold on the tablets round the entrance to the Centre Court before many more names have been added. As they walk on to the Centre Court for their most testing matches they will do well to glance up at the inscription over the players' entrance:

> *If you can meet with Triumph and Disaster*
> *And treat those two imposters just the same.*

10 JULY 1950

WIMBLEDON WAS TRIUMPH FOR MISS BROUGH

John Olliff

Saturday brought the Wimbledon fortnight to a close and a personal triumph to Miss Louise Brough, who won the women's singles Championship for the third successive year and once again won both doubles titles. The women's singles final, in which Miss Brough beat her American compatriot, Mrs W. Dupont, 6–1, 3–6, 6–1, was so familiar an encounter for the Centre Court that at times it was like listening to a gramophone record which one has heard so often that it has lost its ability to surprise and thrill. It would be ungenerous to add that the record was cracked, but it did not run with its smooth rhythm of former days.

When they reached one set all one did not feel the tense excitement in the crowd which usually greets the final set of a Wimbledon final. Rather did one feel that someone had 'put another nickel in' and the tune started up again for the third time. It was the first set (and not the second set on the other side) which was repeated, and Miss Brough demonstrated clearly that she is far less prone to fall into error than is Mrs Dupont nowadays.

Perhaps the most disappointing player in this event was Miss Doris Hart, who had played so brilliantly at Queen's Club the week before Wimbledon, when she beat both the Wimbledon finalists. Miss Hart was at least expected to give the champion a close match in the semi-final, if not to beat her, but when she missed her chance of leading 5–3 in the first set she seemed to become discouraged and ever after her glorious strokes lacked purpose and her determination evaporated. When Miss Hart was beaten this event was robbed of its chief interest to British followers of the game, who could hardly be expected to mind very much which of the charming two leading American women should take the crown which both had previously won.

23 JUNE 1951

WIMBLEDON IS GREATER THAN ALL HER CHAMPIONS

John Olliff, Daily Telegraph Lawn Tennis Correspondent and former British Davis Cup player

For the next two weeks the Lawn Tennis Championships will be played at the All-England Club; Wimbledon tennis will have its crowded fortnight of glorious life. There are still many people for whom, during the other 50 weeks of the year, lawn tennis is a myth, Wimbledon is a legend, and the word tennis is associated only with the old rackets which are tied together in company with buckets, spades, cricket stumps and Aunty Mabel's umbrella and recline on the platform of Victoria Station, a mountainous symbol of the seaside holiday spirit.

It is not so long ago that lawn tennis was regarded, especially at the public schools, as something not only abstract in form but even vaguely not quite proper, like D.H. Lawrence and hamburger sausages. It is all very well to say, '*Plus ça change ...*' but nothing has changed more in character, or in 'tone-consciousness' than Wimbledon since what now seem the medieval times of the Renshaws and the Dohertys, or even since 1922 when Tilden and Lenglen transferred their glory from the Worple Road to the more rural setting of the New Wimbledon.

True, there are still a few sensations at Wimbledon common to the Worple Road spectator and the winner of a seat in the ballot today. There is still the same thrill of impending drama when the octagonal walls of the Centre Court first peep at us through the trees as we approach the ground. Did not patrons of the old Globe Theatre experience a similar vision and the same thrill before the first-night performance of *Hamlet?* Above all, there is still that first view of smooth, wide expanse of soft green grass lying so quiet and peaceful under a caressing sun. But this is merely the overture. Let us ring up the curtain and on with the play!

Wimbledon has won the battle against the players hands down. She has proved since the war that no player is as great as the Championship of which he is but a small part. *The* Championship, mark you! Wimbledon used to be styled the World's Championship. America objected and other nations supported her. But the wit of the late Sir Herbert Wilberforce, then chairman of the All-England Club, was too much for them and the World's Championship took on the even richer title of The Championship.

Every year since the war Wimbledon has had the dream of its champions scooped off the top by the lure of professionalism. Like an old oak tree she stood firm and regardless as her topmost leaves went down the wind. But Nature ever replaces what it destroys and it was soon proved that the tree itself, and not any of its particular leaves, was dearest to men's hearts. It was Wimbledon that made those players great and not those players that made Wimbledon great. We regret their passing and admit that in their day they seem irreplaceable. But would Wimbledon be a greater annual festival in the sporting life of Great Britain today if Kramer, Riggs and Co were competing? It would not.

We all have our Wimbledon heroes and when they go from us and join the professionals we may race hot-foot to Wembley to cheer them once again, but our cheers will catch in our throats and as we creep away into the night our eyes will be wet, not from the strain of the arc lights but because our stars were not in their right setting. No stage scenery can compare with the natural grandeur of Wimbledon.

The Wimbledon authorities have not remained entirely insensitive to the spirit of the age, and next week will see a coloured American lady, Miss Althea Gibson, competing in the Championship for the first time. Authority has also relaxed its stringent views on dress, though with frowning brows, since the days when the American player John Hennessy was asked to change his white flannel trousers before entering the Centre Court because they were observed on close examination to bear a faint grey pinstripe. It must be admitted, however, that certain ladies from the United States have in recent years bedecked themselves on our sacred lawns in a manner not entirely fitting to an event so regularly graced by Royalty. We are inclined to sympathise with an all-male committee whose obvious duty it is to regulate such matters and to hope that the ladies concerned will so distinguish themselves at the only game they were invited to play that they will need no fancy frills and furbelows to give them the panache they seek.

The committee have been bombarded with complaints from the public about their innovation this year of throwing all Centre Court seats into the ballot and thereby offering standing room only on the Centre Court for those who choose to queue up outside the ground. It remains to be seen how this slightly high-handed action will work out. It gives greatest offence to the young enthusiasts who cannot afford the ten-guinea book of tickets even should they be lucky in the ballot and to those who can only go once or twice in the fortnight. They were happy to queue up all night for a seat; now they have not even this privilege.

When one realises that £65,000 had to be returned to unsuccessful applicants in the ballot for Centre Court seats three months ago, and that no other championship in the world has ever sold out for every day (even including seats sold on the day), one can see how little the high-falutin' title of World's Championship matters to Wimbledon and how very worthy the meeting is to be known throughout the world simply as The Championship.

28 JUNE 1951

VON CRAMM SHOWS REAL CLASS, BUT FAILS

John Olliff
WIMBLEDON, Monday

Baron Gottfried Von Cramm, runner-up to Fred Perry in 1935 and 1936 and to Donald Budge in 1937, brought once again a glimpse of real class to the Centre Court, even though beaten 9–7, 6–4, 6–4 by J. Drobny on the opening day of the Lawn Tennis Championships here today. There will not be a better striker of the ball seen at Wimbledon this year, and at the age of 41 it was merely that he had not the speed of foot to reach the wide ball, nor his former eagerness to bend down to make a forcing backhand, that brought about his defeat.

He showed his class in his forehand return service, his superb sense of timing and touch on the low attacking lob and perhaps, above all, by his service, which was a lesson to all modern players. His first service was always a deadly threat, and his second, hit to a splendid length, swung and broke away viciously. British players of both sexes please mark, learn and inwardly digest the fact that, in spite of the quality of the second service, he never served one double-fault throughout the match.

He told me before he went on the court that the last match he played on grass was in 1939, when he and I won the final of the London Grass Court doubles Championship at Queen's Club. Twelve years is a long time not to play a match on grass.

It is true that Drobny was nervous at the start and Von Cramm was allowed to lead 3–1 without being forced to do more than play orthodox lawn tennis at, as it were, cruising speed. Von Cramm led 40–30 when serving at 3–1, and the subsequent loss of that game undoubtedly cost him the set. At seven all, Drobny broke the service and although Von Cramm fought splendidly to recover the break, Drobny served home the set at 9–7.

Von Cramm went to 2–0 in the second set, but the loss of his service in the next game proved fatal, for Drobny broke through again at four all to take the set 6–4. The third set was much the same story but after Drobny got his break with some powerful passing shots to lead 5–4, Von Cramm magnificently went to 40–0 against the service.

It was now that Drobny played with real determination, and in catching up to deuce he gave Von Cramm no chance to win the next point for advantage; but Drobny, now confident of his domination, took the game for the match with a sure touch, an air of grandness, and an understandable sigh of relief. The discriminating Wimbledon crowd gave voice to their appreciation of a player of great craft as he left the court. Drobny had to play well to win, for there are not many players at Wimbledon this year who could have done so.

30 JUNE 1951

OBITUARY: JOHN OLLIFF

A PLAYER-WRITER OF LAWN TENNIS

John Sheldon Olliff, who died suddenly yesterday on his way to report the Wimbledon Championships for *The Daily Telegraph*, was 42. He joined *The Daily Telegraph* in 1945, succeeding the late A. Wallis Myers as lawn tennis correspondent. During his six years as a journalist he made himself a leading authority on the game.

An all-round athlete and a fine player of any ball game, he topped the St Paul's School batting in 1927 with an average of 40.06. Blessed with a quick eye, fine natural skill and a sturdy temperament, he could have come to the front in any department of lawn tennis, but it was as a doubles player that he excelled. True, he began by winning his spurs unaided by triumphing in the public schools singles Championship in 1923, followed by the Junior Championship of Britain in 1924 and 1925, and the Public Schools again in 1926. He also had a great moment as a singles player in 1931 when he beat F.J. Perry at Bournemouth in the British Hard Court Championship. In that year he won the London Championship at Queen's, a victory he repeated in 1936.

But his victories in partnership were even more remarkable. With H.W. Austin he won the British Hard Court doubles Championship in 1930; partnered by Perry he gained it again two years later and with H. Billington reached the final in 1939. Three times he won the British Covered Court Championship, with Austin in 1930 and 1931, and with D. Prenn in 1934, and the mixed doubles with Miss F. James, now Mrs S.H. Hammersley, in 1936. E.R. Avory was his partner when he won the Argentine doubles title in 1932.

Many times he played for Britain, touring North and South America and India. In 1946 he represented Britain in the Davis Cup, partnering Billington in the match against France. He captained the International Club of Great Britain in 1939 and 1946. In May 1934, in Stockholm, he married Miss Dagny Lindblom, a Swedish lawn tennis player. She and two daughters survive him.

5 JULY 1952

SEDGMAN WORTHY WINNER OF GOOD FINAL

Lance Tingay
WIMBLEDON, Friday

Australian lawn tennis has triumphed at last in the Lawn Tennis Championships. Frank Sedgman beat Jaroslav Drobny in the singles final here today to erase the memory of Australia's four losing finalists in six previous postwar years, and to become the first Australian champion since Jack Crawford in 1933. And a worthy winner, too! Sedgman played the final well and though it was not one that will be remembered as a dramatic fight, like Falkenburg's victory over Bromwich in 1948, or as superb lawn tennis, like Kramer's win over Tom Brown in 1947, it will be recorded as one rather above normal standard.

Sedgman played the match like an efficient miler on the track. For the first lap the other man made the pace. He drew level during the second and went ahead in the third. Just before the bell he got right away while Drobny stumbled far behind. Those who looked for an exciting final were disappointed. It was never that, mainly I think because Sedgman was too efficient. There were few second chances given either way, few scrambles or spectacular recoveries. But on both sides it was expert application of a streamlined power game.

But lack of excitement should not blind one to the fact that it was good lawn tennis. There was no fumbling. More shots than normal raised the chalk. Sedgman did not win on the negative qualities of Drobny's suspect backhand. On the contrary, that backhand took much battering and withstood the strain. Where the Australian got his advantage was in his unique weight of shot. No man covers the court so lightly as Sedgman. It meant that shot for shot Drobny needed rather better strokes to effect a winner. A passing shot good enough to beat the left-hander was not quite adequate to get by Sedgman. Drobny thus worked under greater strain. He was rushed and he cracked in the closing stages.

Drobny thus loses a Wimbledon final for the second time. He has the consolation that on hard courts he is Sedgman's master. As for Sedgman his title as world's best can hardly be disputed. I would hold him the best Wimbledon champion since the war with the exception, of course, of Kramer, who has no peer.

7 JULY 1952

MISS CONNOLLY, SUPREME & CONFIDENT, WINS THROUGH

Lance Tingay

To win the Lawn Tennis Championship at the first attempt is remarkable. To do so when only 17 is memorable though not unique, and Miss Maureen Connolly, who accomplished that feat, will have a distinct niche in the game even if she never comes back to Wimbledon. 'Little Mo' in fact intends to do so, and this being the case, there seems every reason why this chirpy and irresistible Californian will go on winning the women's singles for a great number of years. She should get even better and her game, based on solidity of driving strength, is of the type that endures.

Saturday belonged to Miss Connolly. Her concluding triumph, executed in one of the best women's finals seen for years, came after much adversity. An injured shoulder was in itself a physical handicap. The concomitant fuss, the difference of opinion with her coach who for the best of motives wanted her to scratch, was an even greater mental one. Though Miss Connolly wavered in the early rounds – indeed almost to the point of defeat against Miss Susan Partridge – she never lacked her champion's flair. She got better in the later stages and against Miss Louise Brough, thrice holder of the title, she was supreme and confident.

Miss Brough also played her best lawn tennis of the Championship. She used her wide variety of stroke, her strength of service and power of volley – in fact, all the equipment of the complete player she is. She exploited, too, Miss Connolly's weakness with a slow mid-court ball on her forehand, though in this respect the 17-year-old was less vulnerable than she had been earlier. Against this Miss Connolly replied with some net-work that was relatively indecisive. Her volleying would not have taken her far against Miss Brough. It was the withering criticism of her ground strokes, more especially on the backhand, that brought Miss Brough to defeat. These ground strokes, nimbly taken on the run and full of venom and accurate pace, were the instruments with which Miss Connolly gained her title.

Miss Brough led 5–4 in the first set. The match, so tough up to that stage, was decided in the tenth game. Deuce was called three times before Miss Connolly won it, though Miss Brough, who was serving, never got within a point of the set. From that stage the peak of Miss Brough's game was passed. She wearied, almost faltered and though her zest flickered anew at the end when she saved four match points in the second set, it was merely delaying what was bound to come. Indeed, had Miss Brough after all won the first set I think Miss Connolly would still have taken the match. Miss Connolly is remarkably resolute, which is why she wears the champion's crown. As for Miss Brough, let her fine effort be applauded. It is hard to come back, but she did so as far as the ultimate issue.

26 JUNE 1953

DROBNY BEATS PATTY IN GREATEST-EVER BATTLE

SURVIVES SIX MATCH POINTS IN 4¼ HOURS

Lance Tingay
WIMBLEDON, Thursday

Wimbledon should have ended tonight. Never in the history of the Championships has a match been waged more worthy of the greatest of all lawn tennis finals than the third-round match in which Jaroslav Drobny, the former Czech, beat the 1950 champion, Budge Patty. The score − 8–6, 16–18, 3–6, 8–6, 12–10 − speaks for the closeness and intensity of the four-and-a-quarter-hour match. Only the 15,000 packed in the stadium can forever retell the breathless excitement of the Champagne nature of lawn tennis; of the piquant fluctuations of the fortunes of two desperately heroic men; of the caprices of the goddess of luck; or of the stark drama of two players fighting the menace of encroaching cramp.

The tall, slender American was finally holding the upper part of his right leg between each rally, his face writhed in agony, bravely conquering what must have been a sinking feeling until he could stand no more. He had fallen heavily on the court three times in the long, anguishing final set. Drobny, also almost ready to drop, only just outlasted his gallant rival, for whose performance he had nothing but the highest admiration at the finish.

Only when it is recalled that Drobny fought off six match points against him, that the last few games were played in the dim light of dusk, that Drobny, the eventual winner, appealed against it, and that the referee, Col. John Legg, went to the umpire's chair at ten all in the last set and watched from there Patty serve the fatal game in which he lost the initiative before deciding that there was still light enough; then only can it be realised what a truly great contest this was.

This was the longest singles played in the Championships. The previous longest went to 76 games and, I believe, ran to a greater time, but certainly no match of the pace at which this was played has endured so long. It was a clash of artists with Drobny the worker in oils against the more delicate water-colourist. Never for a moment did the standard fall below the super-fine and even when both were playing in a semi-daze the quality of their instinctive strokes and their superb control of length and direction was maintained in the highest degree.

In the long second set Patty, having saved set points in the 29th and 31st games, produced a characteristically, beautifully stroked cross-court back-hand volley that even Drobny could only stand and admire. That stroke squared the match at one set all. The battle was really joined. Drobny, a little jaded by this setback, dropped his service in the third and fifth games, and was trailing 1–5 in the third set. When Patty served at 5–2 he showed for the first time how taxing on the nerves the match was becoming by over-playing two volleys of the kind that had been hitting the target with regularity a few minutes earlier. Even so, Patty won the set against the service in the next game. Both men dropped a service game in the fourth set, Patty in the third game and Drobny in the sixth. So it was level pegging at six all.

When leading 5–4 Patty had match point but drove out. Two more chances came then in the 12th game and Drobny valiantly saved them both – one with a forehand volley, the other with a gentle push of the ball into an open court. The set went to Drobny in the 14th game and so they came to the never-to-be-forgotten final set. Drobny had a service break in the opening game, then the water with which competitors refresh themselves when changing ends ran out and a fresh canister was requisitioned.

Droby built his lead into 3–1 and began sprinting up and down the base-line between the rallies to relieve oncoming cramp. Very soon after this, Patty was the more affected. It attacked him in the upper part of his right leg and he had to keep massaging himself in the groin. Patty broke back in the eighth game to put the set see-sawing the other way. With Drobny serving at 5–6 the score was 15–40. Twice more Patty stood within a stroke of victory. Drobny drew level with a mighty smash and a forced forehand error from Patty. Still Patty had another chance when he reached advantage. Here Drobny put down a service ace that Patty could not reach. So they ran neck and neck to ten all. At nine all Patty, having fluffed two easy volleys, gave way to his feelings by throwing his racket high in the air.

The end was near. In the 21st game of this set and the 92nd of the match Patty failed to hold his service. Drobny thus led 11–10 with his delivery to come. It was a love game to Drobny. Drobny could at long last now win the Championship. Whether he does so depends on his reaction to his utterly exhausting experience.

3 JULY 1954

DROBNY'S TITLE AT LAST: IT TOOK HIM 16 YEARS

ONE OF WIMBLEDON'S GREAT FINALS

Lance Tingay
WIMBLEDON, Friday

Long endeavour had its reward in the Lawn Tennis Championships here today. J. Drobny is the new men's singles champion, 16 years after making his first attempt. In today's final, one that will rank among the greater Wimbledon contests, he ended two hours 36 minutes' enthralling struggle by beating

K. Rosewall 13–11, 4–6, 6–2, 9–7. When he hit the winning ball he was cheered with an enthusiasm not heard since the war. No longer singles final has been played at Wimbledon, and Drobny, the man of exile, the 'underdog' who had twice failed in earlier finals, had emerged the able victor.

As a champion, Drobny is in many ways unique. A Czech by birth, Egyptian by naturalisation, he is the first singles champion from a nation other than those who have held the Davis Cup – Great Britain, Australia, United States and France. This was his 11th attempt. Only one other, Arthur Gore, played in more Championships before winning the first time. But the lag between Gore's initial effort and success was less than 16 years. Drobny was the first left-handed champion in 40 years. Sir Norman Brookes (1914) was the last.

I said yesterday Drobny would make a worthy champion, and so he has. He is a complete lawn tennis player: the big weapons are his, the stinging service and mighty smash; but so are the refined aspects of the game. If today Drobny won by exploiting a mainly power game, though tempered with discretion, he did so because it was the way to conquer the cunning Rosewall.

To the last ball it was anybody's match, for though Rosewall trailed one set to two, there was the memory of his recovery from a like position in both the previous rounds. To indicate further how close it was, I record that Rosewall was within a point of winning the first set in the 22nd game. The crisis came when Drobny stood 10–11 and 30–40. He had been foot-faulted on the previous delivery, and then had bungled the volley. Rosewall, within one stroke of his first objective, essayed a deep forehand pass. It glided out and Drobny finally squared it at 11 all. Two minutes later Drobny was on top in the see-saw of fortune. Rosewall disastrously lost service to 30 in the 23rd game. Drobny, in front for the first time since he led 7–6, thundered home 13–11.

I suppose the issue was decided then, for on the strength of what happened later I doubt if Drobny would have survived an opening loss. The second set was Rosewall's. Set three had Drobny at his best, most powerful and sure. The first turning point in the adventurous fourth set was in Drobny's favour. The service break was had by him in the seventh game to help a 5–3 lead. At 5–4 he began what in normal course should have been a winning service game. He led 15–0, but did not get another point, Rosewall here shed his weariness with some flashing service returns. Drobny of a sudden became enfeebled. Rosewall was in the match again at five all, and then in front at 6–5, even though in the 13th game both were so tired that they did not know which court to serve from.

Rosewall maintained his lead at 7—6 only subsequently to fall behind 7—8. In that 15th game, which proved so decisive, Rosewall lost the crucial point on a lucky net-cord shot. The Australian made as though to throw the ball at Drobny, who, in turn, shrugged his shoulders as though to say: 'How could I help it?' So then Drobny served again, to win the match. Once more Rosewall sprang to temporary life, while Drobny seemed to falter. The Australian had a point for eight all before Drobny pulled him back. At deuce, Drobny sent a spinning service that kissed the line and proved an ace. He required only the one match point, which came when Rosewall tamely put a service return into the net. Drobny, now the champion, was then cheered and cheered. He turned and held out his arms towards the stands where his wife was sitting.

5 JULY 1954

MISS CONNOLLY A TRULY GREAT CHAMPION

COMPLETES WIMBLEDON HAT-TRICK AT 19

Lance Tingay

The finest champion of these Lawn Tennis Championhips was Miss Maureen Connolly. Of this there is no doubt, and why on Satuurday her third successive singles victory was not more uproariously acclaimed I do not fully understand. In assessing the relative merits of the great among the great there is room for difference of opinion. Whether Miss Connolly is less good than Mlle Suzanne Lenglen, or better than Miss Helen Wills, immortals both, I would not care to say. That she is the best woman player since the war I am certain. She lost just 19 games in six matches in winning her third singles crown. Both Mlle Lenglen and Miss Wills had more overwhelming wins, but not at the age of 19.

After winning last year Miss Connolly's first thought was to improve the weaknesses, if such relative lack of strength could so be termed, of her game. She now has no lawn tennis imperfections that can be properly described as such. She has the ability to flog and kill the ball from anywhere, whether running or still, off the ground or overhead, and from either wing. Perhaps she may now develop as good a drop shot from the forehand as she now has from the backhand, but it would be merely academic labour. She has no need of it to win.

Yet I thought Saturday's crowd less warm in applauding her achievement than they might have been. When in the course of the final Miss

Connolly showed her human frailty and lapsed a little; when her opponent, Miss L. Brough, took this cue to play with skilled resolution reminiscent of her old Championship quality and build a second-set lead of 5–2, the spectators understandably egged on the 'underdog' with frenzied zeal.

Miss Connolly's even more splendid effort when she surged through to take the set was less zealously greeted. It was taken for granted she should play like an easy-running machine. It is, perhaps, one of the drawbacks of greatness that Miss Connolly's cold efficiency should be regarded as a personal characteristic. Off the court Miss Connolly is a charming youngster. She is remorseless only when she begins to play, and has, by hard work, made herself the greatest lawn tennis exponent for two decades.

7 JULY 1956

HOAD THE VICTOR IN RICH LAWN TENNIS FEAST

Lance Tingay
WIMBLEDON, Friday

Lew Hoad beat Ken Rosewall 6–2, 4–6, 7–5, 6–4 to win the men's singles Championship here today and to fulfil three-quarters of a major project. The champion of Australia and France is now champion of Wimbledon, and if, as seems not unlikely, he goes on to gain American laurels he will equal the record of Donald Budge in taking all four major lawn tennis titles in one year.

Princess Margaret and the Duchess of Kent saw a worthy champion gain the most desired distinction in the game. There have been more exciting finals but none since the war where high quality of play has been so well sustained and where both winner and loser played to their best capacity. In a rich lawn tennis feast, the basic issue between the two contestants was clear. Both were artists, but Hoad, befitting his burlier physique, piled his strokes with heavier touch, like the painter in oils who wields a knife rather than a brush. By comparison Rosewall was a water-colourist, his efforts more delicate and less permanent.

Hoad joined a not over-long list of Australian predecessors on the Championship roll: Frank Sedgman in 1952, Jack Crawford in 1933, Gerald Patterson in 1922 and 1919, Norman Brookes (now Sir Norman) in 1914 and 1907. It is tempting to question whether he is as great as they, but I hesitate to say. Such comparisons are made in the light of history rather than in the heat of current success. Among post-war champions, Hoad stands well. Jack Kramer and Frank Sedgman certainly rank above him and possibly also Tony Trabert.

Hoad is an enigmatic champion, inconsistent except in crucial issues. If he equals Budge's famous record he will not do so with the same distinction, for Budge was immune from defeat, not only in the big events but also in lesser ones. Hoad has already suffered many a minor fall. He is a player without half measures, an all-or-nothing man. This accounts for his rather high proportion of errors which, some would say, marred his play. Yet the number of mistakes must be balanced against his startling winners. It is significant that the only post-war final that can be compared with today's match in quality of performance is that of 1954, the year J. Drobny won. Rosewall was also the losing finalist that year. His opposition has twice inspired a touch of greatness, a tribute to his own splendid qualities.

More than most finals it was curiously lacking in emotion. Whether the crowd was partisan it is hard to say, though possibly Rosewall, ranking as the underdog, had the more supporters. Yet there was not much on which to make a choice between one Australian or another, both of the same age, born and bred in nearby Sydney suburbs.

8 JULY 1956

MISS FRY'S WIN HERALDS END OF AN ERA
Lance Tingay

When, on Saturday, Miss Shirley Fry beat Miss Angela Buxton to become women's singles champion at Wimbledon, one had the feeling that here was the end of an era. The stimulation of having, for the first time since 1939, a British finalist did not survive many games of the match.

Miss Fry, who is 29 and a victor at her eighth attempt, belongs, albeit as one of the less rather than the greater, to the school of magnificent American players who have dominated Wimbledon and the women's game generally both before and after the war. Miss Alice Marble, Miss Pauline Betz, Mrs Margaret du Pont, Miss Louise Brough, Miss Doris Hart and, perhaps the finest of them all, Miss Maureen Connolly, make up a roll of names that will live long in lawn tennis history. With Miss Fry's well-merited success this era of unusual excellence has, I think, come to an end. It is possible that in the immediate future one will have to judge the women's game by less high superlatives; in women's doubles one already needs to do so.

In the men's game, also, it looks as though to be more than 30 is to be too old to hold a place at the highest level. Lew Hoad and Ken Rosewall were dominant in both singles and doubles, and both are only 21. The older guard could not endure the pace. Of the three former champions who took the singles field Jaroslav Drobny did not survive the first round and was beaten by the Indian H. Krishnan, who is 20. Budge Patty was defeated gloriously for Britain by Robert Wilson, who is 20. The rugged Victor Seixas battled to the semi-final but, in Wimbledon's most exciting contest of 1956, could clinch neither his lead of two sets to one nor his more crucial advantage of being 5–2 up in the fifth set against Rosewall. Drobny, Patty and Seixas have all gone beyond the 30 mark. They are worn in the leaf by dominating Australian standards.

As I wrote a week ago, it was not a vintage year in the Lawn Tennis Championships. Exciting, yes, and there was hardly a day without its remarkable upsets, but only the singles final and one or two other matches – Rosewall against Arthur Larsen, for instance, Wilson against Patty and, perhaps, Luis Ayala against Ulf Schmidt – produced strokes and shots of the highest calibre. All years will not be great years and even a much less good meeting than this would still enthral as does no other tournament in the world, and I would stress that Lew Hoad, the male champion who has emerged, as expected, is one who will rank high on any merit list of title-holders.

Miss Fry on Saturday beat Miss Buxton 6–3, 6–1 in 52 minutes to become the women's singles champion. To speak of it, as was done, as the poorest final played was rather less than fair. There must be short memories, for, as recently as 1951, Miss Hart beat Miss Fry 6–1, 6–0, and Miss Fry was then so conscious of the occasion that she fell grievously below her best. And in 1939 Miss Kay Stammers won only two games from Miss Marble, though, of course, the American played supremely well.

Before 1914 there was a final which Mrs Lambert Chambers won 6–0, 6–0, which, though I only know it as history, was clearly not a sparkling match. Miss Buxton did give Miss Fry a contest.

7 JULY 1958

BRITAIN'S BEST STILL NOT GOOD ENOUGH

Lance Tingay

The Lawn Tennis Championships ended at Wimbledon on Saturday on a more lively note than had been expected. Miss Althea Gibson, in an excellent final against Miss Angela Mortimer, affirmed her status as women's singles champion with impressive skill and dignity. The final was an attractive one. It had the interest of contrast between the baseliner and the volleyer. Miss Mortimer played well and I doubt, in the first set at any rate, whether she could have done anything more. Her driving has firmness and depth, and Miss Gibson soon learned the futility of a net campaign save only behind the spearhead of her penetrating service.

Miss Mortimer's best, however, was not good enough. For one thing Miss Gibson, stronger from the ground than she used to be, came near to matching her driving power, and Miss Mortimer was impelled to seek extraneous sources to find scoring strokes. The volleying done by Miss Mortimer was brave, tactically correct, but ineffectual. To contrive a win she would have had to break down the strength against her. This she never did. Miss Gibson played like a champion from first to last and, being forced to earn every point, did so with consistent power. Spectators, naturally with a British audience, acclaimed Miss Mortimer's successes enthusiastically and, to begin with, even uproariously. Yet during the course of the match much sympathy radiated towards the defending champion. She endured her setbacks with such firm nonchalance that even the most fervid Miss Mortimer supporter could not but be filled with admiration. I refer here to her foot-faulting.

Mrs Gibson was checked for a minor technical infringement, placing her foot on the line, 11 times in all, nine times during the first set. Once she was twice foot-faulted for a double-fault! The foot-fault rule being what it is, enforceable in relatively few matches, with a full complement of linesmen in attendance, this was a frustrating thing to happen. Yet never in the slightest degree did Miss Gibson indicate disturbance at such frequent penalisation; no gesture, no remonstration, no query even, with the linesman came from her.

It was, in fact, almost inhuman the way Miss Gibson endured the checks. Her coolness can be explained only by the fact that it had happened to her before, notably in the American Championships last year. What with this foot-faulting – a major cause of Miss Gibson's six double-faults – and Miss Mortimer's driving power, mainly from the forehand, Miss Gibson endured a perilous first set which she was within a stroke of losing at 4–5 down. Miss Mortimer then pulled back from 5–6 to six all, but against Miss Gibson's all-dominating net pressure lagged quickly 6–7. She had a point for the next game, but was denied the chance and, advantage point behind, submitted with a double-fault. It was Miss Mortimer's only double-fault but delivered at the most irretrievable stage. In the second set Miss Mortimer built a 2–0 lead, but some of her firmness then drained from her.

Miss Gibson, foot-faulting no longer (at least only twice) gained six games running for the loss of only ten points, to win the match and keep her Championship. It lasted just over the hour. My stroke analysis is illuminating. Miss Gibson hit 31 outright winners, of which 13 were on the volley, 13 by a smash and three on service.

22 JUNE 1959

THEY HAVE SO LITTLE TO SAY OFF COURT

Violet Johnstone meets the women players of Wimbledon

Is there time for anything but tennis in a champion's life? Can she appreciate the opportunities of travel that come with tournaments taking her to Paris, Rome, Athens, Istanbul, the Caribbean, Bermuda, the United States, Canada and South America? Having talked to some of the top women players of today, I regret to say the answer is NO.

I questioned Christine Truman, No. 1 seed at this year's Wimbledon ('It's a great honour,' she says), and who, at the age of 18, might well be called a national figure.

'Out of all the places you have visited during this past year, which sticks foremost in your mind?' I asked her. 'I found the Caribbean trip the most enjoyable,' she said. 'But there are the same sized courts everywhere, you know.'

'Do you manage to do any sight-seeing at all?' 'Very little. If you want to become a really good tennis player, you must discipline yourself. You must make tennis your only aim in life and not enjoy outside activities too much.' How does her family feel about it? 'They get sick of talking about tennis – particularly my brothers and sisters. So I have to watch my step,' said Christine.

'Tennis is my life and it's a good life,' said 19-year-old Maria Bueno, top player in Brazil, and seeded No. 6 at Wimbledon. As she walked on to the court wearing tailored shorts and a shirt, she seemed to take life very seriously, I thought. She served three aces which won her great applause – but still she looked serious.

It made a pleasant change to meet a smiling player in the person of Yolanda Ramirez. Wearing a short pleated tennis dress, piped with red ribbon, she was full of life and gaiety. 'I enjoy playing tremendously,' she said, 'and will continue playing when I am married. But as soon as I have children I will stop.' Being Mexico's leading player, Miss Ramirez says she enjoys many privileges at home. She does secretarial work (English and Spanish) in Mexico City and has no difficulty in finding jobs between tournaments.

Miss Ramirez is over here for three weeks. 'Have you seen anything of England?' I asked her. 'Not really,' she answered. 'You see, sight-seeing means walking and that uses up all my energy. So what about my tennis?' Of all the countries she has visited, England is her favourite. Why? 'Because of Wimbledon.'

Having read all about Althea Gibson's future career as a singer, I looked forward to our conversation. But all the time we talked she could not take her eyes off a match that was going on before us. Miss Gibson has been to England six times. 'Have you seen Oxford?' I asked her. 'No.' 'Cambridge?' 'No.' 'Stratford?' 'No. I like London best,' she said, 'because of the grass-court tournaments.'

Although Miss Gibson is not defending her Wimbledon title this year, she still plays three or four times a week in the States, and enjoys a bit of basketball, bowls and golf. 'I also love the theatre,' said Miss Gibson. 'I saw *My Fair Lady* over here last year and one other play – can't remember what it was now. This year I would like to see *West Side Story* – if I get the chance. But really, I like watching tennis best of all.'

Tennis, tennis, tennis. Was there really nothing else to talk about? Yes there was, with the most feminine and charming of all the players I met – Mrs Beverley Fleitz, that ambidextrous player with two forehands and seeded No. 3 at Wimbledon. 'I don't know which I'm more excited about – Wimbledon or my new home,' she told me. She and her husband are having a bungalow built on Long Beach, and they plan to move in during October. 'It's very modern, with lots of indoor plants,' she said. 'Two sides of the house are made of glass and we've got hi-fi in the patio.'

Mrs Fleitz has help only once a week and has to get babysitters to look after her six- and two-year-old daughters when she practises three or four times a week. As we sat having tea (she is never on a diet and was enjoying ice cream with fruit cake) two of this year's glamour players walked past – Karol Fageros from America, who wears a dress trimmed with gold, and Lea Pericoli from Italy.

'Are you interested in clothes?' I asked Mrs Fleitz. 'Very,' she answered, 'and I think English tennis fashions are fabulous.' As she said that designer

Teddy Tinling came up to her: 'I have your broderie Anglaise creation all ready for you,' he said, then turning to me, he added: 'She's my best model from America.'

Mrs Fleitz is the exception that confirms the rule – for most tennis players are more interesting on court than off court. But still, I thank them for the fortnight that is ahead of us, for I, like millions of other people, will be glued to the television set on every possible occasion to watch one of the year's most exciting events – Wimbledon.

I JUNE 1960

SYNTHETICS WIN AT WIMBLEDON

BUT THE SCHOOLGIRLS' IDOL MUSTN'T WEAR FRILLS

Paula Davies

Tennis fashions at Wimbledon, which have seen sensations from Suzanne Lenglen's headbands to Gorgeous Gussie's frilly panties, will be influenced by practical considerations this year. Permanently pleated Terylene for worldwide travelling and easy care has prompted Teddy Tinling in his designs this year for international players such as Maria Bueno, last year's Wimbledon champion, and our Christine Truman. The best result of all for moisture absorbency and laundering is 67 per cent Terylene and 33 per cent cotton. Big news in styling is the return of the dropped waist-line. Dropping gently but perceptibly, it will influence tennis fashion from the 'high courts' of Wimbledon to the vicarage tennis party.

The Wimbledon Lawn Tennis Championships, climax of the amateur scene, begin shortly, and already there's a feverish anticipation in the air. I asked Christine Truman, whose great height and long powerful legs make her a veritable 'Joan Hunter Dunn', whether she ate, drank and slept tennis. The answer is 'yes' during the season, but she finds time for other interests afterwards. 'I play a bit of golf,' she said, 'and also love listening to light music, particularly records from the shows.'

Christine's dresses are always plain and cut on long classic lines. Once, when she went against this tradition and wore an embroidered dress, schoolgirls wrote to her designer in horror saying: 'You can't put our Christine in a thing like that!'

MISS BUENO BRIGHTEST STAR OF ALL

Lance Tingay

Australia, Brazil, the United States and Mexico won the titles at Wimbledon. The 74th Lawn Tennis Championships, perhaps the last meeting restricted to amateurs, came through two weeks of traditional glory with such success as to make the thought of any change almost a matter of sadness, despite its seeming inevitability. The Brazilian winner was the brightest star. One salutes Maria Bueno for the second year, glad that she has again fulfilled her obvious destiny as the best amateur in the world. Grace, precision and power – Miss Bueno has them all. She makes lawn tennis a game of sharp beauty.

On Saturday, Miss Bueno, the epitome of grace, took four minutes under the hour to beat the hardly less graceful South African, Miss Sandra Reynolds, and so kept the champion's mantle. I doubt if there was any stage at which Miss Bueno's supremacy was in danger. I thought Miss Bueno to be rather below her best and Miss Reynolds, spurred by the occasion, a little above hers. A champion such as Miss Bueno can win like that, since her victory margin was wide enough to withstand a little narrowing.

At all times, Miss Bueno had the lead and those occasions when she showed her human fallibility with double-faults merely allowed Miss Reynolds to make it level scoring. Thus, in the first set, there was 3–1 to Miss Bueno that became 3–3, but the advantage of 4–3, 5–4 and 6–5 all belonged to her. It was fast play, full of sharp, decisive and invigorating rallies. The first set finished 8–6 to Miss Bueno when she won against Miss Reynold's service after the South African had been within a stroke of 7–7. The last three points with which Miss Bueno took the set were won with splendid volleys, almost breathtaking in their power and ease of execution. They were the strokes of an outstanding champion.

Miss Bueno won the second set 6–0 and so took the last eight games without loss. That second-set score, however, did scant justice to the resistance of Miss Reynolds. In the second game, one of two deuces, there were three drop-shot winners projected by Miss Bueno on her return of service to make one marvel anew at her touch and skill. They helped deny Miss Reynolds the fruits of a 40–0 lead. As for the third game, this was worth a set in itself. It was probably the longest in the Championships: nine deuces, with five game points on either side. It wavered for 12 minutes before Miss

Bueno won it and, with her success, the last resistance of Miss Reynolds was broken. The Brazilian lost only three more points in the next three games, since by then Miss Reynolds could indulge only in carefree desperation.

5 JULY 1960
LETTER TO THE EDITOR
WIMBLEDON NAMES

Sir,

Before we say goodbye to the 1960 Wimbledon tournament I wonder if the suggestion could be made to the Lawn Tennis Association that, before going on to the court, the umpire should take the trouble to find out how the competitors' names are pronounced. The BBC commentators might also take the hint.

One has a certain sympathy for Dan Maskell in his efforts to pronounce 'Gimeno', but surely the introduction by the umpire of the ladies' singles final of a 'y' into Miss Bueno's name (Byueno) can only reinforce our foreign friends' conviction that the average Englishman has no aptitude for foreign languages.

Arthur E. Smeeton
Birkenhead, Cheshire

25 JUNE 1961
WIMBLEDON AT THE CROSSROADS

This year's Wimbledon Championships will be the last of their kind if the International Federation decide to admit professionals. Here Col. C.T. 'Teddy' Tinling, for 24 years 'call boy' to the Centre Court, recalls outstanding moments and personalities of the past, and names the greatest of his time.

One summer evening in 1934, just after that wonderful Wimbledon when Fred Perry and Dorothy Round had won both singles titles for Britain, Suzanne Lenglen called on me at my office. She sat on my workroom table, swinging her legs with her effervescent, theatrical charm, slim and youthful, although she was then past 30, and talked of the old days on the Centre Court.

Now, 27 years later, when Wimbledon is going through a critical time, which may change the Championships as we have known them, the moment seems opportune to look back over the greatest years of what will always be the world's foremost tournament.

Since 1924, I have known every one of the star players. For 24 years I acted as 'call boy' to the Centre Court, and saw at first hand the triumphs and heartbreaks of such stars as Suzanne, the two Helens, Bill Tilden, Fred Perry, Don Budge, Jack Kramer, Maureen Connolly, Maria Bueno, Ann Haydon, Christine Truman and a host of others.

For the past few years the game has been kept on its feet by the women, none more than Christine Truman. Schoolgirl idol and the most good-natured person ever to walk the Centre Court, she is the embodiment of all that is best in British sport. It takes two stars to bring the best out of each other, and she and Ann Haydon have been a happy complement.

Who are the greatest players? In placing Suzanne Lenglen and 'Big Bill' Tilden above all their rivals, I am assailed by no doubts. When I was in Brisbane a few seasons ago, to watch the Davis Cup matches, I joined a group of 12 Wimbledon title-holders sitting in a hotel lounge discussing who was the outstanding man of all time. Most of us agreed to put Bill Tilden in a super-class of his own, with Fred Perry the prime *match-winner*. What set Tilden apart was his unlimited repertoire of strokes and his personality. Tilden was a greater player, but his temperament sometimes threw him off his balance. Perry, like Ann Haydon a front-rank table tennis player, had that mental resilience and determination which made him so hard to beat.

Among women I would rank Suzanne first over Maureen Connolly and Helen Wills, whom I consider about equal. The French player had great technical skill and a greater depth of personality than her rivals. Nothing is more certain than that Suzanne 'made' the Wimbledon we now take for granted. Only Suzanne could have justified the Colosseum-like Centre Court in its early days.

The course of my life was determined, when at the age of 13, and having been sent to the Riviera because of my asthma, I happened to be at Suzanne's home club, Nice, at the moment when there was no other available umpire. From then on for some reason she seemed to prefer me to others, and so the link was forged. Suzanne's enemies used to say that she looked like a totem pole; fascinatingly unbeautiful. She had an unhappy complexion and a hawk-like nose, but she walked with the conspicuous and compelling grace.

The procession which I led so often on to the Centre Court of the Riviera consisted of Suzanne, her opponent, Papa and Maman Lenglen, clutching their pet toy griffin, Gyp, with the ballboys and some of her current admirers bringing up the rear. There was never any possibility of doubt about who was the prima donna of the whole show. She could make the easiest show look difficult, while her arms and body were a poetry of constant flowing motion; now she was doing a tremendous reach, the next moment kicking high above her shoulders or leaping across court like a dancer making a dramatic exit. Between games, she would sometimes sip brandy from a flask kept in her handbag underneath my chair, while a constant monologue, advice for Suzanne and criticism of my umpiring, would flow from Papa.

Suzanne's style was incomparable. She hit her forehand driver with a big, round-arm sweep, though she was not a 'good' volleyer. But her accuracy was phenomenal. After one match, I examined the court minutely. On the soft, red shale, the marks of her shoes were grouped just inside the sidelines as tightly as the bullet holes of a crack marksman; one group just short of the service line, the next halfway to the baseline, and the last in the very angle of the corners.

On one occasion, I saw a flash of Suzanne's highly strung temperament. I was due to umpire a final between Suzanne and her partner and Elizabeth Ryan and Randolf Lycett, three times Wimbledon mixed champions. Lycett had to catch an early afternoon train back to England and was in a hurry. Twenty minutes passed without any sign of Suzanne. Finally, Lycett told me brusquely: 'Go and fetch her.' With the innocence of a new call-boy at Covent Garden rousing Callas from her dressing-room, I went. The Lenglen house stood opposite the club. As I approached, the iron gates opened and Suzanne, smiling radiantly, came out. 'I was just coming to fetch you, Mademoiselle,' I said. Her face went as dark as a mistral sky. 'Fetch me,' she said. 'Fetch *me?*' And she turned about, re-entered the house and slammed the door.

The experience stood me in good stead in later years when it was my duty at Wimbledon to prepare temperamental players for their matches, to escort them on to the Centre Court, and to commiserate with them or offer my congratulations when they came off. Temperament is an integral part of such an individual game as tennis. Only because the crowds these days have become small-minded is individualism now frowned upon. Maria Bueno alone since Suzanne has a personality, presence and technique that can produce, in an audience, laughter, tears and thrills by turn.

The men of earlier days, admittedly older, seemed to have more personality than those of today. The famous Four Musketeers, Jean Borotra and his fellow countrymen, Henri Cochet, René Lacoste and 'Toto' Brugnon, were a happy band who combined extreme gallantry, charm and talent. Borotra's unquenchable energy will be concentrated next month on steering the 'open tennis' issue through the annual meeting of the International Lawn Tennis Federation, of which he is this year's president.

Wimbledon in its early days had not yet established those standards of punctuality and responsibility towards a paying public which are now accepted. My task was to get it over to the players that the note on the programme, 'intended order of play, at 2p.m. precisely', meant exactly what it said.

For 24 years I never failed to get a thrill from leading the great champions on to the green, sunlit scene of the Centre Court. The moments when I waited for them behind the last doors to the arena were unforgettable; the coolness and half light; the unique smell, compounded of rubber carpeting and perfume; the long imperial black rolls of honour on the walls, silent yet dramatic and inspiring testimony of great names and deeds, with the quotation from Kipling's *If*; the sunshine filtering through the opaque glass beyond which could be heard the anticipatory hum of 15,000 voices round that awesome, challenging stage on which equality must soon be destroyed to create a champion and cast down a loser — all this for me was part of the magic that is Wimbledon.

The greatest year in the history of modern British tennis was 1934 when Perry and Dorothy Round won both titles. This double victory did something to the emotion-charged Centre Court crowd that nothing else had been able to do; it swung them round to Perry's side when earlier they had not been with him.

Looking back from this distance, over years of failure of British players, it seems incredible that Perry was unpopular at home. But he had impatient mannerisms, and a rooted determination to show everyone that he could do just what he had set out to do. Perry was a wonderful figure of an athlete. On court, he was as tensed as a stalking tiger, and created a sense of flowing lateral movement; linking his shots so that he appeared to be swaying back for the next shot almost before he had completed the last. A tremendous individualist, Perry entered a British tennis scene that was dominated by 'Bunny' Austin and he lifted himself to world-class almost by his continuous rivalry, with its clash of personality and differing backgrounds, with

Austin, who represented the public-school type of Englishman as much as Perry represented the self-made players.

Every champion I have met at Wimbledon has been a supreme individualist with a grand indifference to others, a selfish streak if you like, running through the character. Dorothy Round was no exception. With her strict Methodist upbringing, she became the despair of overseas tournament committees everywhere by her refusal to play on Sundays. How she was able to enter European and some American tournaments, when she knew that the finals were always played on the Sabbath, I never understood.

Dorothy was the first to take a set off Helen Wills for six years. I shared many great moments with Helen. The Wimbledon crowd, who were sometimes upset by this disdainful, beautiful woman, christened her 'Little Miss Poker Face'. But there was a great sensitivity behind the façade. In 1935, after she had survived a match point against her bitterest rival, Helen Jacobs, to win in a tense final set, the champion walked off court without showing the slightest emotion. But as soon as she got behind the door, she fell against me with relief.

In 1933, Helen Wills and Helen Jacobs were still the best players in the world, but their hold was weakening. The rallies were getting longer, and I had sensed Helen Wills's increasing nervous tension the year before. Miss Jacobs had been beaten by the newcomer Alice Marble. Later, Miss Marble had a complete collapse. She was taken to hospital and tuberculosis was diagnosed. 'Teach' Tennant, who was to become the most famous coach of all in association with 'Little Mo', gave lessons for nine or ten hours a day to pay for the treatment to keep her star pupil alive. Alice came out completely recovered and won all three titles in 1939.

Whatever happens at Wimbledon in future years, everyone hopes that it will continue to be graced by members of the Royal Family. Their patronage goes back a long way and King George VI, as Duke of York, was a competitor in 1926. The Princesses Helena Victoria and Marie Louise all but lived there in the old days; Queen Alexandra was a regular patron. But Wimbledon really became established as part of the London social scene in 1907 when the Prince and Princess of Wales first attended the Championships at Worple Road.

Queen Mary became a life-long devotee. She frequently stayed on at Wimbledon long after King George had departed, and once told an equerry to inform the King at the Palace that he should start dinner without her. As the sun slanted lower and lower over the Centre Court roof, Queen Mary always moved back in case the sunlight fell upon her flawless Edwardian complexion. In those days, it was a common occurrence to see four vacant rows of chairs in the front of the Royal Box, with Queen Mary sitting serenely in the fifth row, the flower of European society squashed like sardines behind her.

At Wimbledon, there is a natural dread of anything upsetting the Royal arrangements; which goes right back to that awful day in 1926 when Suzanne Lenglen kept Queen Mary waiting for half an hour. The trouble began when the French Tennis Federation ordered her to break her long doubles association with Elizabeth Ryan, who was American, and to play with another member of the French team. Then Suzanne refused to play a singles match before a difficult doubles against her former partner, Elizabeth Ryan, newly paired with Mary Browne.

Queen Mary had been in her seat half an hour next day before Suzanne made an appearance. She was met with a volley of questions from distraught officials. Suzanne was not built to endure that kind of treatment, and she locked herself in her dressing-room, sobbing hysterically. In despair, Jean Borotra was called from a distant court to plead with the star. He had no success and, later, he was obliged to climb the stairs into the Royal Box to offer his humble apologies to Queen Mary. Suzanne recovered sufficiently to play both matches, but later she withdrew from Wimbledon and turned professional.

Traditions at Wimbledon have often been broken for the betterment of the Championships, and that is why I fully agree with the declared determination of the All-England Club to support an open event in future in which the leading professionals, as well as the top amateurs, can take part. It was apparent more than ten years ago that top tennis could no longer be just a recreation; top players must devote their whole lives to competitive play, and be rewarded accordingly.

When the International Federation meets in Stockholm shortly after Wimbledon, antagonism to the Kramer success symbol, already shown by Australia and several smaller countries, will play a major part in determining whether or not the leading professionals like Gonzales, Hoad, Rosewall, Gimeno and Sedgman will play next year in an open Wimbledon.

Two of the oldest powers in the game, the British LTA and the All-England Club, have come out openly in favour of their doing so, at least as an experiment. It now seems that this progressive thinking may be baulked by the outdated necessity for a two-thirds majority, which, in Paris last year, brought about the rejection of the open tournament proposal by only five votes in 209.

If the International Federation again rejects Britain's expressed desire for an open Wimbledon, backed by the hard-won support of the United States, I would like to see Wimbledon 'go it alone'. After all, Wimbledon is the world's most successful tournament and, nowadays, is the only one showing a consistent and substantial profit. If, by next year, all the great champions who established themselves on this very turf can again appear there, who will deny that Wimbledon will once more have pioneered a new age in tennis.

8 JULY 1961

LAVER CRUSHES MCKINLEY IN 55 MINUTES

Lance Tingay
WIMBLEDON, Friday

Class told, as it always does when the occasion is important, and the 22-year-old Australian, R. Laver, from Rockhampton, Queensland, is men's singles champion. It was a one-sided finale to the Lawn Tennis Championships and was all over in 55 minutes with Laver beating C.R. McKinley, from St Louis, 6–3, 6–1, 6–4. There have been quicker and more one-sided finals, but not many. If my memory is correct, Laver today dispatched McKinley rather more speedily than L.A. Hoad beat A.J. Cooper in 1957, but with rather less devastation than J.A. Kramer against T. Brown in 1947.

Before the Championships began it was generally held that, with N.A. Fraser out of form, the best amateur in the world was this other Australian left-hander, red-haired, slight in build and not especially with the air of an athlete. Laver left no doubt about it today. He was as impeccably good as a player can be. He rose to the occasion nobly and the memory of the event will lie in Laver's last three polished rounds against the Chilean, L. Ayala, in the quarter-final, against the Indian, R. Khrishnan, in the semi-final and, most of all, in the final against McKinley. He wielded flying shots and had bite and penetration in all of them. Overhead he was superb. And he had delicacy of touch and finesse of control as well. In this he stood head and shoulders above McKinley, making him look a wee bit clumsy.

Laver took the first set from 2–3 with four games on the trot. The annihilating nature of his progress was more marked in the second set. Here McKinley took just one game, the fourth, and in only 18 minutes he had lost it with the meagre total of ten points. A player less pugnacious than McKinley might well have given up after those first two sets. His reaction was that of a game boxer who, mindless of having been hopelessly outpointed in every round, refuses to yield to anything but a knockout. No one around the Centre Court, still dusty, dry and productive of the occasional bad bounce for the first time in anybody's memory, could have thought that the knockout blow was not inevitable. The question merely was when it would be delivered.

McKinley was allowed no further progress than his 4–3 lead. Laver, having held his service to 15 – in only two games did the American get as far as deuce – got hold of McKinley's service for the fifth time in all. He did so with three of the most devastating returns of service seen in the whole match. Even McKinley's rubber legs and arms were unable to get his racket near the ball. McKinley managed to project one service winner to save what would otherwise have been a love game. Then Laver served for the match.

Soon he stood 40–15 and two match points. It could be he trembled a little then, for he made one of his infrequent mistakes with a high forehand volley. On the second point, with the crowd hushed as it always is on such occasions, Laver was forced to net a low backhand volley. McKinley had saved another. The reprieve was fleeting. A smart backhand volley and then a short, angled smash took Laver to his standing as champion, and dampened McKinley's explosive energy for the first time this year at Wimbledon.

10 JULY 1961

SKILL NOT LUCK
BRINGS MISS MORTIMER TITLE

Lance Tingay

The Lawn Tennis Championships ended at Wimbledon on Saturday with Miss Angela Mortimer the first British winner of a singles title for 24 years. What immortality there is in lawn tennis belongs worthily to her. The quality of her play is simple and enduring. Were this not so she would not have taken the most prized crown at the age of 29, an age when men are reckoned to be one year beyond their peak and women rather more.

Astute court craft and ability to penetrate searchingly against opposition weakness, superb driving control and command of length, these are the merits of Miss Mortimer's lawn tennis. In Wimbledon champions, personality and character are factors that must also be taken into account. Among lawn tennis players who are usually extroverts rather than otherwise, Miss Mortimer is unusually withdrawn and reserved and I am tempted to describe her as a lonely figure. She is also a much-loved one.

Miss Mortimer, as champion, made one of the speeches at the Wimbledon Ball on Saturday night. It was without doubt the best of the evening, simple, generous in sentiment, brief and to the point, and it reflected the same qualities that enabled her to raise the prestige of the British women's game to its highest peak for nearly a quarter of a century. In short, she is a fine champion and I make the point at some length to clear the ground for the question raised in the tense and exciting final, where Miss Mortimer beat Miss Christine Truman 4–6, 6–4, 7–5.

Would Miss Truman now be champion had she not, when within a point of leading 5–3 in the second set, fallen awkwardly and lacked mobility for the next six or seven games? I have seen too many wavering contests between Miss Mortimer and Miss Truman to take for granted that a strong position by one or the other might not be broken. Certainly Miss Truman looked as though she were winning when the sudden net-cord, her quick return and subsequent fall, reduced her power.

In fact, Miss Truman had the cruellest of luck. At the same time it would be wrong to regard Miss Mortimer as a lucky winner. On her part she had to suffer much. It is not easy to play against a handicapped opponent, nor to have to endure the natural sympathies of the crowd with a stricken opponent. Miss Truman recovered her mobility at about 3–3 in the final set. The next six games were played on level terms and Miss Mortimer's control from the ground mastered the trenchant aggression of Miss Truman to the extent of taking four of them, this rewarding her with the match and Championship.

In terms of academic quality there have been better women's finals. Few have equalled its tension of conflict and emotional appeal, and from the spectators' viewpoint the only really satisfactory outcome would have been for both to have won.

7 JULY 1962

LAVER FINEST CHAMPION SINCE HOAD

MULLIGAN DEMOLISHED IN 50 MINUTES OF RUTHLESS PRESSURE

Lance Tingay
WIMBLEDON, Friday

There was a crisp execution on the Centre Court today when the red-headed Queenslander, R. Laver, became the men's singles champion for the second successive year. In the final, one of the briefest played, he beat his fellow Australian, M.F. Mulligan, 6–2, 6–2, 6–1, in 50 minutes and showed the Queen, who watched, how inevitable the outcome can be when one performer is a class above the opposition.

Laver was stirred by the occasion – and who wouldn't be? – to find his finest game. Poor Mulligan! He, too, played by no means badly only to be out-hit, outwitted and perpetually frustrated. I do not readily recall so heart-breaking an affair for the loser. There were many points that Mulligan, in any other situation, would have won, yet the times he was allowed to do so were singularly few, for Laver seemed to possess winged feet and a magic racket. Mulligan drove himself to the limit of physical effort to make a show. The crowd were keen that he should do so, too, and on the rare occasion he projected a shot comparable in quality with those of Laver they cheered him to the echo. As always, it is the underdog at Wimbledon who is most loved. To have reached a singles final is to earn lawn tennis fame. Mulligan can console himself with that, even if the memory of the match will consist of one long pain. Everything he did was done twice as well by Laver and all he earned from toil and tears was a handful of games.

Laver is a good champion, better and more confident than last year. He has speed, lightning reaction, a wonderful wrist, and all the shots, including a backhand, either sliced or rolled, that must rank the best to belong to a left-hander. I would rate him the best Wimbledon winner since L.A. Hoad without a doubt. His achievement this year is formidable and the titles of Australia, Italy and France already belonged to him before he strode confidently through this Wimbledon field. If the American title goes to him as well, as it could, then Laver will make a unique place for himself in lawn tennis history as winner of all five most important titles in the one year. The so far unique record set up by the American J.D. Budge in 1938 will be surpassed, for in Budge's day the Italian Championship had not risen to be a major meeting and that was one Budge did not get.

Mulligan played well enough to prevent the contest becoming a simple procession. He made Laver earn his points and if he made more errors than normal it was because of the tremendous pressure under which he played. Mulligan snatched what he could and they were crumbs from a rich man's table. The first game he got, the fourth of the first set, was gained against Laver's service, a feat he repeated in the fourth game of the third set. This, though, was not the sort of match where service breaks had much significance. Mulligan himself served 12 times, but on only three occasions did he take the game and, of course, on service strength, he is less well furnished than many leading players.

Including the games he won, Mulligan amassed 16 points in the first set, 19 in the second and 20 in the third. I record the figures so that Mulligan may have full credit for what he did achieve, even if it were not much. Laver gained 88 points in all, 46 of these points were outright winners, a high proportion reflecting the impression he gave throughout of magnificent excellence.

11 JULY 1962

LEADER: AN OPEN WIMBLEDON?

Today the International Lawn Tennis Federation is meeting in Paris, and it will have to discuss whether the Wimbledon meetings are to remain amateur, or whether they shall be thrown open to professionals. Wimbledon holds a unique position. It is closed to professionals, yet there is no parallel world meeting at which a professional world championship is unequivocally decided. Wembley has no such claim to advance. The Davis Cup matches have their own restrictions, and there is no Olympic lawn tennis. Wimbledon therefore remains the only annual meeting which could, by a single decision, be so broadened as to enable the winners of next year's singles to claim for themselves the titles of men's and women's 'world champions'.

There would be gain here, and possible loss. The British Lawn Tennis Association supports the obvious argument that amateur status has long been becoming a farce. True, the rules which define that status are strictly kept. But certain countries are prepared to spend so much money on the training and support of their players that, although the rules are kept, they are in fact mocked. As in many other games, the difference between amateur and professional has become increasingly hard to define. Should we not, therefore – so the argument runs – acknowledge the accomplished fact, and admit the professionals to Wimbledon?

If this were done, Wimbledon standards might improve, but not, the experts say, by so very much. The amateur Laver, for example, might perhaps be able to defeat the professionals Rosewall and Hoad. But what of the rewards which the professionals would expect? A nice silver cup is one thing. But when one's annual earnings, as a tennis professional, amount to five figures sterling, then silver cups lose their charm. Undoubtedly, if Wimbledon went 'open', the cost of the meeting would be vastly increased – and who would find the extra money? Its popularity can be judged by this year's gate of nearly 300,000. Are most of these regular supporters to be turned away because they can no longer afford to pay for a seat? The prestige of awarding world titles could be too dearly bought.

WHY NOT AN OPEN WIMBLEDON?

To admit professional lawn tennis players to the famous meeting would be a gamble – but it might be a gamble worth taking

The Earl of Birkenhead, a member of the All-England Lawn Tennis Club and a former Oxford University player

On Monday a new Wimbledon begins. Once again we shall be conscious of the unique atmosphere that pervades the place, compounded by tension and excitement and gaiety, and our footsteps will quicken as we hear the first round of applause from the Centre Court. The organisation of the tournament will be, as always, flawless, but something will be missing. The older spectators will remember nostalgically those finals when the protagonists were Tilden, Lacoste, Borotra, Cochet and other immortals. Those dead emotions cannot be revived today for the simple reason that in those matches the victor had shown himself to be the greatest player in the world. Today, in the absence of the professionals, he cannot establish that claim. We shall again have the uneasy feeling that tennis of a different class is played elsewhere, and that such a master as Rosewall could certainly beat anyone competing at Wimbledon with something in hand.

This change will not be appreciated by a large part of the audience who are now drawn to Wimbledon by watching the Championships on television and by the prospect of a pleasant day out, and it will not be reflected in the gate. But all who love and understand the game will again be perturbed by the fact that the Championships do not include the best players in the world, and the question will be asked again: 'Why not an open Wimbledon?'

Those who make this very natural demand do not, perhaps, realise the complexity of the problem. The game is governed by the International Lawn Tennis Federation, and agreement on open tournaments seemed almost in sight when this body put the question to the vote in 1960, but the issue was lost by the narrow margin of five votes. Since then, unfortunately, international opinion has hardened against the admission of professionals, and to change the rules requires a two-thirds majority, which is unlikely to be obtained.

The Australians see in the proposal a direct threat to their financial position. They derive their tennis income from the Davis Cup, and they fear that once professionals were admitted to it there might come a time when they could no longer hold it. If they were beaten they could forfeit the challenge round, a great national event like the Derby in England, which brings in as large a return as the Wimbledon Championships. The Australian National Championships are played in different parts of Australia and cannot compare with our own as money-makers.

The Americans are also against open tournaments for different reasons, but opinions there are about evenly balanced between East and West. Their hostility is partly due to complicated internal politics, and partly to a question of taxation. Contributions by rich patrons to tournament expenses are an important item in their finances, and these are allowed to be received free of tax for the amateur game. The American authorities are concerned that this revenue would be lost if professionals were admitted.

The Russian tennis 'amateurs', like all their athletes, are in fact already entirely professional since they are released from all other work and are maintained by the State, but this does not stop the Russian lawn tennis authorities opposing the admission of professionals. Their attitude is due partly to the fact that they wish to win Wimbledon for reasons of political prestige; but they also remember that lawn tennis was once one of the Olympic Games and are anxious that it should be restored, because the Russian Government makes special financial grants to Olympic sports. If open lawn tennis became a reality there would be no hope of this, as the Organising Committee of the Games would rule that lawn tennis was no longer an amateur sport.

Of the other countries most concerned the Italian LTA is financed by grants from the Italian football pools, but the latter only make such grants to amateur games and the Italian LTA would lose its major source of income if open lawn tennis became established. Spain is known to be against the proposal, but France is still in favour of open tennis.

Why then, it may be asked, does the All-England Club (Wimbledon) not 'go it alone' and proclaim an open Championship? The answer is that the All-England Club and the Lawn Tennis Association enjoy a close and special relationship which would make unilateral action by the former difficult, if not impossible, and might well bring the game in England into a condition of chaos. An agreement in 1934 lays down this relationship, and provides that the Wimbledon Championships are conducted by the All-England

Club and the LTA through a body called the Committee of Management. Although some of the most influential officials in both bodies want open tournaments, the decision to break away from the International Lawn Tennis Federation could only be made by the LTA, which is the governing body of lawn tennis in this country. Any motion for an open Wimbledon, even one put down by the President of the LTA himself, would have to go to the vote if it meant breaking away from the ILTF, and at the moment, it is believed, would be defeated.

Some of the objectors take the attitude that instituting an open Wimbledon would be a grave risk as it would entail defiance of the International Lawn Tennis Federation, which would presumably prohibit its members from competing, and also ban British players from Continental tournaments. Furthermore, they add, what is the point in running such a risk when the takings of last year's Wimbledon were up rather than down, and the tournament in its present form is always a sell-out? It is important to understand that certain leaders of the LTA and the All-England Club strongly disagree with this argument. They are disturbed at the decline in the level of play, but without the LTA's agreement they cannot open their great meeting to professionals.

If an open Wimbledon was proclaimed and the ILTF thus defied, this would at first leave a tournament of professionals and British players. It would remain to be seen how many foreign amateurs would defy the ban and join them. No other tournament in the world exerts such a powerful spell on tennis players as Wimbledon and it is unlikely that the bolder spirits would resist it. If some leading foreign players succumbed to the lure others would probably follow.

The attitude of the ILTC would depend on the success of the tournament, and the number of defections. If a large enough number of foreign players decided to compete the ILTC might well be forced to change its mind in order to avoid being placed in a ridiculous position. If the worst happened, and no foreign players dared to come, how gravely would the finances of the tournament be affected? My own opinion is that the prospect of seeing the greatest players in the world in action on the Centre Court of Wimbledon would be so powerful a draw that the gate would not be reduced, but it must be admitted that it would be a gamble on the part of the LTA and one requiring a certain degree of courage.

Such an open Wimbledon, once established, would be an example to the world of how a tournament should be conducted. There would be no question, as some fear, of the proceedings being dominated by the Kramer circus, for each professional would enter individually and be under the firm control of the Committee of Management. Some people might fear that the professionals would demand such large prizes as a price of their playing at Wimbledon that they would be beyond the present resources of the Club. This would be a misapprehension. The question was discussed on a former occasion with the professionals and the Wimbledon authorities were perfectly happy about the amount suggested for prizes, which they considered to be well within their financial resources.

For seven years the LTA and the All-England Club have in vain been exhausting every constitutional means of solving this problem. They have put forward proposals which, if accepted, would have brought to an end the disgusting condition of financial jobbery now rampant in the so-called amateur game. It is, for example, an open secret that some leading players accept presents from promoters of tournaments, *sub rosa,* in addition to their legitimate living and travelling expenses. Surely the time has now come for the LTA to throw its heart over the fence and pass a resolution demanding an open Wimbledon with which the All-England Club would certainly associate itself? It would remain to be seen whether the International Lawn Tennis Federation would boycott such a tournament, and, if so, how damaging the results would be to the finances of the LTA and the All-England Club, and how long the ILTF would be able to maintain such a prohibition.

There is a magic about Wimbledon. It is the cradle of the game and the Mecca of all good players. Amid the cynical corruption of modern 'amateur' tennis it is totally disinterested except in the furtherance of the game. Its organisation is the envy of the world. It is therefore improbable, once the nettle has been grasped, that the International Lawn Tennis Federation would be able to persist indefinitely in an attitude of obstruction.

9 JULY 1963

MISS SMITH EARNS FIRST TITLE FOR AUSTRALIA

Lance Tingay
WIMBLEDON, Monday

Margaret Smith, the most athletic woman to grace the courts, took the women's singles crown in the belated finish to the Lawn Tennis Championships here today. In 50 minutes she beat the American Billie-Jean Moffitt

6–3, 6–4 and an Australian name is now, for the first time, on the roll of singles champions. In eight days' time Miss Smith will be 21, and her two previous Wimbledons, when she was a failure as a favourite, tends to make one forget how much she has accomplished. Four times singles champion of Australia, twice champion of Italy, once of France, once of America and now Wimbledon, this is a record that can be matched with the great players of the past.

No one, though, will think of the doughty Miss Smith in the same context as players like Maureen Connolly or Helen Wills Moody. Althea Gibson and Alice Marble are her predecessors in style, in the adaptation of masculine technique of service and volley to feminine skill. The final today, which was watched by a full Centre Court and without any sense of anti-climax, must be recorded in masculine terms. The shots that mattered were service and volley and service returns, for if the bouncing Miss Moffitt is less obviously a trained athlete than Miss Smith, the big guns of lawn tennis are equally as important a part of her technique.

The start of both was as nervous as I have seen. Miss Moffitt held her service in the opening game after four deuces which held, on her side, three double-faults and on the other some returns of services so frail that the ball hardly reached the net. The rest was better than that, but it never did reach heights when both women displayed their richest talents at the same time. Rallies as such were few, for if the service itself were not a winner, a bold service return was the finishing blow. In the short, sharp exchanges Miss Smith was manifestly superior, even if by no great margin. For one thing her service was generally fast and deadly and not open, as was Miss Moffitt's, to an attacking return.

In the second set, after a tight first game, Miss Smith advanced to 4–0 and nothing seemed to remain for Miss Moffitt but to count her blessings for having, as an unseeded player, got as far as the final. In the fifth game, however, there was the longest rally of the match when Miss Moffitt discomfited Miss Smith with a perfect lob. The Australian was serving but nonetheless Miss Moffitt captured the game to love. There cannot have been one spectator who did not ask himself whether this was to be the dividing point between Miss Smith's success and failure. The feeling was confirmed when Miss Moffitt took the next game to 15, thus reducing the Australian's lead to 4–2.

I suppose the next game was the most important of the match. With her third double-fault of the match Miss Smith, still apparently under the high tension which has marred her success before, put herself game-point down.

Miss Smith then provoked in turn a forehand error from Miss Moffitt, an over-ambitious lob and a mistake on the backhand. She stood 5–2, which was as well for Miss Moffitt took the next game and that would have been four games all instead of 5–3 to Miss Smith.

There was match point for Miss Smith at 5–2. Miss Moffitt saved it with a smash that the Australian could not return. Miss Smith served at 5–3 without success and there was another double-fault by her to stress her tension on the brink of victory. In the next game Miss Moffitt was made to look frail again by Miss Smith's searing returns of service. She fell to 15–40 and though Miss Moffitt saved the second match point with a service winner, it was a sharp return of service from the forehand that made Miss Smith the winner and holder of the Wimbledon title.

3 JULY 1965

EMERSON OVERWHELMS OFF-FORM STOLLE

ONE-SIDED SINGLES FINAL LASTS ONLY 67 MINUTES

Lance Tingay

At the age of 28 the wiry Queenslander, R. Emerson, every inch a skilled athlete, is men's singles champion of Wimbledon for the second year. It was all one-sided brevity on the Centre Court today and Emerson overwhelmed his doubles partner, F.S. Stolle, by 6–2, 6–4, 6–4 in 67 minutes. Emerson thus joins two other Australians, R. Laver, the champion of 1961 and 1962, and L.A. Hoad, the champion of 1956 and 1957, in taking the title two years running. The record of Stolle is more distinctive, but he certainly would not want to have it.

Poor Stolle! He and the German, G. Von Cramm, now have in common the undesired record of having played, and lost, in the final three years running. Von Cramm's years in this situation of sublime failure were 1935 to 1937, when he lost twice to F.J. Perry and once to J.D. Budge. From 1884 to 1886 H.F. Lawford failed in the challenge round against W. Renshaw. Lawford, then Von Cramm, and now Stolle are sure of a place in Wimbledon history. But who wants to be a perpetual also-ran? Stolle, 26, has now played eight important national singles finals and won but one, the French title last May. In a ranking list of the second best he stands without a peer.

But what of the triumphant Emerson? The second Wimbledon title he so ably picked up today makes his tally of important championships up to nine singles, and, if doubles be included, to 24. One cannot, then, dispute his status as a good player, though whether he would be able to hold his own with the leading professionals like Laver and K.R. Rosewall is, in my opinion, doubtful. But I am sure Emerson is a better player than a year ago. His service is more sure, especially his second delivery. His forehand is a sounder stroke. He always was mercurial on the court, and he has certainly lost nothing of his dashing speed of foot.

Wimbledon's last men's singles match for 1965 was disappointing. It was always too one-sided to inflame the passions. Emerson was too good and Stolle was too bad. Emerson did his lively talents full justice. Stolle, alas!, fell far short of his, and the dignity of his power strokes was only hinted at here and there. Finals at Wimbledon often fall short of what they should be according to the record book. The nerve-strain of so important an encounter can intimidate the bravest hearts and inhibit the finest skills. Stolle today was a shadowy representation of what he could have been. His return of service was inadequate, to say the least. In Emerson's first service of the match, the second game of the opening set when he had already broken Stolle's delivery, he trailed 15–40. Emerson still won that game, taking four points on the trot. He served in 14 other games and the total of points gained by Stolle in them was merely 13. On only three occasions did Stolle take a service game off Emerson as far as 30. All this was overwhelming, shattering and a little sad, for it reduced Stolle to being outclassed.

Emerson went to 4–0 in the first 12 minutes of the match, by which time Stolle had got only seven points. Stolle held his next two service games, but in less than 20 minutes Emerson had banked an easy set. The second set was bankrupt for Stolle from the start for here again he yielded his service in the opening game; the only disturbance of the set's inevitable course was when Stolle averted an even bigger overdraft by recovering from 15–40 in the fifth game.

In the third set Stolle held out longer. Emerson had lost a little of his momentum – the momentum, I would stress, of a sprinter rather than a long-distance runner – and it was not until the ninth game that Emerson broke service to take the lead. Emerson served out the match very easily. By that stage no one dreamed he would do otherwise than bring a mundane final to a speedy conclusion.

I do not know what Emerson got up to as they breakfasted in their London flat together in the morning. Somehow he contrived to take away Stolle's talents, lock them up and throw away the key.

3 JULY 1966

BILLIE-JEAN IS QUEEN OF CENTRE COURT

Henry Raven
WIMBLEDON, Saturday

It was not a regal women's singles final in the Lawn Tennis Championships here today, but at the end of it Billie-Jean King became the new Queen of the Centre Court by beating Maria Bueno, the winner in 1959, 1960 and 1964, and the runner-up last year, by 6–3, 3–6, 6–1 in 67 minutes. It was the first American victory in this event, which was a speciality of the United States for so many post-war years, since Karen Susman won in 1962.

This was the result that most people expected. Mrs King, a bespectacled 22-year-old Californian, was seeded fourth in the tournament, but victories over Margaret Smith in the South African final and over Ann Jones, Britain's leading player, in the Wightman Cup, made it clear that she was in tremendous form. Ever since she and Mrs Susman, then a couple of teen-aged prodigies, had the precociousness to carry off the women's doubles title here in 1961, she has shown herself to be a formidable competitor. An aggressive service, a sharp eye and arm for the volley and smash, plenty of pace about the court, and great opportunism and self-confidence are her principal assets. There have been Wimbledon champions with purer styles and more varied strokes. But there cannot have been many who have swept into the attack with so much speed, determination and efficiency.

Because she was pressing so hard with her service, Mrs King served eight double-faults – three of them in one game, which she still won – this after-noon, but apart from that she made surprisingly few mistakes for a player who takes so many risks and attacks so boldly. She kept Miss Bueno under pressure all the time and eventually the Brazilian had to drop out of the race. Miss Bueno scored only three points in the last four games.

She had a chance to break service in the third game of the final set when Mrs King lost a lead of 40–15, but the American held on for 2–1 and that turned out to be the last time that Brazil held the initiative. Miss Bueno lost her service immediately for 1–3, playing a wild and careless game, and she never recovered from that. Presented with her opportunities, Mrs King allowed her no hope of reprieve. She lost the first two points of the next game, but increased the pressure at once and held service for 4–1. The rest was quick and sad. 'I have never played such a bad final before,' said Miss Bueno. After losing two in succession at Wimbledon, she must be beginning to know how Fred Stolle feels.

ARE YOU BRIGHT ENOUGH FOR WIMBLEDON?
Violet Johnstone

Wimbledon spectator fashions must change. Colour television will only succeed there if women spectators play their part. Colour – bright reds and yellows as first favourites – is what Britain's ardent tennis fans must wear in future to bring success in this new TV era. 'This is what I'm going to need to break up the mass of green and purple [the Wimbledon colours] which is going to fill the screen,' said Mr A. Wilkinson, BBC producer in charge at Wimbledon. 'I want spectators in bright red hats.'

Very few of us will be seeing a coloured picture of the Centre Court at home this year, but we will get a chance of seeing it in almost every TV rental shop's window display in and around London and any other area that receives BBC2 programmes.

I had a preview of colour TV at Wimbledon last week. On the left was a picture in black-and-white, on the right one in colour. I couldn't take my eyes off the colour picture. 'Wimbledon is an ideal choice for us to launch colour television,' Mr Wilkinson told me. 'It's an outdoor event which is being transmitted live so that people can't think any of it is faked, which they would undoubtedly think with a film.'

But panning around the spectators – and there is likely to be more of this from now on – the overall picture lacked bright strong reds, yellows, blues. It was a lifeless sea of pale shades. Fashions on court this week will, thanks to Wimbledon's fashion king, Teddy Tinling, have bright dashes of red and yellow trimmings – his apt choice for players including Maria Bueno, Virginia Wade and Lesley Turner.

NEWCOMBE SPRINTS TO TITLE IN 71 MINUTES
Lance Tingay
WIMBLEDON, Friday

The Lawn Tennis Championships maintained its refusal to permit a non-seeded singles champion. The Australian, John Newcombe, took the major men's title this afternoon when he beat the German, Wilhelm Bungert, 6–3, 6–1, 6–1. Australian dominance was accordingly maintained. Newcombe, 23, and a good, solid player by any standard, became the ninth Australian singles champion in 12 years.

Beginning with Norman Brookes, who was the first overseas man to win in 1907, Newcombe is tenth in the line of distinguished Australian victors. Whether he will be a distinguished champion depends on what he does in the future for there was little, alas, that was memorable about his victory this afternoon. This was hardly Newcombe's fault. He put forward a game of rugged excellence. His sterling qualities merited stronger opposition but, as it was, those enthusiasts who queued overnight had scant reward for their weary vigil.

By and large Wimbledon finals do not produce great lawn tennis. The occasion is too big and the atmosphere of the occasion too rich for most players to unwind from the shackling influence of nervous tension. On Bungert's part, today was no exception. The fine genius of this German was blunted and he gave but poor indication of what he can do. While Newcombe's virtues shone brightly Bungert's negative ones were more apparent. When it was all over, Bungert having stayed on court for only 71 minutes and won but five games in all, one could think only in terms of negation. Was there ever a briefer final than this, was there one of such poor combat value or one where the vanquished got fewer games?

In 1962, when Rod Laver swiftly despatched the unseeded Martin Mulligan, the loser then got five games only. Five games was the tally achieved by Ashley Cooper in 1957, though the main cause of that debacle was Hoad's tremendous skill rather than the poverty of the loser. Actually, the briefest final of all time, so far as the number of games assesses brevity, was Fred Perry's 1936 win against the last German to be in the final, Gottfried von Cramm.

9 JULY 1967

ANN JONES MAKES THE CHAMPION FIGHT

Lew Hoad, Wimbledon champion in 1956 and 1957

Billie-Jean King retained her Wimbledon singles title yesterday, which I suppose was what most people expected. But Ann Jones made her fight rather more than the 6–3, 6–4 score might suggest. Although Billie-Jean is only 23, she has had a lot of experience. As champion she had a lot to lose, yet she played as well as she could hope under difficult windy conditions against an awkward opponent. Next year she says she'll have a go at the

Grand Slam, the titles of Australia, France, England and America, which only Maureen Connolly has previously achieved in 1952. She'll find it a hard task. Today she became the first player since Doris Hart in 1951 to win three titles, taking the women's doubles with Rosemary Casals and the mixed with Owen Davidson.

I thought Ann played pretty well. She knew she had to vary her game, to disrupt Billie-Jean's rhythm, but though she tried everything not much of it came off. I understand Billie-Jean spent the whole of April practising eight hours a day in California, a lot of the time against men, and that's probably why she's so sharp at the net and overhead.

Ann had no fewer than 14 game points for six of the games she lost, five of them against Billie-Jean's service. And the fact that she didn't win them was because Billie-Jean played most of them so well, tightening her concentration and getting her first service in. Her service was one of the deciding factors of the match, and if Ann had been able to take even half those game points we might have had a real thriller. There was that long fourth game in the second set, when Ann might have got back in the match, when she had five game points against service. Had she won that, I thought, now that she was beginning to hit her drives lower and making it difficult for Billie-Jean on her first volley, she would probably have taken that set. Of course, Ann did pull back for three all, but in the next game she seemed to hurry a bit too much and was 3–4 down again. She had a bad bounce in mid-court at 15–0, but I guess that happens to all of us.

Ann has this tremendous determination, and a pretty good range of shots. If others had her will to win there'd be a lot more better players around than there are. She doesn't have any great shots, but then she doesn't have any really bad ones. Perhaps her backhand may be a bit suspect. But, above all, she moves beautifully around the court and this is something you can't teach anyone. Mind you, next year I don't feel you could look any farther for the winner than Rosemary Casals. She was all over Ann at the start of their semi-final, but what turned the match was experience. Ann needed to change her tactics at a set down and she did, playing Rosemary at her own game, serve and volley, which Ann doesn't really like – and she won.

I don't expect I shall play much more competitively. I've been asked now to play in the Wimbledon professional world grass-court championship from 25 to 28 August, together with Gonzalez, Laver, Rosewall, Gimeno, Ralston and Stolle. It'll be great to be back at Wimbledon. I'll have been playing with the Brazilian Davis Cup team every day in practice in Durban, so I should be in trim. Then there'll be Wembley in October, then Paris and Barcelona and after that I shall concentrate on building up my school near Malaga, where I hope all the promising young players from Europe will come for coaching and practice. I've got 26 acres there, and if it catches on it could be really interesting. And if, say, the British Davis Cup team wanted to come for ten days before a match, they'd be able to.

I don't think I'll play any more, unless there's open tennis. That would be a new challenge. I've made enough money to be comfortable for the rest of my life. So I don't have to play, but open tennis would be fun. It must come. I don't know what the boys make today, but as an amateur I used to make 600 dollars a week. Now I believe it's nearer 1,200 dollars.

CHAPTER FOUR
THE EARLY
'OPEN' YEARS
(1968–79)

THREAT TO WIMBLEDON'S FUTURE

Lew Hoad

Wimbledon, we all know, is going to be different, more exciting we hope, with open tennis. But I can't help feeling that in the arrival of what had to come sooner or later, there is a potential danger, a threat to Wimbledon's pre-eminence in the world of lawn tennis. Up to now, Wimbledon has been the queen of championships. There's no better organised, more enjoyable tournament anywhere. The grounds, the courts, the atmosphere, all are unique. No one could possibly hope to compare with Wimbledon while it was amateur, but now that it is open, its prestige can be challenged – in cash.

The great thing about Wimbledon up till now has been that nobody made anything out of it. Amateurs, who can earn thousands of pounds in a year at other tournaments in illegal expenses and appearance money, have still come to Wimbledon just for the honour and the pleasure of being there, for the sense of occasion. Of course, if they did well, their price at other tournaments went up, so they profited in that way, but from Wimbledon they got nothing but genuine expenses. If they're not top-ranked players that has not been much.

Ken Fletcher, who comes over from Hong Kong these days, won the men's doubles and the mixed two years ago, was in the semi-final of the singles – and got £50. The prestige has been the real distinction of Wimbledon, and the players have enjoyed it that way. But now we're playing for money, Wimbledon is going to be rated more by the total cash prize at stake than by the flowers round the clubhouse. Of course, it'll always be a great club, and I don't think they have to worry too much just yet, but the danger's there.

Look at the present situation. Wimbledon this year is worth £26,100 prize money. Forest Hills is going to be worth £40,000 and there's even some talk of next year's South African Championships in Johannesburg being worth £50,000. Even a small tournament like the Pacific South West in Los Angeles has prize money of £20,000, while the US National Professional Grass Court Championships in Boston, which finished last week, with only a tiny entry, was worth £12,500, with £3,000 to the winner.

You have only to look at other professional sports like golf and boxing to see that the really big prize money is not in Britain, but elsewhere, and mainly in the States. Money talks. This month you have had Margaret

Court, Tom Okker and Manuel Santana giving the French Championships in Paris a miss, and going to Berlin. It can only have been because they were getting bigger expenses. It only needs some new association in America to get smart, or some small European tournament to start up during Wimbledon fortnight – which has been unheard of up till now – with say a limited, select entry of 16, and good place money, for some of the better players to be siphoned off from Wimbledon. Let's face it, players are out for what they can get.

Why do you suppose many leading amateurs haven't been at Queen's this week, when for certain they all need grass-court practice? Because they've been elsewhere, at minor hard-court tournaments on the Continent, making money. I think Wimbledon will find that in only a few years it will be forced to raise its prize money quite steeply to keep in line with some of the other big tournaments if it is not to lose some of its glamour.

The grass-court business is another question. There are not many players outside Britain, America and Australia who play on grass more than two or three times a year, and when they come to Wimbledon it's a bit of a toss-up how they get on. If they hit a streak, they can do well, but sometimes they can get bundled out early on. Sometimes, too, I don't think the standard of play at Wimbledon is as good as people try to make out because the players are still trying to get accustomed to the different surface. Although as an Australian I like playing on grass. I have to admit that there's sense in the suggestion that the Davis Cup should be confined to hard courts. It would be good for the game and would encourage some of the Europeans and South Americans.

Australia have won the Davis Cup 15 times in the last 18 years, the United States the other three. Any country, like Italy, Spain, Mexico or India, which has fought its way through in recent years, has played on hard courts most of the way. Some team then turns up to play the challenge round on grass, only eight days before the competition, with the temperature around 95 degrees. What chance have they? It's a hell of an advantage if you play regularly on grass – and of course only having to play the challenge round. All you have to do is prepare for that one match. Mind you, Australia are in a bit of a fix now, unless they decide to make the Davis Cup open, because they are left only with Bill Bowrey and Ray Ruffels. They were probably banking on John Newcombe not turning professional for another year or two. He'd said he wasn't interested. I think 'Newk' is the nearest there is in the game at present to another potential Laver. He's developed at about the same age as

Rod did. He hasn't got Laver's flair or left-hander's advantage – but I think he has a better service, and he's tremendously steady, an ideal professional.

One thing that has to be sorted out – before next year – is to make sure the nominated amateurs and top professionals from the same country do not get drawn against each other as has happened this year. Nominated players are always placed apart in the draw and the same should be done with professionals. I don't think you can criticise the seedings for this week too much, though I'm surprised to find myself at seven. I expected something like 12, considering I've not really played since last September. I had a bit of trouble with my arm last week at Queen's, nothing much, just a bit sore after suddenly playing competitively again twice a day, especially on grass. Because the ball shoots and leaps and rarely comes through true you are never hitting it with the centre of the racket and this jars and puts tremendous strain on the forearm. I don't think I've had anything like it for ten years playing mostly on wood, but it seems fine now.

6 JULY 1968

LAVER'S TITLE IN HOUR OF SUPREME SKILL

Lance Tingay
WIMBLEDON, Friday

When Rod Laver, now undisputed world lawn tennis champion, enters the Wimbledon Championships next year, it might be as well if he were given the prize money and asked if he minded stepping down. The tournament might then become more exciting. If Laver continues to play as he did in the final today, there will be no contest worth the description. Laver beat Tony Roche 6–3, 6–4, 6–2 in an hour. If not the briefest of Wimbledon finals, it was among the most shattering.

That this remarkable left-hander would dominate the first open Wimbledon was expected. There have been favourites in the past who have gone through the meeting as a whole more one-sidedly, notably Jack Kramer in 1947. Laver, though, has achieved lawn tennis immortality, not by being the champion of the first open Wimbledon, but by climaxing the achievement with a display of such immaculate mastery that, given a repetition, no other man in the world could hope to hold him in check.

One knew Laver to be a maestro. He was when he was an amateur, as witness his unique performance in taking the six big championships, those of Australia, Italy, France, Wimbledon, Germany and the United States in 1962. After that he dominated the more confined world of professionalism. It could not be more fitting that so splendid a performer should win the premier open championship. He paced himself well during the course of the fortnight. He paced himself perfectly in the final. Poor Tony Roche!

He is a good player and he played quite well this afternoon. Yet all he could do, all he was allowed to do, was be a foil to his opponent's high skill. How galling it must have been for him to play his heart out, to reach standards of stroking that were first class, only to be permitted merely an ignominious hour on the court. The highest tribute I can pay Roche is that he did well enough to make Laver bring out his finest game. The more searching his shots, the more Laver raised his own standards.

I suppose the most striking aspect of Laver's high quality is his ability to make a shot of virtuosity when under pressure. It was heartbreaking for Roche to project what would normally have been a sure winner, merely to provoke the unplayable. Two efforts of searing passing shots by Roche were instances in the second set. Most players would hardly have seen the ball, so fast did Roche project it. Laver answered with a stop volley that died as soon as it passed over the net. Afterwards he admitted there was luck about it, but then he is the sort of man who creates such luck. A rally or two later a similar deadly ball was projected by Roche. This time, Laver made the same response with unerring touch, and with intention in every split second of his quick reaction.

Had the game been chess Roche would have retired, for there was hardly any point in continuing a one-sided contest. Clearly, there was nothing he could do against such mastery. Roche manfully kept on despite the odds. Even when Laver reached 4–0 in the third set he played his best, and his courage was rewarded with two more games. At no time did Roche break through Laver's service. In all, there were three games and five rallies when he was within two points of doing so, but always Laver surely took back the chance. Roche may console himself that this was Laver's third Wimbledon title – and his hardest yet. In 1961 Laver beat Chuck McKinley for the loss of only eight games and, in 1962, he brought down Martin Mulligan for the loss of only five. Roche managed nine games with Laver's standard of performance at its highest level. I doubt if there are many players in the world who could have done so well. With Laver in this mood, and with the incentive of the most coveted prize to spur him on, the money prize of £2,000 was probably irrelevant.

BILLIE-JEAN PROVES HER GREATNESS
Lew Hoad, Wimbledon champion in 1956 and 1957

Billie-Jean King must surely be ranked among the great women players after achieving her third singles win in a row at Wimbledon today, beating Judy Tegart in straight sets. She's won everything, and there's not much more she can do. Now she must limit her appearances as a professional if she is to stay at the top and keep fresh. Yet I was surprised to hear her explain at the press conference immediately afterwards why she suddenly went home a month ago, scratching from the tournaments at Beckenham and Queen's. She felt she'd had too much tennis and that she couldn't win Wimbledon if she didn't have a rest. But it's only five weeks since she and the other professional girls – Rosie Casals, Ann Jones and Françoise Durr – were complaining in New York that they hadn't been playing enough, only three matches in 30 days or so.

Today's final wasn't all that exciting. Billie-Jean seems more concerned these days with what's going wrong with her game rather than what's going right – all these odd little gestures with her hands. Mind you, she never looked like losing. Judy Tegart has done very well, but she just hasn't quite got the ability or the experience at this level to play a third key match in a row, after her victories over Margaret Court and Nancy Richey. She fairly hit the ball sometimes, but Billie-Jean has a good all-round game, served well and hardly missed a single low volley. The big difference between Billie-Jean and the other girls is that whenever she's in doubt she throws up a deep lob and then, instead of staying back like the rest, she comes to the net to take the initiative.

I don't think, however, that women's tennis is all that suited to professionalism. The present crowd have probably just jumped on the bandwagon, wanting to make money and to be sincere and open about their status. It seems to me odd to have professional women athletes, except perhaps in ice-skating. That's just my opinion – maybe others won't agree.

Ann Jones has probably missed her big chance this year, having been a set and 5–3 up against Billie-Jean in the women's semi-finals. I think Ann has improved tremendously since last year. She's more aggressive, coming in behind her service, and she beat Mrs King at Madison Square Garden. She needs a lot of tennis, and is probably suited to the professional scene.

Margaret Court has lost a bit of confidence, though she was always suspect in a winning position. This was confirmed when she lost to Judy Tegart.

Rosie Casals was perhaps unlucky against Maria Bueno, but she's still basically the best of the lot. A couple more years and she should beat everyone. At present she's inclined to be erratic because she doesn't know what to do when she's in front. And I feel it doesn't do her any good having to go round all the time with Billie-Jean; she's dominated by the champion too much.

On the men's scene, compared with last year this was a tremendous Wimbledon tournament. We've had some superb matches, particularly in the first rounds, matches like Ralston against Richey, Moore against Gimeno, which have been as exciting as you could wish to see. The standard has improved and it's all going to help more young players to come into the game. But it's obvious the professionals are going to have to think a bit about their position. I know they've had four in the last eight of the men's singles, two in the last four, and that Rod Laver justified his position as the world champion.

In doubles, too, the professionals have five pairs in the last eight, but they realised suddenly for the first time in years that they can't just go out and do as they please. Only the top professionals have proved themselves, and the others are going to have their work cut out from now on to stay near the top. Where it's going to hurt most in the professional game is among the promoters. It's going to be tough, I would think, trying to sell their players, because the public realise they're not the best in the world now some of them have been put in the shade at Wimbledon.

And take a player like Gimeno, with the rival National Tennis League. It's been recognised over the past few years, among the players at any rate, that Gimeno was the second or third best in the world, and he got to the semifinals of the open tournaments at Bournemouth and Paris. But where is he now after Wimbledon, losing to Ray Moore in the third round and being beaten with Gonzalez in the third round of the doubles by Ashe and Pasarell?

Of course, the professionals had everything to lose this year, nothing to gain, and I think it's difficult to judge emphatically on one tournament. I reckon if the whole thing was played again there would be fewer surprises. Gonzalez, Gimeno, Buchholz, Rosewall and myself, for instance, had never seen many of these other guys play, so one had no idea till one got out there how to play them. Not only that – with all that rain in the first week we couldn't get any practice on grass and then suddenly the pressure was really on at the beginning of this week with the sun beating down.

Many of the amateurs, Ashe, Okker and the rest, probably played above themselves, and now they have to live up to their new reputations. Only time will tell. I think the professionals will come back, as Tony Roche said after the final, whatever the prize money ... probably they'd even come back for nothing. But it's up to Wimbledon to increase the prize money. Already it's apparent that Wimbledon is not going to be the top tournament in this respect unless it does something. The winner at Forest Hills, for instance, is going to get almost three times as much as here at Wimbledon.

It seems to me from what we've seen this year that tennis has changed in the last few years. The players find it difficult to get into any sort of rhythm; no match ever seems to be safe. Players have been getting into trouble even with a two-set lead, and I think this is because the leading amateurs – Ashe, Pasarell, Riessen, Graebner, Okker, Cox and others – are always going for the big shot. They really hit their returns, so the server never quite knows what's coming back at him. I don't think this is a good thing in the long run because it leads to being erratic. I don't say a few years ago we were better, but I think we were more consistent. It's the present trend which has helped to produce some of the upsets.

10 JULY 1968

LETTER TO THE EDITOR

SATURDAY FINAL

Sir,

In reply to an earlier letter, when Mlle Lenglen came to Wimbledon she revolutionised women's tennis with the result that she became the greatest draw in the game so everyone flocked to see her. It was generally accepted by the press and never contradicted by Wimbledon that it was due to this draw that the women's final was changed with the men's final to the Saturday.

Now that the television shows far more men's games, I have the impression that it is the men's tennis which has the greatest draw today. In these circumstances I have wondered for some time why the change back was not made. If the men's final was played on the Saturday more men would be free to see it either live or on television.

Gilbert C. Geear
Hook Norton, Oxfordshire

5 JULY 1969

NEVER-SAY-DIE ANN JONES IS WIMBLEDON QUEEN AT LONG LAST

Lance Tingay

Ann Jones gave British lawn tennis one of its finest moments in the Championships yesterday when she beat the American Billie-Jean King 3–6, 6–3, 6–2 to become the women's singles champion. A splendid triumph and a rare one! The only other British singles champion at Wimbledon in more than three decades was Angela Mortimer, in 1961. Although there is little point in balancing one fine achievement against the other, I think the performance of Mrs Jones must be held the more prestigious. The three big wins she had to take her crown were, first, against Nancy Richey; second, against Margaret Court, this being the match in which she played her most splendid game, and yesterday against Mrs King, the champion of the three preceding years. All this was brought about at her 14th challenge and at the age of 30, a time when lawn tennis skill is generally held to be diminishing.

There are doubtless many factors that brought success at long last to Mrs Jones, and certainly one of them was the fervent wish of about 15,000 spectators that she would pull it off. There was a time during the final when the patriotic zeal of the crowd threatened to be less than fair. Indeed, I have the feeling that when Mrs King's game began to fall apart, as undoubtedly it did, it was because she was tired not only of playing against Mrs Jones, but almost every person in the stands as well. In the first game of the third set, when the crowd was becoming so loud and vociferous in its partisan support, and with it anti-American, Mrs King expressed her feeling by ironically curtseying to a section of them. Then, when it was obvious that Mrs King was not resenting their partisan outlook and obvious, too, that Mrs Jones could win the title, the crowd warmed to the American almost more in the imminence of her defeat than they did in her previous victories.

Mrs Jones brought off her victory, watched by Princess Anne and Princess Margaret, in 71 minutes. The quality of the play was mixed, as it so often is in a match on which so much depends, and the victor played less well than she did last Wednesday when she beat Mrs Court in the semi-final. Nor did Mrs King reach the same standard of play as she did in any of her last three finals, particularly in 1967 when her victim was Mrs Jones. But it was a contest of rapt excitement nonetheless. Afterwards Mrs Jones summed it up by saying: 'I got better and she got worse.' She could not have been more accurate.

The opening set belonged to the American pretty well all through, save for the first game which Mrs Jones, who was serving, took to love. The pattern of Mrs King's success was familiar, a good service, nearly always to the opposition backhand, and a decisive volley against the floating return. At this time there was little snap about Mrs Jones's game. One may always judge her form by the extent to which her backhand under-spins the ball in frailty or cuts it with more venom. But having played many floaters in the opening set, which went beyond recall in 20 minutes, Mrs Jones began to play some good points, not only behind her own delivery but also against the service.

It was not long before these good points were furthered into good games and I would mark the time when she transformed herself from a beaten player into one with a sporting chance as the third game of the second set. Here she broke Mrs King's service for the first time. Two games later she did as much again and it built up to a lead of 4–1. She was never more sharp nor more effective than at this stage. But the patriotic hopes that her winning zeal bestirred were checked. From 4–1 Mrs Jones lost ten points in succession. She seemed to have hurt her leg and the fear was of a cataclysmic American victory. With her lead whittled to 4–3 and standing 0–30 in the eighth game, Mrs Jones recovered; equally, Mrs King began to lose herself more and more.

Mrs Jones took the set 6–3 on her second chance when her opponent, forced to stretch widely, missed a forehand volley. This, then, was level pegging, and Mrs Jones became almost as dominant in the third set as Mrs King had been in the first. As her confidence mounted, that of the American obviously diminished. Mrs King's early crispness was replaced, if not by lassitude, at least by an inability to hit the ball well and true. Mrs Jones took everything Mrs King offered her with interest. Soon she was 5–2 in front and serving for the title. She began this game with a double-fault, not a happy augury, and yielded it to 15. For patriots this was an unhappy moment.

But Mrs King, if she were being offered the chance to come back, could not take it. In the next game she was 15–40 and two match points down. These she saved and got to game point. But when Mrs Jones held on and reached match ball for the third time, the American contribution was a double-fault that gave Mrs Jones her Championship.

5 JULY 1969

LEADER: UP WITH THE JONES

Congratulations to Mrs Ann Jones for her splendidly well-deserved win on the Centre Court at Wimbledon yesterday. Her achievement is the climax to a truly great tennis career. On Tuesday Mrs Jones is to receive her MBE from the Queen, awarded for 'services to lawn tennis'. Securing the Wimbledon 'crown' makes a delightfully fitting prelude to this occasion. All the more satisfactory in that she won her match against Mrs Billie-Jean King fairly and squarely with no ifs and buts about it. While some may have been anxious in the opening stages that her gruelling semi-final on Wednesday might have taken too much out of her, she found her form magnificently from the middle of the second set and thoroughly deserved her victory. Praise for Mrs King, a well-liked loser. Pleasure that Britain has won a world sporting event — one sphere where national fervour remains blameless.

6 JULY 1969

MRS JONES AGAIN

Ann Jones, who had failed to win a title in 15 previous Wimbledons, won her second of the tournament when she and Fred Stolle beat Judy Tegart and Tony Roche 6–3, 6–3. Miss Tegart was wild and erratic and Roche almost made too many mistakes. By contrast, Mrs Jones and Stolle missed very little indeed. Their returning of service was quite admirable. It was all so very easy for Mrs Jones that she must be wondering now why Wimbledon has always seemed such an Everest of a tournament for her.

6 JULY 1969

NON-VINTAGE LAVER – TILL CRISIS THREATENS

Henry Raven

In two hours and a quarter on the Centre Court, Rod Laver at the age of 30 made himself the unique modern Wimbledon champion by winning the men's singles title for the fourth time with a 6–4, 5–7, 6–4, 6–4 victory over his fellow Australian John Newcombe in the final yesterday. This was his longest final and as he said afterwards, the toughest that he had been forced to play since he gained his first success at Wimbledon in 1961. The set that Newcombe earned was the first that Laver had lost in any of the finals that he had won.

His victory put him one title ahead of Fred Perry and Bill Tilden, the other post-1914 champions to win three times, and it put him further on the way to the Grand Slam of the four major singles titles – a feat which he achieved as an amateur in 1962. He has already won Australia, France and Wimbledon. Only Forest Hills, where he lost badly last year, remains. This was one of Wimbledon's closest men's finals for several years – it was the first, in fact, to go to a fourth set since Roy Emerson beat Fred Stolle in 1964 – but it was not one of the fortnight's best matches, and certainly Laver was not at his most devastating or his most spectacular. He woke up to play well when he was in danger at 1–4 in the third set, but up to then the match had not produced the same quality or excitement as his brilliant counter-attack against Arthur Ashe or his swift demolition of Cliff Drysdale in the rounds that preceded it.

Laver had found matters easy at first. He had taken the first set, mainly because Newcombe's service had suddenly lost power and accuracy under pressure in the ninth game. Laver attacked and captured his service at a cost of two points. Everyone sighed. It had been so easy. The inevitable Laver victory was approaching. After that the pattern of the match changed a little. The pace, on a fast court, became deliberately slower, almost soporific. Laver was still sluggish at the start of the third. He presented the fourth game to Newcombe with a double-fault and saw his challenger move to 4–1. Then, he said afterwards, he felt that he began to see things more clearly. He served well for 2–4 and, suddenly attacking again, at 30–0 on Newcombe's service in the seventh game produced a sharply angled backhand half-volley which completely beat Newcombe. That was the turning point. That let him back into the match. 'It was a pretty chancy sort of stroke,' he said later with the grin of a player who is used to taking chances and seeing the attempt succeed. Laver, moving lightly, disguised his shots shrewdly and, hitting sudden fierce winners, won seven successive games and that more or less ended the affair. Newcombe struggled vainly to catch up, but Laver always kept ahead of his pursuer. The last shot, which was worth £3,000 to Laver, was a smash.

28 JUNE 1970

TAYLOR CRUSHES CHAMPION LAVER

Henry Raven

Rod Laver's reign at Wimbledon has ended. After two years of absolute supremacy he was beaten 4–6, 6–4, 6–2, 6–1 in one hour and 53 minutes by Roger Taylor, the 28-year-old British professional. It was a great day for Britain and Yorkshire. Taylor stuck grimly to the world champion, serving ruggedly and forcing him to play all the shots that he most disliked. Perhaps Laver, at 31, is not quite the force that he was last year when he brought off the first Open Grand Slam, but Taylor won yesterday because he chained him, restricted him and bludgeoned him to defeat.

Laver has always disliked playing against left-handers and it certainly looked like that yesterday. Taylor, who has had two and a half years as a professional to size up the Australian's weaknesses, found him serving less well than usual. Laver gave him nine double-faults and a great many short second services, which the British player punished fiercely. Taylor also tested him with a plentiful supply of those short, slow returns that John Newcombe had used so profitably against Laver in the final last year. He used a reverse American twist service into the Australian's body most effectively and he hammered home his volleys and smashes fiercely. He looked strong and dominating. Laver, usually the most imaginative and confident of competitors, began to look frail after the first set and seemed more and more vulnerable as the match continued.

The persistence of Taylor's attack was the great feature of this dogged victory. He was remorseless, whereas Laver never looked comfortable. The battle of services was always in the British player's favour and Taylor broke for the first time in the fifth game of the first set. Laver held him off then, taking Taylor's service for the set, from 40–0 in the tenth game. That was the last time that Laver was in any sort of command. Thereafter he showed a few glimpses of his old self but more and more the formidable, aggressive Yorkshireman ruled the play. From the moment that Taylor won the second set it began to seem more and more likely that Laver would suffer his first defeat at Wimbledon since Neale Fraser, another left-hander, beat him in the 1960 final.

Taylor broke at once in the second set, Laver double-faulting twice. The Australian broke back, at 4–4 he faulted again, after fighting back from 0–40 to deuce and saving two British advantage points. Taylor served his way smartly to take the set at 6–4. In the third set Taylor again broke service in the first game after another fine British backhand return down the line and another of those weak Australian second services. Some powerful serving and volleying took Taylor to 4–2, and he broke service again for 5–2. A glorious backhand cross-court return on a second service made Laver 15–40. Again his first service was at fault and he visibly hesitated when he came in behind his second. That was a sign of the extent to which his confidence was cracking. Taylor hit a vicious top-spin forehand pass from the baseline and though taken to deuce on his own service, took the set with a thundering first service. He broke twice in the fourth set and then it was clear that the end was near. Taylor's play was full of flourishes of power. Laver looked dejected and inhibited. At the end there was a tremendous British roar of applause.

4 JULY 1970

MRS COURT EARNS TRIPLE CROWN IN MEMORABLE FINAL

Lance Tingay

Margaret Court, of Australia, won the women's singles crown for the third time in the Lawn Tennis Championships at Wimbledon yesterday by beating Billie-Jean King, of the United States, 14–12, 11–9. Had Mrs King won the title, for the fourth time, equal justice would have been done. The general course of the women's singles this year had been flat and unspectacular. The event was retrieved by a final that was magnificent and memorable, one of the finest played. Not only that, it was the longest. The 46 games played between Mrs Court and Mrs King, lasting two hours 27 minutes, exceeded by two the previous record of 44, set in 1919 by Suzanne Lenglen and Dorothea Lambert Chambers.

And the 26-game opening set was not only the longest played in a women's singles final but the longest of any Wimbledon singles final, men or women. How can one talk of the weaker sex after a match like that? From start to finish each player strove to impose her game on the other. It was the demanding serve-and-volley technique all the way. The cut-and-thrust of attack was pushed back by defence, with one fine shot being countered by another that was even better. One could not see how the issue could be resolved.

It is academic whether there have been better finals. Perhaps there have been one or two. This, though, was among those that will be long remembered and, as I have said, had the American instead of the Australian got the decision sporting prowess would have been just as well rewarded. I suppose that if Mrs King had won any of the games in which she served for the opening set – at 5–4, 7–6 and 8–7 – she might have been the winner. She would have proved as fine a champion as Mrs Court, and the pity is that one of these brave contestants had to lose.

5 JULY 1970

ROSEWALL FAILS TO TURN BACK THE CLOCK

Henry Raven

This is the year for giant-sized matches and high emotions here. After the longest women's final in the history of the Championships, John Newcombe beat Ken Rosewall yesterday by 5–7, 6–3, 6–2, 3–6, 6–1 in the first five-set men's final since Ted Schroeder beat Jaroslav Drobny in 1949. It lasted two hours 42 minutes – just a little too long for Rosewall at 35. Newcombe, nine years his junior, regained the title he won as an amateur in 1967. Rosewall keeps the honour of being, with Gonzales, 'the best player who never won the title'.

Looking back, in the bleak light of another cold Wimbledon afternoon, the real wonder was that Rosewall, older, lighter and forced to always run to score his points, managed to stretch out the contest for so long. The crowd were with him, responding to every stirring of resistance in the last hour of the match. And he came back in the fourth when Newcombe suddenly lost control gracefully and bravely – but time, youth and strength were all against him. Newcombe had to struggle through the first set, saving three game points at four all, missing a set point in the next game and then finally losing his service in the 12th game, but when that was over his greater power, both of service and of ground stroke, told. Rosewall's service, which had been apt to betray him in crises all through the fortnight, became easy for him to plunder with weighty returns that kept low on the dusty court, and his forehand volleying was superb.

Often the match looked like a meeting between a heavyweight and a lightweight and in the second and third sets Newcombe landed so many fierce punches that it seemed impossible that Rosewall could recover in the fourth. Some of Newcombe's forehands were of the highest class and achieved a maximum effect. He lobbed better than Rosewall, too, and although his defences were often pierced by superb cross-court backhands, and shots which ran down the line as though they were on rails, he could suddenly summon up surges of strength – as he did in the fifth set – which would enable him to take command in a crisis.

By the end Rosewall looked utterly forlorn. He had been a finalist in 1954, when Drobny beat him, in 1956 when he lost to Lew Hoad and now Newcombe, who belongs to another lawn tennis generation, had robbed him of the chance of being the oldest champion since Tilden, who won at 37 in 1930. It had been a great achievement to reach the final. He had done well to take Newcombe to a fifth set after seeming to be beaten, but he could do no more. It was one of the best and most moving Wimbledon finals for years.

3 JULY 1971

EVONNE IS QUEEN: MRS COURT
LOSES CROWN IN 63 MINUTES

Lance Tingay

Wimbledon had a story-book finish to the women's singles yesterday when Evonne Goolagong, charming, fresh and only 19, beat the title-holder Margaret Court to make herself the most popular overseas champion since the Brazilian Maria Bueno won for the first time in 1959. Miss Goolagong is by no means the youngest player to emerge as Queen of Wimbledon, nor even the best, for the elite Maureen Connolly was both younger and more efficient. In terms of popularity, measured by appeal of personality rather than national sentiment, this engaging Australian has had few equals.

Mrs Court, denied from winning the event for the fourth time, must have felt she was competing not only against her doubles partner but 14,000 spectators in addition. And how wrong a top coach can be! Vic Edwards, the Australian trainer who has been almost a foster father to Miss Goolagong for many years, was bold enough, when he brought his protégée to Europe for the first time last year, to declare that she might win Wimbledon by 1973. He was two years wrong in his forecast. Nor did he hint that she might take the French Championship into the bargain, a feat she accomplished a month ago.

What a joyous hour was had by the spectators, many of whom had queued overnight! Think of a brown koala bear and you have something of the affection that Miss Goolagong attracts towards herself. Spectators willed her to win, not unsportingly but with manifest preference. That this mass support shared in the reasons for the victory is, I think, certain. For Mrs Court's obvious nervous apprehension must, in part, have been induced by it. The score, 6–4, 6–1, after 63 minutes on the court, does small justice to the closeness of the struggle. Ten of the 17 games went to deuce, many of them more than once.

The basic conflict in the match was Miss Goolagong's happy gifts against a highly trained and sophisticated athleticism of Mrs Court's pressure game. One can never imagine Miss Goolagong playing to a studied plan; rather she goes out on the court, feels the strength of what opposes her and circumvents it by the light of nature. The tighter the situation, the more likely is the new champion to produce the unexpected killing shot from a seemingly lost position. It was like that yesterday when, in the heavy, hazy humidity of the Centre Court, she denied Mrs Court the attainment of what would have been her 83rd major title.

Mrs Court started slowly and, had 15–40 been implemented, would have stood 0–5. Miss Goolagong, standing 4–0, was nearly brought back to four games all. Mrs Court played with a champion's authority, her pressure then irresistible to recoup most of her disadvantage. But she did not recoup enough. Had Mrs Court got to four games all, and in that fateful game Miss Goolagong was 15–40, I daresay she would have retained her title. This, though, was the situation the champion-to-be revelled in. She climbed back to be 5–3 and won the set two games later, despite Mrs Court twice having a point to make the score five games all.

Miss Goolagong was obviously vulnerable on her weak second service and her forehand was generally unpredictable. When she lost the opening game of the second set it looked as if these factors might prove her undoing. When she began to get her first service consistently into the court the prospects altered. The struggle was close and in the course of the next six games, Mrs Court had a point for that by which Miss Goolagong advanced to 3–1, five chances for that which made it 4–1 and two for the 5–1 tally. In the last game of all, Mrs Court began with a double-fault, fell to 0–40, salvaged three match points bravely, and double-faulted (for the sixth time in all) to concede the match and Championship to the irresistible and bubbling Miss Goolagong.

It is worth recording that Miss Goolagong is only the second Australian to win the Wimbledon women's singles, her rival yesterday being the only other Australian to do so. The only other teenagers to win in post-war years were Maureen Connolly, Karen Susman and Maria Bueno.

MRS KING TAKES FULL REVENGE ON MISS GOOLAGONG

Lance Tingay

Billie-Jean King, a masterly player by any standard, equalled a post-war record at Wimbledon yesterday when, with a forthright, expert and almost one-sided victory over Evonne Goolagong by 6–3, 6–3, she dispossessed the title-holder. Mrs King accordingly took the crown for the fourth time, equalling the record of her fellow American Louise Brough, who, having won three times running, came back again after a four-year interval. In this case Mrs King has come back after a three-year gap.

The expert took the victory, the vanquished all the sympathy. When after the 50-minute match the Duke of Kent went on court to give the trophy to the champion, Mrs King was greeted by the crowd with polite warmth. The applause when Miss Goolagong came to receive her second prize was almost rapturous. This was the reaction throughout the match, the plaudits evoked by the coups of Mrs King being but a dutiful response compared with the enthusiasm given to those of last year's winner. If Miss Goolagong, understandably because of her warm and enchanting personality, continued to win the hearts of all who watched her, she won less against the harsh realities of lawn tennis form.

Mrs King was not yesterday so rigorously efficient as in her semi-final against Rosemary Casals. The two double-faults in the opening and third games stressed that she has not become a machine, oblivious of the tensions of a great occasion – yet despite these double-faults she still managed to build a 3–0 lead. I called the match one-sided, and that perhaps is a little unfair to Miss Goolagong, for she was beaten more than overwhelmed. At the same time, there was no point in the match when the Australian looked a threat. The best she did was in the first six games of the second set, when she held her own. Indeed, in the first, third and fifth games of that set, Miss Goolagong played with a venom and skill that was wholly admirable. She served superbly, so much so that Mrs King was thankful merely to get the ball into court.

This deadly rapier work of Miss Goolagong, however, was not maintained. She began the seventh game with a double-fault and though she set this by her and climbed to 40–15, it was a game that marked the transition of the Australian from overdrive to a lower gear. Mrs King performed throughout, despite the slight indications of nervousness here and there, like the tremendous professional she is. Asked afterwards when she had begun her preparations, she responded: 'When I shook hands with Evonne last year' — referring, of course, to her defeat by the Australian in the semi-final.

This rigorous approach to professional lawn tennis is certainly not equalled by Miss Goolagong, whose more happy-go-lucky air constitutes her charm. Miss Goolagong's happy talents took her to the top in 1971, as winner not only of Wimbledon but of the French title as well. She has now lost both to Mrs King. Many suspected she would find it hard to maintain her status against the steely, dedicated and completely equipped American.

15 JULY 1972

LETTER TO THE EDITOR

WANING POPULARITY OF A WIMBLEDON CHAMPION

Sir,

After the Wimbledon ladies' singles final Mrs King was reported to have said in an interview: 'Why can't I have some of the applause and encouragement of the spectators?' During her first years at Wimbledon, when she was Miss Billie-Jean Moffitt, the plaudits of the crowd were hers in full measure, and only in the last few years has her popularity waned.

The reason for this change is not far to seek, for her petty outbursts of bad temper when close line decisions go against her, often with gestures to match and all coupled with occasional snatches of games-womanship, have all contributed to the decline in popularity with the Wimbledon fans, who are as fair a crowd as you will find anywhere. The remedy lies in Mrs King's own hands, for if she plays the game in the same spirit as Miss Goolagong, whom I have never seen question a line decision and who can smile in defeat, she will soon recapture the hearts of the Centre Court crowds.

Stan Smith appears to be another in the same category as Miss Goolagong, and from players such as these Mrs King has much to learn in court etiquette. For a player of Mrs King's class and great ability it is surely up to her to set an example in court manners and behaviour.

R. Gamblin
Southend-on-Sea

STARS WILL BOYCOTT WIMBLEDON

JUDGE SAYS PILIC MUST NOT PLAY

Lance Tingay, Brian Silk and James O'Driscoll

Most of the world's leading tennis players are being told to boycott the Wimbledon Championships starting next Monday because of a High Court decision yesterday upholding the suspension of Nikki Pilic, the Yugoslav player. The boycott confirmed early yesterday by the executive of the Association of Tennis Professionals had already been promised backing by Stan Smith, the reigning Wimbledon champion, John Newcombe, Ken Rosewall, Arthur Ashe and Mark Cox. Women players are not affected.

Pilic, 31, has been suspended until 30 June by the International Lawn Tennis Federation for failing to play for his country in a Davis Cup match. With the backing of the Association of Tennis Professionals, he sought an interim injunction against the Wimbledon authorities observing the ban, claiming that the suspension was unjust. But at the end of the three-day High Court hearing Mr Justice Forbes ruled that Pilic's suspension did not breach rules of natural justice. The judge dismissed Pilic's application and ordered him to pay the costs of the action, unofficially estimated at £5,000.

The decision to confirm the boycott came at a four-hour meeting in the Westbury Hotel of the executive committee of the association. Mr Cliff Drysdale, president of the association, said more than 70 of the 97 all-male membership had already given undertakings to support the boycott. 'This is the last tournament in the world the fellows want to miss. It is a sad thing the International Lawn Tennis Association chose this time for this confrontation. We feel Wimbledon is being used by the federation.'

Mr Drysdale said that although the voting at the executive meeting was not unanimous, he felt the boycott would get 90 per cent support from the membership. Seven members of the executive voted in favour of a motion to boycott the Championships. Two abstained, including Pilic, and one voted against. But it was thought last night that not all the players who have provisionally declared support for the boycott will in fact refuse to turn out. Some, like the Romanian Ilie Nastase, who is No. 2 seed, may be under orders from their own national tennis associations to compete. And another inducement is the Wimbledon prize money: £5,000 for the men's singles champion and £3,000 for the runner-up. All first-round losers get £150.

Evidence at the High Court hearing was in private. But giving judgment in open court, Mr Justice Forbes said Pilic claimed the original suspension imposed on him by the Yugoslav tennis authorities was unjust because he was not properly notified about the disciplinary hearing at which he was suspended and did not attend. Mr Justice Forbes said Pilic had been given an opportunity to make representations to the Yugoslav association. The judge commented: 'The curious thing is that in all the evidence I have heard there is no reason put forward for his not playing in the Davis Cup match.'

Originally Pilic brought the case into court *ex parte* — that is a case where an application is made seeking temporary relief when the defendant named is not in attendance — but later all parties in the action were legally represented. After the High Court hearing, Mr Herman David, chairman of the All-England Club, said: 'I think it has established the authority of the governing body of the game and that in a sense it is a test case for all branches of sport, considering the revolution that is going on now.'

28 JUNE 1973

LETTERS TO THE EDITOR

ASSAULT ON WIMBLEDON VALUES

Sir,

My uncle, William T. Tilden, won the Wimbledon tennis tournament a number of times during the 1920s, so our family have never quite lost our feeling of admiration for the Wimbledon Club and its members, and the tremendous contribution made there towards international goodwill. The unprecedented assault we have just seen made upon it by the Association of Professional Tennis Players is appalling in view of the shadow of personal gain never before having arisen over the sponsorship of all the best aspects of world competition in tennis.

Obviously, the definition in regard to amateur standing as against professional still applies, and players primarily interested in making money cannot achieve that purpose without major alterations to the established ways of this tournament. Ever since the professionals have participated there have been rumours, at least, of their displeasure with the facilities. It is to be hoped that the committee will now draw up the games from the less sensational players, who will perhaps have a little more appreciation of this great club. As for the tennis enthusiasts, they should be pleased that a spirit of sportsmanship for its own sake may once more prevail.

Miriam T. Ambrose
Aldeburgh, Suffolk

GOOD SPORTS

Sir,

Surely a second-class Wimbledon with first-class sportsmen is to be preferred to a first-class Wimbledon with second-class sportsmen?

L.R. Mackintosh
Caseytown, Devon

9 JULY 1973

MRS KING COLLECTS FIFTH TITLE: QUIET KODES TRIUMPHS

Lance Tingay

This year's Wimbledon Lawn Tennis Championships, surviving their original troubles admirably, will be remembered for the men's singles victory by a quiet Czechoslovak, the able but unobtrusive Jan Kodes, and for the overwhelming triumph of Billie-Jean King at her 13th attempt. Of the many Californians who have excelled at Wimbledon, Mrs King ranks highly. This year, for the second time, she took the triple crown, winning the singles, women's and mixed doubles, the latter two titles with the same partners as in 1967, Rosemary Casals and Owen Davidson. She won the singles for the fifth time, a post-war record, and brought her total of Wimbledon titles up to 17. Only one player has exceeded that – Elizabeth Ryan, another Californian, who took 19 titles, but, unlike Mrs King, never won the singles.

The climax to Mrs King's achievement came in the belated finish yesterday. In the mixed doubles semi-final, she and Davidson were hard pressed to beat the Russians, Alex Metreveli and Olga Morozova, but had an easier passage in the final, where they defeated the Mexican–American partnership of Raoul Ramirez and Janet Newberry.

Kodes beat Russia's Alex Metreveli 6–1, 9–8, 6–3 to provide the most one-sided men's singles final since the first open in 1968, when Rod Laver defeated Tony Roche. It was not to be expected that it would come up to last year's memorable climax between Stan Smith and Ilie Nastase. It fell, indeed, far short of that. Wimbledon's first red flag final, like some others, had the players inhibited by the grandeur of the crown they were striving to take. Kodes came nearer by far to doing his own talents justice. He was sharper all round, seasoned by his wider experience of the big occasions. Metreveli's forehand suffered most and his errors on that side eased the Czechoslovak's task enormously.

There was just one occasion when a tight match seemed probable. Metreveli was 5–4 in the second set, having lost the first in only 18 minutes, and Kodes, after being 40–0 on his own service, slid temporarily to having set point against him. The Russian missed this chance hopelessly with a forehand return of service in the bottom of the net. Kodes won the tie-break sequence by seven points to five and it was Czechoslovakia all the way after that.

Mrs King's fifth Wimbledon singles final was also her easiest. Chris Evert was utterly overwhelmed in the first set, which lasted only 16 minutes, and she won only nine points. If Miss Evert, still only 18, made more mistakes than normal in this one-sided spell, it was understandable. Mrs King played as impeccably as any woman could, without error and with almost every stroke – serve, drive or volley – a copybook example of its kind. Later, Miss Evert got into the match. Desperation tightened her game and her own pacemaking made her opponent recoil somewhat. The youngster was in front at 4–3 and at 5–4, but she got no further and Mrs King won by 6–0, 7–5, looking more professionally competent than ever.

Nastase, whose loss in the singles seven days before was the major failure of the meeting, had the solace of a doubles title. He and his American partner, Jim Connors, worsted the Australians John Cooper and Neale Fraser, after a long struggle in which only the fifth set was one-sided. For Mrs King the women's doubles has become almost a routine. This was her ninth personal success in the event, the fifth time in harness with Rosemary Casals.

On the surface this Championship was no different from others of recent years. It seethed and sparkled and was full of tension and enthusiasm, and was still a British social occasion. Nevertheless, changing times could be detected. Most striking, of course, was the boycott by the Association of Tennis Professionals, reflecting a professional union militancy undreamed of a decade ago. Its effect on the attendance was unnoticed. The total, excluding yesterday's free admission, was 300,172. This was 1,276 more than 1971, the last year all the leading men competed and then the second-highest figure. It may be calculated that for each of 79 men who kept the boycott, 16 more spectators attended in 1973.

The need for the International Federation and the ATP to come to terms is obvious. Discussions have taken place on the formation of a joint committee to administer the professional game. In this, the management committee of the ILTF have acceded to the ATP's demands. The deadlock is on the composition of the committee. Neither side will budge and the ILTF go to their annual meeting in Warsaw next Wednesday to ask their own members to ratify a set of proposals that so far the ATP have rejected.

There was a reflection of changing times, too, on Saturday. Nastase, after winning the men's doubles, scratched from the mixed and did not stay to have the doubles trophy presented to him. At the Lawn Tennis Association Ball in the evening, where the singles champions are by tradition feted, Mrs King did not turn up and her husband, Larry King, made the response on her behalf. Mrs King, of course, had a full day of play, with more to come yesterday, but it is not long since the obligation of the champion in this respect would have been regarded as overwhelming.

8 JULY 1974

FIERCE CONNORS TOO POWERFUL FOR ROSEWALL

Lance Tingay

Wimbledon 1974 will be remembered most of all because the singles titles were won by two young Americans engaged to marry, Jimmy Connors, 21, and Chris Evert, 19 – each of whom is double-fisted on the backhand – and because of that the coaching manuals can hardly be the same again. It will be remembered also as one of the wettest meetings on record, though despite the four days plagued by rain, it finished easily. It was also the best-attended tournament, with the final figures around 306,000 – 5,000 more than the previous record set in 1967.

A nostalgic memory will be the man who fell at the last fence, Ken Rosewall, 39, contesting the men's final for the fourth time without success. There was a sad overtone to the singles final on Saturday, when Connors beat him 6–1, 6–1, 6–4. One cannot deny Rosewall played badly. One could have wept for the simple shots he missed. Equally, one cannot dispute that Connors performed superbly. If ever a player turned round the sympathies of a Centre Court crowd by the sheer quality of his game, it was this rather brash young man. What a fierce and compelling game this left-hander played. It was surging, dynamic stuff. Practically every shot he hit was a bold one taken early, aimed fast to the lines with minimal margin of error, and he missed extraordinarily few.

He pulverised an off-form Rosewall utterly. The Australian took the opening game, but lost the next six and won only seven points in the course of them. The punishment continued. Connors went to 4–0 in the second set, this making a sweep of ten games running, though, as it happened, Rosewall got more points – eight of them – in the long opening game to the second set than he had in the six preceding it. Only in the third set did Connors's tour de force lose momentum. There was a brief spell when Rosewall hinted that he might come back. He managed to lead 2–1 and three times came within a point of advancing to 3–1. Artistic shots, especially from the backhand, hinted at his old brilliance with the return of service.

Connors, nonetheless, got that set back under control, and very quickly the crowd lost all hope of a Rosewall recovery. They were now in the mood to appreciate the standard of the American's performance. Serving for the match at 5–4, Connors went to 40–0. Rosewall denied him two match points but on the third he put his backhand return of service into the middle of the net. The match had lasted 93 minutes and though far short of being the most one-sided men's singles final played at Wimbledon, it was not a contest in which the loser had shown any hint of winning. Poor Rosewall! Tremendous Connors!

5 JULY 1975

MRS KING VOLLEYS CRUSHING WIN OVER MRS CAWLEY

Lance Tingay

It was a great day for the United States in the Lawn Tennis Championships yesterday, which was Independence Day, for both the titles that were decided, the women's singles and the men's doubles, went to them. For

Billie-Jean King, who took the singles, it was as splendid a moment as she has had in her 15 years as a competitor at Wimbledon. She gained her sixth singles title, and that was her 19th Wimbledon title in all. She now stands as a record maker, equal arithmetically with her fellow Californian Elizabeth Ryan. But since Miss Ryan won no singles titles the place of Mrs King as the premier monarch of Wimbledon must be undisputed.

Yet it was a sad day for Wimbledon also. No one begrudged Mrs King her fine glory for so good a player as she is certainly deserved it in every way. But no player so richly talented as Evonne Goolagong Cawley, and assuredly no player so well loved as she, deserved to suffer so calamitous a fate as befell her on the Centre Court. She was routed 6–0, 6–1 in a women's singles final that was almost pathetic for its one-sidedness. How could a player so good as Mrs Cawley perform so badly? One has seen her cast away matches in a dream before. Indeed, such has often been the case with her, and 'walkabouts' and Evonne Goolagong are a commonplace of the story of the game in recent years. On this occasion it was not that Mrs Cawley played in a hazy kind of dream, rather it was that she just played poorly. But when she returned service it was an open invitation to Mrs King to volley away a winner. And volley away winners aplenty she did. Mrs King played well. She made hardly an error on her own account and she was sharp and her concentration never faltered, not even when it became obvious that her opponent was never going to make a real match of it.

A bewildered and almost grieving Centre Court crowd watched Mrs King swallow the first ten games of the match without her opponent even reaching points for a game. When at last Mrs Cawley broke her duck there was a cheer. The crowd, perhaps still hopeful that one of their best-loved players might yet show something of her proper form, exuded sympathy. But Mrs Cawley got her solitary game and that was all. The match as a whole lasted only 39 minutes. It was almost embarrassing in its absurd one-sidedness and the total number of points won by Mrs Cawley was 24. And this was a Wimbledon final! In the history of the event there have been just two finals that can compare with its devastating brevity and lack of pressure against the victor. In 1951, in an all-American contest, Doris Hart beat her friend and doubles partner Shirley Fry by 6–1, 6–0. Go back further to 1911, and there was a final more one-sided, too. In that year Dorothea Lambert Chambers, perhaps the finest of the pre-1914 generation, beat another British player, Dora Boothby, 6–0, 6–0.

What of Mrs King's record? She now has six singles, nine women's doubles and four mixed doubles. She may still add to this tally, for though she has declared her retirement from singles she said afterwards she would come again and compete in the doubles. As for the singles, this last brief affair yesterday was her 8oth match. It was the 71st time she had won — 71 wins, nine losses is not a bad record for a hotly competitive field like Wimbledon.

6 JULY 1975

SM-ASHE-D – THE FALLEN CHAMPION

Henry Raven

The odds-on favourite fell at Wimbledon. Jimmy Connors, who devastated Ken Rosewall to win the title last year and had swept through this time without losing a set, was beaten 6–1, 6–1, 5–7, 6–4 by Arthur Ashe in one of the Centre Court's most dramatic post-war matches. It was a most remarkable match and a brilliantly designed victory. For a fortnight Connors had surged and thundered, confident, athletic and aggressive. He came here as the ruler of Wimbledon and Forest Hills and the conqueror of Rod Laver and John Newcombe in two much-publicised challenge matches in Las Vegas. He had beaten Ashe in their previous matches — one victory on clay at Boston and two South African finals on cement at Johannesburg. He had been explosive and uninhibited. Ashe had struggled, notably against Tony Roche in a long semi-final, and had lost sets to Bob Hewitt and Graham Stilwell.

But yesterday he gained one of the most impressive tactical victories that Wimbledon has seen for many years. He contained Connors astutely, seldom allowing the speed that he likes, varying the pace, lobbing more than anyone remembered seeing Ashe lob before, and using slice shrewdly to the younger player's double-handed backhand. He was always making Connors stretch and commit himself and he volleyed far more than usual. Ashe has always worried about his volleying. His low forehand volley has been a weakness which he has discussed on many occasions. But this time he was astonishingly cool, confident and decisive at the net.

'What was the reason for the improvement?' someone asked. 'He hits the ball at 100mph and it is easy to volley well if all you have to do is stick your racket out,' said Ashe. He was helped by the fact that the younger American did not serve well. In the first two sets — as the Centre Court crowd, drawing in its breath and opening its eyes wide — Ashe took command and Connors seldom troubled him with a first serve. His length was disappointing and his approaches lacked their usual weight and accuracy.

Superficially, it was the old bright, brash Connors, hungry for points, indulging in small dramas with the crowd ('Come on, Connors,' shouted one man. 'I'm trying, for Chrissake,' he replied) and occasionally hitting brilliantly spectacular shots, but he was slower than usual. Connors almost came back. He won the third set after Ashe had held no fewer than seven points to break his service in three separate games, and led 3–0 and held a point for 4–1 in the fourth. 'Who knows what might have happened if I had got 4–1? I might have been two sets all and flowing well,' said Connors. But Ashe, methodical, disciplined, restrained, stopped him then and that was his last chance of keeping the title.

It was an intellectual victory. Ashe, the black men's champion, winning the title in the first all-American final since 1947, outwitted him, dictated the pattern of play, never allowed him to play an easy shot, and never allowed him to gallop away with games with his usual noisy, exuberant, extrovert fashion. Connors kept on trying. There was a world of difference between his attitude to the match in the first two sets, in which he won only two games yesterday, and Evonne Cawley's feeble submission to Mrs King in the women's final. He hunted and chased, but Ashe always kept him a long way from his target.

Connors held service in the first game and then Ashe held service to love. Those who thought that the match would be as comfortable a walk-over for Connors as Mrs King's win against Mrs Cawley had been stirred in surprise. Connors led 40–15 in the next game, put a backhand volley into the net, and then missed a forehand after Ashe had mis-hit a smash for deuce. Another Connors backhand into the net took Ashe to advantage point and then came the first moment of theatre. Connors smashed and the ball seemed to be well out. The line judge ruled it in. Ashe looked at him incredulously, and there was a major demonstration by the crowd. 'Out, out, out,' they cried. The line judge gesticulated to the umpire, but the shouting continued. Eventually the umpire quietened them and said: 'The linesman defers to me. The ball was out.' That gave Ashe the game, the break and the initiative. Connors made a gesture to the umpire as he changed over.

That was merely a beginning. Ashe broke him again for 4–1. The tactical plan was working. Connors wasn't being allowed to hit the ball freely. Sometimes he would generate tremendous pace, but the shots would fly out of court. Then he was broken again for the set. The second set followed the same pattern. Ashe had him in chains, but towards the end there were signs that Connors was beginning to break free. The serve worked better. If he was still having trouble with those slow kicks to his backhand, he was guessing right on some of Ashe's deliveries to his forehand. He saved three set points before Ashe made it two sets to love.

The third was always closer. Connors was broken for 3–2, but broke back immediately. Then as those game points mounted up against him he frustrated Ashe again and again until it came to 6–5 and 30–30. He beat Ashe with a forehand return of service and then with a passing shot to take the set. He was back in the match. Everyone looked at Ashe to see whether he was still as calm and cool under the new pressure. He slipped to 0–3 in the fourth, after holding a point to break. A forehand pass and two brilliant volleys from Connors cost him his service in the second, but he again made Connors's forehand look vulnerable, to come back in the fifth game, and that was the end of the champion's chance. Ashe played the last games firmly and strictly, breaking in the ninth game. Connors had won the first point and then, after a good serve to Ashe's backhand, had misjudged a high return. He could have smashed it, but he let it fall in and it died an inch inside the baseline. A backhand pass made it 15–30 and then, countering a backhand return of service, Connors put a low forehand into the net. On break point there was another soft return from Ashe and Connors half-volleyed out.

Five–four and the title to serve for. Ashe, meditating between points as he has done throughout, sat with his eyes shut, breathing deeply. It was the ultimate test of nerve. Against Roche, he had served two double-faults in the last crisis, but here the end, the fulfilment of the great ambition, was cool and efficient. Connors put a backhand into the net, but reached 15–15 by way of a wonderful sprint, dive and cross-court winner. Ashe beat him with a forehand volley for 30–15. A serve to the backhand took him to match point and a smash finished it.

Ashe said afterwards: 'This is my second greatest win. The Davis Cup in 1968 would be the first. I guess this is co-No. 2 with Forest Hills because I am American and you want to win your home championship. I was physically in very good shape and if it had gone to five sets I would have felt very confident, because he has not played five sets in the tournament. If you are never tested you don't know what you will do in a tricky situation.'

5 JULY 1976

BORG SUBDUES THE GENIUS OF NASTASE IN ONE-SIDED FINAL

Lance Tingay

The tournament by which the Lawn Tennis Championships completed 100 years of history will go down as the hottest and driest in living memory. It will also be remembered as one in which youth was dominant. Björn Borg won the men's singles title for Sweden with a meteoric display against the Romanian, Ilie Nastase, on Saturday, to succeed at the age of 20, the third youngest of all time. Chris Evert, who became the women's singles champion the day before, is 21, so the joint ages of the singles champions is only 41. That is not a record, for in 1891 Wilfred Baddeley was the youngest-ever men's champion at 19 and Lottie Dod took the women's title for the third time at the same age, making their joint tally of years a mere 38.

This year's tournament, the 90th meeting, can only be known as Borg's Wimbledon. He was a revelation, not so much in his consistency of form in the early rounds – to a background of speculation that with a pulled stomach muscle, for which he was having pain-killing injections, he was likely to withdraw at any moment – but in his tour de force in the final. The last really shattering display in the last match was perhaps Lew Hoad's devastating treatment of Ashley Cooper 19 years before. For Borg it was a dream performance, when all that he must have dreamed about doing on court was translated into reality.

Yet when the contest started the signs were that this sort of performance was going to be put forward by Nastase. The pace of the rallies, aided by the lightning surface of the baking court, was that of a frenzied knock-up. Out of this exchange of electric pace Nastase emerged in the lead by 3–0. He had three points, all at advantage in a game of five deuces, to become 4–0. Whether that would have made a difference to the outcome of the match one can only speculate. It is certain, though, that Borg saved himself from a crippling deficit by at last holding his service in the fourth game. The Romanian's dominance was then checked and later thrust back.

Borg took the lead for the first time at 5–4, initiating his break of service with a brilliant backhand passing shot that became more and more his typical killing weapon. I am tempted to say that Nastase began to retreat into nervous frailty – by comparison, that is, with what he had been – and surrendered his title chances to young Swedish vigour and enterprise. In fact, what had become a one-sided final revived into one of exciting uncertainty when Borg served vainly for the match at 5–4 in the third set. He reached match point, exactly one hour and a half after the start. With both men at the net Nastase saved the point with a forehand volley, a typical Romanian coup when his speed and genius was functioning well. Borg lost the game. Was he to let his winning impetus slacken?

For four games the match held some hope of Nastase recovering. Then, helping his own destruction with a tame volley error, he dropped his service in the next game. Borg, now 8–7, boomed out the following service game to love and, having been on court one hour and 49 minutes, was singles champion of Wimbledon at 20. No opponent took a set from him. Such unscarred champions are rare. The last was the American Chuck McKinley in 1963 and Tony Trabert did as much in 1955. Don Budge was the only other and he did it in 1938.

Borg plays his backhand double-fisted – and what a searing shot it was on Saturday! I daresay his return of service was the key with which he turned his splendid victory. One thought Nastase to have abnormally speedy reactions and quick eye. There were occasions when Borg made him look slow by comparison.

12 JUNE 1977

COUNTDOWN TO WIMBLEDON CENTENARY

WHEN KITTY WAS QUEEN OF HEARTS . . .
AND TOP PRIZE WAS A VOUCHER

Mark Andrews

The women's champion at this year's centenary Wimbledon will walk off with £10,000 and the runner-up £7,000 . . . a far, far cry from the prize money that Kitty McKane received when she won the same title 53 years ago. 'Ten thousand pounds,' she said without a trace of envy, but with a certain wistfulness. 'It's a lot of money for two weeks' work. My prize was a five-guinea voucher from Mappin and Webb, the London jewellers.' In those days, she recalled, they used to try to save up the prize vouchers won at other tournaments and then get something worth having, like a dressing-table set, a ring or necklace or bracelet.

The 1924 Wimbledon winner is now 81-year-old Mrs Kitty Godfree and living not far from Wimbledon. She is one of Wimbledon's oldest surviving champions and remembers the day in 1924 when she beat the immortal

Helen Wills of America to win that voucher. 'I very nearly lost that match in the second set. I'd lost the first 6–4 and was 3–1 down in the second and I remember saying to myself, "This isn't any good what you're doing so you must try and do something else. It's no good being defensive, you've got to start to attack." So I decided to attack.

'If it came off I might win and if I didn't, well, I was losing anyhow, so what did it matter. So I started to go out for shots. Luckily for me one or two of them hit the lines and perhaps I had a net-cord and gradually things began to turn round. I won the set 6–4. Then I can't help thinking that Helen must have felt a little bit anxious. The third set was a ding-dong battle up to four all and then, eventually, I did win and that was the Championship to me and I must say I was very delighted and very relieved that I'd managed to pull it off.'

Of Helen Wills, Mrs Godfree recalls: 'She was a player who concentrated very much indeed. She showed no emotion of any kind and I think she was concentrating to such an extent she hardly realised that the match was over. I remember we went up and shook hands, and then thanked the umpire. She looked up at the man and asked him what the score was in the final set. That rather surprised me. I would have thought that anyone would have known what the games were in the final set of a championship. But I think it was just intense concentration.'

Dress in those days was not the revealing and casual affair it is today. 'There was a certain amount of decorum,' said Mrs Godfree, 'especially on the Centre Court. Queen Mary was very interested in Wimbledon. I think the powers-that-be wanted to make quite sure nothing would be done that would give offence to Queen Mary. So we wore a tennis dress, below the knee, and stockings. It was a year or two later that a player came over from South Africa and was about to go on court when someone said she'd have to wear stockings. She said she couldn't because she hadn't got any as they never wore them in South Africa. So that was that, and after that we all gave them up.'

Mrs Godfree still plays at the All-England Club. 'I play with friends and we have a lot of fun, but it is only fun and anything that's out of my reach I leave it and say, "Good shot". But the girls of my day are no worse players than the players of today. What is different is the degree of dedication. You can't get very dedicated over a voucher, can you? But you can over £10,000. It's very natural that you become a bit keener.

'But the only reason the game has speeded up is because the balls are now harder and the rackets are more highly strung. The ball comes off the ground quicker and that's improved people's smashes, drives and serves. Of course they play more. But I had a marvellous time. We were pure amateurs, we played for the fun of the game, had a certain amount of prestige and of course we got a lot of travelling.'

Mrs Godfree, who hasn't missed a Wimbledon since 1919, ranks Maria Bueno of Brazil as the best of the post-war stars. 'A beautiful player, a fine volleyer, a fine service and good ground strokes. I think on the whole she was the most delightful player to watch. But if you go back to before the war then I think of Suzanne Lenglen. She won the women's title six times and was the most beautiful player I've seen and the most successful. I think that if she was playing today, at the age of about 20, she could have speeded up her game. I wouldn't have put it past her to beat all the players playing today.

'But, you know, the girls today don't look as if they're enjoying their tennis. They work very hard at it, and they're dedicated. Now if you enjoy being dedicated I'm sure that's all right. None of us in my day was as dedicated.' She wasn't envious, but if she were 60 years younger she'd be a formidable opponent. Even now she has a grip of steel and her parting shot was 'yes, I know, very useful for top shots'.

21 JUNE 1977

WIMBLEDON MEDAL SNUB BY CONNORS
Mary Ellen Synon

Jimmy Connors, men's singles champion in 1974, snubbed the Duke and Duchess of Kent at Wimbledon yesterday when he ignored the presentation of centenary commemorative medals to past champions. While more than 40 former champions, including Fred Perry, René Lacoste, Jack Kramer and Doris Hart, lined up on the Centre Court to receive their medals from the Duke, Connors was practising on Court No. 13 with Ilie Nastase. Connors finished training at three minutes to two and would have had time to join the latter part of the ceremony and receive his medal.

Connors – No. 1 seed for this year's Championship – will not get his medal. Major David Mills, secretary of the All-England Club, said: 'Medals will be sent only to former champions who made every attempt to get there. They will not be given to anyone who was here, but had the discourtesy not to collect it.'

Another former champion, John Newcombe, told Connors that he had made an error of judgment, but the 24-year-old American was unrepentant, and said later: 'I was with my doctor – that's Ilie Nastase – and couldn't go.'

Connors has an injured right thumb and the object of his training session with Nastase was to give it a thorough test. He declined to confirm that he has a broken thumb rather than a bruised one, and said: 'It is sore, but playable.' He appeared yesterday to be playing his shots with a good deal of freedom.

22 JUNE 1977
CONNORS RESPONDS TO CROWD'S BOOS IN WINNING STYLE
Lance Tingay

Jim Connors, who had appeared to be transforming himself into a Wimbledon favourite most people wanted to lose, won his first match in the Championships yesterday with such bonhomie, after being booed on to court, that he cajoled the crowd towards forgiving and forgetting. Connors went on to Centre Court against Middlesex left-hander Richard Lewis soon after four o'clock. There was applause which was obviously for Lewis and there was booing – not vociferous, not overwhelming, but booing nonetheless – which was very obviously for Connors. It was the reaction to the brash action of Connors the day before in preferring to practise rather than receive his centenary commemorative medal along with 40 other singles champions who had travelled from far and wide.

I can think of only one precedent to such a happening. It was at the Jubilee celebrations of 1926 that the immortal Suzanne Lenglen was held to have been discourteous to Queen Mary by being late. When she went on to court in a mixed doubles with Jean Borotra the hostility of the spectators was obvious, and Borotra had to do plenty of clowning to try to win them over. It is not on record, though, that she was actually booed. Connors was booed. The spectators made their point. Connors reacted as one might have expected. He grinned ruefully to his mother, who was in the stands, and got on with the job.

Afterwards he tried his best to convince that his slight to the Duke and Duchess of Kent on Monday was the outcome of a genuine misunderstanding. 'But,' he said, 'you can't bring back yesterday whether you like it or not.' His attitude on court reminded me of his final against Arthur Ashe in 1975. Then, as he was being brought to relatively abject defeat, a heavy-throated enthusiast bellowed that he ought to do better. 'I'm trying my best, for Chrissake,' he yelled back with such sincerity and boyish humour that the crowd were won over to his misery.

There was a measure of that yesterday. At least Connors persuaded the spectators to suspend judgment. He played tolerably well, too. He laughed and hit rousing winners with typically heavy skill. That he was out to outclass Lewis was fairly obvious, and Lewis, in resisting defeat to the extent of 6–3, 6–2, 6–4, did his own talents reasonable justice. Lewis, who had nothing to lose, put up a brave fight and the number of outright winners he projected was not inconsiderable. He would have done even better had he served with more consistent accuracy on his first penetrating delivery.

This service speed had one effect for which he never strove on the practice court. It was in the fourth game of the match when Connors was, as it were, still on probation. Connors failed to get out of the way of a fast fault sent down by Lewis, and it struck the American in his most vulnerable spot. As Connors doubled up with anguish, which fortunately was very fleeting, his very misfortune seemed to bring him sympathy. At least he had good cause to forget the injury to his thumb. When he left the court, Connors received a more or less normal amount of applause.

23 JUNE 1977

LETTER TO THE EDITOR

KEPT WAITING

Sir,

After Monday's performance let us hope Jimmy Connors wins the men's Wimbledon title. Perhaps the Duke and Duchess of Kent would like a game on an outside court while Mr Connors waits for his trophy.

R.F. Evetts
Faversham, Kent

2 JULY 1977

COURT AND SOCIAL: COURT CIRCULAR

BUCKINGHAM PALACE, 1 JULY

The Queen and The Duke of Edinburgh this afternoon visited the All-England Lawn Tennis and Croquet Club, Wimbledon, to mark the Centenary of the Lawn Tennis Championship Meeting.

Her Majesty and His Royal Highness were received upon arrival by the President of the All-England Club (The Duke of Kent) and The Duchess of Kent.

The Queen presented the Ladies' Singles Challenge Trophy to Miss Virginia Wade.

The Lady Susan Hussey, Sir Philip Moore and Major Robin Broke were in attendance.

2 JULY 1977

VIRGINIA TRIUMPHS AT LAST AND WIMBLEDON CROWD GOES WILD

Lance Tingay

The Centenary Championships and the Queen's Jubilee Year could not have combined better in the women's singles at Wimbledon yesterday, when Virginia Wade celebrated Her Majesty's presence by winning the crown for Britain. At just about two o'clock, immediately before the Queen sat down, they played 'Land of Hope and Glory' and there was the atmosphere of a festive occasion, rather like the last night at the Proms. An hour and three-quarters later, the cheer that went up could have been heard in Putney High Street — so loud, prolonged and frenzied was it. Miss Wade had beaten Betty Stove, of Holland, 4–6, 6–3, 6–1, to ensure that a British player was Queen of Wimbledon again.

Miss Wade was expected by many to beat Miss Stove easily. She did not do that. The fact is made evident by the score, and when she lost the opening set after 38 minutes the earlier euphoria of the crowd was dimmed. I say she lost the opening set because that is what she did. Equally, Miss Stove lost the second set. And then the Dutch girl lost the third set. It was that sort of match. The result was memorable. The manner in which it came about was to be remembered only by those who have a taste for the grotesque.

It would be absurd to say that Miss Wade did not do her talents justice, since, after all, she won the match and title. But her display in this match compared ill with her brilliance in the semi-final against Chris Evert. Indeed, in retrospect, one can see that Miss Wade won the 1977 Wimbledon when she brought down the champion, Miss Evert. It seemed likely at the time. Nor, for that matter, did Miss Stove play half as well as she might have done. Curiously enough, there were rallies in which the Dutch player, who took everything that happened so well and sportingly, produced a quality attack well in excess of anything that Miss Wade offered. Some of Miss Stove's volleys, especially from the backhand, made her look the copybook aggressive player to the last inch. Equally, she produced an awful lot of rubbish, when simple forehand returns were such that the captain of a club side would have wondered if she were good enough to be selected.

The tension that pervaded the match came more from the ineptitude of the players on the day than from their real capacity. It happened that for the first point of the match, with Miss Wade serving, Miss Stove projected a positive winning lob. It took Miss Wade five minutes and four deuces before she managed to win that first game. Then, when Miss Stove served in game No. 2, she began with a double-fault. She was destined to serve nine in all during the course of this chequered contest. She fell to 0–40 in that second game but pulled it round nonetheless.

Game No. 5 was one of British foreboding. Somehow, Miss Wade seemed to have lost the confidence she exuded during the last few days, and was falling more and more into uneasy, fidgety, fumbling errors which have characterised some of her Wimbledon performances in the past. A bad Wade game was followed by one from Miss Stove that was even worse, to make the score three games all. Then Miss Wade hauled back a game from 0–40 to lead 4–3, and the temperature of British patriotism rose high again.

But Miss Stove drew level. Miss Wade contributed two losers in the next game, Miss Stove two winners, and that was a love game against the serve with Holland in the lead 5–4. Despite a double-fault in the next game and a point for five games all, Miss Stove won the set. In the last game, there were two good rallies – they were scarce enough to deserve a note – and on the last Miss Wade made a volley error from the backhand to lose it. Then British hearts were able to sing again. Miss Wade cut down her proportion of errors and Miss Stove accentuated hers. At any rate, Miss Wade went to 3–0. She had a point to lead 4–0, and another to be 4–1, but Miss Stove climbed back to 3–3 – and all was tense once more. Miss Wade must have sensed her responsibilities then. Miss Stove seemed to assume that the task was beyond her, winning only three points in the next three games, all of which left Miss Wade in possession of the set 6–3.

She went on to lead 4–0 in the decider as the quality of the play became more reasonable. The crowd warmed to the situation, and every winning shot by Miss Wade, and every losing one by Miss Stove, was great with acclamation. The Dutch girl contrived to win the fifth game, but by then Miss Wade was too close to the title to be deterred. She lost one match point, but took the second with a forehand return of service that forced Miss Stove to volley to the net. Thus came about Wimbledon's rare moment of British triumph. And how sportingly Miss Stove took the enthusiasm that even caused her double-faults to be applauded. Miss Wade has now collected her finest lawn tennis crown. Her other major triumphs were the US Open in 1968, the Italian in 1971, and the Australian in 1972.

3 JULY 1977

KING BORG'S TOUCH OF GOLD
Henry Raven

Classics cannot be contrived or ordained by man. But in the end, after all the 100 years of Wimbledon, the Centenary title was won by Björn Borg over Jimmy Connors in a final which was to take both men into realms of glory and leave the younger, urgent and unflappable Borg the undisputed king. The battle ebbed and flowed for three hours and 13 minutes before Borg, all massive concentration under his coloured headband, was to hammer the final winner into a despairing lunge by Connors and bring to an end a match which rippled with greatness from first ball to last.

Borg won 3–6, 6–2, 6–1, 5–7, 6–4 to retain the title he won in 1976 and establish himself as the only European player, apart from the British, to take Wimbledon two years in a row. Now Borg can emulate Fred Perry by becoming the first player to win three successive singles titles since Wimbledon abolished the challenge round in 1922. And Borg is still only 33 days beyond his 21st birthday.

On Wimbledon's hottest day, with the Centre Court cloaked in brilliant sunshine, the fifth set became a powder keg that was to ignite into a climax that will always give this final the label of total quality, brushed with gold. As Borg hunted for salvation in the fifth set against the left-handed Connors, he swept into a lead of 4–0, so much in command that his grip on the title looked unbreakable. Against anyone else, it might have been. But Connors was in this final because his guts had taken him there, and his instinct to survive and fight did not desert him. Slowly, convincingly, Connors peeled off one game after another to reinstate himself in the match at 4–4. When he broke Borg's serve to level the set with a volley into an unprotected court, Borg retreated to the baseline, his head bowed, his hair falling down like a canopy of uncertainty.

Connors was strutting again after four games of compounded fury. Two games was all he needed to regain the title he last held by pulverising Ken

Rosewall in 1974. Maybe, as his elation bounced off Borg's despair, he saw himself as champion and vitally committed to maintain his momentum at this critical time. Serving, Connors won the first point with a volley. But he did not place another first serve. He double-faulted, was out of range against a drop volley from Borg, and then missed a backhand — two break points to Borg. Connors made another backhand error, and Borg was 5—4 ahead.

Borg could not lose hold of the rope which now dangled from Wimbledon's summit. He went for the first point on his service as though he was serving for his life. Connors tossed up a lob and Borg leaned into his smash for an outright winner. Next, Connors pushed a forehand into the net (an error which had been the cause of so much of his downfall earlier in the set). Borg's next move drilled into Connors's forehand and the American could not lift the ball. Three match points. How could Borg fail now? In the next rally, the Swede unleashed a backhand down the line, and Connors, tumbling towards it with his sinews as taut as wire, could only clip the ball into the crowd and realise, after all the colossal warfare, that his chance had gone. Again.

4 JULY 1978

IT'S CRIMINAL, SAY ARRESTED TENNIS TOUTS
Brian Silk

The shifty-eyed man meeting people off the coaches outside the All-England Lawn Tennis Club at Wimbledon yesterday, provided a glimpse of a crumpled orange No. 1 Court ticket with a face value of £3. 'Twenty-five quid to you, mate, and you won't get a better buy anywhere else.'

The touts moved quickly through the crowds mindful that their business was not illegal so long as they caused no obstruction of the pavement. Overheads have been high this year with a string of touts being hauled before the magistrates and fined for obstruction. 'I've been nicked twice and it's cost me 70 quid,' grumbled one elderly man. 'They're bleeding us dry. It's criminal.'

Putting a stop to the profiteering has not proved easy, as Major David Mills, secretary of the club, explained. 'I'm afraid there's nothing we can do about the touts. We've tried to prevent it but we found it's just a waste of time.' It is a simple matter to trace the numbered tickets back to the original recipients. 'But we have found that a ticket can change hands dozens of times before it gets to the tout,' said Major Mills.

Three touts were complaining about the lack of business when another strolled by. 'Watch it,' he said. 'That copper in the green cardigan has got his eye on you. He's hiding behind the van over there.'

5 JULY 1978

LETTER TO THE EDITOR

GOOD FOR THE TURF

Sir,

Complaints all round, our climate is disrupting play on the finest grass tennis courts in the world. Why is the turf so good? The climate is ideal.

(Mrs) F.M. Lawrence
Churchtown, Gloucestershire

8 JULY 1978

MARTINA CLAWS HER WAY TO TITLE FROM NADIR OF MISERY

Lance Tingay

The Lawn Tennis Championships acquired a new women's singles champion yesterday and one worthy of the honour – the Czechoslavak Martina Navratilova, 21, who beat American Chris Evert, a narrow and generous loser, 2–6, 6–4, 7–5. Wimbledon, which was blessed with warmer weather, lived up to tradition with a women's final that was better in playing standards than many, and enthralling in some of its excitement. It lasted one hour and 43 minutes, and until the final two minutes not even the most fervent supporter of one side or the other would have presumed to foretell the winner, so even was the battle.

Perhaps it was ordained early this year when Miss Evert, queen of lawn tennis for so long, indicated that she was to compete less. Miss Navratilova, a No. 2 and never a No. 1 until this season, dominated the early American scene to a striking degree. Those who watched the BP Cup matches at Torquay five years ago, when she was 16, could hardly fail to take notice of the super athlete from Czechoslovakia. Her penchant for the super-aggressive serve-and-volley game betokened both ambition and skill beyond the normal. Her subsequent career was not without setbacks, for as a young Czechoslovak in America the delights of Western life were tempting. She was left to her own devices without normal family guidance when she became a refugee.

This season, with no fitness problems, Miss Navratilova's skill came into its own. Yesterday, on Wimbledon's Centre Court, she proved her supremacy where it mattered most – and against the one player most fitted to dispute it. The Wimbledon programme identifies Miss Navratilova as from the United States, which could mislead the historian of the future. A resident in America she certainly is, but she has yet to acquire citizenship.

It was windy yesterday and that fact alone precluded perfect skills being shown. The mistakes that were made did nothing to lessen the excitement of a rousing contest. In the first set it must be confessed that Miss Navratilova's supporters wept for their heroine. The Czechoslovak, despite her splendid serving skill and volleying capacity, appeared unable to do much on her backhand than give points to the other side. So it was that Miss Evert took the opening set 6–2. Miss Navratilova was hard-pressed to avoid falling to a deficit of 1–3 and, after two games all, she did not get another game. The crisis game was when she fell to 2–4, a long one of two deuces which seemed to be filled with Czechoslovak backhand mistakes. For Miss Navratilova the nadir of her misery was the final game of the set when she suffered a net-cord against her, double-faulted and generally found the ground strokes of Miss Evert overwhelmingly too solid.

With that set done, Miss Navratilova shed the slough of uncertainty which had plagued her performances on big occasions in the past. Having pocketed the second set 6–4, Miss Navratilova pursued her winning course at the start of the final set, when she found it comparatively simple to force opposition errors and went to 2–0. She might have been 3–1 in due course, but Miss Navratilova made some costly errors in a long fourth game and it became two games all. The pendulum had swung the other way. Miss Evert, abandoning her defensive pastures, began to attack. She advanced to lead 4–2, having taken four games in a row, the last to love. There was some Czechoslovak luck with a net-cord and a lot of fine attacking shots in the next two games which brought the score level at four games all. That was after one and a half hours on court, and as yet no hint of who was to win.

Miss Evert came within a point of losing the next game but took it after one deuce, and a memorable lobbed winner, to be 5–4. She now needed the finishing burst – but could not find it. Indeed, the surge came from Miss Navratilova. The Czechoslovak, now more buoyant than at the start, won a love game to level the score. Then she broke Miss Evert's service to 15, and took another love game to win in a flurry of overwhelming success against depleted American resistance. There have been greater women's singles finals, but not many. At the end Miss Evert ran to her conqueror and affectionately stroked her hair. What a generous gesture by the former champion.

10 JULY 1978

BORG'S ALL-ROUND MASTERY CRUSHES BRAVE CONNORS

Lance Tingay

The climax of the Lawn Tennis Championships on Saturday, when Björn Borg won the men's singles for the third year running by beating Jimmy Connors 6–2, 6–2, 6–3, set new standards in a meeting which has always weaved a rich design in the tapestry of the game's history. There have been some fine men's singles at Wimbledon over the years, in which the winner has played punishingly well, but I doubt if such overwhelmingly good tennis was ever before produced to crush so fine a player. It was Connors himself – there is irony in this in view of what was done to him on Saturday – who demolished Ken Rosewall with fearsome power in 1974; there was Lew Hoad's awesome mastery over Ashley Cooper in the year of his second win in 1957. And Jack Kramer played what seemed a perfect game when he hit his American compatriot, Tom Brown, off the court in 1947 in 48 minutes. I will not go back further than the war.

All these at the time furthered the dimensions of the game. Borg, just 22, reduced to almost ineffectiveness a rival who was only just short of his own high standards. It was a question not of a giant routing a player of lesser breed, but of one heavyweight ousting another. When, in the first set, Borg, having trailed 0–2, won the next six games in a row, it was, so far as Connors was concerned, like seeing a contender for the world heavyweight title taking a count of eight in the opening round. He was not quite knocked silly but it was obvious that his only chance of keeping on level terms was to produce a superhuman effort.

One must give Connors credit for the fight he put up. It was obvious that had Borg relaxed in any way, the American would have come back at him and charged ahead. But Borg never fell short of his own tremendous standards. In attack he was superlatively good, delivering a service that was often unreturnable — a cannonball. He played stop volleys and acutely angled volleys that were breathtaking in their touch and audacity. In defence (and Connors was always counter-attacking him), his backhand passing shot across the court was a dream. It was small wonder that there were spells when Connors was made to appear frail. I dare say that at no time in his top career was he forced to make so many mistakes in mid-court.

Borg hardly faltered from first to last. One cannot talk of a crisis in a one-sided contest, but I dare say things could have been different if, in the second set, Borg — who was serving — had not climbed from his o—40 deficit to increase his lead to 3—1. Connors, put out of the match once he lost his starting lead of 2—0 in the opening set, was not allowed to get back into it. For 119 minutes Borg strode the Centre Court triumphantly. The Swede is not the most elegant of players and, in grace and style, there have been finer champions. But for rugged effectiveness and all-round mastery of every shot it could be that he has no equal; how one would have liked to see him matched against Rod Laver at his best!

Borg, who despite his skill and enormous earnings remains a pleasantly modest young man, has now won 21 singles matches at Wimbledon without defeat and his three Championships in as many years equalled the record set by the then British Fred Perry in 1936. Perry, appropriately, was the first to greet Borg in his triumph on the court. The odds against Borg's taking the title for the fourth time in succession in 1979 cannot be very long. Connors will doubtless continue to resist him and is breathing hard for revenge. 'I'll follow him to the ends of the earth to play him,' he said. If Borg plays as well as he did on Saturday, Connors will not stand a chance. Yet it would be unrealistic to expect this super player readily to repeat the standard the Wimbledon final inspired him to find.

30 JUNE 1979

LETTER TO THE EDITOR

THEN AND NOW

Sir,

If there be anyone else still living who played in the Wimbledon Lawn Tennis Championships when held on the original ground at Worple Road as well as when held on the present ground at Church Road, he or she will no doubt recall that play on the original ground had to stop every time one of the not infrequent trains thundered past on the nearby railway line, though perhaps wonder whether all the changes have been for the better. However, '*Tempora mutantur nos et mutamur in illis* [Times change and we must change with them.].'

Clinton McIlquham
Steverton, Gloucestershire

6 JULY 1979

BORG HUMILIATES CONNORS – AND NOW FOR TANNER

Lance Tingay

So far as the men's singles is concerned, the Lawn Tennis Championships at Wimbledon should have ended last night, because Björn Borg was so impressive a semi-final victor that all who watched him must have felt like proclaiming him the champion on the spot. Borg, whose quest for a record fourth successive title will end in the final against Roscoe Tanner tomorrow, beat Jimmy Connors 6–2, 6–3, 6–2. He won in 106 minutes.

His performance was of Homeric standards. I suppose of all the leading men in the game today, Connors more than any other has the capacity to make his opponents look puny. His weighty attacking shots, hit with pace and depth, are punishing and intimidating. Connors grinds his opponents into the ground. But this fine player, currently the champion of the United States and the Wimbledon winner in 1974, was yesterday made to look insignificant. So good was Borg, so high did he raise the standard of his play, so impeccable was he in nearly everything he did that the mighty Connors was humiliated.

After the match, which was three minutes briefer than the final between the same men a year ago, Connors hurried to his chauffeur-driven car without changing and sped back to his London hotel. It was an ungracious farewell to Wimbledon. But one could sympathise with his chagrin. It is hard, to say the least, to have claimed to be the No. 1 player in the world, as did Connors with a good deal of justification, and then in the spectacular setting of the world's greatest arena be made to look not much better than a beginner. Borg was awesomely good. When Connors projected a heavyweight stroke that would have been an outright winner in normal circumstances, the Swede's response was, as often as not, an even finer stroke. The linesmen earned their keep. Connors hit testingly near the lines, but Borg allowed himself even narrower margins. And how seldom did he miss!

It was a titan duel from the start. Connors had the advantage of serving first and this in the normal way of things gave him the psychological advantage of the lead. Even so, he was hard pressed to sustain it. Connors was in front 1–0 and 2–1 in the opening set, but he fell behind when his service was taken in the fifth game. It was a tightish game that Connors yielded after just one deuce, and his losing stroke was a backhand into the net. This was the first shot played by either man that was not first class.

Borg proved in this game his ability to win, but he was under pressure to hold his lead and Connors had one chance to break back in the next game. Even so, Borg was more and more the iron man. One became conscious of the great gasps Connors was making, as he always does every time he hits the ball. They became more like the anguished cries of some dying animal.

Borg won the first set in 38 minutes, having taken five games in succession. And in the second he unleashed his pressure weapons with even stronger emphasis. He had served fairly well in the first set, but now he began to serve with unstoppable power, losing only one point as he served four times. In another 38 minutes he was two sets in front, with Connors looking distinctly shaky.

Yet there was some ammunition left in Connors's locker. He broke Borg's service – it was the only time – in the opening game of the third set and advanced to a lead of 2–0. The start of a comeback? The threat lasted no longer than the fourth game, and the turning point, I believe, came when Borg won a 20-stroke rally to prevent Connors going to game point for a 3–1 lead. The Swede became once more irresistible. He took the next six games to win the set 6–2 and earn his place in the final. He had sent down 11 service aces during his supreme example of controlled aggression.

8 JULY 1979

KING'S TRUMPS

Billie-Jean King, of the United States, now 35, set a record when she gained the doubles title with Martina Navratilova at Wimbledon last night to pass the 19 titles achieved by her fellow Californian, Elizabeth Ryan. Mrs King has won six singles titles, ten doubles and four mixed doubles, compared with 12 doubles and seven mixed titles gained by Miss Ryan, who collapsed and died at Wimbledon on Friday evening at the age of 87.

'You have to admit it's bizarre,' said Mrs King, after she and Martina, the singles champion, had defeated Bette Stove of Holland and Wendy Turnbull of Australia 5–7, 6–3, 6–2 in the final. Mrs King recalled the time when she was playing at the age of 13 and Miss Ryan had watched her. 'When I heard she had passed away my whole life passed in front of me,' she said. 'It has taken a lot of joy out of winning.'

The final had a nervous ending, but the result was not in doubt. Mrs King and her partner won eight games in succession to lead 5–0 in the final set, but Mrs King then lost her serve. Against Miss Stove's serve, there were three match points, but all those chances were lost. Then Martina decided it on her serve, closing with a winning volley, and hugged Mrs King while the Centre Court gave a standing ovation.

Miss Navratilova is Mrs King's latest partner for a Wimbledon title – the others were Karen Susman, Rosemary Casals, Maria Bueno and Miss Stove. 'Twenty titles is a new stance, but sometime someone is going to break it,' forecast Mrs King, who has recovered from three knee operations and a foot operation to maintain her remarkable career. She praised the part of doubles in the game, and said: 'Doubles is more creative than singles will ever be. There is no comparison. It is always important to me that I could play any event well.' Well, she proved her skill and endurance yet again.

9 JULY 1979

'GRAND SLAM' NOW ONLY PEAK LEFT FOR BORG TO CONQUER

Lance Tingay

Wimbledon 1979 will need a bigger entry than usual in the annals of lawn tennis, for records were written anew, the chief one being the achievement of Björn Borg in winning the singles for the fourth successive year and establishing himself as outstanding even among the titans. There was the indefatigable skill of Billie-Jean King recording 20 Wimbledon titles, surpassing the total of 19 that was established in 1934 by Elizabeth Ryan. If Mrs King built the record sketchily in a shaky women's doubles final, it is not surprising since Miss Ryan had died at Wimbledon the day before. There was a record in that with Borg retaining his title, and Martina Navratilova keeping hers, neither singles titles changed hands for the first time since 1921, the last year of the challenge-round system. The boys' singles Championship was won by the Indian Ramesh Krishnan, whose father, Ramanthan Krishnan, won the same title in 1954. The total attendance at Wimbledon was 343,044. This was an all-time high, which was inevitable, perhaps, since for 1979 an extra 1,088 seats were available.

What a mighty player is Borg. He is 23 and he has won four Wimbledons in a row, involving 28 consecutive singles victories, the French Championship four times, including this year and last, and the Italian Championship twice. Is there anything more for him to do? There is. Yes, he still has to take the US Open Championship – and how Jimmy Connors will battle to prevent him doing that – and he has yet to win the Australian title. He has not yet approached the achievement of the Grand Slam, which is simultaneously holding the Championships of Australia, France, Wimbledon and America. No one could doubt his ability to do so and the question is just if and when he will.

Borg is the best player since Rod Laver. Whether he's as good or better is a nice talking point, but Borg certainly has scope to take his stupendous playing record to greater heights. He won the final against Roscoe Tanner by 6—7, 6—1, 3—6, 6—3, 6—4. It was a very good match and reflected great credit on Tanner. One may take Borg's conduct of it for granted and it was a champion's performance. It could be said that Borg played less well than normal. He was more impressively dominating when he beat Connors in the semi-final and Tom Okker in the quarters.

If Borg played a rougher sort of match it was because Tanner's able tactics forced him to do so. Tanner served well, with 14 stinging aces, and harried his man from the net continually and exhaustingly. The purists would say Tanner's lawn tennis was hit or miss. Of course it was and it had to be if he were to live against Borg's mastery. Tanner lived for nearly three hours against the Swede, led by one set to nil, led by two sets to one and I dare say had he been able to implement his threat to make it four games all in the final set he could have taken the Championship.

Some may be curious as to the other men who have won the Wimbledon singles four times in succession. Laver did it, not in consecutive years but in a continuous spell of personal competition, 1961, 1962, and then in 1968 and 1969. In the challenge-round days, when title defence meant playing one match, the New Zealander Tony Wilding won for the fourth consecutive year in 1913, Laurie Doherty for the fifth year in 1906, Reggie Doherty for the fourth in 1900 and William Renshaw for the sixth year in 1886.

CHAPTER FIVE
THE 1980s

THE MAN IN THE HIGH CHAIR

George Feifer

Telegraph Sunday Magazine feature

It is men's semi-finals day of the All-England Championships at Wimbledon in 1976. Almost all Centre Court matches at this stage are tense affairs, but this one, between Björn Borg and Roscoe Tanner, is more tense than most. On the last point of the tie-break, which will end the crucial second set, Borg sends up a deep defensive lob. Tanner charges back to play it, turns, loses sight of the ball ... which lands on his foot, inside the baseline. What is the rule here? Will the silk of Wimbledon's ordered perfection be scratched? The 14,000 spectators hold their break. But not to worry. Although the umpire has seen no such occurrence in a lifetime of tennis, his 30 years in dozens of chairs have given him a sixth sense, not only about the rules themselves, but also about how to interpret and share them as if they derive from Natural Law. His enunciation of 'Game and second set to Borg' — in a voice which blends theatricalism, unquestionable authority, glorious amateur sportsmanship and the serene conviction that there will always be a Wimbledon — is intoned without a second's hesitation.

The following day a headline in Llanelli, the South Wales town once synonymous with the manufacture of pots and pans, announces: 'Local dentist in Wimbledon drama'. But dental surgeon Edward James in fact felt no more — or less — drama in that point than in tens of thousands of others he had umpired at Wimbledon and elsewhere. It was but one instant in an umpiring career dedicated to turning all extraordinary events on the court into, mediatorially speaking, utterly ordinary (in the sense of calm) moments of play.

'I think the first thing to say about umpiring is that you must do a lot of it in order to develop the necessary confidence. You can go through a match and do nothing but announce the score. But to retain command of unforeseen, unusual situations, I know no substitute for experience. Like a flier, you must log up the hours.'

The many hundreds Edward James has logged since he began at Wimbledon in 1961 include those of the 1977 ladies' final and the mixed doubles final last year. Unless the hard-working, easygoing sportsman somehow falls on his face, he is most likely to be entrusted soon with the finals of the men's doubles, then the men's singles — the pinnacle of Wimbledon and, therefore, of world umpiring. 'If I'm asked, I'll have to accept, won't I? Umpiring depends on a sense of duty. But I've no special ambition for "the big ones". It's just that someone has to do them.'

Sense of duty is a common denominator among Wimbledon's 280 umpires, most of whom began, as did James, taking the chair to help out at their local clubs. But if the 'typical' umpire is a London civil servant, this one's background is quite different. He was born 50 years ago in Llanelli, the son of a dental surgeon who died when he was 11. He missed the discipline imposed by his father and, after a spot of adolescent unruliness, attended a Surrey school. There, his self-discipline flowered, together with an enviable athletic career. The young James dabbled in hockey and cricket (he captained Caterham's second XI), sprinted and, 'of course', played rugby.

At Guy's Hospital, which he entered after national service, he was the inter-hospital sprinting champion, equalling, in 1951, the record of the 100-yard dash (ten seconds dead) set a quarter of a century earlier (at Guy's, he competed against Roger Bannister, who ran for St Mary's). He played first-class rugby, too, and continued to after returning to practise in Llanelli in partnership with someone who had worked with his father. Quick-moving, James scored often from his usual position on the wing.

Although he had begun to take tennis seriously during school holidays, it remained the game at which he was least proficient. Re-settled in Llanelli, he played at the Lawn Tennis Club – and volunteered to help out with its umpiring chores. The club host a ladies international (England versus Wales) and the Carmarthenshire County Championships every year. 'As my playing ability diminished, my umpiring seemed to improve. Never mind, even good coaching at the right age wouldn't have made me a top player.'

Hearing of a shortage of qualified umpires for Wimbledon in 1961, James offered his services much as he had done for his own club. With a recommendation from the Welsh Lawn Tennis Association, he went to work almost immediately as an umpire and linesman on Wimbledon's outside courts, logging his hours. In five years, which is roughly average, he had worked his way into the inner circle of around 60 umpires who handle the 'show courts', No. 1 and Centre.

The combination of skill he has acquired in his Wimbledon and other umpiring has something in common with those of a circus master. Not least of them, and very important, are those that a voice coach might have taught. 'It's no mumbling, or keeping your head down. You must be in charge and heard to be in charge. And if you can peal out, "Game, set, match and tournament to …" before the crowd erupts – ah, that's a test.'

Remaining impartial is easier. James says this might seem harder at one's home club, umpiring a match with an especially admired local girl, than at Wimbledon, where he maintains a discreet distance from the players. 'But wherever it is, you *never* allow personal preferences to interfere. A ball's either in or out, no matter who hit it. You're there to do a duty, aren't you?' Concentration – of the kind needed to supervise a three-ring circus – is another prime requirement. 'One learns how to rest between games, just as the players do. Because from net-cord to scoreboard you must see every-thing – which means sensing what "everything" might be. Anticipation. Timing. And even in a four-hour match, *peak concentration* throughout.'

Unlike those who think a dental surgeon occupying a Wimbledon chair odd, James believes his vocational training sharpens him for his hobby. 'Just as in dentistry, one needs to concentrate powerfully, know exactly what's going on everywhere, see very clearly, control all phases of the operation, and not make mistakes.' As a dentist, he says he tries to 'combine courtesy and firmness. I try to treat players coming on court a bit as if they were patients coming into my surgery. I want to make them feel welcome; must treat them with respect. It's far easier if a rapport can be established from the beginning – which means letting the players know I'm there to help them.'

James has the distinction of umpiring the last Wimbledon match which Björn Borg *lost*: a 1975 quarter-final against Arthur Ashe, that year's eventual singles champion. Declining to discuss known troublemakers in detail, he quotes the counsel of a former president of the Umpires' Association: 'If you can't think of something complimentary to say about a player, say nothing to the press.' But he is full of praise for the game's gentlemen, espe-cially for Borg, whose behaviour he admires as exemplary.

By going 'open' just as tennis in general was changing from a seemingly genteel game to a big business, Wimbledon also opened itself to ungentle-manly stresses and strains. James deplores the growing influence of money on the game, and the corresponding deterioration of manners on the court. Yet he himself has managed to avoid unpleasant incidents, and even claims to feel no greater pressure in the chair. The real increase in pressure, he quips, is in his Llanelli appointment book as he prepares for his annual 'holiday' in late June. (Unpaid, apart from expenses, he does however regard Wimbledon fortnight as a kind of holiday.) And in the often 'fallacious' second-guessing of the press and slow-motion television replays? 'Those commentators aren't placed to see the ball. The linesman is, and when I'm there, I call them as I see them.'

The domestic life of the earnest but jolly James reflects his emotional equilibrium — and, it goes without saying, his love of sports. His wife of 18 years presides over their comfortable house, the former residence of RAF Pembrey's commanding officer. Their four children — two elder daughters at Cheltenham Ladies College, a son and daughter still at home — play a variety of games eagerly and proficiently, but without obsession.

It seems unlikely that anything can cause the steadfast James embarrassment on the court. He is too experienced, too full of composure, too willing to admit an error if he makes one. 'If two players on opposite sides of a net hear a let, you play one, even if *you* didn't happen to hear it. That's just common sense. If you, God forbid, blank out and call the wrong score, you listen to the reaction. Fourteen thousand howls can be a wonderful and very quick corrective.'

Nevertheless, he admits to butterflies when he takes to the show courts. 'If you're not secreting adrenalin, you probably shouldn't be in the chair. Because although an umpire should be heard and not seen — and although nobody remembers him unless he's made an awful hash of it — he must, in fact, put on a performance. In a way it's terribly simple. You're there merely to see that the play is fair, that nobody breaks the rules — and to keep score, communicate what's going on. But in other ways it's not quite that simple. On the show courts you're in charge of a team of 13 officials. You're *in control* of the entire show.'

'Control', 'discipline' and 'aura of command' punctuate James's reflections about his avocation. The Wimbledon incident which gave him most trouble came during a semi-final of the 1978 men's doubles, when a player on his No. 1 Court thought that the Centre Court roar for Martina Navratilova's win of the ladies' singles had drowned out a call of 'fault'. He did not return service. A courteous James ordered the point to be played again, to the outrage of the team who felt victimised by his decision. Sympathetic as he was with the aggrieved players, he told himself: 'I believe my decision was correct; I must be strong.' He was, but felt saddened that the incident seemed to impair the further play of the angered team. In such matters, James is sustained by his confidence that getting on with it is the important thing. 'You're a patient I like very much, but you've come to my surgery with certain symptoms — which it's my duty to judge on their merits. If the tooth doesn't come out now, the matter will only get worse ... It's all to do with discipline.'

He is also sustained by his wit. 'Yes, I as a person can make mistakes,' he smiles boyishly. 'But when you are the foot-fault judge on the Centre Court at Wimbledon, you are, my good man, above reproach.'

5 JULY 1980

EVONNE CAWLEY –
WIMBLEDON'S NINE-YEAR WONDER
Lance Tingay

Wimbledon, despite some more rain, had some of its most rewarding moments yesterday with Evonne Cawley winning the women's singles Championship for the second time by beating Chris Lloyd 6–1, 7–6. It was a richly popular win, gained in slightly more than 90 minutes by a supremely satisfying player, and notable for several reasons. Mrs Cawley, 28, regained the title nine years after her success in 1971, and the only other player to leap such a gap was the American, 'Big Bill' Tilden, who won in 1930, having previously succeeded in 1921.

It was the first victory for more than 60 years by a mother. Mrs Cawley, who has a daughter, Kelly, three, emulated the performance of Dorothea Lambert Chambers, who had a family when she took the singles title in 1914. It was also the first time a singles Championship has been decided on a tie-break since that sequence of abbreviated values was introduced in 1971. Mrs Cawley won it by seven points to four, the crucial point coming when she broke service to lead four points to three after Mrs Lloyd sent a forehand drive over the sideline after a long rally.

The match was interrupted for an hour after Mrs Cawley had dominated the first set and taken the lead 1–0 in the second. This 30-minute spell was as fine as anything seen on the Centre Court this year. It was feminine grace and beauty brought back into the game. One felt that what was taking place deserved to be transformed into a ballet and with all the rhythm of shot that Mrs Cawley brought to her play there was sparkling and telling pene-tration. Mrs Lloyd played with poetic touches also but more defensively. She was entirely outplayed in the first set.

The second period of magic never quite recaptured the spirit of the first. Both players rose to heights only to fall into spells of error. There was a 3–0 lead to Mrs Cawley when the Australian threatened an overwhelming victory, but she remained at the back of the court and merely tried to be steadier than her opponent. The set see-sawed. Mrs Lloyd took four games in a row and with the lead for the first time at 4–3, she pressed somewhere towards the title. Mrs Cawley regained the lead, though only after a game of five deuces at 5–4. Mrs Lloyd claimed it back at 6–5. One felt that had the issue been taken to a final set, she would have won hands down. It never reached that because Mrs Cawley – again displaying her fine play at the net – forced it to 6–6 with the tie-break following to strain the nerves of both.

I dare say the Mrs Lloyd of a few years back would have taken control of such a sequence. Mrs Cawley proved to have the steelier arm on this occasion and those who regretted that so sporting a player as Mrs Lloyd had not taken the title for the third time, were compensated in seeing a player equally as sporting for the second.

7 JULY 1980

REMORSELESS BORG
JOINS SPORT'S IMMORTALS
Lance Tingay

Wimbledon, 1980, the 94th of the Lawn Tennis Championships, will stand in the records as the wettest since 1927, but will be remembered for its jewel of a climax. This was a men's singles final that lies with a handful of matches in being classed as the most enthralling and richest in quality of all time. Björn Borg began the meeting as a lawn tennis hero. He ended it an even greater one, now in possession of the singles for the fifth consecutive year and, at the age of 24, transcending the confines of lawn tennis in the certainty of sporting immortality.

It takes two to make a notable lawn tennis match. It became an outstanding singles final because John McEnroe, 21, resisted so superbly. Another reason to make the last day of Wimbledon memorable was the fact that this young American was booed as he went out to play, and cheered for his gallantry as a loser three hours 53 minutes later. Borg beat McEnroe by 1–6, 7–5, 6–3, 6–7, 8–6. It must be said that at the start, for all of the first set, and for much of the second, the Swede was untypically frail.

McEnroe was venomously sharp. The champion could not read his services at all and it was a disconsolate crowd, overwhelmingly in support of Borg at this time, that witnessed his discomfiture. Borg weathered the storm created by his own failings and his opponent's surging strength. He narrowly averted the disaster of a deficit of two sets, which would surely have come about had he not, in the ninth game of the second set, saved three break points in a long game on his own service. This was the turning point of the first period, the end of Borg as a clumsy, inept champion. In the 12th game he projected one of his screaming backhand returns of service across the court. It helped him break McEnroe's service for the first time (hitherto he had not come anywhere near so doing) and gave him the second set 7–5. At last the final had become an open issue.

And what a vibrant issue it turned out to be. Borg became more effective, McEnroe less. There was a hotly contested seventh game in the third set, in which Borg recovered from 0–40 and won after 20 points. It quelled McEnroe's threat to climb back into the set, in which he had fallen behind by having his service taken in the second game. Borg, after nearly two hours' play, led two sets to one towards his fifth Championship.

It was not yet a vintage contest, but it became so in the fourth set. Borg, getting a break, served for the match at 5–4 and went to 40–15. Then, after rather more than two and a half hours, Borg was poised with two match points to quell the presumption of McEnroe. The American, first with a backhand pass down the right and then with a drive volley, never played more boldly or more effectively than on these crucial points. The set came to the tie-break. Theoretically I would say that this abbreviated sequence is too much of a gamble on which to risk a Wimbledon Championship. Yet, its excitement, in such a situation, transcended most thrills in sport and for the 20 minutes or so which this tie-break endured on Saturday, tested the heart of all who saw it. Borg, six points to five and then at seven points to six, had two more match points which he was not allowed to win. McEnroe, at 8–7 and 9–8, had two set points. Borg, at 10–9, 11–10 and 12–11, had three more match points. Then came McEnroe's third, fourth, fifth and sixth set points. McEnroe finally won his seventh set point. It gave him the sequence 18–16, and every shot in the course of these throbbing exchanges, recorded in the scorebook as a set 7–6, was a positive one by both men. Certainly, in a final, the like of such bold, brave hitting had not been seen before, it did not fall far short of the longest tie-break played at Wimbledon. That took place in 1975. It was between the Indian Premjit Lall and – guess who? – the then champion-to-be, Björn Borg.

All this was just the preliminary to the set that counted most. It was nearly 50 minutes later before the identity of the champion became known. In the fifth set Borg was in the ascendancy throughout. He fell to 0–30 in the opening service game but did not lose another point on his delivery until he was putting himself in front at 5–4. McEnroe, fighting a rearguard action, hauled himself up from 0–40 in the eighth game, otherwise the match would have ended sooner. It was a complete reversal of the opening stages of the match, when Borg could not handle McEnroe's service. In this resounding climax, McEnroe could no longer cope with the deliveries of Borg. The end came in the 14th game of the set, and the 55th of the match, when Borg broke service to win. Characteristically, his closing shot was a searing backhand that won his eighth match point.

Borg thus won his fifth Championship and 35th successive match at Wimbledon. The unique record of the Swede is 105 sets won, 19 lost, 742 games won, 475 lost. For McEnroe it should be said that his resistance was heroic and Wimbledon will remember it more than his lack of grace in other matches. Who else has saved seven match points in a Wimbledon final? What a fighter! What a champion who beat him!

17 JULY 1980

LETTER TO THE EDITOR

A TROUBLE WITH TENNIS

Sir,

Wimbledon is over for another year and I still find it strange that the server is allowed two attempts to get that ball into the service court. Players and spectators alike enjoy tennis for its rallies rather than its aces, so would not the game be improved if this server's advantage were withdrawn? It might then be found possible to abolish that abomination the tie-breaker.

A.L. Poole
London E18

12 JANUARY 1981

PETERBOROUGH: END OF SERVICE

Lance Tingay gives place today as Lawn Tennis Correspondent of *The Daily Telegraph* to John Parsons. His retirement ends nearly 29 years of service to this newspaper. Latterly his annual lawn tennis rankings have carried more weight with a lot of enthusiasts than the computerised product that now determines the seeding lists of most tournaments. Tingay has, of course, seen every day of the last 43 Wimbledons.

His standing in lawn tennis journalism on both sides of the Atlantic has been, in the words of a former colleague and rival, Peter Wilson: 'Unique not only for his encyclopaedic knowledge ... but for the wonderfully generous way in which he has put this at the disposal of younger or less well-informed colleagues.'

The spacious Tingay style owes a little perhaps to his passion for the works of Anthony Trollope, about whom he has built up an enviable library, including a short story he found in America that was unpublished here. He rectified that omission with a limited edition.

22 JUNE 1981

LOOK WHAT'S FOR TENNIS

Serena Sinclair

Tennis, anyone? More to the point, tennis clothes, anyone? As Wimbledon fortnight dawns, the sports shops brace themselves for a sudden thud of demand. Everyone who ever wielded a racket in youth gets that re-awakened desire to play tennis yet again, however clumsily, and the look round the shops this year is a fruitful one. The colours are enchanting – lots of soft baby ones, but lemon yellow stands out. Lemon with white seems the coolest mix to wear on this summer's courts, and you get it from several ranges, from different countries.

The irony about these pretty colours on the courts is that they come just when spectators all round the world are wearing frothing pure white. In fact, it has probably never been easier to get regulation tennis whites from a non-tennis store than now. White Bermudas, for instance, are everywhere. So are short white shorts, white muslin baggy zouaves. Any number of all-white outfits could be assembled in a twinkling.

Softer shapes are this year's tennis-gear news: a one-piece bloomer in cotton jersey, with elasticised waist, for instance. Or the tennis skirt that swings wide from a hip band, with the skirt as full as a skater's, all cut on bias.

What do you wear to cover-up when the tennis game is over and you are suddenly chill? More and more of the sportswear firms now do poplin jackets to match the T-shirt and shorts. You will find a pretty pink one from Switzerland to go with T-shirt striped in wine/pink/white, while others are striped in lemon/lilac/white. These jackets, of course, are ideal holiday companions and look just as good over white jeans or slim skirts. Tennis wear and real clothing (i.e. spectators' clothing) are closer in many ways this summer than ever before.

23 JUNE 1981

McENROE FACES FINE FOR TANTRUMS

Roger Heywood

John McEnroe lived up to his reputation as the 'superbrat' of tennis at Wimbledon yesterday. He described the umpire Mr Edward James as 'an incompetent fool', called the referee Mr Fred Hoyles a four-letter word, was penalised two points, and will be recommended by Mr Hoyles to be fined by the committee.

Afterwards McEnroe, aged 22, and the No. 2 seed, said: 'What I did was bad and wrong. Why do I do it? I'm only hurting myself. I would say it was my own fault but the guy did a lousy job. If he's incompetent then surely I have the right to say so. If I play badly I lose and if he makes eight or ten bad calls then he should be replaced.'

His display of tantrums occurred on No. 1 Court on the opening day of the Championships, when he beat fellow American Tom Gullikson, 7–6, 7–5, 6–3. His frustration took control of him when Mr James, the umpire, declined to reverse a number of linesmen's decisions. McEnroe called some decisions 'the pits of the world'.

At one point he tried to break his racket in two. This resulted in a public warning from Mr James for 'misusing your racket, Mr McEnroe'. The climax came in the third set when after another outburst from McEnroe, Mr James announced: 'I am going to award a point against you because you are rude.'

McEnroe demanded that Mr Hoyles be sent for and when Mr Hoyles refused to quash the penalty point McEnroe abused him as well. Mr Hoyles said afterwards: 'He said he refused to be penalised by an incompetent old fool and he called me a four-letter word. It was not a very serious one.' Nevertheless it cost McEnroe another point for 'insulting the referee'. According to the rules under which the Championships are now played, an offending player is warned once, then penalised a point twice, then penalised a game and then disqualified. McEnroe was three-fifths of the way through the system.

28 JUNE 1981

MANNERS AND TENNIS TANTRUMS

Lance Tingay

When, on the opening day of this year's Wimbledon Championships, a young man of 22, in the hearing of not only nearly 8,000 spectators but of a television audience of millions, berated a courteous umpire as an 'incompetent fool', one felt that lawn tennis manners had sunk to their lowest depth. However, those who, like myself, have spent a lifetime closely concerned with what I would claim to be the supreme combination of athleticism and artistry are not unused to seeing the image of a splendid sport marred by offensive behaviour. Bad manners on the big occasion make news; good behaviour is still taken for granted; and there always have been both. At this time the greatest player is, indisputably, the Swede Björn Borg. In victory or defeat, who behaves better?

Has the game changed all that much? There must be many who remember the German Gottfried Von Cramm, three times a losing Wimbledon singles finalist in the 1930s. His court manners were impeccable. When he lost one of his finals against Britain's Fred Perry, in a contest abysmally one-sided because he had pulled a muscle in his thigh in the opening game, he kept the injury to himself lest he mar the glory of his opponent's victory. Getting nearer today, who does not remember Christine Truman, now Christine Janes? Was ever a player more generous on court? Her sportsmanship shone in every match she played.

The sinners highlight the saints. Good behaviour would be less memorable but for the bad, and the pages of lawn tennis history are full of the latter. There is a book published in the 1890s which adjured players not to brandish their rackets before linesmen and call them blind old so-and-so's. There have always been impossible players. The heights of infamous behaviour reached by the Romanian Ilie Nastase will be known to all. There was a peak of sorts only last year in the Davis Cup tie at Bristol. A suspension was the outcome. Yet more than 50 years before, another Romanian had made his mark by outrageous eccentricities of behaviour. He was Nicholas Mishu, notorious for serving with his back to the net and for making a target of any passing bird. His opponents were constantly distracted. He does not, though, appear to have been suspected of doing it deliberately.

Players themselves tend to be more tolerant of bad manners, always provided that they are without malice aforethought. Players have no time for the cheat; bad manners and cheating are not always the same thing.

That at least must be said in defence of McEnroe. He would never claim a point that was not fairly his – or his, at least, in his own opinion.

No one would defend the use of bad language, but there were certainly obscenities and blasphemies to offend spectators in the years before the Second World War. The New Zealander Cam Malfroy, who was something of a mixed doubles specialist, shocked many an old lady at British tournaments. Bob Hewitt, first an Australian and then a South African, played last at Wimbledon two years ago. He learned to swear in Afrikaans. It did not stop a clergyman at the Midland Counties Championships at Edgbaston from lodging a complaint to the organisers. Nor did it stop Roger Taylor, a few years later, from giving him a cut eye in a dressing-room after a match. The most offensive language I have heard on court came from a pretty woman, now a model mother and an exemplary person in every way. Behaviour on court and off it are often very different things.

I doubt if the scale of bad lawn tennis manners has altered all that much over the years. What has changed is its style. As elsewhere, authority tends to be questioned rather than accepted, and the astronomical earnings of players like McEnroe do not help. One may dismiss him as an impossibly brash, gifted young man. It is odd that he should be so, since his background is not from a back street in Brooklyn but from the American equivalent of a public school and Oxbridge.

About 25 years ago another American, Earl Cochell, offended lawn tennis authority by punching the referee of the US Championships on the nose. He was suspended for life. That, in terms of sporting discipline, is the equivalent of capital punishment. Many would like to see 'capital punishment' brought back in the game, but bad manners, however atrocious, perhaps hardly merit so drastic a remedy.

The professionals themselves, through their Association of Tennis Professionals, have supported the Code of Discipline with commendable enthusiasm. Indeed I am not so sure that the players as a whole do not behave better than they did a few years ago, when the first pressures of the big earnings that arrived with open lawn tennis in 1968 came about. People in the game do not delude themselves by assuming that there was a golden age years ago when all behaved perfectly. I saw 'Big Bill' Tilden, as a pro, behave appallingly because he had lost. I saw Pancho Gonzales, another of the all-time great players, behave like a spoiled child when frustrated. Yet somehow McEnroe has contrived to be more gratuitously offensive than most. He has everything a man could want – except good manners.

3 JULY 1981

ASTOUNDING BORG REVIVAL BEATS CONNORS IN EPIC STRUGGLE

John Parsons

Björn Borg, champion extraordinary, kept an ecstatic Centre Court crowd spellbound for three hours 18 minutes last night as he brilliantly fought back from two sets down to survive one of the most inspired matches Jimmy Connors has played at Wimbledon. Borg, who now meets McEnroe tomorrow in a repeat of last year's final, for his sixth consecutive title, eventually won what developed into one of the Championships' epic struggles, 0–6, 4–6, 6–3, 6–0, 6–4.

The drama and excitement of the final set was quite remarkable. It had looked as if Connors, whose tennis in the first two sets had evoked memories of the unbeatable form he showed in winning the title seven years ago, was likely to fold. Instead he charged back, bolder and more vibrantly aggressive than ever before, spectacularly saving four break points against him in the third game and three more in the fifth, while in between, Borg saved two break points in the fourth game, both with aces. Nothing epitomised the rich quality and intense passion of easily the most inspiring match at Wimbledon this year than those three games.

No one wanted to see Borg's incredible record broken – it now stands at 41 consecutive victories – and no one wanted to see Connors lose either. Connors was splendidly aggressive from the first point, whereas Borg, who collected 13 points in the first set he has lost 6–0 at Wimbledon since a fourth-round match against Jamie Fillol in 1975, looked unbelievably out of touch at the start. Eventually towards the end of the second set, by which time he had already suffered the break which was to put him two sets down, there were signs of the Borg revival which then rapidly developed both in power and accuracy. Coming as it did in a semi-final, this was an even more incredible escape for Borg than when he was last two sets down here against Mark Edmondson in the second round four years ago.

The final turning point in a match full of tantalising twists and turns was the seventh game of the final set when Connors overhit a forehand at 30–40. Connors twice had chances to level at 4–4 in the next game but Borg hit three aces, taking his total in the match to 16, and then, serving for the match, he took the game to 15. For a man who had lost his last nine contests with Borg, Connors was magnificent. It may just have been his last chance of winning Wimbledon again, but whatever he may do here in the future he could not have written himself a finer epitaph.

LETTER TO THE EDITOR

WIMBLEDON MANNERS

Sir,

I was interested in reading Lance Tingay's article about the relations between players and umpires at Wimbledon as I was the chair umpire of the match in which Fred Perry beat Gottfried Von Cramm to take the title in 1936. I can substantiate Tingay's assertion that Von Cramm kept his injury from all but a few of the many thousands who watched the match. It was, of course, obvious to Perry, who asked him if he would prefer to retire, but Von Cramm was determined not to detract from Perry's victory.

I think I can claim to understand, in some measure, the players' point of view, as I competed at Wimbledon three times myself, and in fact was beaten in the first round of the Championship in the year when I umpired the final. Some years before, those of us who were eliminated in the qualifying competition were offered the opportunity to umpire at Wimbledon. To us it meant seeing all the great players in action, as well as free lunches, teas, and car parking, and also the privilege of buying a seat at the back of the Centre Court for the following day. All these perks, which were not offered to ordinary competitors, were much appreciated by hard-up students like myself!

On their part the Championship organisers got a number of relatively young, keen-eyed umpires who learned that officiating at an important match is no easy task. I was privileged to umpire 'on the line' and 'from the chair' for most of the great players of the 1930s including Perry, Austin, Von Cramm, Tilden, Vines, Allison, Borotra, Cochet, Crawford etc., and I never received more than an 'old-fashioned' look, although I was the youngest umpire to officiate on the Centre Court. Furthermore I never saw an umpire's final decision questioned.

The rudeness and bad behaviour of certain players in recent years, particularly McEnroe, Nastase and Connors (my ears have heard a more blasphemous version of 'Jeez' than Tingay's) does little credit to themselves or to the game. A disturbing outcome of this insufferable behaviour is that a section of the crowd applaud it. Unless the authorities take immediate steps to stamp it out it won't be long before the spectators will have to be 'caged', as at soccer matches, to prevent invasion of the courts.

In conclusion, I am of the opinion that, in spite of their undoubted talents, the game would be better off without certain players, happily only a small minority, and the men's events at Wimbledon could again truly be called the gentlemen's Championship. I have nothing but admiration for the sporting behaviour of the ladies who compete at Wimbledon.

Leslie Newman
Wimborne Minster, Dorset

4 JULY 1981

McENROE WINS CROWN ON MERIT AS BORG'S CHAPTER CLOSES
John Parsons

John McEnroe, master of tie-breaks, undoubtedly became the new Wimbledon champion on merit as he lowered the curtain on Björn Borg's unrivalled run, in a gripping, rather than spectacular, men's singles final. Whatever his many, much-publicised shortcomings, so tiresomely displayed earlier in the Championships, which leave him facing fines totalling £7,500 of his £26,135 prize money – if upheld by the Men's International Professional Tennis Circuit – McEnroe at least left the Centre Court on the right note after his 4–6, 7–6, 7–6, 6–4 victory.

Not only did he produce the most courteous bow to the Duchess of Kent, after the Duke had presented him with the gleaming trophy, but he paid a most gracious tribute to an opponent who had reigned supreme for almost six years. 'I feel great because I so wanted to win Wimbledon,' said the controversial New Yorker, relaxing for almost the first time since he arrived in England a month ago. 'And I especially feel good because I've beaten a great champion who is one of the finest players who ever lived. I couldn't have picked a greater guy to beat and I'm very proud to be Wimbledon champion.'

It was just a pity that McEnroe's pride was not deep enough to persuade him to attend the Championships' dinner, where many title-holders of the past, among them Kitty Godfree (1924 and 1926), Fred Perry (1934–36), Yvon Petra (1946), Budge Patty (1950) and other great players, such as Ken Rosewall, were ready to acclaim him. On the day, however, he was the better player, mainly because, as he agreed, he chose the right occasion to produce his best serving form of the fortnight, whereas Borg's first serve, so important to a player whose volleying is none too punishing, hiccupped badly.

Borg's defeat was infinitely more than the loss of a Wimbledon final on an overcast Saturday afternoon in July. The time – 5.29p.m. on the electric scoreboard as McEnroe hit the high forehand volley which floated past the Swede and dropped in by a foot – marked the end of a remarkable chapter in lawn tennis history. Since his quarter-final defeat by Arthur Ashe in 1975, Borg, 25, has won 41 consecutive singles matches and the title five times. One doubts whether those of us privileged to have followed his majestic progress will see anything like it again.

Everyone knew this defeat had to happen some time and that McEnroe, such a canny and positive tactical player, was the man most likely to be Borg's successor, even though the title of gentlemen singles winner hardly seems an apt description in all the circumstances. The main disappointment was that although Borg's defeat came in a competitive and compelling enough final, it was certainly not a vintage one. With that first serve betraying him worst of all, despite ten aces, one almost sensed an air of despondency in Borg's approach to those decisive middle-set tie-breakers, while towards the end of the fourth set he also tired visibly.

McEnroe missed just one first serve in each of the tie-breakers, taking the first 7–1 and the second 7–4. It meant that in 15 tie-breakers McEnroe has played at Wimbledon over five years, he has now won 12. Even more significantly, he has won nine of the 13 on different surfaces against Borg, and although the match lacked the explosive intensity of Borg's semi-final with Jimmy Connors, the highlight of the fortnight, this was because McEnroe deliberately denied Borg the pace he feeds off, and mixed his game adroitly with soft chips, dinks and slices.

The third-set tie-break was probably the most important for, leading 5–4 in that set, Borg, who had taken the opening set with a flurry of well-disguised winning ground strokes, had four chances to lead by two sets to one. Umpire Bob Jenkins sorely stretched McEnroe's tolerance level when he overruled the baselinesman, which left the American at 15–40, facing the first two set points. There was no protest from McEnroe, merely that look of agonised disbelief as he rested in his haunches to regain some composure – and then repeatedly served, volleyed and smashed his way out of trouble in a thrilling, tense game spanning six deuces. Borg had led 4–1 in that third set, but lost his break partly on the unluckiest of net-cords, and then a terrible bounce which highlighted one of Wimbledon's most urgent problems – how to reverse a general deterioration of the top three courts, once the envy of the world.

The noisy interruptions of a crowd more suited for Wembley than Wimbledon, and more concerned with individual rivalry than appreciating the tennis, also rings alarm bells. Sorry though most people would be to see it happen, it may be necessary in the long term to replace the standing areas with rows of extra seats.

6 JULY 1981

'BLACKBALL' AND £7,000 FINES FOR CHAMPION McENROE
Roger Heywood

John McEnroe has become the first Wimbledon singles champion not to be made an honorary member of the All-England Lawn Tennis Club. But this was only part of the controversy which has soured his victory over Björn Borg. McEnroe received the world's premier tennis trophy from the Duke of Kent on Saturday. The new champion made a rare but only fleeting smile. Within an hour of the presentation he was told that the Wimbledon committee had recommended a further £5,000 fine for his abusive behaviour in the semi-finals. Because of the 'aggravated behaviour', the fine for Thursday's game against Rod Frawley was in addition to the £750 penalty imposed for abuse to officials on the first day of the Championships. He has also been fined £373 – plus a recommended £1,250 – for accusing a line judge of 'cheating'. This takes McEnroe's total Wimbledon fines to well over £7,000 and a possible 21-day world ban on him by the Men's International Professional Tennis Council.

McEnroe's immediate response to the snub by the All-England Club, in refusing to make him an honorary member and then giving him a maximum fine under the rules of the game, was predictable and in tune with his behaviour over the last fortnight. He refused to confirm that he would return next year to defend his title, and then became the first men's champion not to attend the annual champions' dinner at the Savoy Hotel. It was claimed by the McEnroe camp, naturally loyal to the champion who had won his title on American Independence Day, that he had asked the

Wimbledon committee for eight seats at the tables and he had been offered only five, the traditional number. But the obvious reason for McEnroe refusing to attend the dinner was that he would be asked to make a vote of thanks, as champion, to the All-England Club for their success in organising the Championships. This he could not do.

It inevitably put added strain on Mrs Chris Lloyd, who as the popular women's champion, had to make the major players' speech of the evening. 'Sir Brian Burnett, chairman of the All-England Club, said, in John McEnroe's absence, that I should make two speeches,' she quipped. 'Unfortunately, I can make only one, because I have not John's vocabulary. But I apologise, as an American, for the fact that he is not here.'

16 OCTOBER 1981

WIMBLEDON 1982 FINAL ON SUNDAY

John Parsons

The All-England Lawn Tennis Championships at Wimbledon will be extended by one day next year, with the men's singles final taking place on the Sunday. Another radical change, also announced today, is that all Centre Court tickets for the last four days, including the standing area, will be sold in advance so there will be no need for anyone to queue overnight.

The move to a Sunday men's singles final in line with most other major tournaments, was foreshadowed during this year's Championships and it will provide two major benefits. Not only will it ease pressure on the scheduling of matches, allowing the women's final to revert to its previous place on the second Saturday as was the case years ago, but the huge worldwide television audiences for both finals is expected to produce an additional £400,000 for the Lawn Tennis Association to plough back into the game.

The decision to make even the standing room area round the Centre Court all-ticket for the last four days is essentially to compensate the club's neighbours for the extra day's inconvenience. These tickets will be allocated by ballot, the arrangements for which will be announced later. But it is also hoped that this move will help to curb some of the rowdier elements who attended, particularly for this year's final between Björn Borg and John McEnroe. At the time I described the atmosphere with the rival chanting as being more like Wembley than Wimbledon, and many readers of *The Daily*

Telegraph wrote to endorse their dismay and alarm at the trend. In a statement, the Wimbledon management committee says that without an improvement in the situation they will seriously consider turning the Centre Court into an all-seat arena.

26 JUNE 1982
LETTER TO THE EDITOR
BASKING IN MEMORIES

Sir,

A recent letter reminded me also of M. Jean Borotra. He was known as the Bouncing Basque, and always wore a beret on court. While he was playing a doubles match on Centre Court a ball accidentally went into the spectators' stand. A lady handed it back. M. Borotra, who removed his headgear before receiving it, then bowed over the lady's hand.

Gabrielle Foster
Hunmanby, North Yorkshire

2 JULY 1982
LETTER TO THE EDITOR
BOTHER WITH BOUNCE

Sir,

A main criticism by tennis players of grass courts is that the bounce of the ball is unpredictable. I note that at Wimbledon the grass is cut in alternate swaths. Cricket pitches have always been cut up and down on the same line, thus eliminating the lines down the pitch, and ensuring that the grass is all laying the same way to provide an even bounce. Tennis balls do not have a seam to cause deviation on pitching, but they are much lighter than cricket balls and I would have thought that their bounce could be influenced by landing on grass with a nap alternating every two feet or so.

P.G. Powell
Norwich

4 JULY 1982

FIGHTING CONNORS DEPOSES McENROE IN LONGEST FINAL

John Parsons

Jimmy Connors, who said all along he was producing his best fighting tennis since he first became champion in 1974, proved the point handsomely yesterday when he took the title from John McEnroe in Wimbledon's longest final. The Centre Court clock was just ticking round to four hours 15 minutes as Connors brought up a cloud of chalk with the serve which climaxed his 3–6, 6–3, 6–7, 7–6, 6–4 victory, and then went to hug his wife, Patti. It was the first time since Bill Tilden in 1930 that any player has regained the Wimbledon title after so much as an eight-year gap. McEnroe's defeat means that Don Budge, in 1938, remains the last American who has successfully defended the title.

McEnroe served 19 aces. But he was so inconsistent in other aspects of his game that he could not benefit from Connors letting him off the hook after service breaks in the first and third sets of a match which only came alive as it grew in length and intensity. The only solace for McEnroe, who sat in his courtside chair, head slumped in his lap for minutes after the defeat, was the granting to him of the honorary membership of the All-England Club denied him a year ago.

It was undoubtedly true that McEnroe has worked desperately hard to keep his temper and feelings in check over the past fortnight, but there will be many who will be surprised by the membership award in view of the fact that he did not again become champion. He was, after all, warned in at least three matches, fined £280 for verbal abuse to an official in his semi-final against Tim Mayotte on Saturday, and invariably stretched the rules to such a limit that the improvement in his behaviour was relative rather than total.

For more than the first two hours, the match looked like being a considerable let-down. There were long, tedious spells, interrupted admittedly by some wonderfully spectacular rallies and shots, but also by some equally spectacular, almost inept, errors. In the third set, for instance, Connors, who led 3–1, served eight double-faults, two in the second game, three in the fourth, two more most wastefully of all from 30–30 as he served for the set at 5–4, and the last in the tie-break which he lost 7–2. In the end, however, it was his serve which eventually brought Connors back into the game for the only other double-fault of significance was his last, ironically the 13th, on his first match point.

The first game of the fourth set emphasised Connors's expression later that it was a match in which it was 'kill or be killed', for it lasted ten minutes, contained five deuces, and also a return to exciting winners after a set riddled with mistakes. In fact, the fourth set was the most competitive of all as, for the first time, both players seemed to lose some of the tension which had gripped them so fiercely hitherto, although increasingly it was noticeable that the best chances were falling to Connors. Twice in the sixth game he had chances for a break, but a backhand error cost him the first, while a magnificent McEnroe smash retrieved the other. Connors finally levelled the match in a second tie-break, this time 7–5, and fully deserved to do so if only for the amazing reflex volley he produced to rescue the serving break against him at 2–3. It was one of the most thrilling points of the afternoon. McEnroe played a superb drop shot which Connors just returned. McEnroe then hit a volley which by most standards would have been a decisive winner, but Connors's counter-volley was even more remarkable.

Connors was hardly a popular champion when he defeated Ken Rosewall, one of Wimbledon's favourite sons, in 1974, but now the crowd was ready to hail him lustily. Twice, at the change of ends, there were even soccer-style strains of 'There's only one Jimmy Connors' ringing from the standing room. The first time his supporters broke out in song, Connors played that disastrous tenth game which cost him the third set, but the second time it inspired him to break most propitiously. In the third game of the fifth set he did so in a confidently flamboyant style which was the beginning of the end of McEnroe's resolve.

On his second break point, Connors leaned back and then launched himself into a drilled backhand down the line which was loaded with all the pent-up aggression which has not quite been controlled enough to earn him a Grand Slam title since the US Open in 1978. Serving to stay in the match, McEnroe, though mentally and physically weary, produced one final bold act of defiance by holding to love and winding up the game with his 19th ace. Connors, however, was riding high. One could sense the enjoyment in every shot he played and two stunning volleys, plus a forehand which clipped the baseline, took him to the point of triumph. For McEnroe there was only despair and more to come with defeat in the doubles.

Connors, who collected £41,667 compared to McEnroe's £20,833, said: 'It was a life and death struggle in the sense that it was all-out-guts play. We both gave everything we had and that is why I like playing McEnroe. He brings out the best in me because he fights for every ball.' Connors, who was warned for an obscene gesture, said: 'I didn't intend to insult the line judge. I was abusing the electronic machine he was operating.'

8 JUNE 1983

PAT'S JOB: TO PUT THE TENSION INTO WIMBLEDON'S TENNIS

Kenric Hickson

Pat Menon is a quiet, modest woman who during the Wimbledon fortnight is the friend, expert and mentor on whom most of the stars depend to get their rackets strung to the particular tension that best suits their style of play. While lesser mortals go into sports shops and buy a racket off the shelf, for professional players the tension is all important.

Most top players like a tension of around 65lb, but McEnroe is exceptional and demands tension at the extreme end of the spectrum. McEnroe will have 40lb. Yet Borg, a top-spin player, would have nothing less than 70lb and sometimes asked for 90lb. 'Borg travelled with about 60 rackets and would often take ten on court,' Pat says. 'With the type of game he played, the strings just didn't last. Normally, I can thread and stretch the 34-foot-long gut in about half an hour, but stringing for Borg used to take longer – and if the gut broke, as it sometimes did because of the extreme tension, I would have to start all over again.' The weather has a considerable influence on tension. Gut is very absorbent and if the grass is damp, even if it is not raining, the ball picks up moisture and transfers this to the strings. The gut swells and the result is loss of tension.

Pat learned the art of stringing from her husband 'Remy' Menon, who died seven years ago. He was an Indian who came to Britain before the war and learned and practised stringing as a hobby. By chance, he met Art Larson (US Forest Hills champion in 1950) and was asked to string for him. After that, other players brought their rackets to 'Remy', until he had built up a large and select clientele who regarded him as the best in the world. At her flat, Pat has a treasured collection of photographs and letters from tennis stars past and present. Billie-Jean King wrote: 'Without your help, Remy, I could never have won Wimbledon.' A photograph of Arthur Ashe is signed: 'To Mr Menon, the Master Stringer.'

Some rackets are strung with nylon but most players insist on gut, which is not (and never has been) cat-gut, but is made from the intestines of sheep and cattle and comes mainly from Australia. It takes about seven sheep to make one length of gut.

Pat knows most of the players. She said: 'Jimmy Connors is my favourite. He often comes to my flat and brings his friends and other players with him for a cup of coffee. Billie-Jean is great fun and she has a tremendous sense of humour and Evonne Goolagong Cawley is lovely.'

During the Wimbledon fortnight Pat works in the glass-sided hospitality office at the Gloucester Hotel, Kensington, where many players stay during the Championships. She usually starts stringing about 7a.m. and is often there until midnight or after. 'Sometimes the players come in looking a bit worried and anxious about their game and I give them a cup of tea and try to reassure them. I don't give preference to any player. They all take their turn and I don't think I have ever failed to get anyone on court on time.'

Pat would love to watch the Championships – especially the finals on Centre Court – but she is so busy stringing she cannot get away. She keeps a television set switched on while she is working and so keeps in touch with what is going on. 'It is important to know each player's style,' she explained. 'Because you string the racket to suit the player and it helps to see them in action.'

Pat has seen many changes since she was first associated with Wimbledon. 'Perhaps the biggest change has been in the spectators and their behaviour. It used to be rather a sedate occasion, but today there are more young people who are a bit unruly at times. Now it is almost back to the gladiatorial atmosphere when the crowds went to see the Christians thrown to the lions. Clapping faults and mistakes is just bad manners.' As for the players' behaviour, 'they're not as disciplined as they were years ago, but it's all due to the pressures of the game. When you think that £60,000 can rest on one point it is not surprising they lose control sometimes.'

Do women players get more nervous and tense than men? 'Not really,' said Pat. 'They like to chat about their families. I remember Martina Navratilova was over the moon when her mother was able to come out of Czechoslovakia to see her win the Championship. She regards Wimbledon as the highlight of a tennis player's career – which it is.'

The Wimbledon Championships keep Pat busy for only two weeks in the year. For the remaining 50 she works at her shop, The Racquet Shop in Shepherds Bush. With rows and rows of rackets and racket frames waiting to be strung it is a veritable Aladdin's cave for tennis buffs. One wall is almost covered with photographs of tennis stars bearing appreciative dedications to Pat, and there is a composite cartoon of a number of players signed by each in such terms as 'Pat, you're the greatest, Jimmy Connors', and 'Pat, I love you, Ilie Nastase'. She says: 'The shop is rather off the beaten track and we don't advertise. We rely on our reputation and on the recommendation of satisfied customers.'

Wimbledon is the highlight of Pat's year, but there are two other prestigious events at which she and her partner Mike Rickman provide a service: the Benson and Hedges tournament at Wembley and the world doubles at the Royal Albert Hall. One of the most unusual and unexpected engagements for Pat was the international tennis tournament in the Middle East – the Gold Tournament at Dubai. The organiser, who had seen her working at the Gloucester Hotel and knew how much the players depended on her, invited her, all expenses paid. 'It was a wonderful experience,' she recalled. 'I had the red-carpet treatment. Waited on hand and foot at this fabulous luxury hotel. Unfortunately, it was a one-off event and has not been held since. I'm waiting for the next one now. If I should be invited I would be off like a shot.'

4 JULY 1983

NAVRATILOVA: BEST OF GENERATION

John Parsons

Martina Navratilova tried to put Andrea Jaeger at ease before their Wimbledon singles final on Saturday by practising with her how they would curtsey to the Royal Box. From playing the consoling big sister in the dressing-room, however, Miss Navratilova swiftly became the teacher, giving the overawed pupil the sharpest possible lesson once the match began. Despite the degree of respectability which Miss Jaeger managed to provide in the second set, when she won 37 of the 79 points, it was still the shortest, drabbest final since Billie-Jean King outplayed Evonne Cawley 6–0, 6–1 in 1975.

Whatever chance Miss Jaeger may have had of denying Miss Navratilova her fourth title in four finals, depended on her applying early pressure on the champion. Instead she could hardly keep the ball in court and the first set was over in 15 minutes. Miss Jaeger won only nine points and started thinking she should take as much time as she could between games because the match was sweeping past her so swiftly.

Her hint of a threat in the second set, when she at last found range and control, was too little and too late, though it was possibly sabotaged in part by a call which, to say the least, was bitterly unkind to the teenager. Trailing 2—3 she was holding a game point when Navratilova hit a drive which looked well out over the far sideline, but there was no call from New York official Judy Lessing. So instead of being 3—3 Miss Jaeger then lost seven points in succession to trail 2—5 and though she had three break points when Miss Navratilova served to retain her title two games later, it was by then a forlorn effort.

That Miss Navratilova allowed her opponent even a game after crushing her so mercilessly in the first set, suggests she still lacks the ruthless streak of Suzanne Lenglen or Maureen Connolly. Yet she is unquestionably the finest and fittest woman player of the present generation. No one can seriously dispute this when she has just won Wimbledon without dropping a set for her 24th title in 18 months, during which she has lost only four of 139 matches. Such has been her powerful supremacy that the question of how she might fare on equal terms against men has inevitably been raised. 'I think I'd qualify for some of the events,' she said. 'But I'd have to get stronger and work a lot harder. I think I am quicker than a lot of men but their serve is so tough to return. If they were allowed only one serve, though, it would be a different ball game.'

For Miss Navratilova, the remaining challenge in tennis for her is to reach her full potential. 'Until that happens, I won't stop,' she said. Meanwhile, Miss Jaeger, 18, whose lobbing was so astute and successful against Mrs King, but disastrous in the final, knows that there are several lessons she still has to learn in the game — including, at Wimbledon, how to curtsey. Just as she forgot so many basic principles of match play during the final, she also forgot the lessons Martina had given her about curtseying when she approached the Duke of Kent to collect her runners-up medal.

29 JUNE 1984

TENNIS BEHAVIOUR PROTEST FROM THE BALLBOYS' HEADS

John Izbicki, Education Correspondent

Head teachers of schools who supply the Wimbledon tennis tournament with ballboys and ballgirls have expressed 'serious concern' at the bad behaviour of some of the players and the poor example they are setting children. Mr Richard Davies, director of education for the London borough of Merton, the home of Wimbledon, has passed on the heads' concern to the All-England Club, who supervise the tournament. The heads, all from Merton schools, expressed their concern at their monthly meeting.

Mr John Attree, headmaster of Garth High School at Morden – a school which has been supplying ballboys for Wimbledon throughout his 11 years as head – said last night that the behaviour shown by some players was intolerable. 'It astonishes me that the British public tolerates the behaviour of players like John McEnroe. He is undoubtedly a great player but his antics on court set a bad example.' Mr Attree, who at the age of 57 has taken early retirement ('Only another 19 days to go as head,' he told me) recalled his youth when he was a Wimbledon ballboy. He said: 'Players behaved quite differently then. Some lost their cool from time to time but there were never the temper tantrums we have to witness today.'

Mrs Daphne Haugh, headmistress of Rowan High School for Girls, which has six ballgirls on the Wimbledon courts, said that youngsters always admire and copy excellence. 'That's great and we would encourage them to do so. We want them to see how and why players win the glittering prizes – through perseverance and total commitment. But unfortunately, children will also copy the nasty things in their heroes. You can see it now on any tennis court where youngsters play. They will throw down their rackets, swear, thump their fists on the ground and so on.'

Mrs Haugh, who played tennis at county level for Northamptonshire and Worcestershire, said tennis players were not alone in causing concern among teachers. The lifestyles of pop stars left much to be desired. 'If a child's hero takes drugs, who are we teachers or parents to say that drug-taking is wrong? We strive hard to maintain the highest possible standards in our schools, but schools reflect society and all is far from well.'

Mr David Giles, head of Tamworth Manor High School, Mitcham, said that McEnroe was by no means the only culprit. 'We want to see the sport played the way it was intended, for the example of players has a rub-off effect on pupils,' he said.

Commander Charles Lane, who has trained Wimbledon's ballboys and girls for the past 18 years, said the teachers' fears were 'groundless'. 'The boys and girls are not influenced by the behaviour of the players which will not affect them in the very slightest – why should it?' He said they only did the job for a fortnight and they were warned about the behaviour of some players during their pre-Wimbledon training.

Among many letters received by *The Daily Telegraph* on the subject, Karen Brown, aged nine, of Ottershaw Christ Church Middle School at Chertsey, Surrey, wrote: 'If we behaved like John McEnroe in games or PE, we would be sent out. He is very rude.'

John McEnroe said yesterday that microphones should be taken off courts so that television audiences could not hear foul language from the players. He said: 'I intend to bring this up in the future and I hope that other people will feel the same way and we can have something done about it.'

30 JUNE 1984

PETERBOROUGH: WIMBLEDON'S CHAMPION ROUND

Amid the razzmatazz surrounding next Monday's centenary parade of past ladies' champions and the 50th anniversary of the first of Fred Perry's three successive singles titles, there is some surprise that no mention has been made of his fellow champion that year, Dorothy Round. A Methodist Sunday school teacher, Miss Round, who died in 1982 at the age of 73, was blessed with an uncanny composure on court which helped her to the Wimbledon ladies' singles title in 1934 and 1937. As Perry's partner, she also twice won the mixed doubles.

Christine Janes (née Truman) and Virginia Wade are among those who feel some tribute should be paid. 'Dorothy Round has never been a figurehead like Fred Perry has,' Miss Wade, the first woman member of the Wimbledon Committee, told me yesterday. 'But that's maybe because she was a mere woman.' A Wimbledon steward recalls that such was the euphoria over Perry's and Round's double triumph that the BBC, in its national news, played in their honour the *Trumpet Voluntary* by Jeremiah Clarke. Times have indeed changed.

30 JUNE 1984

CONNORS'S PIECE OF HISTORY

John Parsons

Jimmy Connors made history at Wimbledon last night when his 6–4, 6–7, 6–3, 6–4 defeat of fellow American Marty Davis enabled him to beat Arthur W. Gore's record of 64 singles match victories at the Championships. Gore,

Wimbledon's oldest champion when he won the title for the third time in 1909, spread his career over 39 years. For Connors, champion in 1974 and 1982, this is his 13th year of competition.

It is a pity that Connors was not able to produce one of his more scintillating performances to coincide with this remarkable landmark. He won well enough in the end, but it was only in the fourth set that he became the bright and breezy player one expects. Connors tended to lift his game just often enough to keep himself in command, except for a spell in the second set when his serve faltered badly, his game in general stuttered and he also collected a warning for verbal abuse. This happened at the end of the seventh game when Davis went into a 4–3 lead after a sideline call which left the reigning United States Open champion raging wildly at the official concerned.

I JULY 1984

THAT TWO-SETS-DOWN FEELING

Oliver Pritchett

Do you sometimes feel in life that you are serving to stay in the match? When you look around you and consider your circumstances do you get the sense that there are three break points against you? I have come to the conclusion that the real fascination of Wimbledon on television is not the tennis – serve and volley, serve and volley, let – but that it turns us all into philosophers. Staring at the bright green screen we find that the words of Dan Maskell and the other commentators contain an important message. Most of us are, in a way, fighting back bravely on one of life's outside courts.

In fact all sports commentators have a way of sending you off into a world of speculation. The reason the whole population watches hours and hours of snooker on TV is not for the game itself, but for the metaphor. 'He is 36 behind and there are 35 points left on the table.' The commentator breaks the tragic news in a whisper. A million philosophers nod gravely at the screen. It was while watching the 157th frame of some marathon sponsored by a cigarette company that I composed my own epitaph – 'He died requiring snookers'.

You switch on the TV set to watch the tennis and it is always in the middle of a match. The first thing you see is two men seated on chairs beside the umpire's step-ladder, drinking Coca-Cola from cardboard cups and staring gloomily at their feet. By studying their faces you can tell which one is winning. The one who looks most agonised about his feet is two sets up and has, according to Dan Maskell, 'found his touch'. This is clearly bad news.

Before there is a chance to see how he will be affected and whether he will recover from his grief, Harry Carpenter briskly tells us that it is time to go over to Court No. 3 where a game English girl is battling to overcome her nerves. Or else we are treated to a succession of scorecards which make the screen hum and which inform us that an unknown South African has beaten an unknown Peruvian in three straight sets. Now, here is another cause for speculation. What is the Peruvian going to do with himself for the rest of the fortnight? Perhaps he will go sight-seeing and, if so, I wonder which of our ancient monuments would delight a disappointed unseeded Peruvian.

And what is the matter with Jimmy Connors's racket? Between every point he picks fretfully at the strings and peers at them. Obviously the mesh is not quite even, some of the squares are not properly square. It makes you want to get out of your armchair and go over and have a closer look, to try to help him straighten it out.

Early last week, when refusing to give a TV interview, John McEnroe said he was going to let his racket do the talking. Now he punches the strings and listens to it like a tuning fork. One of these days that racket is going to utter and it will receive a public warning for abusing an official.

'Magical touch!' says Dan Maskell, but I missed it because I was worrying about the towels. Wimbledon must have more towels than all London's hotels put together. One of the players adjourns to wipe his racket handle or his neck and I am now calculating the laundry bill. When Ivan Lendl changes ends how does he know which is *his* towel?

Never mind if you missed the wonderful cross-court volley; you can always tell who won the point because the camera picks him out first, walking to his place looking utterly disgusted with himself.

Then there are moments of true drama and suspense. The high-ranking, high-earning star has just put his lightning first service into the net. I hold my breath. Now, under the cold stare of the player, the ballboy must run at a crouch across the court, pick up the ball without stopping and scamper to safety on the other side. The suspense is hard to bear. That is one more time that he has managed it without falling flat on his nose. Surely his luck cannot hold out for ever.

Take me away from all this, Harry Carpenter. Take me back to Court No. 3 where the game English girl is still battling with her nerves. Soothe me with a buzzing scorecard. Give me an aerial long shot of a tie-break between an unknown New Zealander and an unpronounceable Bulgarian. What news of the lonely Peruvian? Return me to Desmond Lynam interviewing somebody in front of the fake studio shrubbery and let me wonder for a few moments if his moustache is really symmetrical.

It is a strain on the emotions and on the brain. By the end of Wimbledon you are overcome by a terrible sense of foreboding and unease. You know that feeling: you are 40–0 down and it is Miss Navratilova to serve.

9 JULY 1984

MRS LLOYD INSPIRES GREATNESS IN NAVRATILOVA

John Parsons

It was abundantly appropriate that in the year of centenary celebrations for women's tennis at Wimbledon, the singles title should be held by Martina Navratilova, the greatest woman player in the game today – and possibly of all time. Equally, it was right that she was engaged in such a sparkling and often exciting final before drawing level at 30 wins each with Chris Lloyd, who had been the finest in her time and still yearns to be so again.

Miss Navratilova, best of all, knows that the 7–6, 6–2 victory in 83 minutes which made her the first player since Billie-Jean King (1966–68) to win Wimbledon in three successive years, might even have been prised from her grasp. Although Miss Navratilova's added power, which stems from incredibly hard work, proved decisive in the end, especially on the serve, the challenger, lively and so determined, had the chances to push the world champion to breaking points. 'Martina doesn't give you many chances and I definitely had one or two,' said Mrs Lloyd. 'Maybe I played tentatively, but she also served so well.' That summed it up, for Miss Navratilova, under attack, no longer looks the frail-looking waif of a few years ago. Then, her serve would swiftly become the first indication of vulnerability. Now it is her first to last strike weapon.

Mrs Lloyd, Wimbledon champion three times, began brilliantly. She hit a variety of winning shots, ranging from the customary passes and drop shots to aggressive play at the net which gained her two service breaks in the first three games. For the first time in the Championships, Miss Navratilova became unsure and her forehand suspect. But by the fifth game, her serve was beginning to find its stinging depth and accuracy – and that changed the course of the match. It came to the rescue most of all with an ace when

Mrs Lloyd, who had led 4–3, 30–0, next had an opportunity with a break point at 4–4. It could have left her serving for the first set. Then, in the tie-break, after Mrs Lloyd had double-faulted at 2–5, another ace settled it for Miss Navratilova on her third set point.

That opening set had been as much a scorcher as the 100 degrees of heat in the bowl of the magnificent Centre Court which, on such a day and with such superb competitors at or near their peak, must make it one of the most emotionally inspiring sporting venues of the world. Although limited to eight games, the second set was only marginally less rewarding than the first. One always felt that Miss Lloyd's best would not, in the end, be quite enough. But she was still running freely, still going boldly for her shots and still demonstrating outstanding character. Following one stunning drop-shot winner in the third game, even Miss Navratilova bowed in deference to such marvellous skill. Alas for Mrs Lloyd, from 40–30 she double-faulted and then was broken by two spectacular winners by her opponent.

Miss Navratilova felt the seventh and eighth games of the first set were the crunch. 'That was when she was coming to the net and putting pressure on me,' she reflected. Yet the three break points Mrs Lloyd held at 1–2 in the second set, with two more at 2–3, mainly saved by fierce serving and all-out aggression, were also significant.

Even when Miss Navratilova was poised for the title for the fifth time in seven years, Mrs Lloyd refused to yield until the fifth match point, drilling first a backhand and then a forehand past the champion, before another fine serve, sliced and swinging this time, brought the victory cheers. The £90,000 first prize and the title were Miss Navratilova's, but much of the honour also went to Mrs Lloyd who, for the second successive match, raised her form to the level she has been seeking all year.

9 JULY 1984
CROFT LANDS GIRLS' CROWN

Annabel Croft provided a heartening British climax of Wimbledon when she fought back after losing the first set to the South African, Elna Reinach, 15, in the final of the girls' singles. Miss Croft's 3–6, 6–2, 6–2 victory made her the first British winner of a junior title at Wimbledon since Ann Haydon Jones in 1956. Miss Croft, the third seed, was often caught by Miss Reinach's drop shots early on, but the Kent girl, whose form and mood has been transformed since Paris after several months of disappointing results, came back strongly.

9 JULY 1984

LLOYD VICTORY TASTES SWEET AGAIN

Roger Malone

Wimbledon enthused last night over the rare luxury of a British flavour to the title line-up for the second successive year, when John Lloyd partnered Wendy Turnbull, of Australia, to retain the mixed doubles Championship. They overcame the No. 2 seeds, Steve Denton, the fierce-serving Texan, and Kathy Jordan, of the United States, the singles semi-finalist, by 6–3, 6–3. Last year, when Lloyd and Miss Turnbull, 31, beat Denton and Billie-Jean King in the final, Lloyd, from Essex, became the first British man to win a Wimbledon title since 1936.

After last night's win, in which Miss Turnbull's steadfastness proved a perfect foil to his quickness, Lloyd, the British No. 2, commented that he felt less pressure this year because the historical breakthrough had been made. 'Our partnership now is 20 per cent better than last year,' he added. Asked about the qualities of their partners throughout the tournament, Lloyd pinpointed Miss Turnbull's reliable first serve and solid volleying. The experienced Australian highlighted Lloyd's 'good crossing at the net, where he intimidates the other woman', and his ability with his returns to keep the opposition guessing.

23 JUNE 1985

SEEDS OF SUCCESS

Sebastian Faulks

Our brief annual love affair with tennis begins tomorrow: a fortnight of flashing hemlines, bulging thighs and bad sportsmanship. Beneath the dark, echoic stands of Wimbledon excited young girls tremble and pulsate like characters from a Mills and Boon romance as hunks of seeded manhood brush past. Here two worlds meet: the clubby, awkward formality of the All-England Club, and the billion-dollar brashness of the cultureless orbit of the pro where such standards as exist are defined by the relative snob value of the designer's name on shorts or sunglasses.

It has all the elements of cheap fiction: money, clothes, good looks, prestige and hostility. The additional element of Wimbledon is the gladiatorial setting of the Centre Court where the covered, narrowing oval seems to gather and focus a collective tension on to the two players below.

It could equally provide a superior romance, in which (one fantasises) a surprise British qualifier, previously unknown, battles through to the final. He arrives to play McEnroe wearing an old Fred Perry shirt and carrying a single wooden racket. McEnroe misbehaves as usual, but his opponent pleads continuously on his behalf. So bamboozled is McEnroe by this display of sportsmanship ('Do have it again, John') that he unaccountably surrenders a two-set lead and returns to New York a sadder and a nicer man.

There are in fact no surprise qualifiers. After the top hundred ranked professionals there are two or three hundred more, almost as good, hustling a living on the edge of the game, sleeping in their cars, doing part-time jobs and hoping for a break. 'It's like Los Angeles,' said Vijay Amritraj, the Indian ranked 49, 'where every waitress has a film script tucked in her back pocket.' Such players compete in qualifying tournaments before Wimbledon begins and there are no good-hearted amateurs in the final draw. Which is not to say there are not plenty of quite reasonable people. 'I have been on the tour for ten years,' said the Pole Wojtek Fibak, 'and it is really rather pleasant.' Amritraj agreed. 'Ninety per cent of the people are really nice. They're not spoiled brats with too much money.'

There was a crisis point about five years ago when the behaviour of the top men was so bad it began to look as though sponsors would pull out their investments and the game would starve for lack of cash. The moment has passed, and the next generation seems not to have copied the manners of its elders. The women are self-evidently more civilised. Although some of the French girls can become hysterical and the Americans Kathy Jordan and Pam Shriver have a terse way with words on court, there is a friendly feeling among them in the players' lounge. Even the surly Navratilova is a different creature without a racket in her hand. Pam Shriver, who with the Czech Hana Mandlikova is heiress apparent to 'Chris and Martina' (they are often referred to as a unit), is much liked off court. She said: 'Our life is a combination of excitement beyond words and tedium beyond words.'

At Edgbaston, where the women gathered for some pre-Wimbledon shower-dodging, the atmosphere in the sitting-out room resembled that of an exotic girls' finishing school. Away from the ageing television cameras, they seemed much younger as they tuned up their Sony Walkmans, shot pool, knitted and played the fruit machine (a jackpot for Gabriela Sabatini, the 15-year-old Argentine prodigy. Coals to Newcastle, one couldn't help thinking).

Suppose, then, you are a young woman player among this number and tomorrow is your first Wimbledon. If you are an American, it will not be as important to you as the US Open, but to most other nationalities it still represents the high point of the year. Tonight you will stay at the Gloucester or the Kensington Hilton in London, probably sharing a room with another young professional, and tomorrow you will be picked up by an Austin Rover and driven down to Church Road, SW19.

There is a large new administrative building inside the gates, and a good deal of the grass where people used to picnic has been concreted over. Wimbledon has responded to the complaints the players were making about it and now tries to cosset them in the way they require. 'I would rather sit on a beach in California with a can of beer than go and play tennis at Wimbledon,' said the American Eliot Teltscher eight years ago. 'It always rains, you can't get a practice court, transportation is bad and the players are not considered by the people who run it.' But Teltscher plays tomorrow, seeded 13.

You find your named locker in the changing-room on the ground floor of the ivy-covered main building. It's surprisingly like your local club in some ways, only larger. Lesser players change upstairs (ladies) or by Court Six (gents). Wimbledon is keen on preserving class distinctions and some players (previous champions, other elected members) are allowed to change in the Members' changing-room.

This causes friction; a young thruster from Milwaukee may have to change in the junior dressing-room while an elegant old favourite, some way down the rankings, may get into the main one. On Day One you have to clamber over other players doing stretching exercises and fight your way through the bodies to the door. Off for practice now, since you may never have played on grass before and the change, in the words of the BBC's Gerald Williams, is 'a complete culture shock'.

The practice courts are far away at the north end of the ground beyond a former rugby pitch. Here you catch your first sight of what Ginger Rogers has called 'the most beautiful legs in the world'. They belong to Hana Mandlikova, the capriciously gifted world No. 3, a young player of wonderful elegance.

The Mills and Boon story comes alive here when you anxiously survey the other women. The competition (in the beauty stakes) is much higher than in the butch days of the mid-1970s. 'Chris has got her hair right at the eighth attempt,' sighed Ted Tinling, the diamond-earringed dress designer who is now the 'player liaison officer'. And here is young Gabriela Sabatini, who reached the semi-finals of the French Open. She has a soft, warm handshake, lowered eyelashes, and affects not to understand English. Before playing her, Pam Shriver said: 'If I ever lost to a 14- or 15-year-old I'd die right on court.' She lost. Sabatini's tennis, according to the British girl Annabel Croft, is 'incredible'.

Annabel herself is a charming girl of the kind you might meet – if you were lucky – at the Farnborough Young Conservatives dance. Her candour and good sense seem all at odds with this weirdly separate world where every day you have to prove yourself anew. Here, too, are the ballboys and girls who have keenly volunteered to take two weeks off school to be trained by Dr Arthur Jonathan, a beaming South African with a PhD in the 'psychology of skills acquisition'. The ballboys' favourites are the Americans Vitas Gerulaitis and Billie-Jean King, who used to give them sweets, and Johan Kriek, the South African, who last year gave them some rackets he no longer needed, thus proving again that you can't judge a man by his behaviour on the court.

Practice is over, and you have seen from *The Daily Telegraph* this morning that your match is not on till later, so it is time for lunch in the players' restaurant. This is not a pleasant sight. Here, at last, we encounter the Men. There is an appalling poundage of surplus muscle requiring to be fed. Ambling up to the food bar in loose-fitting tracksuits, one of them, such as the fabulously hungry American Gene Mayer, may begin: 'I'll take the steak pie … and is that a cheese omelette? OK, let me have some of that … and a side salad … Is that fish? No, I don't want that. Give me the pork in cider.' And so on.

It is only at the major Grand Prix tournaments that the men and the women play together, and relations between the two are not as they might be. The men never bother to watch the women unless they have a particular friend or share a coach, and some of them resent the amount of money the women now earn. 'I make 150,000 dollars a year, but, sure, I'd get creamed by the 100th-ranked guy,' said Pam Shriver. 'But so what? They're nowhere near as friendly as they should be. I reckon it's good if I can get five guys a day to say "Hi" to me.'

In the evenings the men go out together and eat; they go to cinemas or discotheques. It's not all lavish. 'There are some men,' said Amritraj, 'earning 100,000 dollars a year and they never go to anything more than the Wimpy and the pizza place.' But it's fun. For the women it's different. 'I live a bit like a hermit,' said Annabel Croft. 'I eat alone. I have no actual life at all. I pack and unpack four times a week. My social life is non-existent.' She speaks to her parents on the telephone almost every day.

And as for the love life ... There are always spare girls hanging around outside the men's dressing-room and they can select a girl from the crowd and ask if she would like to go out to dinner. But the women players? Nothing. Even Gabriela Sabatini only writes letters.

If you do squeeze a 'Hi' from one of the men, it may well be from the gentlemanly Tim Mayotte, one of the many better-mannered younger generation of Americans, or from John Lloyd, recently voted 'best-looking pro on the men's tour' in *International Tennis Weekly*. It probably won't be from Gerulaitis, who is not a great admirer of women players, or from the dangerous-looking Australian Mark Edmondson, whose enormous haunches are the despair of shorts manufacturers.

Now it is time to complain to the referee. This is an old Wimbledon custom and one that referee Alan Mills, a former Davis Cup player for Britain, is well prepared for. You will probably want to complain about the scheduling of your match, and later on (since you're a real pro) about a penalty point given against you for bad behaviour. Mills, a Liverpudlian, keeps his door open to players and sometimes even upholds their grievances. Be warned, though, that he has the television on in his office upstairs in the No. 1 Court complex and can see trouble brewing in televised matches, especially those involving 'Our Friend' — as McEnroe, whose name no one seems to want to soil their lips with, is universally called.

Last year when McEnroe insisted that Mills be called on to adjudicate on a linesman who had been foot-faulting him, he was surprised to see Mills pop out of the crowd on the baseline. Having seen the problem coming, he had already slipped into the crowd and observed the linesman's performance which, he said, was impeccable.

You will have noticed from the scoreboards that it is now time for your match and, as Mills and Boon would have it, you are on the Centre Court. Having sat quietly in the locker-room for half an hour, you are called down to the waiting room. This is a small white cell at the back of the main building which, even when empty, has an appallingly tense atmosphere. On its white brick walls is the odd picture — a photograph of Maureen Connolly ('Little Mo'), a pencil drawing of Björn Borg and Our Friend, posed in this very room, gnawed by nerves.

This is the worst part of the day, a bizarre and unnecessary torture which ends with the arrival of the Master of Ceremonies, Peter Morgan, who leads you over the step at the back of the clubhouse and takes you the half-dozen paces across the path to the green screens at the back of the Centre Court.

He tells you which royal personage will receive your curtsey. Clutching a bag full of rackets you step into the arena.

One or two reflections while you're playing. Your opponent may be a liked colleague, but won't be a friend. With the exception of a few Americans, like the No. 3 doubles seeds Ken Flach and Robert Seguso who were at Southern Illinois University together, there are not many real friends on the tour. The crowd watching you are surprisingly well rated by the pros. They are less *chic*, it is true, than the French, many of whom go merely to be 'seen' in their Rigatoni sneakers or Netsuke wristbands; but they are less partisan than the Italians (heaven help the man who plays Panatta in Rome), and less abrasive than the Americans in New York. 'I'm not disappointed with Wimbledon,' said Jimmy Connors in a recent interview, 'but I much prefer to play in front of an animalistic atmosphere like in New York.'

Your umpire may be a dentist, a doctor or a banker and is unpaid for his hazardous hobby. The officials are players of varying standards themselves and are without exception big noises at their local clubs. Why anyone should volunteer for the job is a mystery. The chief umpire, Peter Webster, another Liverpudlian, who is a colonel in the Royal Corps of Signals, said he once offered the players at a tournament the chance to sit in the chair. None of them would do it. 'They all said it was a mug's game, but the truth is they didn't want to upset their colleagues on court. They were frightened.' Last year he had a thank-you letter from the Women's Tennis Association, but not a word from the men. Rather the opposite in fact.

Your game is now in full swing. The hours of waiting have been for these few moments. On a drizzly day at Edgbaston, Anne Hobbs warmed up six times for a rain-interrupted match. Pam Shriver remarked of the same day that it had 'seemed like four days'. But when the ball is going in, it seems worthwhile. One can forget how much even a mild-mannered girl like Annabel Croft simply enjoys winning.

Many of the most successful players have borne grudges of some kind that have made them angry and desperate. When Connors lost Wimbledon to Borg he said: 'I'm going to follow that son of a bitch to the ends of the earth and beat him.' Likewise Our Friend, of whom a fellow pro commented: 'Some people hate him, some dislike him, but most just ignore him.' Another, less fluently but more crisply, put it: 'Dis guy is complete nuts.'

The end of the McEnroe–Connors era may mean that tennis will become like golf, with any number of players able to win big tournaments. It may also, thinks Wojtek Fibak, bring greater specialisation, with clay-court players not bothering to compete on faster surfaces. It will also be a relief. One male player lamented: 'What a champion McEnroe could have been. With that talent, those hands ... But he is a disgrace, he will never be a champion like Newcombe or Ashe or Rosewall. He is the most complete player since Laver and twice as quick. Maybe it is the way he was brought up or something ...'

Your match is over and you have won. You now go to a small room under the main building where you are required to be interviewed by the gentlemen of the press before going on to the BBC room where Gerald Williams will give your hand a friendly squeeze. 'I was married to a tennis pro for eight years,' he said, 'and you can't sleep with someone for that long without feeling a sympathy for the way they tick. People respond to Christian warmth, I think. Of course I do sometimes ask trite questions. I see it later and think, "How could I have said that?"' His dream interviewees are Billie-Jean and Vitas; but don't worry, he won't give you a grilling.

On now to two American TV interviews, upstairs to change and out on to the clubhouse steps where a crowd of young fans are held back by crash barriers. This may be the best part of your day as you wait for the courtesy car to take you back to your hotel. Perhaps your driver is Katrina Williams, a model who does fashion shows. Perhaps it is Toby Berridge, a cheerful redhead who takes Wimbledon fortnight as his annual holiday from a fabric design company and who had the misfortune to drive Chris Evert back after she had lost the Grand Slam. Romance is not forbidden, but it is difficult to arrange, since you cannot be sure which car will be around when you need a lift. One girl driver did become engaged to a player, but he broke it off.

Next day the saga continues. The officials always ask you for your badge, even if you have been on television all day. There are 20 or 30 little things that irritate the players, but the older participants forgive them. 'When I first went there,' said Pam Shriver, 'I rebelled against the authority. But the longer you play there, the more you appreciate it.'

And so begins another day of warming up, waiting, eating and more waiting. Many of the girls bring friends and relations on tour with them to keep them company; some have husbands and some bring girlfriends, though it is hard for players below the top 50 to afford anyone else's plane ticket.

Only in Vijay Amritraj did there seem a spark of genuine romance. 'I was born in Madras, and when my younger brother was born my grandfather had a dream that one of us would play at Wimbledon.' He is going back tomorrow, even though he injured his left hand so badly during the Stella Artois at Queen's that it hurts when the ballgirl throws him the ball to serve.

And if you should battle through each round, defeating the loneliness and the tedium as well as the opposition to meet Chris or Martina in the final, and if you should manage against all the odds to win that one, too, then your prize that evening at the Wimbledon Ball, with its sparkling jewellery and ranks of sun-burnished manhood awaiting your pleasure, is a dance with the Men's Champion.

That currently looks likely to be either the hysterically abusive John McEnroe or the spectral and monosyllabic Czech Ivan Lendl. Second prize, as you by now have no doubt guessed, is two dances.

5 JULY 1985
WIMBLEDON FLOODED IN STORM
Guy Rais

Wimbledon was hit by a 20-minute downpour yesterday which left the Princess of Wales sitting in the back of a soaked Royal Box while cleaners mopped up around her. The storm started as the Princess, in a light summer dress, arrived for the two men's semi-finals. Within minutes one of the Centre Court entry tunnels was under three feet of water, and the Royal Box, covered in green tarpaulin, was drenched.

Water overflowed from gutters and drains. Tennis fans, in flimsy summer clothes, fled as the rain soaked even the covered seating area. The flooded entry tunnel provided a makeshift 'swimming pool' for 22-year-old Anne Rundle, from Chingford, East London, who jumped in the water as part of a student bet. According to the London Weather Centre, the All-England Club got an estimated one and a half inches of rain – three quarters of the average July rainfall – in 20 minutes.

8 JULY 1985
BECKER TAKES TITLE AND MAKES HISTORY
John Parsons

Wimbledon rose to acclaim a remarkable new champion yesterday as Boris Becker, still more than four months away from his 18th birthday, stormed to a 6–3, 6–7, 7–6, 6–4 defeat of Kevin Curren in the final. In a three-hour 18-minute contest which began almost tamely but then developed into a gripping feast, Becker became not only the youngest winner in the 109 years of the Championships, and the first German to triumph, but above all, the first to do so unseeded.

Despite the prediction of Johan Kriek after Becker had beaten him in the Queen's Club final that this amazing youngster would win Wimbledon, it was still almost impossible to believe it had happened. Yet exactly a year after he left Wimbledon in a wheelchair, nursing torn ankle ligaments, which needed an operation, there was this strapping young man standing centre stage on the Centre Court holding aloft the gleaming golden trophy which all the greats of the past have held before him.

As Curren came forward to a sympathetic runners-up reception, Becker, whose attitude during the past fortnight has not always won universal approval, sportingly applauded his opponent. He might also have reflected how his opponent's game had never struck the right note. Curren, who admitted later that he had played an 'horrific' game, to be broken the first time he served, which was enough to cost him the opening set, never went even remotely close to recapturing the explosive serving form which had knocked out former champions John McEnroe and Jimmy Connors in previous rounds.

Becker described the gusty Centre Court as being like Paris (clay) in the middle and Wimbledon on the sides. Both players faced problems in dealing with fierce serves which kept low. But Curren's difficulties were two-fold. His own serve lacked its expected intensity, with his first-serving ratio never advancing beyond 50 per cent, while he was always under pressure from Becker's rousing deliveries, even though in the end the ultimate ace count was marginal, 21–19. Becker, who climaxed the opening set with his fourth ace, had dropped only six points on his own serve to that stage and to add to Curren's problems, the former South African, who is now an American, started foot-faulting – always a sign of tension creeping in.

Yet with Becker not really in his most explosive form, and the match still waiting for a major ignition, one still felt that if Curren could overcome the tentativeness which was so often holding him back on overheads and first volleys he might take control. In retrospect it might only have meant Becker lifting his own game that much sooner, for although Curren retrieved three break points from 0–40 at 3–3 and went on to level the match from 0–3 in a 7–4 tie-break, with two superbly directed backhand passes, it was resilience in the face of adversity which transformed the match.

After his break for 4–3, Curren was invariably struggling to stay with an increasingly urgent, fist-clenching opponent and there were almost moments of tension between them as the contest moved towards its final, most compelling session. With Curren a set point down when serving at 4–5, Becker delayed the crucial delivery by turning away. Curren, after slamming an unstoppable serve past his opponent to make it deuce, firmly demonstrated his displeasure. Early in the fourth set, too, after Becker had moved ahead by clinching the second of the tie-breaks 7–3 on his eighth set point, there was more irritation when the German's exuberance at breaking in the first game overflowed. There was no lingering malice, however. There was no time for that. Becker, diving and tumbling, kept going wholeheartedly for winners, while eighth-seeded Curren was preoccupied in trying to scheme a way back.

Becker, almost two years the junior of the previous youngest champion, Wilfred Baddeley, in 1891, was in no mood to offer him even a glimmer of a chance. In fact, the pressure remained on Curren despite his growing ratio of aces as he was forced to save more break points in the fifth game. It was far from one of the greatest Wimbledon finals. There were too many startling errors for that. Because of the excitement of watching such a charismatic new prodigy and the historical significance surrounding his success, it is one which will always be remembered. With Curren looking increasingly disconsolate as the game ran out on his chance of breaking back, he double-faulted to go match point down in the ninth game, but Becker drove his backhand into the net.

Serving for the victory which made him the youngest winner of any Grand Slam tournament, two months ahead of Mats Wilander when he won in Paris for the first time in 1982, the crowd gasped as Becker began with a double-fault. As three other seeds, Joakim Nystrom, Tim Mayotte and Anders Jarryd had discovered, Becker shrugs such inconveniences aside as if they had never happened. In next to no time, after his 21st ace, he was holding two more match points at 40–15 and despite one further double-fault to prove that he really is human, another huge service was enough to bring that now familiar victory salute.

As for the future, Curren said: 'He can be No. 1 in the world one day. He is only 17 and he has got so much time – and a lot of room for improvement, especially his volley. He is still going to grow and I am sure he is going to get stronger.' Such a message will no doubt send a chill of apprehension down the backs of others who, on past performances, were seeded at Wimbledon this year while young Becker was overlooked. For the record, Becker became men's singles champion at the age of 17 years, 228 days. At precisely the same time as this piece of history was being made, the junior title was going to Mexico's Leonardo Lavalle. His age – 17 years, 358 days.

21 JUNE 1986

DAN MASKELL'S TOP TEN

Telegraph Sunday Magazine feature

Dan Maskell has been the voice of tennis on television in Britain for more than 30 years. A former professional player, he has attended every Wimbledon Championship since 1924, and has not missed a single day's play since 1929. In more than 60 years of watching and commentating he has seen – and, often, played against – every great player of modern times.

What more acute judge could there be of the qualities it takes to make a great Wimbledon champion? With that in mind, and to celebrate the centenary of the men's singles, we asked Dan Maskell to draw up his list of the top ten men's singles players of all time.

'If you really are talking about the ten greatest male players at Wimbledon you have got to bring in names like William Renshaw, who won the men's singles seven times in the 1880s; Reggie Doherty, who won four times in the 1890s; and his brother Laurie who won five times in the 1900s. And Anthony Wilding, the great New Zealander who won four times between 1910 and 1913. But it seems to me that the known and modern period of tennis comes after the First World War. So I have drawn my ten from them.'

Rod Laver, Champion in 1961, 1962, 1968 and 1969 – 'The pioneering left-hander who achieved the unique distinction of twice winning a "Grand Slam" of the world's four major tennis titles, as an amateur in 1962 and as a professional in 1969. A beautiful mover with a brilliant match temperament.'

Björn Borg, Champion five times consecutively between 1976 and 1980 – 'A great player who never really volleyed. He was basically a baseline, hard-court player, and to win on grass at Wimbledon so often was a magnificent achievement. His two-handed backhand was a colossal stroke. A wonderful ice-cool temperament. He has left his mark on world tennis.'

Bill Tilden, Champion in 1920, 1921 and 1930 – 'A virtuoso, with a cannonball serve and about five different styles. His play generally was quite fantastic, even though he was not a great natural volleyer. An enormous man with a majestic presence on the court.'

Fred Perry, Champion in 1934, 1935 and 1936 – 'One of the fittest men who ever played tennis. The gods gave him a beautiful figure for the game. They also gave him a very sensitive hand. His forehand drive is legendary. A highly competitive man, he took tremendous pride in his performance and had a great love of playing for his country.'

Don Budge, Champion in 1937 and 1938 – 'The first man ever to win the "Grand Slam" of men's singles championships around the world – in 1938 – he had perhaps the world's most devastating backhand in terms of power. He was very strong, a beautiful server, wonderful volleyer and a true all-court player. A great American patriot who also had enormous self-confidence.'

John McEnroe, Champion in 1981, 1983 and 1984 – 'With astonishing reflexes and speed at the net, he has the full equipment of shots for grass and is one of the best volleyers from below the height of the net that I have seen. The most extraordinary thing about him is that after one of his temperamental bouts, he can come back and play a point as though nothing has happened. That is very rare.'

Henri Cochet, Champion in 1927 and 1929 – 'A lovely forehand and touch, with a sharp, short backhand and a marvellous low volley. Never a notable server, he still made it into a weapon by following it in. At his best he was incredibly fast at the net, and a naturally early taker of the ball.'

René Lacoste, Champion of 1925 and 1928 – 'A great tactician who led the French Davis Cup teams so successfully. He had relentless backhand accuracy and a supreme control of length, so that players found it extremely difficult to come in to the net against him. He was very much a player's player.'

Jean Borotra, Champion in 1924 and 1926 – 'The great entertainer, who was also one of the greatest volleyers and overhead players of all time. But his technique was as far removed from the textbooks as you could find, with a jabbed backhand and a forehand of no aesthetic beauty. He always played with a smile on his face, and his famous berets were always in evidence.'

John Newcombe, Champion in 1967, 1970 and 1971 — 'The "jet-age tennis player" because he could play all over the world — Australia one day, San Francisco the next, New York the next, indoors or outdoors, under floodlights, on any surface and at any time. He was tough enough to do it. There were no frills about his stroke play. A great sportsman.'

'Naming just ten means that I have to leave out Lew Hoad (champion in 1956 and 1957), and I find that impossible. He could play such devastating tennis that he could replace anyone on the list: so I have to make him 11th man.'

23 JUNE 1986

WHAT A MONOTONOUS GAME, SAID THE FIRST CHAMPION

Lance Tingay

It is one of the ironies of lawn tennis and the Wimbledon Championships in particular that a fervent cricketer, who was far from enthusiastic about a new-fangled game, should be uniquely famous as the first champion. He was Spencer W. Gore and he became the first winner on Thursday, 19 July 1877, when, having won the four earlier rounds, he took the final 6–1, 6–2, 6–4 against William Marshall. The match should have been played on the preceding Monday, but the day was wet. Despite the postponement, 200 spectators paid a shilling (5p) each to see the climax of the first real tournament of a sport in its cradle years.

The meeting had begun at the All-England Croquet and Lawn Tennis Club in Worple Road, Wimbledon, on Monday, 9 July, and with an entry of 22 for the only event, the men's singles, could easily have finished on the Saturday. But from the start the organisers decreed a break for the Eton and Harrow cricket match at Lord's, then an absolute must for the sporting social world. The worthy Gore must have heartily approved. He was 27, had been the Harrow cricket captain ten years before, and remained a keen cricketer all his days until his death in 1906 at 56.

He was a Wimbledon resident and by profession a surveyor and land agent. His brother was Bishop Gore of Birmingham. He translated his rackets prowess (another sport at which he represented Harrow) to the lawn tennis court, and was so effective that his sportsmanship was questioned. His style was to come up to the net and volley. He could even reach over the net to make his shots more effective, so much so that they had to bring in a rule banning this tactic. The following year, however, when Gore sportingly defended his title, a tea planter, Frank Hadow, who was on leave from Ceylon, shrewdly frustrated him by lobbing.

I say 'sportingly defended' because Gore was by no means keen on a game at which he had excelled. He was to write 'that anybody who has really played well at cricket ... will ever seriously give his attention to lawn tennis ... is extremely doubtful; for in all probability the monotony of the game as compared with others would choke him off before he had time to excel at it'. So Gore's name did not afterwards appear in the annals of lawn tennis. None the less there has been no champion more sure of immortality with the sport. He was the first of his kind.

As for the first woman champion, she did not appear until Wimbledon had survived its cradle years and became a healthy infant. Not until 1884 was the chauvinistic curtain lifted to allow women to compete, albeit only when the men's singles had been completed. Maud Watson was the first of a distinguished line. She set a curious record, not only being the first champion but by beating her own sister in the title match. For years the records had it that in 1884 Miss M. Watson beat Miss Watson 6–8, 6–3, 6–3. Only in more modern times did anyone seek to find who the vague 'Miss Watson' was. She was Lilian, elder sister of the 20-year-old Maud, and as was the convention in those days, universally described as such, the distinction of identifying initials being reserved for the lesser sisters.

They were the daughters of the rector of Berkswell, near Coventry. They were born in Harrow where their father had been a mathematics master at the school – he may well have taught Spencer Gore. Maud competed at Wimbledon three times in all, winning for the second time in 1885, but losing in the challenge round in 1886 to Blanche Bingley, later Mrs George Hillyard and a multiple champion.

23 JUNE 1986

THE BACHELOR WHO FATHERED KILLER SERVING

Lance Tingay

Lawn tennis began on the vicarage lawns of England and the young men and young ladies enjoyed themselves by scooping the ball to each other over the net. When the first Championship was staged at Wimbledon in 1877 the competitors echoed that gentle style. Both men and women served underarm, only the more energetic males hitting the ball at shoulder height. Few took the risk of hitting the ball early, and even the unorthodox Spencer Gore, the first winner, hit it at no great pace.

The champion of 1879 and 1880 not only learned on the vicarage lawn. He himself was a vicar, of Burneston in the North Riding of Yorkshire. The Rev. John Hartley's gentle retrieving craft, learned as a real tennis player at Oxford, outlasted all opposition. Until, that is, 1881, when Hartley was trounced 6–0, 6–1, 6–1 in the challenge round by a 20-year-old from Cheltenham, William Renshaw.

William triumphed on the shattering merits of a fast overhead service, accurate volleying and pace generated by taking an early ball. He was the elder of twins, Ernest was less robust, but they were held to be as good as each other. No one would claim that the Renshaws would be able to hold a candle to the modern play. Their rackets, the ball and the relatively poor courts of their time would clearly make it impossible. Yet it was modern lawn tennis they played. It was their style and technique that became the standard. If ever two men should be made posthumous honorary members of the Association of Tennis Professionals it is William and Ernest Renshaw. William won the Wimbledon singles seven times. No one has done as much. As a doubles pair they were almost invincible and, indeed, put the Americans in their place. In 1884 two Boston brothers, C.M. and J.S. Clark, were chosen as a representative US pair and came to England to challenge the best of the British. In two challenge matches at the All-England Club, the Americans won only one out of seven sets.

The Renshaws would have eschewed the financial side of ATP, inheriting wealth from their father. They were the first charismatic champions. Crowds surged to watch them, so much so that the London and South Western Railway built a platform beside the club in Worple Road, running special trains for the tournament. Their generosity and sportsmanship was a byword. N. Lane Jackson, a famous figure in the football world and a lawn tennis referee, recorded how, when running a provincial tournament, he was beset by a financial crisis. Ernest learned about it when Jackson announced his imminent departure for London. He said: 'Oh, don't go for that! I'll let you have £600 with pleasure.' The sequel almost has a sting in it. When Jackson repaid the loan, which in those days would have bought a high-quality house, Ernest remarked that it was the first time he had ever been repaid.

The fame of the Renshaws rests not now on their wealth (in money terms some ATP members might not be impressed) but in their creative talent. When they came into the game, learning on an indoor asphalt court in Cheltenham, they took part in a pastime; after a year or two they had turned it into a sport.

Neither twin had a long life. Ernest died in 1899 when he was 38, William in 1904 when 43. Neither, as far as it is known, was married. William won five doubles titles with his seven singles at Wimbledon. Ernest took one singles with his five doubles. For a decade they were without a peer, and the standard they set has been the bedrock ever since.

24 JUNE 1986
SWEET TREAT

Wimbledon's traditional strawberries and cream dish has been reduced in price this year as a 'special treat at the 100th Championships'. After many complaints, the treat now costs £1 compared with £1.35 in the first week and £1.50 in the second week of last year.

7 JULY 1986
CROWN WHICH MEANS SO MUCH TO MARTINA
John Parsons

Before Martina Navratilova stepped on to the Centre Court on Saturday to repel Hana Mandlikova's latest abortive challenge, her coach, Mike Estep, told referee Alan Mills that Martina would win – from 2–5 in the first set. Estep, who has helped to coax and build steel into Miss Navratilova's approach, as much as her tennis, no doubt sensed that the younger player would make a typical whirlwind start, blow herself out and then despite brave flurries, would be given another big-match lesson. So it was. Miss Navratilova won the women's title 7–6, 6–3 in 72 minutes to carve her name even more proudly and deeply into tennis history in the tournament which means more to her than any other.

Later, Miss Navratilova was constantly reminded that she had equalled Suzanne Lenglen's record of five consecutive singles titles, had dropped only two sets (both to Chris Lloyd) in 34 unbeaten singles since the semi-final of

1981, and was only two short of surpassing the record of eight singles wins by Helen Wills Moody. She said: 'It's never hard to get up for Wimbledon. Other tournaments are not so meaningful as they once were. When you start and you get to the semi-final of, say, the Poldark Open, it's thrilling … you think it's the big league. But you can win 150 of those tournaments and if you haven't won Wimbledon, you haven't really won. I've never felt scared by Wimbledon – only excitement. I can't wait to be back. Every year when I toast the New Year I say, "Here's to Wimbledon". It's so special; I feel part of it. I feel I belong here, I feel the sense of history; I feel that as long as the earth is in one piece there will always be Wimbledon.'

It was perhaps hardly surprising, therefore, that even when Miss Mandlikova was drifting glorious backhand passing winners, or stepping in smartly to volley effectively, that far from looking irritated or upset, the world No. 1 had a warming glow about her as if she knew the pattern would change. Fitting, too, in the year of 100 Championships, Miss Navratilova – possibly an even greater player than the legendary Lenglen – should be presented with the trophy which is so familiar to her by Kitty Godfree, 90, Wimbledon's oldest living champion. Miss Godfree was beaten by Mlle Lenglen in the 1923 final before winning the first of her two titles the following year.

There were other factors, apart from Miss Navratilova's supreme confidence and inspiration for the occasion, which conspired against Miss Mandlikova, who was hoping to complete her own collection of all four Grand Slam titles. Drizzle in the opening few games made the court slippery and at 5–2, because she had already lost her footing a couple of times, Miss Mandlikova decided to change her shoes. It had a disastrous effect on her concentration and then her conviction. The dampness also made the balls heavier and as the lightweight Miss Mandlikova, who has possibly shed too much weight, said later: 'I think that helped her instead of me. The balls became very heavy and I felt she had the power to hit the ball harder than me.'

7 JULY 1986

BECKER POWER WRECKS LENDL IN THREE SETS

John Parsons

Boris Becker brought the 100th Wimbledon Championships to a resounding climax yesterday by the spectacularly impressive fashion in which he retained his title. On the Centre Court, which seems to inspire this wonderfully gifted teenager to greater heights every time he steps foot on its cherished turf, Becker, 18, still the youngest champion, took two hours two minutes to beat Ivan Lendl, the world champion, 6–4, 6–3, 7–5.

At 0–3 in the third set and even more so at 4–5, 0–40, when Lendl was holding three points to carry a high-powered and fascinating rather than classic final at least into a fourth set, Becker seemed suddenly to be under critical pressure. Yet, as so often this year, when rewriting the record books – not least by becoming the first unseeded champion – Becker demonstrated that this is the time when, almost instinctively, he becomes most dangerous. On the first of those set points, the West German teenager pounded down one of his 150mph serves and moved in serenely to put away the perfect backhand volley. On the second, the performance was repeated.

By then, as he said later, he could tell from Lendl's face that the Czechoslovak did not know what to do about trying to pass him on the big points. He went for a crunching backhand return, but once more Becker's brilliant net play was too much. During this set Becker's supply of aces, and many other ruthless service winners, which had been so significant in curbing Lendl's challenge earlier on, had expired. At that moment, however, the flow resumed. An ace, Becker's 14th and last of the afternoon, gave him game point. His equally huge service winner that followed made it 5–5. It was an incredible way for anyone to save a game at this level let alone in such circumstances.

If Lendl, the reigning French and United States Open champion, did not realise then that after seven Wimbledon attempts he was still going to be denied his first Grand Slam tournament title on grass, the next two games painfully confirmed it for him. At 30–30 in the 11th game Becker ripped a stunning backhand past him from baseline right to the other. Lendl, who had won four of their previous five contests, but never had to face the West German's explosive skills on his ideal surface before, was so bewildered that he then missed an easy forehand volley.

So Becker could serve for the title and even in this game he produced one of those magical acrobatic touches which make him and his tennis so attractive and popular. At 15–30 Lendl hit a fine backhand down the line. Becker dived full length as the ball hit the tape and almost 'died' as it dropped and was still on the floor. Yet amazingly he played a backhand winner into open court. Two points later – appropriately both of them service winners from a man who struck 102 aces during seven matches in the fortnight and dropped only two sets compared with seven last year – Becker was champion again, waving joyfully to his parents, his coach Gunter Bosch and his chain-smoking mentor Ion Tiriac.

In his excitement after being presented with the trophy by Wimbledon's oldest living men's champion, Jean Borotra, 87, Becker let the lid fall to the ground as he was being greeted enthusiastically by the Duchess of Kent. The Duchess, who to the delight of the crowd left the court arm-in-arm with Borotra after he had first kissed her hand, asked Becker if his ambition was to win Wimbledon five times like Björn Borg. 'I said, "See you in three years then",' recounted Becker who, from the moment he had walked out in the first round, said he 'always felt good out there. It seems like my court.'

22 JUNE 1987

THOU CANST NOT BE SERIOUS, VARLET!

Lance Tingay

In an age of ruthless professionalism in tennis which has seen the abandonment of many old values and the introduction of changes like tie-breakers and magic-eye service calls, it seems anachronistic that the scoring system remains untouched. Why not 1–0, 2–0, 3–0 and game instead of all that 15–30, 40–0 and deuce business? And how did this peculiar lexicon come about in the first place?

The short answer is simple. It was borrowed from the parent game of tennis – by which I mean 'real' tennis, played in a courtyard, and already ancient when Henry VIII was the champion of England. But why that way in tennis? Not even Henry VIII knew why. An historian, Jean Gosselin, writing in 1579, declared that the game's origins were lost in antiquity. But there is documentary evidence that it was firmly established in 1435.

It must be remembered that real tennis goes back to the Middle Ages and to France, where 'jeu de paume', the terms still used, was a favourite sport among courtiers. Picture the rectangular stone courtyard with a clock face at one end. After each rally the marker (a necessary adjunct to the old game) was moved one quarter – to the quarter-past position, then half-past, then quarter-to, and on up to the hour. Thus 15, 30, 45. Yes, 45. Until the mid-18th century it *was* 45, not 40. Then, as happens in speech, it became contracted.

Another explanation also rests in the wide use in the Middle Ages of the sexagesimal system, with 60, not 100, as the natural base. The French played tennis not just for 'love' (a term that has for long meant nothing) but for crowns and écus, the smaller coin being 15 units or one quarter of the whole. Every rally comprised a bet. So the debt progressed, 15, 30 and so on to the larger coin. It was instant calculation.

The word 'service' has a simple explanation. Henry VIII and other such dignitaries had a servant put the ball in play. That was the 'service' provided. What of the word 'tennis' itself? The French used to cry 'tenez' (for 'ready') at the start of play. 'Tenez' to 'tennis' was a simple Anglicisation. And 'deuce'? It means two more points are needed to win. In French they cried 'à deux'. There you have it.

A century from now these explanations will doubtless still be sought by new generations of tennis aficionados. And by then it will be necessary to explain to them other curiosities lost in the mists of time – like the origination of 'code violation', and who was it said: 'You cannot be serious, man.'

6 JULY 1987

GLEEFUL CASH DESTROYS LENDL'S BIG DREAM

John Parsons

Pat Cash became the first Australian since 1971 to become Wimbledon champion, with a masterly serve-and-volley display which even illustrious predecessors, such as Rod Laver, Lew Hoad and John Newcombe, would have found difficult to surpass. Then, having maintained almost relentless, faultless pressure for the 7–6, 6–2, 7–5 victory which left Ivan Lendl a bemused and frustrated runner-up for the second successive year, Cash, whose career was almost wrecked by back injuries two years ago, conquered a second daunting challenge.

Ignoring the customary tradition and protocol of waiting patiently by the umpire's chair, while the carpets were rolled out for the Duke and Duchess of Kent to conduct the presentation ceremony, Cash could not contain his desire to 'share victory with the people who have helped me and mean most to me'. Having turned immediately after putting away the forehand volley on his first match point, to throw a ball towards the box where his family, friends and coach were sitting, he decided to join them.

Clambering through the astonished but delighted crowd and finally pluck-
ing up courage to test the strength of the scorebox roof, which was the
only route then open to him, he fell into the arms of, among others, his
father, Patrick, his long-serving coach, Ian Barclay, and the mother of his
baby son, Anne-Britt.

It was a typically extravagant gesture from a young man who many
among his fellow countrymen argued would never be sensible or mature
enough to win major titles. He has answered all such doubts, never shared,
incidentally, by his Davis Cup captain, Neale Fraser, with a perfectionist's
path to the game's greatest prize, which also makes him the only former
Junior Boys' winner at Wimbledon, apart from Björn Borg, to go on to win
the senior title. After his second-round defeat of fellow Australian Paul
McNamee, Cash said he did not know how well he was playing. On a Centre
Court so hot that even the Royal Box eventually adopted shirt-sleeve order,
he produced grass-court tennis of the highest quality. He conceded only 15
points on his own serve throughout the two-hour 45-minute match, and
went through the second set without dropping even one – a remarkable
feat in a Wimbledon final.

7 JULY 1987

SECRET PILGRIMAGE INSPIRED NAVRATILOVA'S SUCCESS

John Parsons

Martina Navratilova, whose emotional affection for Wimbledon grows
stronger with every visit, made a secret, solitary pilgrimage to the Centre
Court on the eve of this year's Championships, in search of the inspiration
to defend her title. The world champion certainly found what she was
looking for. She told the story when, for the eighth time since 1978 and the
sixth year in succession, she was one of the guests of honour at the Champions' Dinner at the Savoy on Sunday night.

Sharing the excitement and joy of her outstanding triumph with this
year's other title winners, champions from the past, leading officials of lawn
tennis around the world and 'the friends who have kept faith with me
during a long year', Miss Navratilova said: 'When I arrived back at the house
[within walking distance of the All-England Club] after losing in the final at
Eastbourne, there was a moment when I wondered if I should keep playing

any more. I decided to take a walk to think things out. I went down to the club and into the Centre Court. The canopy was up so I went in beneath it and just sat there trying to figure out if I wanted to be there again.

'After a few minutes I knew there was nothing I wanted more than to be there again. I plucked a tiny piece of grass out of the court, taking care to make sure the groundsman would not notice. Then I also looked in on Court No. 1, plucked a rose from Mrs Fraser's garden [Mrs Fraser looks after the dressing-room for the leading women players] and, as I walked back, picked up a nicely shaped piece of rock from one of the car parks. The rose didn't last very long; the grass is now pretty yellow, like the Centre Court, but the rock will stay in my racket cover for ever, as a permanent reminder of winning this tournament.'

Miss Navratilova's evocative story is further evidence of the unique atmosphere which captivates even the most stern-minded professional and helps maintain Wimbledon's undisputed reputation as the tournament which means most to the players. She also revealed how Neale Fraser, 53, Wimbledon champion in 1960 when Australian men's tennis ruled the world, had not only helped Pat Cash towards his men's singles victory, but also had a hand in her own win. It was Fraser, like herself a left-hander, renowned for his direct serve-and-volley game, to whom she turned to help her perfect those sharply spun serves, swinging away from the Steffi Graf backhand, which proved so decisive in the final. Miss Navratilova had recalled the pictures she had seen of the Fraser serve when she was a young schoolgirl in Prague, in the only tennis book which then seemed to be available in Czechoslovakia.

15 APRIL 1988

GOLDEN GIRL

Karol Short, the 'Golden Goddess' of tennis, who was banned from wearing gold lamé underpants at Wimbledon 30 years ago, has died of cancer in South Miami, Florida. She was 53. A former Wimbledon semi-finalist, she was once ranked fifth in the world. In 1958, after she wore the gold lamé underpants in the French Open, Wimbledon officials banned her from the tournament, because the panties 'might put her opponent off'. She was reinstated when she agreed to cover them with white lace.

COOKING: FEAST OF SPORT

Thane Prince serves for tennis and other summer occasions

Socially, the English summer centres on sporting events. Crowds of spectators flock to Henley, Ascot, Lord's and, of course, Wimbledon. And for many, the fun is as much to do with the eats as with the sports. Unlike a winter picnic, these summer alfresco meals should be delicate and elegant, served with sparkling wines and eaten from china plates. It's not unusual to spot crystal glasses and even floral centrepieces among the feasts spread behind the parked cars.

My tennis lunch has an exotic flavour. Try starting with falafel. These highly seasoned Middle Eastern meat balls are excellent for nibbling with drinks to whet the appetite; alternatively, an instant, peppery, smoked mackerel pâté served with high-baked water biscuits.

Oriental Chicken Salad combines different tastes and textures for an eye-catching one-dish meal. Soy sauce, sesame seeds, stem ginger and water-chestnuts give an Eastern flavour to chunks of cold chicken and Chinese noodles, with beansprouts, scallions and red pepper added for colour and crunch. Leave the chicken to soak up the dressing overnight and add the prepared salad vegetables just before you set off.

Wimbledon wouldn't be Wimbledon without strawberries, though, caught as they are between the end of the Continental crop and the start of the English one, they can often be scarce and costly now. Make a frangipane and strawberry tart as a delicious way of stretching your strawberries. As this tart really needs no further gilding, it also solves that cream-on-a-picnic dilemma.

French bread and cheese plus cold wine, Centre Court seats and sunshine: you are all set for the perfect day.

FALAFEL

225gm/8oz dried chick peas soaked in 2pt water for 24hr
1 medium bunch spring onions
3 cloves of garlic
Large handful parsley
Rind and juice of medium lemon
1 tsp salt
1½ tsp ground cumin

1½ tsp ground coriander
1 tsp bicarbonate of soda
Black and cayenne pepper to taste

Place the chick peas in a food processor with the bicarbonate and the salt. Process to break up and add the roughly chopped onions and the garlic. Continue to process until you have a mixture resembling breadcrumbs.

Add the parsley and chop into the mixture, then add all the other ingredients and process briefly.

You do not want a smooth paste; rather, a crumbly mixture. Form this into balls the size of walnuts and fry them in about 1in of oil over a medium heat for about 2min each side. Drain and serve cold.

PEPPERY MACKEREL PÂTÉ

175gm/6oz peppered smoked mackerel fillets
75gm/3oz cream cheese
1–2 tbsp lemon juice

Blend skinned fish and cream cheese in food processor until fairly smooth. Add lemon juice to taste and place in a bowl in the refrigerator overnight for the flavour to develop.

ORIENTAL CHICKEN SALAD

4 boneless skinned chicken breasts
175gm/6oz beansprouts
75gm/3oz Chinese thread noodles or similar pasta
1 medium bunch spring onions
1 medium red pepper
1 small tin water-chestnuts, drained
3 pieces stem ginger (in syrup)
1½ tbsp sesame seeds
Dressing
1½ tbsp soy sauce
1 tbsp dry sherry
2 tbsp syrup from stem ginger
1 tbsp wine vinegar

5 tbsp peanut or sunflower oil
Pepper to taste

Poach the chicken in water with bay leaf, slice of onion, carrot and a stick of celery for 15-20min until cooked, then allow to cool in the liquid for about 30min.

Cut chicken into 1in cubes and place in a large dish with the water-chestnuts and ginger, both slicked into fine matchsticks. Sprinkle with the sesame seeds. Having mixed the dressing ingredients well, pour one-third of the dressing, toss and leave in the fridge overnight.

Finely slice the red pepper into strips 3in by $^1/_8$in, cut the onions into 3in strips and slice finely; wash the beansprouts well. Cook the noodles according to the instructions on the packet, drain and reserve.

Before serving, mix all the ingredients together with the reserved dressing.

STRAWBERRY AND ALMOND TART

750gm/1½lb strawberries
100gm/3½oz blanched almonds
100gm/3½oz butter
100gm/3½oz caster sugar
1 tbsp plain flour
1 egg, plus 1 egg yolk
1 tbsp almond liqueur (opt)
9in flan dish lined with sweet shortcrust pastry
To glaze
4 tbsp apple or redcurrant jelly

Place the almonds in a food processor and process until finely ground; add the remaining ingredients except for the strawberries and jelly; mix well.

Pour this frangipane into the prepared pastry shell and bake for 20–25min in pre-heated oven 350°F/180°C/gas 4 until golden brown. Remove from the oven and allow to cool.

Carefully place the cleaned, hulled strawberries, pointed end up, in circles on the tart starting at the outside and continuing until the pie is covered.

Thin the apple jelly with 1 tablespoon of water and boil 1min then allow to cool and brush the glaze over the berries. The basic tart may be baked the day before but should not be filled with the strawberries or glazed until the day it is to be eaten.

DRINKING: GAME SET

Roger Voss packs the picnic basket

It's thirsty work, watching tennis. During Wimbledon fortnight we will buy around 12,000 bottles of Champagne from the marquees, and almost certainly bring in even more than that in picnic hampers. And the wine that goes in those hampers – whether you are going to Wimbledon or to any other of the summer's great sporting or social events – is what often makes the difference between a good picnic and a memorable one.

Sparkling wine – with Champagne at the top of the list – is the most pleasurable way of setting the scene while the hamper is being unpacked. Two alternatives to Champagne are definitely worth considering. One is a Crémant de Loire, from Marcel Neau, made in Saumur, but following stricter rules than sparkling Saumur. This wine is fragrant, light and creamy, with what tastes like a touch of chardonnay to give it a hint of richness (Majestic Wine Warehouses, £4.99). The other is Raimat Chardonnay from Catalonia, a well-balanced, highly refreshing wine, heavier than the Loire wine, but also very elegant (Victoria Wine Company, £5.49).

An alternative aperitif, ideal for summer drinking, would be white port. Drink it chilled, with a twist of lemon, topped up with soda or tonic. Good examples are Taylors Chip Dry (Davisons, £6.99) and the slightly sweeter Cockburns Light White (Tesco's larger stores, £5.99).

When the picnic gets going, I find that still wines to go with cold meats would be the Vernaccia di San Gimignano 1987 of San Quirico. From the hill-town of San Gimignano in Tuscany, it has rich, earthy flavours, balanced by a lime-juice freshness (Sainsbury, £3.55). An alternative would be a light red, which can then be drunk cooled. I have just tasted the Listel Rubis Rouge, which comes from France's largest vineyard, in the south near Montpellier. This has a touch of strawberry ripeness balanced by a hint of tannin – highly refreshing (Thos Peatling, £3.15).

And when it comes to strawberry time, the only sparkling wine to have is Asti spumante. It needs to be fresh and well chilled, but at its best it has a touch of honeyed sweetness balanced by some acidity. A good example is the St Michael Asti Spumante, light and fresh and utterly delicious on a warm day (Marks & Spencer, £3.99).

And finally, a reminder – don't forget the corkscrew.

29 JUNE 1988

LONDON PROPERTY: NO ONE HERE FOR TENNIS!

David Hoppit

As a place in which to live for 351 days of the year the village of Wimbledon has few equals; but when the cheers of the faithful fans ring in their ears many residents feel a compelling urge to be somewhere else. Of those who do stay a few of the more enterprising profit from the invasion by selling strawberries on the lawn, or parking tickets for their coveted drive: the going rate of a parking place is at least £10 a day – 'for a good charity'. A house within a drop shot of the tennis courts is coveted, and some even have a gate directly on to the grounds. Some flats have a view of the outer courts.

However, there is much more to Wimbledon than tennis. There is the 1,200-acre common, established by Act of Parliament in 1871; it has 16 miles of bridleway, golf courses, football pitches, ponds for sailing boats and a million trees. As a place for kite-flying, the common is rivalled in London only by Hampstead Heath; house prices fly almost as high, as do rents, especially during 'the fortnight'.

Even before tennis put the village on the map, the building of the railway altered the image of the area. It went from a backwater to a desirable residential area in a matter of a few years. Wimbledon is a mere nine miles from the West End, and just 11 minutes by train from Waterloo. It is hard to imagine somewhere with 70 recorded species of birds being so close to our capital.

Agents, like residents, seem to stay around for a long time. Ms Renatta Belchamber started her business, Townchoice, about 15 years ago; Hamptons are also well established. Andrew Lever, at Hamptons' office, explained that property up to £300,000 has shown a 15 to 20 per cent increase in value since last autumn. On the rental side agents are finding that a furnished house costing about £450,000 to buy can command a weekly rent of between £700 and £800.

5 JULY 1988

EDBERG REVERSES ROLES ON DISPIRITED BECKER

John Parsons

Stefan Edberg, one of the least likely lads when the tournament began, emerged handsomely as Wimbledon champion yesterday when he suddenly and comprehensively outplayed Boris Becker, the former champion. Almost 23 hours after he began the much-delayed and twice-interrupted final, Edberg's tennis, which is quite the reverse of his droll nature, soared to a fresh peak from the start of the second-set tie-break to an astonishing 4–6, 7–6, 6–4, 6–2 triumph.

So, when it seemed as if the rain would never move away and Wimbledon 1988 might never end, it was the sweetest possible revenge for Edberg, the first Swedish winner since Björn Borg's record five-year reign ended in 1980. Not only had Becker beaten him with more than a hint of gamesmanship in the Stella Artois final at Queen's Club three weeks ago, but also in the WCT Finals in Dallas in April.

Beyond that, Becker, never before beaten on the Centre Court, was on record as saying he always felt he would have a mental mastery over the Swede who had so frequently double-faulted against him at crucial moments in their matches. 'It was the other way round today,' said Edberg, who could surely have been forgiven a wry thought, if not a smile, when Becker lost the crucial opening game of the fourth set on his seventh double-fault and a cry of 'Bye bye, Boris' came from the crowd.

Becker looked slightly the better all-round player when this first men's singles final to be spread over two days eventually resumed at 1.04p.m. yesterday, slightly more than two hours late. He continued the recovery he had made from 0–3 and 2–3 on Sunday night by making it 5–3, while Edberg, who was openly urging himself to 'concentrate', seemed all at sea with his service toss. There was a further one-hour 40-minute interruption before Becker was able to serve out of a three-part opening set of 40 minutes' playing time, within a 20-hour 28-minute time span.

After fighting his way out of trouble caused by two double-faults in the second game of the second set, Becker looked poised for another significant breakthrough when Edberg double-faulted to 30–40. The 1985 and 1986 champion, however, whose defeat robbed West Germany of a spectacular victory to set alongside Steffi Graf's singles and doubles triumphs, misread the spin on Edberg's next serve and once this chance was lost he found himself increasingly under pressure. Becker claimed that had he taken that break point the match would have been over. Winning the second set 7–2 in the tie-break was the key for Edberg, 22. By the end of the third set he could see that Becker, who collected a caution for racket abuse, was becoming irritable and disillusioned. That lifted his confidence even more.

More than once, including the extraordinary match point, Becker went for what looked more like an intimidating rather than common-sense point. Edberg, who an hour after making his Centre Court lap of honour with the gleaming golden trophy was still saying 'it's just hard to believe I've won it; it hasn't sunk in yet', was certainly surprised by the way he won the Championship point. He mistimed a shot which flew off the frame of his racket. Becker, with all the time in the world, slammed a backhand into the net. 'Boris only had to play it back into court but instead of trying to play the ball he went to hit it into my body,' said the new champion. 'It was a stupid thing to do. He didn't know what to do in the end. I didn't give him a chance.'

16 JANUARY 1989

LETTER TO THE SPORTS EDITOR

KEEP RIGHT ON TOUTING

Sir,

Those people who are trying to reduce the profits of Wimbledon tennis ticket touts 'in order to bring more profit to the sport' are making a big mistake. The touts do a great service to those lovers of the game who have been unlucky in the draw and are unable to stand in a long queue for hours. If people wish to spend money on such tickets, knowing the original price of the ticket, instead of on video recorders and things like that, of what concern is this to the Wimbledon authorities?

Many people are selling properties at prices and profits well above the original or even real value of the property. Does anyone denounce them for taking these profits? Why should the touts be hounded for making a profit?

Incidentally, those fortunate enough to get a ticket from a tout are just as likely to spend money in the museum, refreshment areas and shops as those who queue to get in. I have depended on touts at Wimbledon for many years and I am grateful to them and hope they will be left to continue in peace.

Patricia Barnard
Saffron Walden, Essex

LETTER TO THE SPORTS EDITOR

WIMBLEDON SINGLES

Sir,

I have received from the All-England Lawn Tennis Club one ticket application form in response to my request for one form for each member of my family. Also enclosed was a letter saying that only one application per household or company address will be accepted to increase the chances of success for all genuine applications. I have been going to Wimbledon for 30 years and have taken my children every year since they were so small that they had to be lifted over the turnstile. The youngest is now 15. Can somebody please tell me what is a 'genuine applicant'?

(Mrs) Marion Heath
London SW19

I SAY! MY 65TH WIMBLEDON

SUNDAY TELEGRAPH 7-DAYS MAGAZINE

Sixteen times British professional champion, Dan Maskell hasn't missed a day at Wimbledon since 1929. Russell Davies pays fond tribute to the definitive voice of tennis commentary.

No prizes this year for the TV critic who mocks Dan Maskell's perennial Wimbledon cry of 'Ooh I say!' It's an old joke, for one thing and, for another, it overlooks the notable fact that Dan Maskell retains his capacity to be surprised by tennis. There cannot be a sporting broadcaster anywhere who knows better than Maskell what shot ought to come next. He has seen all the players, analysed every conceivable shape of rally, yet a winning stroke from an unpromising position still brings him the tribute of astonishment. It says a lot for the game, and the resourcefulness of its players, that this is possible. 'Truly remarkable!', as another of Mr Maskell's catchphrases has it.

Eighty-one this year, Maskell has reached that stage in life where the calendar is thronged with impressive anniversaries. It is 40 years, for example, since he started broadcasting from Wimbledon, on radio at first alongside Max Robertson. Going further back, this year sees the 65th anniversary of

Maskell's first visit to Wimbledon to witness a Championship match. Sitting in seat D4 – just in front of the TV commentary position he would occupy in 1951 – he saw the 1924 ladies' final between Kitty McKane (later, and still, the delightful Mrs Godfree) and Helen Wills.

'When I used to play with Helen Wills,' Maskell says, 'I would remind her that I saw her beaten. She never lost another singles match at Wimbledon; she was eight times champion.' We can be sure Maskell saw those wins: he hasn't missed a day's play at the Championships since 1929.

Those were the days of full skirts and the extravagant balletic swoops of Suzanne Lenglen, with whom Dan Maskell played three times in her professional days. 'She was in many ways a natural exhibitionist. It was her theatre, you know. One of her great forehand shots, if she got a half-court ball about waist-high' – he leaps up to demonstrate on one of Wimbledon's sunny grass fringes – 'as she hit it, her body would be parallel to the ground, feet out here. In those days, style – as with cricket and most sports – was very much the thing that attracted attention. The gutsy-gutsy guy with a somewhat agricultural style was always thought to be a poor champion.'

Maskell himself, though conveniently raised in nearby Fulham, was ineligible for amateur Wimbledon, and contented himself with winning the British Professional Championship 16 times. He had taken the self-supporting, professional route from the start, working at Queen's Club as one of 30 ballboys. 'Twenty-seven of those,' he says, 'eventually became teachers of tennis, or squash, or both, all over the world.'

His own appetitie for all the racket-and-ball games was such that various mentors did their best to corral him into their preferred specialism: racquets, for instance, which he still considers 'a glorious game', and real tennis, which he abandoned after showing exceptional promise. 'Great pity, you know,' said the game's leading propagandist at Queen's, 'you've got just the buttocks for it.'

His contract as head pro at Queen's still had a year or so to run when a call from the chairman of the Lawn Tennis Association summoned him to be the first permanent coach to the All-England Club at Wimbledon. He held the teaching post from 1929 right through to the 1950s, when age began to take the topmost edge off his game. ('I always thought it was a good idea if the coach could beat the player,' he explains.)

Among the major triumphs of his coaching regime had been the Davis Cup, regained by Perry, Austin, Hughes and Lee under his guidance; but he derives almost as much satisfaction from the change he wrought in the atmosphere of lawn tennis between amateur and professional. The old Gentlemen/Players distinction had been somewhat sharply drawn: 'You had world champions at Queen's who were not allowed to go into the Members' Room, the Members' Dining Room, the lounge or the bar. If you wanted to have a drink with a Member, you stood outside the bar with him. It was a way of life then, nobody thought they were being hard done by.' Yet the Wimbledon post proved things could be done differently. Even Queen's gradually relaxed its puritanical attention to status and, in 1953, Wimbledon made Maskell an Honorary Life Member.

Two years later he was made training manager to the Lawn Tennis Association, his expertise in teaching by now indispensable. This was not just a matter of long experience on the courts, but of an understanding acquired in the most distressing circumstances of wartime. Maskell put in five years with the RAF at its rehabilitation centre at the Palace Hotel, Torquay. 'It changed my life ... I'd been dealing with fit people all the time, now I was helping chaps who were badly knocked about in every way, burns and bad injuries and so on, motivating them to will themselves to recovery. I learned a great deal about human nature, and a great deal about myself.' On one occasion he was asked to take an exhausted anaesthetist away and make sure he had a relaxing weekend. In their absence the Palace Hotel was bombed and Maskell's deputy killed on duty.

Awarded the OBE for his service, Maskell emerged with one philosophy that proved especially useful in the post-war sporting world: 'The psychiatrist at the Palace Hotel always said to me, "If you want to avoid the psychiatrist's couch, adaptability is the best bet". Adaptability in this world of change.' When Open Tennis came in, therefore – even though Maskell had insisted it would never arrive in his time – he was able to go along with even its less pleasant consequences. 'They became greedy. What perhaps one didn't expect was that the game would be so quickly surrounded by entrepreneurs and agents, people tending to exploit players. And what I do find hard to accept is these chaps who say they're forced to play too much – yet when they have a chance for a break, they're playing an exhibition match, perhaps getting injured when they should be resting. This is absolute hypocrisy.

'But ... the money is there. I'm a man who believes in the power of the market. I'm a Thatcherite in that sense. The market regulates things badly, but better than any other method. As for standards of behaviour, well, we've lost our standards in all walks of life, and sport tends to reflect the state of society. We have suffered in tennis far less than in other sports. I think we have made mistakes. If John McEnroe had been disqualified here that first time when he behaved so badly ... yes, the authorities have been weak.'

But these bad habits are not yet necessarily ingrained in the game. 'The Junior Championship was played here just a few weeks ago, on the hard courts, one of the best I've seen for years. I didn't see any behaviour at all that one could frown at. In fact I saw some quite chivalrous behaviour. I'm not nearly as depressed about the future of the British game as I was a few years ago.'

As the Championships approach, Maskell prepares the elaborate charts and listings that will sustain his commentaries. Colleagues tease him about these; but he remembers the one time when he did neglect to prepare fully, feeling that he knew the order of play and everybody in it. 'I was terribly bad. Within 15 minutes I'd made two or three silly mistakes – I wasn't keyed up.

'I remember Henri Cochet, one of the great French Musketeers, who used to change next to me here at the Club. He'd just come off court, having been badly beaten by an Englishman in an early round, and he was at his locker. I said, "Henri, I can't believe the result, whatever happened?" "Dan," he said, – Maskell spreads his hands in the Gallic gesture of helplessness – "I 'ad no feeling under the heart, I was dead". As a commentator, too – it's rather like playing a match – I have to have that little windy feeling under the heart as I go in. The day I don't get it, that's the day I shall say, "Time to go".' And that's the day we, the viewers, will begin to realise how much we miss the good old 'Ooh I say!'

24 JUNE 1989

A LADY AND A CHAMP

John Parsons

One of Wimbledon's greatest champions will as usual be keeping abreast of events at this year's Championships through television at her home in Carmel, on California's Monterey Peninsula. But this year Helen Wills Moody will be paying particularly careful attention, waiting to discover whether Martina Navratilova can break her record of winning the women's singles title eight times. The record has stood for 51 years. Mrs Roark, as she is now, was intrigued by Miss Navratilova's decision to cancel her participation in all European clay-court tournaments this year to concentrate so firmly on preparing for the grass – and what most would see as her last realistic attempt to annex the record just for herself.

'She's a splendid player and if she can win again on what is such a specialised surface, she'll certainly deserve it,' says the former champion, who was kept in equal suspense a year ago, when Miss Navratilova led by a set and 2–0 in the final. 'It was so exciting, but Steffi is such a powerhouse,' says Mrs Roark, who, whatever happens, will probably never have her record of remorseless consistency and efficiency at Wimbledon surpassed. For while Miss Navratilova's eight titles has spanned 16 years, Helen Wills Moody played at Wimbledon only nine times. Her one defeat in 56 singles matches was at her first attempt in 1924 when, aged 18 and already the United States champion, she was beaten in the final by Britain's Kitty Godfree, after leading by a set and 4–1.

Mrs Roark recalls the handful of losses she suffered, while winning the French title four times in five attempts, the United States women's singles crown seven times in nine years and the Olympic gold medal in 1924, more than her countless victories. 'Defeat sometimes leaves a more lasting impression on you. You think more about them,' she says. 'Tennis is such a hard game to analyse as a player. Against Kitty, for instance, I think I lost my concentration. It was my first time playing on Centre Court and that is a tremendous thrill which many never experience. Kitty probably thinks she started to play better. There was no doubt she rose to the occasion.'

Certainly that is a match Mrs Roark remembers far more clearly than any of her eight titles, five of which were gained without conceding a set and which probably would have been even more but for one year when she had injured her back and another when she was taken into hospital with appendicitis while in Paris. In fact she didn't lose a set in singles at Wimbledon between June 1927, when she took three sets to beat Gwen Sterry in her opening match, until the final in 1933, when another British player, Dorothy Round, who was champion in 1934 and 1937, also took her the full distance.

As Alan Little, the Wimbledon librarian, and Lance Tingay, my predecessor as lawn tennis correspondent of *The Daily Telegraph*, have written in their paperback review of women's champions, published by the Wimbledon Lawn Tennis Museum: 'On the court, Helen Wills Moody was as efficient as a machine, with a depth and pace of drive that was never broken down. She never showed emotion. Her sobriquet was "Poker-faced Helen" and nothing could have been more apt.' They insist she was 'almost, but not quite, as invincible as Suzanne Lenglen, whom she succeeded as queen of lawn tennis' and who she herself says was 'the best player I ever faced'.

Clearly relishing the memory as it unfolded in her mind, Mrs Roark says: 'Those were the days when players really had to run around a lot. It wasn't simply a matter of rushing to the net. Suzanne's game was so well thought-out. She would manoeuvre her opponents, usually with a shot to the far backhand of the court, followed by a drop shot, making them run the furthest distance, until they were worn out. She could also play at the net if she wanted to and put away overheads with the greatest of ease. If she had a weakness at all, it was her stamina, especially in later years when she became so slender.'

Mrs Roark, who also won 21 of her 30 matches in Wightman Cup contests against Britain between 1923 and 1938, accepts that overall tennis standards today are higher. Yet she is equally adamant that the finest players from the past would hold their own with those of today. She would certainly back her ground strokes of 50 years ago against those of today, especially in this generation of double-handed backhands.

'I feel sorry for those who start out with a two-handed backhand,' she says. 'Apart from anything else, they lose four to six inches in reach. I was talking to some youngsters about it the other day telling them they really ought not to play double-handed but the only reply I was given was, "Chrissie [Evert] does it". You can't argue with that.

'I belong to another age when life wasn't so complicated. Nowadays it's a throwaway age,' she sighs. 'You could argue all day whether tennis is as much fun as it used to be. I kept on for so many years because I enjoyed it. Now I think I'd easily be very worried if I thought there were all these dollars at stake. I often ask myself whether I'd have been so happy playing tennis today from the sheer enjoyment point of view.'

Mrs Roark thrived in an age when, instead of flying overnight from Los Angeles to London, it would take five days from Berkeley, where she was born in October 1905, to reach the east coast of the United States by train, after a change in Chicago, and then at least another five days on a boat to Europe. While many of the current players traverse the world with a couple of holdalls and another bag full of rackets, Mrs Roark and her leading contemporaries would fill a wardrobe trunk, with separate sections for evening dresses, as well as tennis wear and shoes. There were parties on board ship every night. 'We danced all the way across the Atlantic, although I never stayed up late and I was thinking about the tennis,' she recalls. The time to relax completely was after matches had been played and won and she still recalls, with obvious pleasure, visits to the theatre in London – 'because it was always so good' – and listening to Maurice Chevalier in Paris.

If Suzanne Lenglen was her greatest opponent, then 'the other Helen', fellow Californian Helen Jacobs, was certainly her most noted rival. Tennis legend abounds with tales about the alleged bitterness between them, although both deny it strenuously. The champion of whom it was said 'she never smiled but nor did she ever frown' certainly enjoyed winning the Pacific South West mixed doubles title against Helen Jacobs in Los Angeles in 1938.

Don Budge, the first man to win the Grand Slam and her partner on that occasion, recalls how when they broke back on Henry Culley's serve after saving three match points 'she threw her arms around me and said, "You're a dear". Everyone always said at the time she hated losing to Helen Jacobs. I'd never seen her show such emotion.'

I suspect that the lady herself, who admits to being 'so envious' when she sees people running around today playing the game which was so much her life, would have loved nothing more than the chance to decide her Wimbledon record with Miss Navratilova on a tennis court, rather than on paper, in the way the passage of time now, perhaps cruelly, demands.

10 JULY 1989

GRAF SHOWS SHE IS STILL WORLD'S BEST

John Parsons

Steffi Graf resumed her now customary parade of world major titles at Wimbledon yesterday after again denying Martina Navratilova the record ninth singles Championship she fought so bravely to achieve. A stunning ace down the centre line, her fifth of the match, on her first match point, completed the West German's 6–2, 6–7, 6–1 victory in one hour 32 minutes – and restored her supremacy following defeat in Paris four weeks ago.

Yet though the outcome, a day later than planned, was the same as last year, when Miss Graf conquered Wimbledon for the first time and ended Miss Navratilova's six-year reign, the world champion was pressed much more vigorously than many had predicted. That did not seem likely early on. For although Miss Navratilova was moving reasonably well and hitting most of her shots more crisply and confidently than in several of her earlier matches, she took only ten points after leading 2–1 in the first set. It was the classic example of the difference between one great player, who many, including Chris Evert, believe has still to reach her best, and another who can no longer guarantee the powerful magic of the past.

Yet there are few more stout-hearted competitors, especially at Wimbledon, than Miss Navratilova, who was starting out on a second century of matches after playing her 100th in the semi-final. She had gone to inordinate lengths to prepare for the occasion, including bypassing Paris and other clay-court tournaments to give herself maximum time to adjust to grass. When the opportunity suddenly came for her to rekindle her dream of annexing the eight-title record she shares with Helen Wills Moody, who won the last of her titles in 1938, her response was fitting. Though Miss Graf, who never moved more than marginally close to the awesome level she reached when a set and 0–2 down last year, clawed her way back from 2–5 to 5–5, in a fascinating second set. But Miss Navratilova levelled the match by sweeping through the tie-break 7–1.

Miss Navratilova deserved the sympathetic but appreciative reception she received. At least, until that final break point eluded her, she had kept running for everything. For most of the second set and particularly in one of the finest tie-breaks she has played at the Championships, Miss Navratilova offered more than a few reminders of why, at her peak, she was for so long the best player in the world. Serving at 5–3 for the second set, Miss Navratilova looked a lonely figure when, having netted a close-in volley to be 15–30, she then saw a backhand cross-court from Miss Graf drift past her and drop on the line. Yet her spirits were lifted again in the tie-break when she played a superb forehand pass from the baseline and, with Miss Graf making a couple of uncharacteristic errors, took it in such handsome style.

Unhappily for the former champion, the superb volleying she so often produced in the second set later deserted her, although, in fairness, that also coincided with a significant rise in the quality of Miss Graf's returns. Whereas all too many of them had been sailing back a couple of feet above the net, easy prey for Miss Navratilova as she bounded in eagerly behind her serve, once they started skimming the tape, so that the volleyer was forced to play the shot from below the height of the net, it was quite a different matter.

7 SEPTEMBER 1989

'DAD'S ARMY' REIGN ON CENTRE COURT

John Parsons

The war clouds were already gathering over Europe when Bobby Riggs and Alice Marble took both Wimbledon titles home to the United States in the summer of 1939. During the seven years which elapsed before the Championships could be staged again, most of the courts remained open and the home of the All-England Club remained a hive of activity – but very little of it had anything to do with lawn tennis.

The famous concourse outside the main entrance, which nowadays crowds throng to watch leading players and Royal Box guests arrive, became the parade ground for soldiers, including the Irish and Welsh Guards, who were billeted on the cricket and golf club grounds across the road. Fields now used as car parks were either ploughed up as arable land or became a farmyard, with pigs, hens, ducks, geese, cows, rabbits and even a donkey. The members' tea room and kitchen became a canteen, the reading room a dormitory with iron bedsteads, the changing-rooms became first aid posts as, at various times over the years, the National Fire Service, Red Cross, Civil Defence, ARP, St John Ambulance, and eventually 'Dad's Army', the Home Guard, were based there. An opening, large enough for stretchers to be pushed through in an emergency, was knocked into the outside wall of the men's main dressing-room, while members' lockers were filled with splints and bandages.

As for the Centre Court itself, by 1945 it resembled a scrapyard. Although it escaped the worst of at least 16 bombings, which left craters and crumbled masonry throughout the grounds, there were several direct hits which destroyed part of the roof and 1,200 seats. Edwin Fuller, the head groundsman, and one assistant did their best to keep most of the courts in reasonable condition and members of the various services based at the club were allowed to use them.

A skeleton staff, including club secretary Major Dudley Larcombe, who died during the war, his secretary Nora Cleather, and Marie Bumpas, who helped out one day a week, kept things ticking over until the club was eventually derequisitioned in time to stage the 1946 Championships. It was an astonishing feat. When Col. Duncan Macaulay, an assistant referee at Wimbledon before the war, became secretary in January 1946, he discovered, among other things, that after no income for six years the club had only £100, not enough to pay salaries let alone stage the Championships. Funds had to be borrowed. Most of the groundstaff had not been demobbed, mowers no longer worked, there was broken glass and girders everywhere and finding staff was almost impossible. Far more essential post-war jobs still had to be done.

There were other, equally fundamental problems. Britain still had rationing of food, clothes and other essentials, including soap, which the players would need after their matches. Everyone rallied round, not least the members who pooled their clothing coupons and organised a collection of old tennis shoes and plimsolls so that the ballboys, then from Dr Barnardo's, could be fitted out and not have to run around the courts bare-footed as had originally been suggested.

At 2p.m. precisely on Monday, 24 June 1946, Don Butler, from Britain, and D. Scharanguivel, from Ceylon, walked out to begin play on Centre Court. Wimbledon was in action again. The strawberries had never tasted better, even if sugar was rationed and real cream was still unobtainable.

CHAPTER SIX
THE 1990s

LETTER TO THE SPORTS EDITOR
FAULT IN INTRODUCING SEATS AT WIMBLEDON

Sir,

There seems to be no end to the knock-on effect of the Hillsborough disaster. The Centre Court standing room terracing at Wimbledon is now being dug up to be replaced by seating because it is considered by the local council to be unsafe. What nonsense. For nearly 70 years this terracing has been occupied by mostly young people who have given the Centre Court a unique atmosphere, without any trouble or danger. The replacement seating will considerably reduce the capacity of the Centre Court and thousands who enjoyed the matches on this court will be unable to afford to go, and will be unable to obtain seats anyway as they will be heavily oversubscribed.

H.J. Baldwin
Caterham, Surrey

CAPTIVATED BY A STROKE OF GENIUS

From Jaroslav Drobny to John McEnroe and Maria Bueno to Monica Seles, 'it is the assertion of individual brilliance that attracts me'. On the eve of Wimbledon, Paul Bailey recalls great players of the past 40 years and outlines the irresistible qualities that make tennis 'the most dramatic and psychologically interesting of all sports'.

I remember coming home from school one summer afternoon and turning on the wireless – this being the early 1950s, few people used the word 'radio' – and hearing a man's voice rising higher and yet higher. Was he one of Dr Dale's patients, having a screaming fit in Jim's consulting room in *Mrs Dale's Diary*, I wondered? Obviously not, for the set was tuned to the Home Service, not the Light programme. Who was this man, and why was he so excited?

I listened, curious to discover what would cause such a state of near-breathlessness, for he seemed to be taking gulps of air in mid-sentence. 'It's deuce once again,' I heard him say. 'And now it's Patty's advantage.' What on earth was 'deuce'? 'And now it's back to deuce.' I was quite mystified.

And this I remained for the rest of the broadcast, although by the end of it had worked out that 'deuce' meant that the players had 40 points each, that an advantage was advantageous, and that 'love' was a daft way of saying someone hadn't scored. The game of tennis sounded very dramatic as described by Max Robertson, the commentator on that occasion. And *sound* dramatic it did to me for years, until I paid my first visit to Wimbledon in 1959.

There were no facilities for playing tennis in the grammar school I attended in south London. In pre-yuppy Battersea, we were encouraged to play football, cricket and — it still amazes me — fives. I hated sports with such intensity that I was prepared to risk a caning or take on extra homework rather than display my ineptitude at the crease or on the pitch. Cricket I especially abhorred, although I delighted in its surrealistic terminology — 'silly mid-on' and 'silly mid-off'. I ducked or closed my eyes whenever the ball was bowled to me, inspiring derisive laughter and mocking applause from the other boys. I made four runs once, and only once, and my achievement so angered the startled bowler that he despatched me immediately afterwards. To be hit for four by me was an insult no self-respecting sportsman could bear.

At the age of 15, when I became captivated by the idea of tennis, it was impossible to give my fascination with the game physical expression. Tennis lessons were costly, and my widowed mother had no money. I had had enough trouble winning a scholarship to see me through drama school, for it was my ambition to be a great Shakespearean actor. (I was learning *Hamlet* on those afternoons when I wandered away from the sports field.)

In the 1950s, tennis was regarded by many as the pastime of the rich and leisured, who had their own courts and held tennis parties at weekends. It seemed to belong in that vanished age between the First and Second World Wars, the age of the Bright Young Things. Despite the fact that England could boast one great champion, Fred Perry, who was famous throughout the world, tennis was considered a game that belonged to Them, not Us. 'Tennis is for cissies' was a phrase I heard often during my schooldays. The question 'Anyone for tennis?' had already entered the language, and could only be asked in a posh voice. 'Anyone for tennis?' suggested drinks trays and cigarettes by Abdulla and buxom girls and rosy-cheeked youths entering through the French windows in a thousand witless light comedies set in grand country houses — the very theatre that Osborne, Arden, Wesker and Kenneth Tynan were about to send packing, they hoped, for ever.

I was a professional actor by the time I finally got to Wimbledon. The year before, I had taken a leading role — of a young gangster from the East

End – in Ann Jellicoe's *The Sport of My Mad Mother* at the Royal Court Theatre. I was, in a modest way, part of that theatrical revolution of the 1950s. Tynan had compared me to Brando, but not flatteringly. I arrived at the All-England Club at about 6a.m. that June morning, and queued for admission until noon, when I was fortunate to obtain a seat in one of the uncovered areas on the Centre Court.

Max Robertson's vivid commentaries had prepared me for the game, but not for the crowd. The fans I had waited in line with were most definitely Us, but the men and women in the covered stands were Them with a cut-glass vengeance. There was scarcely an open-necked shirt to be seen among the regimental and public school ties, and very few of the ladies from the shires were hatless. Wimbledon was, like Ascot, a place to be seen at, and Jennifer was no doubt lurking somewhere in the Members' Enclosure with her diary open, Cartier biro in hand.

The unseen match that converted a hater of sport into a lover of tennis was played between an exiled Czech, Jaroslav Drobny, who gave his country as Egypt, and an ebullient American, Budge Patty. It lasted more than five hours, and contained innumerable deuces and advantages – those same deuces and advantages that were making Max Robertson breathless with excitement when I turned on the wireless in expectation of nothing special. I recalled the atmosphere of tension and high drama Robertson had conveyed to me as I stared at the spectators that first afternoon. Had they been witnesses to that 'titanic struggle'? They looked far too reserved, too remote from the earthy and everyday, to enjoy such a passionate involvement.

In the following years, when my appearances behind the magazine counter in Harrods far outnumbered those on stage or television, I progressed to the covered stands, as a result of persuading my tennis-loathing friends to apply for tickets in the annual ballot. I enjoyed studying the reactions of the crowd almost as much as the tennis – more so, at times, for there were several dullish Wimbledons when the best players were all turning professional and the All-England Club was clinging on to its amateur status, in defiance of reason. Watching the worthy Jan Kodes was no substitute for the pleasure of seeing Pancho Gonzalez and Ken Rosewall at their peak.

Two characterisitics – one engaging, the other less so – marked the crowd then, and now. It was pleasing to hear, and join in, the applause for an artist of the game – like the Mexican Rafael Osuna, tragically killed in a plane crash, or the Italian Pietrangeli, or the two Krishnans, father and son – who stood only the remotest chance of winning the tournament. The gifted underdog still enjoys the crowd's favour and encouragement. But when it honours an indifferent British player with its support – emitting a collective sigh when he or she makes an entirely predictable error – I groan inwardly at the nationalistic nonsense it is expressing.

For tennis is a game in which individual talent is allowed to assert itself, and I care not a jot whether the player is Swedish, American or Indian. Our national inability to produce the likes of Laver and Gonzalez, both of whom came from poor families, may have something to do with the fact that boys and girls from the back streets of Bradford or Newcastle – and London, in my experience – have been denied the opportunity to learn how to play. (Footballers and their male supporters are called 'lads' by managers and commentators on radio and television. Is it possible to imagine English tennis players becoming 'lads'? Hardly.)

It is the assertion of individual brilliance that attracts me, in all its diverse manifestations – the wiliness of Rod Laver, the extravagant theatricality of Gonzalez, the battling determination of the mature Jimmy Connors, and – yes – the irrepressible genius of John McEnroe, on those magical days when he has let his personal demon work for him instead of against him.

In the not-so-egalitarian Wimbledon of the 1960s, when the vicarage-lawn mentality held sway, the arrival of a black player, Arthur Ashe, was a matter of some concern for Them in the covered stands. 'I don't mind Indians,' I heard a picture-hatted woman say to her companion, 'because they're close to us, in a manner of speaking. But a *Negro?* Playing *here?*' Had she said the same thing about Althea Gibson, who won the Championship before pursuing a doomed career as a film actress?

Ashe played what I consider the most lethally beautiful tennis I have seen – in 1970, when Wimbledon was at long last a professional tournament. His opponent that day was Rod Laver, who regarded Ashe with disbelief as one winning shot after another, perfectly placed and timed, reduced him to impotence. Laver shook his head frequently, and even looked up at the sky for explanation. Ashe's speed was such that many sports writers compared him to the panther or the cheetah. His tornado-like display did not continue into the second set, and Laver was to win with ease against a depleted adversary.

The player I remember with most admiration, however, is Ken Rosewall, whose return to Wimbledon was especially welcome. I had seen him at the Royal Albert Hall and other London venues, but he was at his grandest on the Centre Court, where his consummate artistry could be enjoyed in surroundings worthy of it. His overdue arrival at Wimbledon came after the spectators had endured a surfeit of serve-and-volley tennis, Might pitted against Might. The late David Gray, who wrote about the game for the *Guardian,* compared one such grisly encounter to a Havergal Brian night in the concert hall (Brian's symphonies, of which there were many, go on and on, relentlessly).

Rosewall's play made one aware again of the possibilities that are there for an artist to seize on. His serve was really never more than adequate, but what a repertoire of shots he possessed to compensate for this sole weakness, particularly those he executed at the net, with the daintiest of touches. He never argued with a linesman or umpire, kept a handkerchief in his shorts to wipe the sweat from his hands and face, slicked his hair down with Brylcreem, or similar oil, and seldom displayed emotion. His feelings were entirely in his tennis, which was of the heroic kind. Skill, he insinuated, can outwit and outlast brute strength. That skill was wonderful to behold.

Words drew me to tennis, words that described the courage of Drobny and Patty as they battled for long hours. I am glad that I didn't turn the switch to another station on that summer afternoon, for I might have denied myself the pleasure of watching the most dramatic and psychologically interesting of all sports. I would not have seen Laver win match upon match after seeming to lose them, picking up the pieces at a dangerous moment in the third set and wearing down his recently optimistic opponent for a further two. I'd have missed seeing Maria Bueno, noblest of all the women champions, whose face registered dismay and joy and pride, and Doris Hart, who triumphed over polio in childhood and always reminded me of Eleanor Roosevelt.

Had I not listened to Max Robertson, I would probably not be watching the tennis at Wimbledon next week, and therefore not delighting in the exuberant double-handed strokes of the wonderfully gifted Monica Seles, whom Ted Tinling, the designer who died recently, declared the most exciting player he had seen since his beloved Suzanne Lenglen. It was Tinling who designed the memorable outfit for the otherwise unmemorable Gussie Moran, which included a pair of frilly knickers. He was banned from Wimbledon back in the staid 1950s for doing so, in the days when They did not approve. Now, despite the vulgar wealth and bad manners of so many tennis stars, the game, paradoxically, is what matters.

25 JUNE 1990

NAVRATILOVA READY FOR THE KIDS

Billie-Jean King

Wouldn't it be just great if this turned out to be the year of the oldies? Martina Navratilova and Ivan Lendl winning at Wimbledon after the successes of Andres Gomez in Paris and Hale Irwin in the US Open golf. It could happen.

Let me make it abundantly clear. I admit I have a vested interest in that I have spent almost 50 days this year working with Craig Kardon in trying to get Martina into the best shape she has probably been in for Wimbledon. I really think we have succeeded and that this is the best chance she has had of claiming that record ninth women's singles title, which means everything to her. It would bring her total peace of mind. Not only has she had an extra year working with Craig and me, but Steffi Graf's clearly not playing as well this year, while Monica Seles and Jennifer Capriati are still so young.

One change we have made is to Martina's serve. The other night we were looking at an old Wimbledon tape and her backswing now is shorter, which is something that we were working on last year but just did not have the time to improve. Her perception last year that six weeks' preparation was a long time, no longer applies. I had asked her, when she first talked to me about coaching her full time – but I couldn't because of my commitment to Team Tennis – not to go to Australia last year, but she decided to do so. Also she can come over the backhand now and hit it flat, which she could not do a year ago when she was slicing every time, making it very defensive.

The big difference I have noticed in Martina is that whereas in the past she has always wanted to blame someone else, now she really takes full responsibility. I believe she thinks she could actually coach now, whereas a year ago she wouldn't have known where to start.

Earlier in the year when Craig and I told her we wanted her to play on clay she thought that was really quite funny. 'Playing on clay to try and win Wimbledon?' she asked us. We replied: 'Yes.' She was in shock. We had to push and pull pretty hard to convince her on that one, but it was essential. Playing on clay is for grooving your shots. It is being in the trenches. It is for being able mentally to sustain a rally. It is really for the mental and emotional parts of her, the two areas she needed to work on most.

Physically she loves to pump iron and work out, but she has to be more balanced than that as an athlete and she has worked really hard in confronting both the mental and emotional aspects. Craig has been great for her as a coach and a person. She knows he is there for her and is not just someone who is being paid to work with her on court. He and I get along great, too. We have done since day one. I think she knows that she does not have to win for Craig and me, whereas last year I believe she felt she had to win for us to be all right with her. All we ask is that her attitude is right.

We talk things over a lot and we have little bets. She has to pay us £1 every time we think her attitude on any point has been wrong. The first game in any second set is what we call the caviar game, because her friend Judy Nelson told her she would give her a can of caviar every time she won it. Martina responds well to these fun things. Obviously we want her to win because we know how much it means to her, but she has grown so much as a person. That is what is so important. Martina knows there is nothing more we could have done. She was ready for Wimbledon three weeks ago. I told her then that I was getting bored because there was nothing more I could tell her.

As for her rivals, there is certainly not the same intensity about Steffi Graf this year. She is not so focused. Whether it has anything to do with matters involving her father I don't know, but that must be rough on her and would certainly make sense of what has been happening. I knew a year ago that she was getting more emotional and told Martina, though she had not noticed it. I told her: 'Something's not right with Steffi.' Now it is very apparent. Normally she would never lose a tie-break after leading 5–0 and 6–2, which she did in the first set of the final in Paris. I really needed to have seen Monica Seles play on grass this year to get a true feeling about her chances. I am surprised she was not at Eastbourne. She would have been but she is tired from too many tournaments.

Right now she is the No. 1 player, especially on clay courts. Arantxa Sanchez Vicario has also played too many tournaments and is exhausted. Mike Estep, Martina's former coach, took a look at her schedule when she asked him to come aboard and couldn't believe it. She has just run herself into the ground. By the time the French came around this year she could forget it. She had no chance because she was so tired from too much tennis. She might be better off here because she has since taken a little bit of a rest. I know Mike is going to try to persuade her to serve and volley more and be more aggressive. She has a good volley and should be at the net more, though her main game will always be from the baseline, as with Jennifer Capriati.

Jennifer is a little bit like the Jimmy Connors of women's tennis. She hits hard and flat off the ground, but she will come to the net. She is trying to develop an all-court game and her first-round match against Helen Kelesi is going to be tough. I have always thought that Kelesi has not come close to reaching her potential. If she ever became wholly disciplined and really made the effort she could jump way up. So far she has always been an underachiever and I have told her that. She could be top ten or even higher and really be special, but she needs to make that total commitment. If Capriati was to beat her, I think she is capable of doing damage because she hits through the ball so well. Anyone who hits that hard off the ground on grass, is going to do more. The ball is going to groove, rather than sit up as it does on clay.

Jennifer just loves it out there. I think the only thing which is going to keep her back right now is lack of experience. That is the only reason she is losing a few matches now. She hurries. She does not slow down enough or think enough about where she's going to put her serve. She has not quite become the thinking player that she probably will be. She is very bright and smart. We are really lucky with Jennifer and Monica in this age when so many youngsters are pretty spoiled. Under the circumstances they are two nice, kind, good people. That is important. Too much is put on whether you're a champion or not. Tennis is almost secondary in the whole picture.

Monica is interested in tennis history. She asked me for a copy of my book, *The History of Women's Tennis* ... and has read it. I was in total shock. She is the only youngster I know who has wanted it. Last year, when she was at Wimbledon for the first time, Jennifer, I gather, spent some time in the tournament's museum. That is what you look for – youngsters who want to take in the whole picture. These two may eventually have something like the Evert–Navratilova rivalry. Most coaches talk about conditioning and technique. To me that is just scratching the surface. The emotional and mental aspects are also so important. Champions do get tight but they find a way out a higher percentage of the time. We spent hours confronting Martina, gently sometimes, much more abrasively at others. You have to be able to sense what is going on in her mind.

Last year, despite what she thought, she really was not as fit as she should have been. Craig and I felt that from as far back as May, but it was not until after the US Open that we put it to her that she needed to do a lot more aerobics work. Now she is probably in the best shape that she has been in for the tournament. People talk about her being 33, but what and where you are is far more important than age.

I think Ivan Lendl will win the men's singles. I hope he does. It would be great. He is standing in closer on his returns and you can tell that he has paid the price. I heard him say recently that he had to know that he had done everything to try to win this time and that he did not want to think later on: 'If only I'd done this or that.' Things have not come easily for him.

That is why we made Martina go on the clay courts. We kept telling her that every day you have to be in the trenches. Now there is nothing more we can do. Three weeks ago I told her: 'That's it, you're in great shape.' She really wants her place in history and I believe she can achieve that. Then she will go for my record (20 singles and doubles titles at Wimbledon), too. I just wish I had thought about that a little more and rather earlier in my career. It was only at the very end, when someone pointed out to me that I already had 17 and I knew Elizabeth Ryan's record was 19, that I made it my goal.

30 JUNE 1990

WIMBLEDON DIARY: MONICA'S DILEMMA

When quizzed as to why she was not out and about in the same pink pants she had worn at the French Open, the engaging Monica Seles explained how it was not worth the risk. 'What am I going to do if someone tells me I can't wear them?' she asked.

– LM

4 JULY 1990

WIMBLEDON DIARY: IN THE HOT SEAT

Lori McNeil stopped off at an information desk to ask how best to get to Court Three. The official in charge, too busy to look up, asked of Miss McNeil if she would be wanting a seat. 'Only at the change-overs,' returned Miss McNeil.

– LM

13 JULY 1990

LETTER TO THE SPORTS EDITOR

HELEN WILLS WAS ON WAY TO RECORD

Sir,

Since Martina Navratilova's win at Wimbledon, a great deal has been said about her record (nine singles wins) beating that of Helen Wills Moody (eight wins), but an essential difference has not been stated. In the days when the tournament was for amateurs, and before international air travel, it was a major undertaking for anyone living in California, as Helen Wills did, to make the journey to Wimbledon.

From the time when Suzanne Lenglen turned professional in 1926 to some time in the 1930s, Helen Wills was unquestionably the finest female player in a class by herself. Until 1933 she never even lost a set, let alone a match. But in 1931, 1934, 1936 and 1937 she simply couldn't be bothered to make the journey. If she had done so, she would finally have been champion nine and perhaps even ten or 11 times.

Cecil Gould
Chard, Somerset

23 JUNE 1991

20 THINGS YOU OUGHT TO KNOW ABOUT WIMBLEDON

Russell Davies

Courtesy of the Wimbledon Lawn Tennis Museum, the new Wimbledon Compendium (available at the club at £4.95) the BBC's Wimbledon 91 magazine ... and a little shrewd guesswork

1 – The costume worn by Mr Andre Agassi in the gentlemen's singles this year will be predominantly white. Entering the arena in a swan's-down cape, he will doff this to reveal white lederhosen and an off-the-shoulder shirt made of laminated dish-cloths boiled in whitewash. The shirt will be designed, as ever, to ride up and reveal the musculature of Mr Agassi's torso. His bodily hair, like his facial stubble, will be bleached white. He will, however, be wearing black socks.

2 – Your correspondent will wear an old hat, in order to signal that these disputes over costumes are just that. They have been going on, at least, since Bunny Austin turned up in shorts on the Centre Court in 1933; and reached a crisis in the 1960s. An *Evening Standard* cartoon showed an umpire asking: 'Is there a dress designer in the court?' while officials tended a female player, collapsed in a heap of ribbons and flounces and furbelows on the ground. Preserved in the Wimbledon museum, this may well be the funniest cartoon ever drawn by Jak.

3 – Only 25 days of Wimbledon competition have been completely rained off since 1877, when the gentlemen's singles began. This total may well reach 30 in 1991. The number of days on which play has indeed been possible, but only between the hours of 6p.m. and 8p.m., in a goose-pimply dusk latticed with drizzle, is not recorded.

4 – In spite of complaints about the price of strawberries, the Championships expect to shift some 23 tons of them during the fortnight. They will act as the chasers to approximately 12 tons of salmon, the entire menu to be washed down with 300,000 cups of coffee and tea. Emergency provision of hot chocolate and Horlicks is being considered this year.

5 – The Donnay Ultimate Pro, a racket partly designed by Agassi between costume fittings, now costs £179.99, the same price as the Yonex RQ380 Wideboy, as used by Navratilova, Seles and Cash. However, there is nothing new under the rain when it comes to metal-frame racket design. In the 1920s, there was a vogue for the 'Birmal' racket, made of aluminium (presumably in Birmingham), and strung with piano wire. It did not win many matches, but it played a spirited version of 'Yes, We Have No Bananas'.

6 – Racket technology matters more now than it used to, as Björn Borg presumably realises after attempting a comeback with a wooden-frame racket. It is quite possible to produce an almost unbeatable racket: indeed, one has already appeared in the form of the 'Vilsbiburg' or 'spaghetti racket', a complicated double-strung affair designed by Werner Fischer in Germany. This implement created spins that were so nearly unreturnable that Herr Fischer's effort had to be banned.

7 – Major Wingfield, the Victorian codifier of Lawn Tennis, originally called it by a Greek name, 'Sphairistike'. Sceptics abbreviated this to 'Sticky'. Had those nomenclatures caught on, we should all suffer from 'sphairistike elbow', and young men would appear at French windows and call: 'Anyone for sticky?' A favourite interview line at Wimbledon would be: 'I felt good, but she played real power sticky out there.'

8 – Profits from the Wimbledon Championships are known as the 'Financial Surplus', as though it came as rather a surprise to have money left over. It doesn't, though. Last year's Financial Surplus amounted to £9,620,856.

9 – White tennis balls, much prized by traditionalists, are becoming quite rare. It is said that one must travel to Italy nowadays in order to find them on sale. Yellow balls were introduced at Wimbledon in 1986.

10 – During the late Victorian era, it was polite society that 'only a cad would hit the ball away from a lady instead of to her'. A modified version of this principle became a crucial part of the amateur player's standard tactic in mixed doubles: 'Only an idiot would fail to hit the ball straight at the lady, and as hard as possible.' Nowadays, that doesn't work, either.

11 – The inscription over the doorway to the Centre Court reads: 'If you can meet with triumph and disaster/And treat those two imposters just the same.' If I were a competitor, this would annoy me intensely, partly because I prefer the spelling 'impostor', but mainly because it doesn't go on to say, if *what*? I would be tempted to crayon in: 'You'll be Slobadan Zivojinovich, my son', or something to that effect.

12 – Weather again, from the official records, 1965: 'A wet first week.' 1968: 'The first week was the wettest on record.' 1974: 'Three very wet days.' 1978: 'A dull and wet meeting.' 1980: 'One of the wettest meetings on record.' 1982: 'The meeting was one of the wettest on record.' 1985: 'Rain on the first six days … 1½ inches of rain falling in 20 minutes.' 1988: 'Rain interfered on each day of the second week.' 1989: 'Rain badly interfered with the programme.' 1991: And the best of luck.

13 – Another cartoonist, E.H. Shepard, illustrator of the *Pooh* books, once made the suggestion that a 'Brighter Wimbledon' could be arranged if the

size of the racket came in inverse ratio to the ability of the player. Boris Becker would thus play with a tiny racket, while Jason Snurge would have a kind of giant oval screen with a handle attached. Something like this appeared to be happening in 1954, when the enormous Dunlop Maxply racket was produced. So huge was it, however, that the wooden frame warped under the tension of the strings.

14 – Jason Snurge of Surbiton lost in the Qualifying Rounds this year, to J.C. Poppiqotl.

15 – The boys' singles Championship is worth keeping an eye on, since it has been won in the past by Borg, Lendl, Cash and Edberg. When will last year's winner, L. Paes of Indonesia, make his mark?

16 – 'If tennis is your game,' the advertisement for Du Maurier cigarettes used to run, 'smoke the cigarette that keeps you fit.' This large claim was made on the basis that Du Maurier had filters. Today, smoking is banned in the stands of the Centre and No. 1 courts.

17 – Catering again: Wimbledon is 'the largest single sporting outdoor catering operation carried out in the United Kingdom'. So large that 20,000 meals are provided for the caterers' own staff.

18 – The last gentlemen's singles champion to wear long trousers was Yvon Petra in 1946. The immediately post-war tournament seems to have been something of a half-hearted affair, since the 'Financial Surplus' was recorded as a 'nominal amount' of £750. At that, London Transport alone claimed they had ferried 176,000 people there.

19 – The last time a Briton won a Wimbledon title was … four years ago. Unseeded, Bates and Miss Durie won the mixed doubles. Anything is possible.

20 – It is certainly time I bought some new tennis shoes. The ones I have bear the bold commercial endorsement of somebody called Ilie Nastase. I cannot be serious.

WIMBLEDON DIARY: MISSPENT YOUTH

Stefan Edberg's ability to get neither bored nor uptight when there is nothing to do may have had its origins in childhood years spent in Vastervik. In the latest issue of *Sports Illustrated,* Franz Lidz tells how, as a boy, Edberg and his friends would spend long hours 'sitting by the road and speculating on whether the oncoming clunker was a Volvo or a Saab'. Said Edberg: 'Ninety-nine per cent of them were Volvos – so it wasn't much fun.'

– LM

TENNIS STARS MUST BE
WHITER THAN WHITE
Taki

On and off the tennis court, Pete Sampras, last year's US Open champion, is a gentleman, which made him a popular victor even among the rowdies in the borough of Queens, New York. His manners also helped Sampras, of Spartan descent, make mincemeat out of his opponent, the ghastly Andre Agassi. The reason I am being beastly about Agassi is simple. His behaviour is as appalling as the luminous green and pink Spandex shorts that he has made his trademark. He even had the poor taste to spit on a referee during the Open, claiming he accidentally missed the ground.

Just compare Agassi's attitude to that of the great gentleman of tennis, Baron Gottfried Von Cramm, who played in the 1936 Wimbledon final without admitting he had a debilitating injury, in order not to mar the victory of Fred Perry. If Von Cramm were alive today, he would more than likely throw his racket away for good. The Baron would not be alone. One of the reasons I no longer follow tennis closely is that the sport is overrun with prima donnas who make posturing and gamesmanship the main event. This is not only bad in itself, it also reduces pleasure in the game.

With the exception of Stefan Edberg, Sampras and most of the women, who lag far behind the men in egotism, the players try to bend the rules. Some cheat downright or 'tank' matches (playing to lose so that they will be available for another tournament but also collect an appearance fee). It was not always thus. My old Davis Cup doubles partner, Nico Kalogeropulos, an ex-junior Wimbledon champion, and twice in the last 16 of the adult version, was among the most popular players on the circuit during the 1960s because of his sportsmanship. In France he was almost revered. During the 1964 French Championships in Paris he was playing Pierre Darmon, France's No. 1, in the quarter-finals. On match point in his favour Nico went to the net and Darmon passed him. The linesman called the passing shot out, but Nico, better placed to make the call, signalled in. As a result of Nico's chivalry, Darmon eventually won, but the headlines the next day were all in favour of the Greek. Nico's private life was on a par with his on-court behaviour. Compare him with Fredy Huber, the American champion now dead, who twice during his life had brushes with the law. For whom would one root if Huber and Nico played each other, as happened many times?

It is impossible to avoid the fact that the conduct of star players strongly affects one's views of them in the sporting arena. Mario Andretti, the champion racing driver, was once quoted as saying that a competitor is right to try to cheat and that everyone does it. He rationalised it as outsmarting one's opponent. What I would like to know is the difference between cheating in sport and cheating in the stock market. To me there is no difference, yet when was the last time an athlete went to jail for cheating?

The great Bill Tilden was a gent on and off the court, kept his homosexuality private, but was jailed for it. Martina Navratilova revels in her lesbianism, yet remains very popular with the public. I believe Tilden got a raw deal, just as raw as the public is getting from Navratilova, because she sets a bad example. No matter how liberal one might be, it is normal to root for a feminine young player when she is up against such a creature – just as it is normal to root for Stefan Edberg, because of his impeccable behaviour on and off the court, when he is up against Mr X, managed by a crook.

Needless to say, I am on the side of the greats of yesteryear – Lew Hoad, Rod Laver, John Newcombe, Budge Patty, Manuel Santana – all wonderful sportsmen and great role models for the young. If one was to compare them with, say, the McEnroes and Connorses, one would conclude something has gone very wrong with tennis, perhaps with society itself. A cheat in life cannot be regarded as a sports hero, just as a sports star who cheats cannot possibly be straight in life. And, to me, cheating includes gamesmanship *à la* McEnroe. By his tantrums throughout his career he has broken the concentration of his opponent, yet he has got away with it because of his drawing power. I would much rather watch Rosewall play Seixas, or Patty playing Drobny. If I want to see thugs, I can always watch pro-wrestling.

1 JULY 1991

CROWD WINS PLAUDITS ON DAY FOR THE REAL FAN

Lewine Mair

A real crowd came to Wimbledon on the first occasion of middle-Sunday play. They lit up the Centre Court with Mexican waves as they waited for the opening match. Then, when the time came for Gabriela Sabatini and Andrea Straadova to put in an appearance, they clapped the ballboys, booed the umpire light-heartedly — and let out a roar for the players. When it came to the knock-up, they counted the shots while their cheers reached a crescendo as Sabatini arched her back to hit one practice smash after another. But they settled at once as the umpire called for quiet, endorsing his plea with a 'Shush!' which reverberated throughout the stands.

No one was going to let the side down. Though the police had voiced fears that if a person were to go to the toilet someone might pinch his seat, the fact was that those who had bedded down together on pavement had been transformed, overnight, into old friends. They had begun to gather at midday on Saturday as news came that the public would be allowed in yesterday on a first-come, first-served basis with tickets costing £10 for the Centre and No. 1 courts and £5 for a ground pass.

Scott and Jan Barribal, who had met in a Wimbledon queue in 1983, were among the earlier starters. 'Like winning the pools,' was their reaction to the chance of buying a Centre Court ticket. Catriona Hardie, a light sleeper in her own bed, had slept like a log in a black bin bag on Church Road with none of the usual pre-Wimbledon worries as to whether she would be as well dressed as the next person. No one, apart from a few debenture-holders, was in his or her Sunday best yesterday.

Two thousand strong at 11 o'clock on Saturday night, the queues yesterday morning reached 14,000 and the fairways of the Royal Wimbledon Golf Club. By all accounts, there was applause for every early-morning golfer lucky enough to be holing his putts. Of the first five at the front of the queue, four wanted to see Jimmy Connors while the fifth was after a ground pass. 'There aren't,' he explained to a bemused gathering, 'enough big enough names on the Centre Court or No. 1 Court.'

Chris Gorringe, Wimbledon's chief executive, was biting his fingernails as Wimbledon waited for ten o'clock and the gates to open, even though his worst fears — that as many as 100,000 might have gathered — had long before been allayed. The predicted chaos never materialised. A shriek went up as the gates opened and people leaped through the turnstiles and across the forecourts, pausing neither to buy programmes nor to rent cushions. Those who appeared first up the Centre Court shoots looked as disorientated as shoppers at a sale. Where were the best seats? The answer was that each and every seat was a bargain at £10 as against the £25 of the day before.

At a midday press conference, Mr Gorringe, who talked of the 'last night of the Proms' atmosphere, promised the staff would be well rewarded for putting in an extra day. This was going to come as good news for the WC attendants and the litter collectors, all of whom were under the impression that they, in contrast to the court-coverers whose fee had been doubled, would be getting nothing.

Though he made the point that the All-England Club did not intend to repeat the exercise of arranging play for the middle Sunday, Mr Gorringe agreed they would be giving 'a lot of thought' to the business of building on the public's goodwill. Mr Gorringe, who took advantage of a rain break to thank spectators, describing them as 'the most enthusiastic Centre Court crowd we've ever known', had not arranged any last-minute Royals for the Royal Box. However, the relevant seating was to be taken by an illustrious list of past players – Owen Davidson, John Newcombe, Tom Okker, Ken Rosewall, Manuel Santana, to name but five. They were joined, a couple of times, by Martina Navratilova who, try as she might, could not conceal the envy for those who were playing on the Centre Court on such a day. 'The real fans are here,' said Navratilova, echoing the words of Sabatini. 'They should do this every year.'

WIMBLEDON DIARY: UNDERARM SCOOP

Chris Gorringe, the chief executive of Wimbledon, has an underarm service. The news was leaked to the press yesterday, with Gorringe acknowledging, cheerfully, that it was indeed the case. A good enough player to have competed in the British Junior Closed Championships at Wimbledon, Gorringe decided on his underarm approach after watching Björn Borg's final with Roscoe Tanner in 1979.

'Since it was clear,' said Gorringe, who had all his life thrown in the occasional underarm service, 'that I was never going to have a serve like either of them, I decided to swallow all pride and try it.' He has never regretted it, pointing to how he is affected neither by sun nor wind.

– LM

WIMBLEDON DIARY: OVER THE TOP

Jennifer Capriati, 15, is armed with a very different service from the one with which Lottie Dod, then 15, won the first of her five Wimbledons in 1887. Whereas Capriati has what Tom Gullikson describes as 'potentially the strongest service in the women's game', Lottie Dod served underarm on the grounds that the service action placed too much strain on one of her sex.

– LM

ONE ACE AND WILL-POWER OF 4,000 FANS HELPED ACHIEVE LIFE'S AMBITION

Nick Brown, the unfancied Briton who defeated No. 10 seed Goran Ivanisevic, describes his moment of triumph on the greatest stage lawn tennis can offer

Wimbledon '91 will have many memories for me. The fantastic support and encouragement I received during all my matches from the public was second to none. The feelings I experienced when 4,000 people were willing me to win were breathtaking, unforgettable; their expressions of emotion when I had achieved my task quite unbelievable. The biggest moment occurred at 4.45 on the first Saturday.

After three and a half hours on Court 13 playing Goran Ivanisevic, one of the favourites for the title and the tenth seed, I found myself on match point. I felt calm. The crowd were suddenly very quiet. Today was going to be the day I buried the ghosts of those matches where I had missed my chance. I served ... the crowd erupted with applause. I had served an ace and the match was over. The crowd were giving me a standing ovation, cheering. I turned to all four corners and clapped back. I just wanted them to know how much their support had meant to me. They were superb. They made me proud to be British. The walk back to the Centre Court changing-room through the packed gangways seemed to take ages. My next buzz was the live interviews for the press and TV and the following day the Sunday papers were just tremendous, an uplift not just for me but all of British tennis.

My first experience of Wimbledon came as a 14-year-old in 1976. At that time I was very keen to improve my tennis and I remember how excited I was at seeing players such as Ilie Nastase, Jimmy Connors, Roscoe Tanner (with the lightning serve) and, of course, my teenage idol, Björn Borg. My excitement made the four and a half hour journey from Warrington with my father pass very quickly. I remember camping outside the grounds of the All-England Club in the hope of getting into the standing area on Centre Court to see the men's semi-finals and, at two o'clock, I witnessed the first balls being struck on the sacred turf. I couldn't help wondering if I would ever get the chance to play there.

I found Wimbledon tremendously exciting and inspiring. Being a part of the unique atmosphere that surrounds the Championships certainly found a place in my heart and increased my love for tennis. In 1982 my ambition to play at Wimbledon was realised. I remember I was so nervous I hit four balls out – over the backstop at the end of the court – and that was only in the knock-up!

But it wasn't until this year that I was able to fulfil two of my life ambitions: to win my first singles match here and to play on the greatest tennis stage in the world – Centre Court. I only hope that these positive things of Wimbledon '91 will inspire young players to work hard at their games and never give up and show them that success is a great reward. I also believe that the press deserve praise. There has been very little negative press and the positive approach has been appreciated by the players and will do no harm in the promotion of the game in Britain.

I was also thrilled at being a part of Wimbledon history as much as I was the only British player to be involved in a singles match on a Sunday when tickets were sold on a first-come, first-served basis, which gave an opportunity to people who normally would not get the chance to see tennis played at this level. The players also appreciated the carnival atmosphere of these new Wimbledon fans with their 'Mexican waves' and flamboyant cheering. I am sure those fans and probably many more would love the Sunday experiment to be repeated.

This year has seen many changes in British tennis. Tony Pickard's appointment as Davis Cup captain has already had a great effect. His knowledge and experience has been a great benefit to all the players. Bringing in more successful coaches from outside will enhance British chances. I, for one, would love to pass my experiences on to the younger players and put something back into the game. For now, I am focusing towards the Davis Cup tie against Austria in Manchester in September. Another British win will lift British tennis even more. I hope the British players there will receive the same support as I did on my 'lucky' Court 13.

8 JULY 1991

HOW TO SUPPLY BETTER SERVICE FOR SPECTATORS

Fred Perry

The final between Michael Stich, whose legs always seem to be too lean to hold him, and his brawny compatriot, Boris Becker, shooting for his fourth title, demonstrated the brilliance of the serve-and-volley game. But, as in the two men's semi-finals, where similar-style opponents faced one another, it lacked the excitement of matches between players of opposing styles. Too much biff and bang with too few rallies the spectators could get their teeth into.

Serve-and-volley players have dominated the men's event. Matches between such exponents, although the tennis may be brilliant, does not provide much excitement for the spectators as the points are over too quickly and the matches inevitably lack variety. Perhaps the time has come for a rethink in the service law. So many players are well over six foot these days. Add three feet for the arm, and two feet three inches for the racket, plus the five or six inches they jump off the ground, and the ball comes down from a height of some 12 feet. As most of the big servers are nearly two feet inside the baseline when they hit the ball, their advantage is astronomical. Make them stay behind the baseline with one foot on the ground until after they hit the ball and their advantage would be diminished. If service lines were to be moved three inches closer to the net, it would also make a vast difference in the service supremacy.

The tactics of moving and dancing around between the first and second serves when receiving the ball is becoming more prevalent and must be disturbing to the server, particularly as it invariably happens in the backhand court at game point. Some players do a pretty good imitation of the samba or the cha-cha-cha. It is not necessary and could well be classed as 'gamesmanship'.

It would also be a help if umpires were more uniform in their interpretation of the 'code violation' rule for racket abuse and other infringements. Some are notoriously lenient while others clamp down hard. During the Championships, Goran Ivanisevic was given code violations for racket abuse on two different courts the first time he banged his racket on the ground. The same penalty befell Guy Forget when he first did it on No. 1 Court against Becker. John McEnroe's racket bit the dust at least five times in his first match with Sandon Stolle. Despite the fact that it once went from the baseline to the player's chair, a distance of 39 feet, he was not penalised. In the French Open, a middle-ranking player was fined heavily for wearing a company patch judged to be too large, then got fined again for arguing about it. Can it be simple inconsistency on the umpires' part, or does it make a difference who you are?

In my playing days, the unwritten law was that you staked everything on trying to stay in any match against a player of Latin temperament, the theory being that no matter how much trouble they gave you, sooner or later they would collapse. Saturday's women's final was a perfect example. When it mattered most it was Gabriela Sabatini, from Argentina, who succumbed to the pressure, allowing Steffi Graf to complete the first part of a German double in the singles. Graf, whose tennis has for long been in the wilderness, came from the brink of defeat to win her third Wimbledon crown in a most intriguing and emotional match. Sabatini, winner of their last five meetings, served for the Championship at 5–4 and again at 6–5 in the final set, when the roof fell in. Graf refused to surrender when all seemed lost, while Sabatini wilted under the pressure of the occasion.

WIMBLEDON PREVIEW SUPPLEMENT 1992

FOND MEMORIES OF ARTISTRY AND WOODEN RACKETS

Michael Parkinson

Where I grew up it was easier to find a man who had met the Dalai Lama than to come across someone who owned a tennis racket; there were far more Viking burial grounds in the area than tennis courts and a tennis ball was what you learned football and cricket with until the real thing came along. It hadn't always been that way. There had been an awakening of interest in the 1930s when Fred Perry won Wimbledon, but the manifestations of that enthusiasm — one grass court and two hard courts in the local park — had been neglected and forgotten, and put to uses other than those for which they were originally designed.

I don't know, but I would guess that 50 years on little has changed, which is why we are still waiting for the next Fred Perry. The best gauge of our neglect of tennis is the absence of champions. Although there have been changes of late, indications that the sport is waking up, it is still severely hampered by a mixture of traditional class attitudes and the absolute theory that tennis is a pleasant pastime designed for the delight of a privileged few.

Wimbledon stands as a monument to the view it is, first and foremost, a social event. The only difference between Wimbledon and Henley is the water, plus the fact that marginally more people get legless at the rowing than at the tennis. But the accents are the same, the costumes are interchangeable and the general ignorance about what the athletes are doing is something else both sets of spectators have in common.

Judging by their reaction, the average Wimbledon spectator has a skimpy knowledge of what is going on, which is why they laugh at McEnroe's brainstorms when they ought to sign a petition to have him committed to a safe place. They collude with Connors and encourage his antics without realising that it's part of a game-plan to upset and discomfort his opponent. They sit enraptured through a serve-and-volley game (nowadays so enhanced by the equipment that it has taken monotony to new heights) when they ought to be demanding their money back.

Worst of all, they queue up to see women play tennis. At this point I feel I must make all the normal disclaimers. I have nothing against women playing tennis providing they don't expect me to watch; some of my best friends are women who play tennis, too; no, I have not suffered a bad time with a traffic warden who looked like Martina Navratilova. It is simply that they compare so badly with the men. At its best tennis is a graceful and thrilling spectacle. When I remember Rosewall, Hoad, Laver, Nastase, McEnroe, Borg and Edberg, I see elegance, artistry and power. I cannot for the life of me think of one woman tennis player I have seen who has approached those heights of athletic excellence. Nor will they ever, not because they lack the skill but because they do not possess the strength. Having said that, it could be argued that the modern equipment which threatens to make the men's game so predictable has substantially altered the women's game for the better, by giving them the power they require to make things more interesting.

I have several ideas for improving the game of tennis. First of all I would demand a return to the wooden rackets of old so we might see some of the artistry of shot missing from the modern game. I would banish the two-service rule. It strikes me as barmy that a player be given two chances to do what they ought to get right first time. Think what an easy game golf would be if we were allowed two off the tee. Wouldn't taking a penalty at soccer become a doddle if you knew that there were two strikes at goal? What else? I would outlaw grunting by players. This would mean disqualification for Connors, Sabatini and Seles. Sports psychologists tell us that the explosive noises made by these players are not affectations but necessary expulsions of air to release tension. I would also ban sports psychologists.

Another solution to the problem would be to encourage the spectators to make more noise, so we hear less of the players. I have never been able to work out why a sporting contest should take place in total silence. Why the reverential hush, the cloistered quiet? This is a gladiatorial encounter we are witnessing, not some great religious ritual. It was interesting that Jo Durie was indignant and upset when a spectator broke the golden rule of silence recently and told her after she had lost her game that she was 'rubbish'. Why should she be upset? He had, as he pointed out, come a long way to see some tennis, paid good money through the turnstile and been disappointed. Why shouldn't he make his complaint to the appropriate person: namely the player? It seems to me that tennis is one of the few games where the players can make as much noise as they like and abuse whoever they want, while the spectators are allowed no such privileges. Can this be fair?

For all its faults, it remains a beguiling game and Wimbledon fortnight is one of the great occasions of the sporting calendar. It also provides us with the opportunity to ask what is wrong with this country when we can provide the means of holding the world's greatest tennis tournament, but cannot produce the players to compete in it? The answer is, of course, that not enough children in Britain are given the opportunity to play the game. How many public tennis courts do you see in towns and cities? How many schools have a tennis facility and a teacher to show how the game is played? How many people watching Wimbledon, both at the ground and on television, have ever seriously played tennis in their lives? In Australia I lived for a while in a hotel, and from my window looked across public tennis courts. They were in use all day long and in the evening under floodlights. At weekends children, from tots to teenagers, were coached in the rudiments of the game. Why doesn't the same happen here?

There is an argument which says that tennis is no different than any other sport in Britain. In other words, we leave everything to chance and give precious little assistance to anyone wanting to take up a sport. I wouldn't argue with that. Our neglect of sport in schools and throughout life is a great and growing scandal. But the problem tennis has is more specific and acute than most other sports. The shortcomings in cricket coaching at school, for instance, are being absorbed by clubs. Cricket has an infrastructure to deal with neglect; tennis hasn't. We keep hearing about the amount of money made at Wimbledon and how it is passed on for the good of British tennis and all we see is a dreary repetition of the dreadful inadequacy of our own players. It's not good enough; in fact it's a bloody disgrace ... but you won't find anyone saying that at the All-England Club. It will take more time yet for the sun to set on that rampart of the Establishment. In the meantime Wimbledon will continue as a uniquely British institution: much more appreciated by the tourists than the natives.

23 JUNE 1992
WIMBLEDON DIARY: ONE FOOT IN THE GRAVE

René Lacoste and Jean Borotra, who won the doubles title in 1925, are still occasional partners for lunch. Lacoste's favourite story concerning his old friend relates to an exchange during their last singles meeting at Wimbledon. Lacoste, who had lost to Borotra in the 1924 final but had beaten him 6–3, 6–3, 4–6, 8–6 in 1925, was comfortably ahead in their next clash when Borotra, in mock desperation, pleaded: 'Please let me win this time ... You've got many more years to play and I'll be dead soon.' Borotra, who was in his late 20s at the time, is 93.

– LM

24 JUNE 1992
WALLY'S TOUGH TALK
PREPARES HIS PUPILS FOR HARD SERVICE
Lewine Mair

Wally Wonfor was looking for trouble. 'Stop biting your nails, Amy,' barked the man who took over Commander Charles Lane's job of preparing ballboys and ballgirls for Wimbledon fortnight. Wonfor turned on Gemma McClusky after the young lady from the Ursuline Convent had uncharacteristically allowed three out of four balls to escape her clutches. 'That was a hor-r-r-r-rible ball change, Gemma,' he said, his 'r's' reverberating around Wimbledon's Indoor Tennis Club.

Gemma looked him in the eye, taking it unflinchingly. That, though, was not the end of the matter. Minutes later he called her to his side. 'What happens,' he snapped, 'to ballboys who make mistakes?' 'They go down a group, sir.' 'That's right,' returned the glaring Wonfor. Then, suddenly, his face lit with laughter. Gemma had spilled balls but not tears. In other words, she had passed an important test. Ballgirls, to adapt the words of the song, 'don't cry'.

'Out here,' explains Wonfor, 'I'm worse than McEnroe. I have to be.' He feels he must prepare the children for everything that is going to be thrown at them, which, in the past, has included a racket. 'Let's face it,' said Wonfor, 'some of the players treat the ballboys and girls abominably. They are the nearest people on whom to take out their frustrations.'

Wonfor, 62, a retired PE teacher, sets out in March with 200 local children aged 15 or thereabouts and drawn from ten local schools. Sixty-six of his intake will fall by the wayside. Giggling girls and those who connive with friends after a telling-off get their cards in the early weeks. As, indeed, do those who refuse to call Wonfor 'sir'. Earrings must be removed at the first training session; long-haired boys may return for a second session only if their locks have been suitably shorn. Those rejected doubtless spend Wimbledon fortnight brooding darkly on the iniquity of it all, but the 134 who make the grade are by no means averse to Wonfor's brand of old-fashioned discipline. Indeed, the aforementioned Gemma is among his staunchest supporters.

'Our PE teacher warned us about him, prepared us for the worst. It was a wise move,' she said. Gemma, who wants to study law, appreciates that Wonfor is wholly fair. 'He's certainly not afraid to tell you where you are going wrong ... All of us know exactly where we stand.' Yes, she had felt the tears welling up inside her when he spoke to her earlier, 'but you can't start crying at Wimbledon. You have to hide it.'

Not all the players, of course, give the boys and girls abuse. The children enjoy working for such as Edberg and Lendl for they will almost always acknowledge the teenagers' help at the end of a match. Pat Cash, Jeremy Bates and Andrew Castle, who have been practising at the indoor centre, have gone out of their way to establish a rapport with them. Martina Navratilova is another who never takes them for granted.

The advent of ballgirls came in 1977. For about four years no more than ten girls were allowed, and they were tucked away on outside courts. The numbers of boys and girls are now roughly equal. Last year, one Centre Court team consisted exclusively of girls. Weighing up the merits of both sexes, Wonfor said: 'Boys are usually the faster but girls generally have the better posture.' There is equal pay, of course. It comes in the shape of expenses, with the teenagers expecting to take home a cheque of £60 to £70. But for most of them, that does not appear to be a consideration. 'I'd do it for nothing,' said Robbie Mallah, a pupil at Tamworth Manor, who thought he would miss the Wimbledon opportunity when he arrived for training with a sprained ankle. He saved himself by the conscientious way in which he sat and learned from everyone else.

It is every ballboy and ballgirl's aim to make Group A, whose province is the Centre Court. But those who begin the fortnight on Centre Court do not necessarily stay there. After Group A have done a couple of duties on Centre Court, Wonfor is liable to give Group B a turn on the third day. 'Why have we been demoted?' the A's will chorus. 'Because Group B were better yesterday,' he will reply. Wonfor chuckles at the thought of the effect such treatment has on the A's when, on the fourth day, they return to Centre Court. Individuals can move up or down the groups. Wonfor recalls one girl who started at the bottom and finished the fortnight by captaining the Centre Court team. He has also known Group A children whose Centre Court appearance so went to their heads that he had to dispatch them to outside courts.

26 JUNE 1992

WIMBLEDON DIARY: FAMOUS? MOI?

It was 8.45 in the evening and Monica Seles and her mother were in the dressing-room after a late-night practice session over the road. When her mother looked out of the door to see if their car had arrived, she was taken aback at the large throng standing outside. 'Who are they waiting for?' she asked. 'Monica,' came the reply. 'Oh,' said the mother, dismissively, 'I thought we were about to see somebody famous.'

– LM

BRAVE BATES A POINT FROM GLORY

John Parsons

Jeremy Bates kept his promise to 'give everything I have to give' on Wimbledon's Centre Court yesterday, but in the end there was only heartbreak for the British No. 1, who had been within a point of reaching the quarter-finals. Almost exactly an hour after a hushed crowd, with Union Flags at the ready, prepared to salute Bates, it was instead Guy Forget, the ninth-seeded Frenchman, who qualified to meet former champion John McEnroe in tomorrow's quarter-finals with a 6–7, 6–4, 3–6, 7–6, 6–3 win.

Three 'killer' net-cords, one just before Bates reached his match point, another which cost him that game and a third during the fourth-set tie-break, all contributed far more to the British No. 1's disappointment than any lack of courage or commitment on his part on Wimbledon's most scorching day for years. Indeed, it was probably the first of those net-cords which did the most damage for it made the difference between Bates being 40–0, with three match points, and 30–15, still offering Forget a glimmer of hope. Had the former been the case there would probably have been no chance for Forget.

The tension at 40–30 could be felt not only within the Centre Court, but throughout the grounds of the All-England Club where several matches were briefly halted as other spectators, following Bates's progress in sound, if not vision, responded excitedly and enthusiastically. As he prepared to serve on the match point, Bates checked because the original toss was not right and he let the ball drop. 'Somebody sneezed, I think,' he explained later. 'Or somebody did something just as I was throwing the ball up. Because it was so quiet you could hear a pin drop and I heard whatever it was just as I was in the motion of throwing up the ball.'

On the second serve, the delivery looked a shade tentative, though Bates, with some degree of disappointment that the idea was being suggested in the first place, denied that the nerve edges had shown through. However, the length of the serve was enticingly short for his opponent and Forget simply unleashed one of those hit-or-miss shots which swept straight back past Bates. A Bates forehand volley which landed a fraction over the baseline then gave Forget a break-back point but, having saved that with a winning serve, the British player provided his opponent with another when he misjudged a return which initially looked to be going out, but had just enough top spin to make it fall in.

It was bad enough for Bates when a second net-cord then cost him the game, but that became cruelty beyond measure when, with Forget leading 3–2 in the tie-break, the tape intervened decisively again, despite an instinctive response from Bates. The British player hit a first return through his legs but, not surprisingly, was well out of position after playing his next shot. The way Bates gestured as he changed ends, now 2–4 down, said it all and the backhand winner which Forget then drilled with spectacular ferocity on the next point really rubbed salt into the wound. Forget hit 31 aces, the equivalent of almost eight games, and with the mental crisis past, the quality, consistency and power of his returns increased also until there were four brilliant winners, two on either flank, as he broke Bates again in the ninth game.

Bates is at least £18,000 richer from his three victories here with more still to come as he continues his mixed doubles partnership with Jo Durie. Another plus is that his world ranking will be boosted from 113 to about 80 – his highest for five years. He accepted defeat philosophically. Of those net-cords and the lost match point, he said: 'That's how the balls run. They certainly went his way in the crucial stages of the fourth set, but you make your own luck. At 5–4, 30–0 I hit a good wide serve and he didn't really hit the backhand very cleanly, but it skipped on top of the net, otherwise I'd have had three match points.'

In a gripping opening set, which lasted exactly an hour, Forget had the advantage of serving first and after the Frenchman had saved two break points in the third game with aces, the British player was forced to hang on. He did so defiantly and, at times, quite spectacularly. Then, in an incredible tie-break, Bates looked to have sacrificed his chances by missing two high backhand volleys, one at 5–4 when Forget's return would have gone out, and then at 9–9 to give Forget his fifth set point but the first on his own serve. Instead Bates responded with a fine forehand pass down the line on the run, followed it with a gorgeously timed backhand cross and then took the tie-break 12–10 with a perfectly controlled backhand volley.

Though the second set slipped away in little more than half the time of the first, after Bates had double-faulted on the first point of the third game, the underdog struck back well again in the third. The opening game was crucial. Bates, despite having problems from a tweaked neck joint, which twice needed treatment, saved four break points, but then broke Forget from 40–15 in the fourth. The way Bates held on to that lead, rounding off the set with an ace, had everyone's adrenalin flowing. And when, after fluffing an early volley in the fourth set, Forget tossed away the white cap he had been wearing, that seemed another pointer towards a home victory.

Almost every point was a nail-biter from then on, especially when Bates broke for 2–1 in the fourth set with a stunning backhand service return and confidently held for 3–1. All he had to do was hold his serve through the rest of the set. On such an occasion and in such circumstances it was an enormous task and responsibility. And that was without taking into account those net-cords.

1 JULY 1992

WIMBLEDON DIARY: THE PLASTIC BAG LADY

Among the stories circulating about the late Kitty Godfree is that concerning how, ten or so years ago, she turned up during the Wimbledon fortnight for her weekly game on one of the courts over the road. While various unknowns went into the dressing-room before her, all armed with five or six rackets and swanky holdalls, this winner of eight Wimbledon titles arrived with a battered Dunlop racket peeping from an old Tesco carrier bag.

– LM

4 JULY 1992

WIMBLEDON DIARY: BLEEPING MACHINE

Bill Carlton, the inventor of the Cyclops or magic-eye machine, was able to explain why the bleeper had incorrectly sounded during the McEnroe–Forget match. The Forget service in question was in by as much as six to eight inches. But the ball hit a stray divot, which in turn hopped over the line and activated the machine.

– LM

5 JULY 1992

WIMBLEDON DIARY: THE LINESMAN'S TALE

The umpires have had plenty of time to swap tales during rain-lashed periods, with one oft-repeated story that of Jacky Smith, a line judge whose patch for a match involving Borotra was the middle-service line. Having had a couple of glasses of wine at lunch, Smith was dozing off when he came round to the sight of a ball finishing two inches outside his all-important line and thundering on towards him. 'Fault,' he cried, before suddenly it came to him that the players were in mid-rally. Showing an admirable degree of mental and physical dexterity, Smith wheeled round and shook his fist at the people to his rear. 'Quiet, please,' he pleaded.

– LM

6 JULY 1992
SILENT SELES HAS NO ANSWER TO MAJESTIC GRAF
John Parsons

Steffi Graf powerfully and exuberantly cast aside all her problems of recent years to produce a performance which ranks alongside the best by any Wimbledon champion. In simple and not always wholly meaningful statistical terms, Graf's 6–2, 6–1 victory, which ended Monica Seles's hope of achieving a Grand Slam, was the easiest since Martina Navratilova beat Andrea Jaeger 6–0, 6–3 in 1983. Like Seles, Jaeger was only 18 but, playing in only her second major final, was overawed. Seles, the world champion who has won six Grand Slam tournament titles, more than anyone of a comparable age, was ruthlessly overpowered as she suffered her worst defeat since her last Wimbledon meeting with Graf, in 1989.

While everything in Graf's naturally aggressive but sometimes expensively impetuous game was working perfectly, there was one familiar ingredient missing from Seles – the grunt. And while she was successful in curbing her habit of the last eight years, it certainly coincided with a similar reduction in the force she displayed in her tennis, especially those ground strokes which brought her to Wimbledon holding the US Open, Australian and French titles.

The final game in many ways typified the whole match. It began with a reminder of those screaming – though this time silent – backhand, cross-court service returns from Seles but, as earlier, Graf never allowed her to home in for enough of them. Three forehand winners by Graf followed, the last as she drove with great power, length and control into the Seles backhand. Then came the match point ace. It was not just the frequency and quality of Graf's winners, especially on serve and off the forehand, which was so impressive, but also the way she maintained them through the rain delays.

The actual playing time was 58 minutes but spread over periods of 36 minutes, two minutes, 11 and ten, with the last taking place in still gloomy conditions, little different from when officials had been reluctant to take off the covers earlier when Graf had been just six points from victory at 4–1 and 15–30 on the Seles serve in the second set. Although Graf struck the first serve of the match at 2.08, it was 7.29 when she bounded in behind that matchwinning ace to claim for the fourth time in five years the title which clearly means most to her.

Who knows, on this form and with the same enthusiasm, she might even threaten Navratilova's record of nine Wimbledon triumphs. At 23, by which time Navratilova had won the title only twice, time is on her side and, as she says: 'I still think I have a few years left.' With the exception, perhaps, of her performance in winning Wimbledon for the first time against Navratilova in 1988, this was certainly the finest tennis she has produced at the Championships. Not only was the vitality and spontaneity back in Graf's game but she demonstrated greater versatility than before.

6 JULY 1992
WIMBLEDON DIARY: QUICK SHOWER

What did the women's finalists do during the rain delays? Seles remained at the club, but Graf, at one point, sought permission from Alan Mills to return to her house, once the home of the old Wimbledon referee, Fred Hoyles. 'We won't need you for about an hour,' Mr Mills indicated, pointing to the approaching cloud. No sooner had Graf walked through the front door than the phone rang, the caller Georgina Clark. The senior tour director of the Women's Tennis Association was asking: 'Can you come back at once?'

– LM

6 JULY 1992
AMERICAN GLADIATOR AGASSI
WINS HEAVYWEIGHT TITLE BOUT
Michael Calvin

One of the many advertising campaigns built around the incandescent personality of Andre Agassi proclaims: 'Just do it.' Well, to the delight of sponsors and schoolgirls alike, he did it. It proved to be a debilitating experience. As Agassi lay spreadeagled, face down on the turf, his mind's eye was filled with images of rejection, frustration and self-justification. 'Oh my goodness,' he said, breathlessly reliving the sweetest moment of his life. 'I couldn't believe it. Millions of things were running through my mind. I was Wimbledon champion. A Grand Slam winner. I thought of the months, and years, of people doubting me. Then I thought of all the people who believed in me. It was just overwhelming.'

He was weeping when Goran Ivanisevic reached him after climbing over the net, into which he had slumped the instant he missed the fateful backhand volley that caused his opponent to collapse. 'Listen, man, you deserve it,' he told him. 'You played great. All these two weeks.' They embraced, like two heavyweight boxers after the most attritional of title bouts. For once, in the maze of mirrors that is Agassi's career, the image matched the reality. For the Centre Court crowd witnessed a tennis match that was closer, in spirit, to the more memorable fights staged in the champion's home town of Las Vegas. The same gladiatorial air swamped the senses; the audience response, from gasps of awe to gleeful celebration of raw power, carried familiar echoes of celebrated desert nights in the car lot at Caesar's Palace.

Both men were enriched by the experience. Agassi proved, beyond reasonable doubt, that he is more than a one-dimensional celebrity. Ivanisevic emerged as much more than a mercurial character with a serve even quicker than his lightning wit. The forging of mutual respect, in the most pressurised of circumstances, was a uniquely powerful experience. When they hugged, they enshrined the purity of sport, so often trampled into the dirt of the market place. 'Any time you are in a match that goes to five sets, where both of you are just doing everything to stay in there, there is a bond you develop,' Agassi reasoned. 'You cannot explain it to anybody else. You are an athlete and you feel it out there in the heat of battle. You are fighting so hard to kill the other one, yet you have so much respect for him fighting back.' Agassi's most critical battle was with himself. If he really resembled his home town, where they compensate for matters of substance with neon light and poor taste, he would not have left Wimbledon cradling the golden trophy with a care reserved for first-born children.

Perhaps we should have taken notice of his recovery from the slump that examined his self-belief earlier this year. Three defeats in Grand Slam finals had eaten into his soul and invaded the darkest recesses of his mind.

He described the experience perfectly before the final. 'You feel like people cheering against you are carrying megaphones,' he said. 'An opponent who's six-foot-two looks six-foot-eight. Someone with a big serve looks like he's packing a howitzer.' Now, as champion, Agassi was able to reflect: 'It is really weird. Any time you look back at a slump it is hard to figure out why you doubted yourself so much. But I did. Going through something like that builds a lot of character.' So, when he awoke yesterday morning, he felt a strange serenity. Nick Bollettieri, his coach, bolstered his confidence as carefully as a man building a house of cards. 'This is yours,' he told him, repeatedly. 'This is your Wimbledon, your tournament. It is your turn today.' The Florida-based coach had 35 years, and several million dollars, invested in the events of a grey, breezy afternoon that captivated television's millions.

Ivanisevic, beneath the veneer of ebullience, had succumbed to superstition. For the six previous days he had eaten the same meal at the same restaurant: fish soup, followed by lamb and chips. Orange juice helped digest a dessert of vanilla ice cream, topped off by chocolate. 'They didn't bring me the menu, they just brought the food,' he smiled. If only his performance had been as predictable. It was not, as had been expected, the tennis equivalent of drag racing, a brief explosive burst of barely tamed energy. Agassi refused to be ruffled by the 37 aces that flew past him. He fed off the crowd, who responded with the mixture of sympathy and admiration reserved for anyone who dares stand up to the village bully.

He was beginning to realise just what he had missed during three years of self-imposed exile from the All-England Club. The Centre Court radiates history, even on days when the weather forecast is required reading. 'I'm kind of sad I didn't come here because, you know, the sport has offered me and my life so much. This tournament has offered me and my life so much. It is a shame I didn't respect it a little earlier. This is the greatest title in the world. It is the greatest achievement I have ever made.'

There are times when even the most charitable soul detects the unseen hand of public relations executives in Agassi's off-court utterances. This was not one of them. He came straight from Centre Court and was speaking from the heart. The real Andre Agassi was standing up and demanding to be counted. 'If my career is over tomorrow, I have had a lot more than I deserved,' he said. 'I have had a lot more than I could ever ask for.' Viva Las Vegas.

McENROE SERVES UP VICTORY
AFTER MARATHON FINAL SET

John Parsons

For some years John McEnroe has dreamed of collecting one more major title before he retires. Winning the men's doubles at Wimbledon may not have been what he originally had in mind but, as he said after taking the title for a fourth time yesterday, partnered by Michael Stich: 'It's the next best thing.' It was played out amid amazingly emotional scenes. More than 6,500 were packed into No. 1 Court with nearly another 1,500 in the grounds – some had queued overnight – principally for another glimpse of the extraordinarily gifted McEnroe as he and the immediate past singles champion took 34 minutes to carry a 13–13 overnight final-set score to a record-breaking 5–7, 7–6, 6–3, 7–6, 19–17 defeat of Jim Grabb and Richey Reneberg.

Apart from underlining the unique appeal of Wimbledon, those who took advantage of free admission to see the 1992 Championships tidied up on a third Monday were witness not only to another classic chapter in McEnroe's career but the longest final in terms of games (83) and time (five hours one minute). McEnroe and Stich both found it 'just so exciting and motivating' to discover the enormous queues snaking their way to every entrance when they arrived, while Cyril Suk and Larisa Savchenko-Neiland were beating the Dutch pair, Jacco Eltingh and Miriam Oremans, 7–5, 6–2 in the final of the mixed doubles.

At 9.21p.m. on Saturday, when it was nearly dark, McEnroe and Stich, playing together for only the second time – but already tentatively booked to continue the partnership at the US Open and Wimbledon again next year – asked their opponents, who had already had two match points on Stich's serve, if they would like to settle it in a final-set tie-break. 'I'm glad now they didn't seem very keen on the idea,' said McEnroe, who had just shared in the fantastic lap of honour reception, which emphasised his own enduring popularity.

Certainly, it was the perfect climax for the Championships, and for the crowd, when McEnroe not only delivered the fabulous top-spin lob which broke the serving stalemate but then served out for victory. McEnroe, still hitting those superb left-handed swinging serves away from the receiver's backhand with almost as much venom as when he last won both the singles and doubles at Wimbledon in 1984, was hugged and lifted high in the air by

Stich after Reneberg's service return finished in the net. The crowd went wild. McEnroe said: 'It was one of the best receptions I've ever had. It was incredible to come back on Monday and find the stadium totally full. The energy was incredible and really pumped us up. It would have been big for us just to have played and won in front of a couple of hundred people. The reception and excitement was just unbelievable.'

WIMBLEDON SUPPLEMENT 1993

FROM STAYS AND CORSETS TO MINDLESS PASTEL SPLURGES

Hilary Alexander

The early history of women's tennis fashion is a story of triumph over rigid social etiquette and even more restrictive discomfort. The first Victorian players wore the sort of clothes they would have worn to a garden party. In her book, *Tennis Fashions,* for the Wimbledon Lawn Tennis Museum, Valerie Warren describes the typical attire of the 1870s and 1880s as 'an elaborately flounced dress to the ground, with long sleeves, high neckline, and a clinched waist'. Underneath were boned corsets, bustles, layers of petticoats, long drawers, stockings and heeled shoes. Aprons were worn with large pockets for tennis balls because it was almost impossible to bend down.

But despite the restrictions, even the earliest women players achieved a personal touch – so often missing today – by embroidering their aprons with elaborate motifs. Pioneering spirits such as Maud Watson and Lottie Dod introduced their own fashion signatures. Maud Watson, who won her first Wimbledon in 1884, wore black shoes and stockings under her bustle-dress and a man's straw boater. Schoolgirl Lottie Dod, five times the women's singles winner, sported a calf-length 'uniform' with a white cricket cap.

Post-First World War women's tennis was rich in on-court flair. The dazzling Suzanne Lenglen electrified spectators in the 1920s with her Parisian silk flapper shifts. The 'Lenglen bandeau' became a cult, only ousted in the 1930s by Helen Wills's trademark white eyeshade. The couturier Ted Tinling both shocked and delighted the tennis world over the next three decades. His signature was prettiness-at-play, interpreted in lace-trimmed knickers for Gussie Moran, a shocking pink lining for Maria Bueno, and some of the most flattering dresses seen on Centre Court for Evonne Goolagong and Chris Evert. His styling was in marked contrast to the tailored functionalism spearheaded by man-made fibres and the earliest sponsors, which continues to this day – apart from a bold, but ill-fated attempt to enliven the scene by Anne White in 1985.

Women's professional tennis wear has today become a cliché; the equivalent of the ubiquitous shell suit. The regulation T-shirt and little pleated skirt 'jazzed up' with some mindless pastel slurge may be function at its best, but is style at its worst. No one is suggesting that the likes of Steffi, Martina and Gabriela should abandon their lucrative clothing deals – where would the game be without them? But surely sponsorship need not be as inhibiting to personal style as stays and corsets once were to freedom of movement.

23 JUNE 1993

WIMBLEDON DIARY: TRABERT'S GRANDSTAND SLAM THREAT

Tony Trabert, who was a Wimbledon winner in 1955, was able to explain why the All-England Club, after years of going its own way, finally stepped into line over the matter of providing new balls rather more often than at the end of a set. It was in 1950 and Trabert and Budge Patty were playing Frank Sedgman and Ken McGregor, who would go on to win the doubles title in each of the next two years. Trabert and Patty won the first set 6–4 and a new box of balls was duly handed out. The next set got under way and, at a time when the score was a mind-boggling 20–20, Trabert advised the umpire that they could do with fresh ammunition. 'Sorry,' replied the umpire, 'but it's against the rules.' The referee was called for and he, too, said it was out of the question. Eventually, after a deal of fuss, it was agreed that they could revert to using the balls which had done duty in the first set. What made officialdom see sense was Trabert's light-hearted threat to slam the old balls out of the stadium.

– LM

29 JUNE 1993

WIMBLEDON DIARY: WHITE LIES

Some among the juniors at Wimbledon are up to their old tricks. They go on court in heavily patterned shirts and, before too long, a colour controller comes running up to explain that he/she must wear white. The junior explains that he doesn't have a white shirt and, hey presto, he is given a spanking new Wimbledon polo shirt. It works every time and, in the case of one competitor, who had best remain anonymous, it has worked twice.

– LM

30 JUNE 1993
BALLBOYS PUT IN THE SHADE

The Wimbledon sunshine has forced an end to the century-old tradition of hatless ballboys. After more than a week of hot weather, the All-England Club have issued blue baseball caps to ballboys and girls after six of them complained of mild sunstroke. 'They are fine now and back on court,' said Mr Wally Wonfor, manager of the 188 ballboys and girls. 'We told them to have a cool shower and lie down. There is a staff of six who look after them and check that they do not overdo it.'

The youngsters are also told to wear a cream containing a high 'sun factor'. It is not the first time that ballboys have covered their heads. At the end of the last century, the job was done by scouts who wore their caps.

1 JULY 1993
WIMBLEDON DIARY: SOFT TARGET

There were 7,500 cushions for hire at the start of Wimbledon fortnight. Now they are down to 7,000. The tally of thefts corresponds, more or less, with the number of silver-plated knives, forks and spoons, all of them bearing the Masters logo, which were nicked this year from the main dining room at Augusta.

– LM

5 JULY 1993
NOVOTNA DENIES SHE MADE THE 'GREATEST CHOKE OF ALL'
John Parsons

Once the euphoria at the moment of victory had passed, Steffi Graf seemed more embarrassed than elated over the manner in which she won her fifth

Wimbledon title against the distraught Jana Novotna. As her coach Heinz Guenthardt said after Graf had completed an astonishing 7–6, 1–6, 6–4 victory when, but for a haunting Novotna double-fault, she would probably have been trailing 1–5 in the final set: 'It was Jana, not Steffi, who turned things round. Steffi played well in the end but she was given a tremendous amount of help.'

Graf, like everyone else, had enormous sympathy for Novotna, whose belief over those last few tortuous games disintegrated even more terribly than the defending champion's game in the second set. 'Yes, I felt bad,' admitted Graf when asked if she felt sorry for her opponent. 'If you're 4–1 up and serving, then you're pretty much in a position that you have to win. I made some important points but she definitely gave me a few and it was disappointing because she played so well and didn't make it.' Indeed, the public tears on the court by both players were repeated and shared with other players past and present in the dressing-room, according to Judy Dalton, runner-up in the first Open Wimbledon in 1968.

Graf had also been lucky in the 1991 final against Gabriela Sabatini. On that occasion, however, the Argentine's serve, especially when she twice served for the match, was so weak that she did not deserve to win. In contrast, on Saturday, when Graf hit back from 3–5 to take the longest tie-break in a women's final 8–6, Novotna had served, volleyed, smashed, opened up the court and generally produced tennis worthy of a champion with such obvious hunger for success. It looked as if she had conquered her notorious tendency to self-destruct. She, like the enthralled Centre Court, must have felt she had one hand on the trophy when, effectively on that one double-fault, the whole mission was aborted. Graf, who had suffered what most presumed was to be her final blow when she double-faulted to go 1–4 down in the previous game, certainly felt she was out of it. 'She had two breaks. The way she'd played the games before and the way I played [winning only two out of ten games after the first-set tie-break] I did think "I've kind of lost it".'

Putting on a braver face in the interview room than she had managed on court where, in one of the most touching moments in Wimbledon's long history, the Duchess of Kent understandingly allowed her to weep on her shoulder, Novotna firmly rejected the obvious analysis that this had been 'the greatest choke of all time'. 'I won against Sabatini and Navratilova because I went for my shots, including aces from second serves. I decided to do the same today because I know I can't play different tennis. The sad thing is that it didn't work so well. I don't see that nerves or confidence have anything to do with this loss.'

Maybe one can give Novotna the benefit of the doubt on the double-fault when she was poised to take a 5–1 lead. But however much she felt compelled to go for broke on the second serve at precisely the moment that percentage tennis was required, it was a grave tactical error. Certainly from then on her nerve went. Novotna, who had been supremely assured on smashes and high volleys earlier, missed one overhead and then netted another as Graf, who had been caught hitherto by several brilliant lobs, responded in kind.

It was a shame that such an enthralling and, mostly thanks to Novotna, such a high-quality contest – the longest final (two hours 14 minutes) since the Margaret Court–Billie-Jean King classic in 1970 – ended with a nightmare scenario. It was Graf's 13th Grand Slam singles title, hardly an unlucky number, lifting her above Billie-Jean King into fifth place in the all-time list behind Margaret Court, with 24, Helen Wills Moody, 19, and Chris Evert and Martina Navratilova on 18.

Novotna was given a tumultuous reception when she returned to the Centre Court barely three hours later only to be disappointed again as she and Larisa Leiland (Savchenko) were beaten for the second successive year (6–4, 6–7, 6–4) by Natalia Zvereva and Gigi Fernandez. They have now won the last six Grand Slam titles. It was 9.08p.m. when Zvereva made it match point by playing two consecutive returns while on her knees. The last thing Novotna needed to be told was that it had not been her day.

5 JULY 1993

WIMBLEDON DIARY: SEEDS OF DISCONTENT

The £6,000 or so worth of hydrangeas which decorate the Wimbledon complex each year are brought over from the Continent. None among the local gardening experts doubt that the flowers can be obtained more cheaply abroad, but feel that an institution such as the All-England Club should support local nurseries. In the opinion of one, Steve Pitkin of S&J Garden Services, such penny-pinching on the club's part merely goes hand in hand with the hefty prices they charge for everything from tickets to strawberries

– LM

5 JULY 1993

FINAL REDUCES GAME TO LEVEL OF TRACTOR-PULLING

POWER PLAY GIVES SWEET MUSIC A HARD EDGE

Michael Calvin

A *Thunderbirds* puppet named Pete Sampras defeated a baseball cap called Jim Courier in the world arm-wrestling championship on the Centre Court yesterday. Or, to put it another way, the world's best tennis player confirmed his superiority over the world's second-best tennis player in the Wimbledon men's singles final. Sampras, claiming his inheritance on an unrivalled stage, should have been the stuff of legend. But he conspired with Courier, his childhood friend, in reducing a game of infinite variety to the level of tractor-pulling. Tennis, as demonstrated over 178 mind-numbing minutes yesterday, is no longer sweet music. It is as harsh and discordant as a heavy metal guitar chorus. Power has corrupted its spirit.

Though the occasion invited trite nationalism – both entourages flourished miniature Stars and Stripes – it was appropriate that Sampras should be crowned on American Independence Day. The final might still be grinding on but for the tie-break. For, just as basketball games could be satisfactorily condensed into the two frantic minutes that habitually signal the end of the fourth quarter, modern tennis matches could be adequately decided by the best of five tie-breaks. To borrow Courier's telling phrase, fashioned by the bittersweet experience of his second defeat in a Grant Slam final in a month: 'That's just grass-court tennis. Let's roll the dice.'

There was the occasional mesmeric rally, and delightfully deft drop shot. The athleticism of the contest was unrelenting. But the story of a match that appeared to chloroform the Centre Court crowd is best summarised by two raw facts. The final was almost an hour old, in the second game of the second set, when Sampras forced its first deuce. Another 40 minutes of bicep-flexing followed before the new champion reached the final's first break point.

The aim of every self-respecting player in this year's Wimbledon – or 'Wimpleton' to use Sampras's approximation of its pronunciation – has been a 'Bee Bee'. Apparently, that is an abbreviation of 'Boom Boom'. Sampras has been plagued by shin splints, in addition to the shoulder strain that has played on his mind, and the suspicion persists that he would have struggled if dragged into a fifth set by the pugnacious Courier. Yet experience has turned the beaten finalist into a pragmatist. Courier reasoned: 'He was tired but when you're serving at 120mph, and then 95mph on the second serve, you don't have to move too much. Maybe if we were in a fifth set his legs would not have allowed him to swing with as much energy. But I'm in his shoes and I'm tired, I'm just going to start firing Bee Bees. Keep firing Bee Bees, don't give the other guy a chance. That's what he did. There are no would-haves or could-haves. It's just that I got outplayed and it's not any easier to take because of that.'

The thought that some unfortunates in the crowd paid touts £2,000 for a Centre Court ticket beggared belief. Even if they contrived to enjoy the simplistic version of tennis on offer, they would have been as well entertained with a chauffeur-driven tour of the Bisley rifle ranges. They certainly did not pay to see incandescent personalities. Courier is the first to admit that without his trademark baseball cap he can enjoy the luxury of well-cushioned anonymity. Few of his actions yesterday, once defeat had been confirmed, challenged the assumption he would have been horror-struck to find himself watching the final on American TV, swigging ice-cold beer from the bottle at his nearest truck stop.

Sampras continued, to the bitter end, to drive diarists to despair. He was asked, ritually, how he intended to celebrate what he acknowledged as the most substantial achievement of his career. 'You know, I don't know,' he said. 'I haven't really thought about it. I'll hopefully get some sleep tonight. I'm leaving for the States tomorrow so maybe I'll have a couple of glasses of Champagne.' Steve 'Interesting' Davis has met his match. Pete 'Prudent' Sampras proved beyond belief that he is not one of nature's hellraisers.

The last all-American final featured Jimmy Connors and John McEnroe. They were hardly angels but they had a presence and vivacity which forced the crowds to respond. Yesterday all Sampras and Courier generated was respect. Sampras admitted his parents, who did not fly to England for the occasion, probably went for a walk during his match. Quite a few other spectators were tempted to do the same. One of the few times Sampras showed any spark, on or off court, was when he was asked whether he noticed the Princess of Wales applauding towards the end. 'Maybe she has a crush on me,' he said.

There were far too few flashes of individualism to make yesterday's final an enriching experience. There is more to tennis than the match suggested. But, to look on the bright side, there is a light at the end of the world's longest tunnel for British tennis. If the trend continues all we have to do to produce a Wimbledon champion is to persuade Geoff Capes to abandon retirement and teach him how to serve.

20 JUNE 1994

GARDEN PARTY TAKEN OVER BY BIG BUSINESS

Fred Perry

When I first went to Wimbledon as a wild-eyed, not-too-successful competitor in the junior Championships, it made a stunning impression that has stayed with me all these years – almost 70, in fact. As an amateur tournament, like all others until it pioneered the change to professionalism, Wimbledon entries were made through other associations throughout the world. They sent players to the tournament in exchange for visits from British touring teams. The draw of 128 was made up by 60 nominations from various countries and about 60 other top players, with the last eight places decided by the qualifying tournament – named 'the blood-bath' by those who had to go through it. I won my way into Wimbledon that way in 1929 so I know all about the trials and tribulations. The woman's draw of 96 was made in a similar way.

The changes behind the scenes have also been enormous. In the pre-war years only the seeded players were provided with transport, everyone found their own accommodation and made their own way to the ground. Players nominated by their country were, of course, looked after by their own associations. Today, competitors are really pampered. If they make the main draw they are housed and transported, locker-room spaces have doubled, the women have hairdressers on hand and competitors with children are provided with babysitters – a far cry from earlier days.

Pre-war Wimbledons were a sedate and smooth sort of garden party when every Centre and No. 1 Court seat was occupied by a tennis nut. The loss of Centre Court standing room has meant the loss of much of the colour and enthusiasm which was so much a part of the scene in the old days. In those days there was no corporate hospitality block-booking Centre Court seats which remain empty while the honoured guests spend the day watching matches on television after a long Champagne lunch. Times have certainly changed.

The most radical change took place with the advent of professional tennis and, with it, television. As amateurs, we played because we loved the game. As professionals, today's players also love the game and play it extremely well, make no mistake. They are also businessmen who get paid well for their expertise. They have an agent, lawyer, coach, ball-hitter, trainer and bodyguard, a regular portable business office. The yardstick is no longer who you beat. It is money.

The new equipment has helped make the game faster. Today's equipment is much lighter, notably the racket head, and there are only 16 main strings. The ball has to be hit extremely hard and more winners, and more mistakes, have crept into the game: a new style entirely. We went on court with three or four rackets, not staggering under the weight of a huge bag with the name of the manufacturer suitably placed for maximum publicity.

Television has revolutionised the game, even leading to a change in the rules. The birth of the professional game meant prize money. This called for advertising, which in turn needed 'names'. Soon, 60 seconds were allowed on the change-over so the advertisement could be aired. The time was later extended to 90 seconds. In contrast, we had to stay on our feet for five sets and were not allowed to towel down during games. We took a quick drink and towelled-down on our way past the umpire's chair.

Television has made tennis popular and who can say that the presentation of the cups to the champions is not one of the most wonderful ceremonies one could want. No such luck with us. We played the final, shook hands, and walked off to the dressing-room. In fact, I did not see the two main cups until 1947, when they were left on display, and did not touch the gold one until 1984.

This year marks the diamond jubilee of my first Wimbledon win in 1934. It is staggering to think that no British male has been able to do it since. The men did extremely well last year and already have had successes in this summer's grass-court season. Let's hope someone does something spectacular. I wish them luck.

21 JUNE 1994

WIMBLEDON DIARY: KEEPING AN EYE OUT

Eileen Ward, who is in charge of Lost and Found, had a couple of inquiries within five minutes of the gates opening yesterday. The first came from a woman looking for the gold watch she had lost last year, the second from a man – mercifully not an umpire – who had lost his glasses. In the five years she has been at this post, this former All-England Club secretary has contrived to reunite several members of the public with their false teeth. Sadly, she could not be of assistance to the gentleman who had mislaid a glass eye.

– LM

WIMBLEDON DIARY: NO BALL!

A Chris Bailey serve to Javier Frana kicked off the Argentine's racket and into the crowd. 'Can I have the ball back?' called the umpire, in the anxious tone of one who suspected he might have to pay for a replacement. The fellow who caught it, to give him his due, had no intention of stealing silently away. Instead, he answered the umpire with a 'No!' which reverberated round the stands.

— LM

23 JUNE 1994

WIMBLEDON DIARY: BORIS'S BALLS

At the end of every day, used tennis balls are sold off to the public, with the Duchess of Kent having featured among past purchasers. After Boris Becker's first-round match, a middle-aged lady, not quite sure of the form, went up to the WRVS information desk and asked, with somewhat unlovely ambiguity: 'Where can I bid for Boris Becker's balls?'

— LM

24 JUNE 1994

PLEASURE AND THE PERILS
OF CENTRE COURT

Fred Perry

To play a match on the Centre Court at Wimbledon is the dream of players all over the world. To be able to watch a match on this hallowed court is perhaps the dream of all enthusiasts as well. It looks so inviting, you feel you could walk out there and in your mind's eye play your dream game without any problems at all. It looks comparatively small and benign. Do not be fooled. I have played on it many times and also studied it extensively with Mr Fuller, the groundsman who travelled widely giving his advice when grass was a predominant surface.

Almost all centre courts have long run-backs between the baselines and the walls of the stands. The space on the sides is not so large, something between 20 and 25 feet before you hit the box seating walls. Not so at Wimbledon. It's about 30 feet to the sighting barrier, another 25 feet to the wall of the stands, and the whole seating area has a roof over it. Paris has no roof. New York has no roof. Melbourne has a sliding roof, making it possible to play indoor and outdoor tennis on the same day. The court itself is always 78 feet long and except for Wimbledon and partly in Melbourne the spectators are in the sunshine, so the ball comes out of a multi-coloured background caused by the sun's rays on the bright clothing of spectators.

At Wimbledon, the ball can be seen for a longer time as the dark background under the roof seems to give a longer sighting. It is still only travelling some 78 feet from baseline to baseline as on all other courts in the world. You think you have more time to prepare for the shot but find you are two or three inches too slow with your racket and the timing is off. For a player making his first appearance on the Centre Court, he has the problems of adjusting and his rhythm takes time. It takes about a set and a half to get the timing right. But you can be in a big hole by that time.

The players come out past the sighting barrier and are immediately faced with over 15,000 pairs of eyes giving them the once-over. Should royalty be present, and they usually are these days, you follow explicit instructions, walk to a spot parallel with the service line, turn to the Royal Box and bow, or curtsey, as the case may be. This makes the tension a little tighter.

Mr Fuller taught me to study the way the mowers had been used. The lines, always dead straight, look beautiful but still have a bearing on the bounce of the ball. Pitching a ball with the grain of the cut causes it to skid and keep slightly lower, coming through a little faster. Bouncing against the grain, it holds up a bit and gives a slightly higher bounce. You have to adjust a little and should the court be damp or slippery, have the ability to make 'snap' shots, either holding the racket back a second or two or pushing it through a little faster. That's where the Europeans fall down. Nurtured on slow clay courts, they are taught a slower rhythm with longer backswings and follow-through. They don't like grass and never have, and believe that playing tennis on it spoils it for the cows.

Hard courts and soft clay surfaces have taken over, leaving Wimbledon as the only grass-court Grand Slam event. With the birth of the computer ranking list, which unfortunately now governs the seedings in all events, we find so many upsets of seeded players. Competitors have become computer specialists, working out the events where the surface suits their personal game. With so many tournaments on the calendar and so few 'names' available, the lesser lights are able to pick and choose their spots to get good rankings. The hard-court and indoor experts get high seedings in their European events because they have done so well on their own surface. They promptly get knocked off because they can't play on the slower surface. Their style of play just isn't suited to it.

The slow-court season of Europe, which ends with the French Open, gives success to the Europeans in particular so they also move much higher on the computer. Then they come to Wimbledon, get seeded on their high computer standings, and almost catch the next plane home because they don't like grass. They have never mastered it and don't even try. Out they go in double-quick time.

Different surfaces call for different techniques. Surely it would be better to rank players on results on each of their own separate surfaces and give them seeding priority according to results on those surfaces. On hard courts, the 'hard and indoor' list could apply and the same idea used with 'slow play' in Europe. A special Wimbledon list could be used for players who know how to play on it. This would prevent good grass-court performers being shunted out of the tournament while seeded 'non-grass-courters' were busy being demolished by those who gained entry, many times by the 'wild-card route'.

4 JULY 1994

SECOND FIDDLE
PLUCKS SW19'S HEART-STRINGS

Fred Perry

The new women's champion had to sit in a chair while the losing finalist received an unprecedented five minutes' standing ovation when she received her prize on her final singles appearance at Wimbledon. Martina Navratilova, second fiddle on the court, took the stage while the champion, Conchita Martinez, waited. I have never seen or heard such a demonstration of affection in all the years I have been a player or spectator at Wimbledon. There has never been such an emotional climax to any match in that famous arena.

The new champion produced an unbroken stream of passing shots that were unbelievable. Navratilova just could not believe what was happening and the slow walk was much in evidence as she tried to figure it out. It was a most intriguing final and a new star was born – a personality the women's game needs badly at this time. Martinez has lived her tennis life in the shadow of another Spaniard, Arantxa Sanchez Vicario. Twice French Open champion, Martinez has received little worldwide attention and not too much in her own country. But one Wimbledon title is far more prestigious than two French. Her media value will leap and her self-confidence will soar. She will become a much better player.

Navratilova has departed the tournament scene. It is a pity but the time has come. She leaves it with dignity and pride. She will go down in tennis history as the greatest athlete and dedicated champion of all time and perhaps the best women's player that ever walked on to a tennis court.

This 108th Wimbledon has been blessed with good weather except for the horrible second day. It has provided more excitement than usual. To lose the women's champion, Steffi Graf, and the second and third men's seeds in the first few days, made a mess of the draw. The standard of tennis has been rather like the curate's egg – good and bad in spots. Unfortunately, British interest in the women's singles was snuffed out quickly. The men bit the dust at an early stage, with the exception of Chris Wilkinson – who survived until the Friday – and standard-bearer Jeremy Bates, who produced his usual grass-court form and stuck it out until the second Monday. The exploits gave British tennis a much needed boost and let's hope it can make further progress. Wimbledon and its grass is one proposition, but what happens when they go abroad to other surfaces? Surely there must be someone, some-where who has the talent, dedication and determination to make the grade.

I watch players these days and find a certain lack of urgency in their approach to the matches. If they serve well they work; if the serve is off they give the impression that next week means another pay cheque so why bother. I do miss that Jimmy Connors attitude. When he was on court, one had the feeling he was saying to himself: 'This guy's not going to beat me.' I don't see that any more.

There has long been talk of speeding up the game and also making it more interesting for the spectators. The ATP came up with a beauty. Reduce the present 25-second allowance between points to 20 seconds. That's going to save a heck of a lot of time! After all, the players have just had 90 seconds to sit down, relax and check with their coaches while the TV advertise-ments are shown. They also propose more spectator involvement by letting them move about and shout during play. That just is not on. Make a noise now or move around and they stop play, as it disturbs them.

The two women's semi-finals and final provided a great finale. Of the last four, three players were in their 30s, with Martinez 22. What happened to the players between 20 and 25? Pete Sampras retained his title as everyone expected. Under the fast conditions there was no one who could even come close to him and his defeat of Goran Ivanisevic was a very routine affair. After the drama and excitement of Saturday's women's final, the boys were on a hiding to nothing as they had no hope of creating the same excitement with their big serve-and-volley games.

28 JUNE 1995

WIMBLEDON DIARY: SPIDERMAN PALMER

Already trailing two sets to love against Scott Draper, America's Jared Palmer played a bad game to lose the lead he had held in the third set. The American's head went down and, in staring at the ground, he spotted a spider. There may have been murder in his heart but, very gently, he took his racket and shepherded the beastie towards the back netting. To the huge satisfaction of those who enjoy their superstitions, Palmer was never in trouble again. With the man they call 'the next Rod Laver' hitting a cluster of wild forehands, the American won 5–7, 3–6, 7–5, 6–2, 6–3.

– LM

6 JULY 1995

WIMBLEDON DIARY: A BIRDIE PUTTED

A small bird, maybe confused by Zina Garrison-Jackson's strange flutterings as she prepares to receive serve, was struck by a lob as Garrison and Katrina Adams lost to Jana Novotna and Sanchez Vicario in the doubles. What was the ruling? All the players wanted to double-check when the match was done, but the umpire was correct. They played a let.

– LM

7 JULY 1995

WIMBLEDON DIARY: BY ROYAL APPOINTMENT

'Kitty', as she likes to be known, was yesterday retiring from Town and County catering after 40 years at Wimbledon, many of them in the Club and

Guest areas. She remembers the days when people would come to the Championships straight after Ascot, wearing much the same fancy clothes and attaching rather more interest in being seen than watching play. She describes today's crowd as 'a little more casual and rather keener on its tennis'.

For 30 years Kitty has served those in the Royal Box, her overriding memory being of how each member of the Royal Family in turn has been equally polite. The nearest she would make to an indiscreet revelation concerned a recent trend. Apparently, the Royals love their sardine sandwiches.

– LM

4 JULY 1996

SIR CLIFF PLAYS WINNING SET ON CENTRE COURT

Giles Smith

Predictably, rain stopped play at Wimbledon yesterday. Completely unexpectedly, Sir Cliff Richard then stopped the rain. The covers were on and the crowd were huddling beneath umbrellas when, from a position at the back of the Royal Box, and easily visible in a bright checked jacket and searingly yellow tie, the singer appeared with a microphone. He raised his voice and his arms, sang 'Congratulations' and, almost at once, the clouds parted. Twenty minutes later, Pete Sampras was back on court.

It was a moment reminiscent, not of sports events, but of old summer rock festivals. At Woodstock, in the 1960s, the crowd were urged to think hard in the hope of raising the collective mental energy to stop the rain. Yesterday, in what will doubtless go down in history as Cliffstock, the crowd had the slightly less taxing task of singing along and waving their arms while Sir Cliff manfully did the rest.

On backing vocals was a unique ensemble of women players, including Virginia Wade, Pam Shriver and Gigi Fernandez. 'Bachelor Boy' was the cue, bizarrely, for Martina Navratilova to turn up. Cliff, who apologised for the absence of his regular band, referred to his backers as The Supremes and said it was a pity they hadn't brought their rackets with them. 'You could have pretended they were guitars.'

Sir Cliff, 55, is no mean tennis player himself and was made a full member of the All-England Club earlier this year, but he had probably never expected to play in public on the Centre Court. His set yesterday steered largely clear of recent pop music trends, settling instead for hits from the 1950s and 1960s – 'All Shook Up', 'The Young Ones' and the richly inappropriate 'Summer Holiday'. Numerous fans of Sir Cliff were left dewy-eyed by the experience, which was some consolation for not seeing the British hope, Tim Henman, who spent a nerve-racking day waiting to make more history against Todd Martin. The more sceptical took comfort in a single fact: at least Sir Cliff didn't do 'Mistletoe and Wine'.

7 JULY 1996

GRAF SWEEPS CLOUDS AWAY

Ronald Atkin

Steffi Graf brought the sunshine to Wimbledon yesterday as she plundered her seventh singles title at the Championships. In a one-hour 28-minute match, played from start to finish under a bright sun, Graf defeated Arantxa Sanchez Vicario 6–3, 7–5. It was the expected confirmation of the German's ongoing domination of the women's game and was achieved despite an aching knee and the sniffles from a virus condition. It was Sanchez Vicario, in fact, who looked a degree or two under the weather. Her ability to chase and retrieve was noticeably less marked than the usual all-in commitment to the cause, though this was in part due to the brilliance with which Graf took charge of this match. She has never, as Sanchez Vicario noted ruefully afterwards, hit her forehand harder or more accurately.

The 27-year-old Graf has now won 20 Grand Slam tournaments and stands second in the pantheon of greats to Margaret Court, who captured 24. This was Graf's 100th tournament title in a career stretching back 14 years, and she has captured the last five Grand Slams in which she competed. All this from a woman whose future has been in doubt for the past two years because of a chronic back condition, and who underwent a second foot operation last December.

In this sodden Wimbledon it was only to be expected that, after the Centre Court fireworks of the MaliVai Washington win a little earlier, the women's final would be delayed by the weather. The players had just started their warm-up when rain started to fall, but after a 53-minute delay the clouds stayed well away. Sanchez Vicario opened with a smart little ploy which only just failed to work, winning the toss and inviting Graf to open the serving. Twice Graf was within a point of losing that opening serve but she hung on gamely. Then Sanchez Vicario was immediately under assault as Graf began to batter her opponent with big, powerful, accurate ground strokes. So grimly were they locked into combat that the first two games lasted ten minutes and the opening four games all went to deuce.

Graf managed the crucial break of serve in the fourth game, however, and it proved the key to the opening set. Sanchez Vicario tried everything to claw back the break, even forsaking her natural way of playing and charging the net. She was also, as ever, poised to punish the slightest Graf miscalculation, but there were precious few of those in a 34-minute first set. There was no sign of Graf's foot coming off the pedal in the second set, either. She surged through the first four games, dropping only two points on her own serve and ruthlessly exposing a Sanchez Vicario weakness on the backhand and occasional untypical wildness with some of her returns. But those on the packed Centre Court who thought they were in for an early tea needed to think again, as the 24-year-old from Barcelona mounted one of her familiar counter-attacks.

As Graf went for the kill at 4–1, moving to the net behind her serve, she was passed and broken. There was a car alarm going off in the background and alarm bells should have been ringing in Graf's head, too, especially when she went for an easy kill of an overhead and was guilty of playing an air shot, a rarity indeed at this level of tennis. That was all the encouragement Sanchez Vicario needed to get back into the match. By now Graf was towelling down frequently. Was the virus bothering her? It certainly seemed so when she served for the match at 5–4. Two double-faults pitched her into dire trouble. One break point was saved with a smash and an exultant Graf skipped away, fist raised, but two forehand errors cost her the game and levelled the set at 5–5. Graf's response was that of a true champion. She went on to the attack, drove two stupendous forehands into the deepest corners, then floated a gorgeous backhand which drifted past the incoming Arantxa. The startled little Spaniard promptly dropped serve by projecting a backhand too long. Stepping up to serve for the match for a second time, Graf seized the chance against an opponent who was clearly tiring at a rapid rate of knots. Match point came up when Sanchez Vicario sent a backhand service return wide, and then a Graf serve was returned into the netting.

Graf was £353,000 the richer but her reaction was a good deal more muted than it had been here a year ago, after what was a much more entertaining match against the same opponent. Their final at the French Open last month had also been a much more emotional occasion. The applause, too, was polite rather than rapturous. Seeing Graf lift the trophy seven times may be verging on the boring for some. The players kissed decorously, Arantxa raised a laugh or two by offering Steffi her runners-up prize and then borrowed the winner's trophy, just to feel what it was like. With Graf in this sort of form, it may be some time before she has an opportunity to hold it for real.

8 JULY 1996

SPORT ON TELEVISION: MARTIN SURPRISED BY PENDULUM'S RETURN

Giles Smith

Astonishing images from Wimbledon on Saturday: skies a colour one can only describe as blue, dotted with strange white fluffy things, and the light full of weird, golden stuff. 'Sunshine,' concluded John Barrett in the BBC commentary box. It's at times like these that you fully appreciate having an expert like Barrett around. Not all of us have memories going back that far. The second week had been nothing but grey skies. Rain brings down upon Wimbledon all manner of crises and miseries. It's frustrating for the spectators, impossible for the players and sheer hell for the commentators. 'Why, they even ran out of fudge in the sweet shop,' Barrett told us on Saturday, in the tone of one about to compose a letter of complaint to the club secretary.

Yet here we were on the last Saturday with the tournament, amazingly, back on schedule and the women's final about to begin. The only evidence of the lousiness of the preceding days was British Summer Time's gift to Steffi Graf — what Barrett unhesitatingly diagnosed as a 'nasty cough'. Or as Virginia Wade put it, removing the matter properly to the realm of tennis: 'Steffi keeps getting into this coughing situation.' What we had to worry about was the chance of this coughing situation developing into a fully fledged ear, nose and throat concept, leading eventually to a play-hindrance scenario. But it didn't pan out that way. Steffi walked off with the silver tray and the cheque for £353,000 — 'not that she'll be thinking about it', Barrett promised us. And Arantxa Sanchez Vicario (try saying that with a mouthful of fudge) was in the role of pugnacious bridesmaid all over again.

This year, for the first time in television history, a microphone was able to pick up the magic which is the Duke of Kent's end-of-tournament ballboy interview. This happens annually, as the Duke and Duchess make their way to the trophy presentation through twin lines of Wimbledon's most underrated servants, but its contents were a mystery until Saturday. 'Did you enjoy being a ballboy?' the Duke asked, before immediately answering himself: 'Frightfully hard work.' Then, further down the line, he stopped in front of another one: 'Did you enjoy being a ballboy? Frightfully hard work.' What one really wanted to hear was a ballboy returning the question: 'Do you enjoy being a member of the Royal Family? Frightfully hard work.' But they're too well trained.

Earlier that morning, Todd Martin (crazy name, crazy guy) had an open door into the men's final slammed in his face by MaliVai Washington (crazy name, crazy city). 'Now there's a change in the pendulum,' said David Mercer, not the only commentator recently to have been thrown by a malfunctioning pendulum. Indeed, is there any chance he bought his pendulum from ITV's Brian Moore? During football's European Cup final at the start of the summer, Moore detected 'a slight little turn of the pendulum Ajax's way'. It's time this pendulum was pulped or replaced by a more reliable electronic light meter.

The only performer at Wimbledon consistently in a position to take advantage of the weather was Des Lynam. The wetter it got, the drier Des became. On Wednesday he guided us through some images from Court No. 1, where Wimbledon's uniformed stewards were leading portions of the drenched crowd in time-passing mime games and renditions of 'Singin' In The Rain'. It would have been easy to capitalise sentimentally on these pictures. Only Lynam would have had the necessary calm to insinuate that being caught up in the middle of all that might have been like finding oneself trapped in a holiday camp staffed by the army. The camera alighted on one of the most active stewards. 'He's a household name,' Des said. 'In his own household, at any rate.'

Shortly, in what was to become front-page news, a professional household name would appear on the Centre Court, wearing one of John Barnes's checked jackets. It was Sir Cliff Richard and – great news – he was holding a microphone. Astonishingly, the BBC were on the scene right at the beginning of this unplanned moment. You'd think someone had tipped them off or something. Still, they definitely hadn't been given a set list. 'Hope he doesn't do "Summer Holiday",' Des said. 'What about "Summer Holiday"?' suggested Sir Cliff, out on the court.

How popular is Sir Cliff? Put it this way: many people phoned the BBC late on Wednesday to complain that his impromptu appearance had not been listed in *Radio Times*. Even allowing for the fact that some of these calls may have come from people who would have liked to have known when Sir Cliff was on so that they could go out and miss him, this is a remarkable testament to the 55-year-old singer's enduring appeal, particularly among the bewildered.

Later Sir Cliff popped up to the BBC booth for a bit of post-gig smooth-talk with Sue Barker, whose outfits this year have provided us with nearly all of Wimbledon's brighter moments. Sue and Sir Cliff had their names linked some years ago, before Sir Cliff decided to release himself as a single. But the old chemistry still bubbles. On Wednesday, he told Sue he was sorry she hadn't been up there on the Centre Court among the women players who pretended to be his backing singers; Sue was, after all, 'a better dancer than Pam Shriver'. The flatterer! No shortage of fudge in Cliff's sweetshop! A shame, you reflected, that the pair never got it together when they seemed to share so much. Not just a love of tennis, but a taste for clothes made out of their mums' sofas. It would have been a marriage made in Debenhams.

23 JUNE 1997
PUTTING THE FAN IN FANATICAL
David Law
Wimbledon 1997 Supplement

Unwashed, fully clothed bodies wrapped in sleeping bags lie on a mattress of empty beer cans, junk-food cases and the previous day's newspapers. You could be forgiven for believing that a wrong turn had taken you to Cardboard City rather than the outskirts of the All-England Lawn Tennis and Croquet Club. As far as the eye can see – up and down the length of the Somerset Road adjacent to the grounds – small tents protect veteran queuers from the cold night air. This is the warts-and-all side of Wimbledon. Civilised people (myself included) happily cast aside home comforts for nights sleeping on the pavement – and all to watch a day's tennis.

To the TV-viewing public, Wimbledon fortnight begins on Monday at lunch-time with Desmond Lynam and Sue Barker casually introducing the opening day's play. But for the 600 or so ticketless people at the front of the queue, the Championships can start as much as 48 hours before a ball is hit. Mike Walsh, an irrepressible queuer of 16 years, takes no chances. Arriving early on Saturday before anyone else, he spends two nights eating from barbecues, drinking coffee from a flask and chatting with friends from queues gone by. But why so early? For Walsh, the queuing experience can be just as enjoyable as the tennis itself.

'It's the whole occasion,' he says. 'We arrive on Saturday every year, and it's like meeting up with old friends. We spend the whole two weeks here and have some great conversations. It's the atmosphere of the place.' This friendly group bring a table and chairs, facilities to cook their own food and arrive early, ensuring a full choice of courts for the following day. But not everyone is as well prepared. First-timers are conspicuous by their lack of luggage – the heaviest bags carried are underneath their eyes after a night spent tossing and turning on the cold concrete.

Hygienically speaking, the Wimbledon queue is nothing to write home about, but no one seems to mind. Male and female Portakabins provide half-a-dozen washbasins and toilets for the 3,000 or so queuers. And there is no danger of oversleeping. Those who are able to sleep receive a free alarm call at 5a.m. each morning from teenage newspaper sellers shouting, 'Wakey, wakey'. However, by that time the smell of freshly cooked bacon has encouraged many people to desert their roadside beds for an alternative queue outside a converted ice-cream van.

The Wimbledon queuers are a cosmopolitan bunch: Australians, Americans, Germans and Japanese converge on SW19, and with so much time on your hands, you soon find yourself merrily chatting away to your neighbour, whoever he or she may be. Tennis is the native language and everyone seems to speak it fluently. By 8a.m. tents are packed away and the queue begins to move forward. A number of welcome sideshows encourage the final hour to pass swiftly with Radio Wimbledon swinging into action over loudspeakers, providing results, reports and interviews with the stars.

As the clock hits 9.45a.m. Mike Walsh and company finally purchase their tickets. They plump for Court No. 2 and hope for a day of upsets. The remaining overnight queuers divide up the Centre Court, Courts No. 1 and 2 ticket allocations at £21, £17 and £14 respectively, leaving the late arrivals and rookie queuers to fill the ground capacity for Courts No. 3–17 at £8 a time.

Later, as the first day's play comes to a close, the queuing Wimbledon faithful return to the pavement and build their temporary city for another night. Darkness descends. Unwashed, fully clothed bodies wrapped in sleeping bags lie again on mattresses of beer cans, junk-food cases and the previous day's newspapers.

27 JUNE 1997
WIMBLEDON DIARY: FALLING FOUL OF FASHION POLICE

First thing yesterday morning, Venus Williams, 17, and her younger sister, Serena, were in the Women's Tennis Association office, discussing the business of their hair beads, which, for the sake of other players looking for ways of filling in their spare time in this sodden fortnight, take 12 hours to thread. Having seen newspaper reports to the effect that the Williamses' beads, if they were to fall out on court as they did at Indian Wells at the start of this year, could get them into trouble, the sisters wanted to know the score.

The pair had the so-called 'hindrance rule' spelled out to them. Namely, that the first time the beads started popping out all over the place, the umpire would accept that it was simply a case of bad luck. If it were to happen for a second time, the Williamses would get a warning – and after a third time, they would lose a point.

– LM

1 JULY 1997
WIMBLEDON DIARY: TAKING THE BOUNCE OUT OF WIMBLEDON

Much has been written about one or two top Wimbledon women whose tennis dresses or shirts have been hanging somewhat unflatteringly over the latest in cropped tops or sports bras. 'The sports bra may not do anything for a player's shape but it is comfortable,' explained one contestant with experience of such things.

Yesterday the manageress in the Harrods lingerie department said that the saggy, shapeless look was entirely unnecessary. She put the *Telegraph* Diary on to the store's PR department, who in turn issued an invitation. Any Wimbledon girls looking, as it were, for a bit of a lift, could come to the store's first floor and avail themselves of a special free fitting service.

– LM

5 JULY 1997

WIMBLEDON DIARY: ILIE'S DISAPPEARING BALL TRICK

Roger Taylor said that he and his contemporaries have been talking, lightly, of how Ilie Nastase would have dealt with Greg Rusedski and his idiosyncratic urge to keep serving with a lucky ball. 'The moment Ilie spotted what was going on,' said Taylor, 'he would have slipped the relevant ball in his pocket. Then, if anyone had challenged him, he would have gesticulated as if to suggest he didn't know what the hell they were talking about.'

– LM

20 JUNE 1998

PROPERTY SECTION: GAME, LET AND MATCH
Christopher Middleton

How would you like to be paid £10,000 to make yourself scarce for three weeks? That is the sort of bonus that some homeowners in Wimbledon will pocket this month, courtesy of 'the greatest tennis tournament in the world'. In June and July, the word 'let' takes on a dual meaning in southwest London, as several hundred local residents hire out their homes and head for the hills. In so doing, they achieve their own version of the Grand Slam: they avoid the tennis crowds, and have an expensive foreign holiday entirely financed by the stars.

Prices for a temporary tennis home start at about £400 for a one-bedroom flat on the rather drab, Quaker-built Southfields Grid (the mile-square expanse of houses that you see in the distance when the camera pulls away from Desmond Lynam). The top seeds, however, tend to drift towards the more glamorous environment of Wimbledon Village where one-bedroom flats go for £500 a week, while a four-bedroom house can fetch £3,000. Most sought-after are big residences within walking distance of the All-England Club. For years, Martina Navratilova has hired the same house in nearby Newstead Way, from where she can hear the cries of the Centre Court crowd and actually watch games taking place on the outside courts. The exact address is closely guarded. Top players don't like it made public where they are staying. No one appreciates the need for secrecy more than Joanna Doniger, who runs the specialist lettings agency Tennis London.

'The players would hate it if their cover was blown. But what they love about Wimbledon is that they get to stay in a real home rather than some anonymous hotel,' she says. 'They genuinely enjoy the fact that the owners' clothes are left in the cupboards and family photographs are left out on the mantelpiece. I've got some players who have taken the same house for the past five or six years.'

To protect their privacy, some stars bring along bodyguards as house guests. And no one – but no one – gets past the front gate. Not even the owners, whose mail is routinely delivered to their temporary accommodation by blazered 'security personnel'. 'It's a very funny feeling going past your house for an entire month and not being able to go inside because other people are living there,' says Sue Wilson, who each year takes the entire family off to her parents' home ten miles down the A3. 'It's still term time so it's pretty disruptive for the children but the money does come in extremely handy for the school fees.'

Around the back gardens of SW19, anecdotes abound as to what people have spent their money on. 'Each year we have a different room decorated on the strength of what we make from Wimbledon,' confides a newly retired civil servant. Others splash out on exotic holidays in the Caribbean or the Canaries. But lying on a beach 3,000 miles away, some houseowners can still hear the sound of breaking crockery. 'You get very nervous the first time you rent out your house,' said one resident who stands to make £2,500 a week from letting out her home this year. 'When we started, we used to leave these notes everywhere about what china they should and shouldn't use; we even pinned up instructions reminding them to tuck the shower curtain inside the bath.' The notes do have an impact. 'I live in constant terror of forgetting to water the owners' plants as per instructed,' confided one regular hirer of a particular Wimbledon home. 'Whatever time I stagger back from the ground, I always feel I have to connect up the hosepipe and refresh the begonias.'

For the most part, the hirers are much better behaved than their hosts expect. 'In six years, the worst we've had is a few broken plates – and one year the carpet needed cleaning,' says one resident. And the deposit pays for it all. Some firms ask for as much as six weeks' rent up front, to set against possible breakages and damage. But problems are rare, says Joanna Doniger. 'Tennis players are not exactly a wild bunch these days – all they're after is a quiet life and an early night.'

The tension in this niche property market revolves around the speed at which the game can change. Both homeowners and agents can be waiting right up until the last minute to know whether or not a particular property is required. 'Last year I got this frantic phone call after the tournament had begun from a French player who'd amazed himself by getting through to the next round, and so didn't have a place to stay,' says Nicola Booth, of Wimbledon agents Cotton Thompson Cole. Conversely, some lets terminate abruptly. 'They're the best kind of all,' confided one veteran Wimbledon resident. 'When they've booked the place for a whole month and the player gets knocked out in the first round. You get all the rental money – plus you're back home early.'

Most experienced Wimbledon landlords say the longest lasting inconvenience is likely to be the continual unearthing of brand new tennis shoes around the house which the players seem to use once and then discard. Life inside may change dramatically during your temporary absence. Sue Wilson remembers one star player who insisted that the house had to have satellite television. 'We told him we weren't connected up to Sky or anything. He seemed to accept it, but when we drove past the house a few days later, we saw this giant satellite dish sprouting out of the roof. But when we got back into the house at the end of the tournament he'd had the connection terminated and the dish removed. We were a bit disappointed at the time – but I think the neighbours were rather relieved.'

22 JUNE 1998

WHY I LOVE WIMBLEDON

Chris Evert

Wimbledon is still the title the players most want to win. If you've got to pick just one to win in the year, then in the minds of most players, Wimbledon will be that one. Even though I'm an American and the United States Open is my tournament, Wimbledon was always the icing on the cake for me, the pinnacle of tennis. I grew up with that. The first match I saw was at Wimbledon on television. The atmosphere is so different from the other Grand Slams. When you go to them, you often feel you're at a baseball game, with everyone screaming. But at Wimbledon, on Centre Court, there's a reverence. You can feel the ghosts of past champions. Also, the Brits really know how to present their events, whether it's Wimbledon, Royal weddings or Ascot. You do it with so much class and respect for tradition.

It's not easy playing there the first time. I was lucky because my first time playing at Wimbledon was in the Wightman Cup. That was on the old

Court No. 1. But then I played my first three matches in the Championships on Centre Court. For a clay-courter, playing on grass was a daunting experience. Suddenly, you have to deal with a surface which is slick one day, really fast and dry the next. Although many people felt my game wasn't suited to grass, I loved Wimbledon – and playing on grass. It forced me to do things I didn't normally do. I had to compromise my game and improvise. You have to shorten your swing and make other technical adjustments. I liked that challenge. It becomes a mental game, as much as a physical one, because the two Grand Slams at this time of the year are so close together. After Paris, where I usually did pretty well (winning the title seven times), there wasn't the time to get used to that success before having to concentrate on preparing for the next challenge.

Since I played at Wimbledon for the last time in 1989, the biggest change in the game has been the extra power which the players get from modern rackets. Despite what some people say, I don't see the women necessarily being better athletes than before. I see extraordinary athletes like the Williams sisters but we had Martina Navratilova in that calibre. We played with wooden rackets so we kept that little bit of finesse which we hardly see in today's players, with the exception of Martina Hingis. There's a lot more top spin in the game because the racket-head speed has improved. More players have a 'western' grip with a more open stance, using the hips, torso and legs a lot more to generate the power. That's why I've been so happy to see Hingis coming along so well because I think the next generation always emulates the No. 1 player in the world and she has so much talent. The Williams sisters have started out with sheer power but I think it is only a matter of time before they also adapt. The best players in the world will always encompass every aspect of the game. If you watch Hingis, you will see that she can wind up really powerful winners when she has to.

These are tremendous times for women's tennis. Tennis is exciting if you have great rivalries – which we had with myself and Martina, especially, and the men with Jimmy Connors, Björn Borg and John McEnroe – or new blood and new personalities. Now, among the women, we have the added element, as we saw at the French, of experienced players such as Monica Seles very much back in the picture, and at Wimbledon, the added mystery of how well Steffi Graf will perform in the short time she has had to get back to form and fitness. I don't think Steffi can win Wimbledon. I'm amazed she's even playing. At the same time, I'm delighted she's back because I want her to retire on her terms, not because her body breaks down and she has no choice in the matter.

Steffi is giving a wake-up call to the youngsters, saying, 'If I'm healthy, I'm still a force', but I just don't know if she has enough time to peak.

As for the Williams sisters, I think Venus will find it too difficult to move well enough on grass to win. History shows that many of the taller, bigger women, such as Betty Stove and Brenda Schultz, have had a problem. The grass favours the more agile. Anna Kournikova had a great Wimbledon last year, though with a rather kind draw, and there was also a little bit of the intimidation factor because players did not know enough about her, which won't be the same this time. But like Hingis, she's a crafty player, she can change her game, rally from the baseline if she has to, and she has a good drop shot. She's also improved a lot mentally since Pavel Slozil began working with her. Anna could play Serena Williams in the third round. That would be the match of the first week.

I go for Hingis, who realises she let the French title slip away. She had the wind blown out of her sails and was defensive the whole match, which is not like her. My second pick is Jana Novotna. Her ground strokes were so much better at the French. I think her nerve will be fine. As for the men, I like the way Yevgeny Kafelnikov plays, Marcelo Rios could also do well, but my heart wants Pete Sampras to win. He's been going through a bit of a slump so it's now or never for him, as far as this year is concerned, and I wouldn't be surprised if Wimbledon, which is the easiest of the Grand Slams for him to win, and which has always been the highlight for him, brings out the best in him again.

24 JUNE 1998

WIMBLEDON DIARY:
MICKEY MOUSE'S DAY OUT

The tradition of animal interference continues to amuse. There was the wagtails' nest on Centre Court in 1990, the occupants' flutterings disturbing the Navratilova final. Last year a sparrow dropped dead out of the sky to be removed by an umpire with the formality one associates with the All-England Club. The mouse that interrupted play on Centre Court in Monday's first-round match between Yevgeny Kafelnikov and Mark Philippoussis looks set to be a repeatable delight. The rodent frolicked around the grass before being ushered out of sight near the BBC commentary box. 'Let's hope he's not the proud father of 27,' quipped one club official.

— SE

25 JUNE 1998

WIMBLEDON DIARY:
LADY IN WHITE (AND RED)

A muddled member of the public rang one of the six Women's Royal Voluntary Service information stands for sartorial advice. 'I know about the dress code of white,' she said, 'but would it be all right if I wore a white dress with red roses on it?'

— SE

6 JULY 1998

TENNIS LACKS THE MENACE OF DENNIS
Sue Mott

There was a moment of sublime and intoxicating beauty at Wimbledon on Saturday. Unfortunately for tennis, it was the moment Dennis Bergkamp struck the ball with the outside of his right boot to claim Holland's late winner against Argentina, shown live in the Wimbledon press bar. 'Jaaaaah!' yelled a bevy of Dutch journalists who should have been watching Jacco Eltingh and Paul Haarhuis in the final of the men's doubles. It was specific and damning evidence that The Fortnight had played second fiddle this year to The Month in France.

But even in its bridesmaid status, at least one individual was on hand to catch the bride's bouquet. She walked out with it at 2p.m., curtseyed to her mate, the Duchess of Kent, won an undistinguished women's singles final 6–4, 7–6, held aloft the silver tea tray and then left the Centre Court with the typically generous-hearted gesture of bestowing her armful of flowers on a woman in the crowd. Jana Novotna had finally succeeded in realising her dream, shaking off the albatross reputation of the perennial loser, with one final forehand clump. As she exulted like a World Cup goalscorer, blowing kisses to the crowd, arms outstretched, looking for a corner flag to dance with, you could almost see the shadow of the dreaded bird lift away from her.

No one could begrudge her. Certainly not the Duchess, who held both her hands and reminded her: 'I told you it would be three times lucky.' Certainly not her fellow finalist, Nathalie Tauziat, who behaved with as great an exhibition of magnanimity as we have seen from a loser at Wimbledon. Having enjoyed a good cry into the privacy of her towel immediately after the match, she was persuaded to embark on a mini lap of honour herself, clutching her demonstrably smaller and less encrusted tea tray, and smiling very French ironic smiles. She understood pretty well what had happened. Novotna was the better player whose coverage of the net, anticipation of returns and innate self-belief were to prove pivotal in the match. The Frenchwoman's essential hope had been that the Czech's mental frailty would increase in inverse proportion to her prowess as the cauldron bubbled to a frenzy. But it didn't. It nearly did, but it didn't.

Novotna's principal wobble came at 5–4 in the second set, serving for the match. Suddenly she was down 15–40, which in her case is more like 15–45. Tauziat, born and raised for her first eight years in Africa, had the animal instinct to sense a wounded beast downwind. Novotna won the next two points but Tauziat eventually claimed the game with an imperious forehand smash. 'I have nothing to regret in this match. I think I gave it my best,' the Frenchwoman said later. But there was nothing so Edith Piaf-ish about her in the deciding tie-break when with a simple netted forehand she gave her opponent an almost unassailable lead. Tauziat knew it. She fell to her knees and punched the turf with her racket handle. The game was up metaphorically. Three points later it was all over.

Now the aftermath. This match tells us many things. It tells us that two nervous players, one with a reputation for 'choking' and one the lowliest seed to reach a Wimbledon final in the Open era, may necessarily diminish the spectacle. 'Did you sleep well?' Tauziat was asked. 'So-so,' she admitted. 'I sleep OK. Not very, very good like a baby but I sleep OK.' It also tells us that two older players – Novotna 29, Tauziat a year older – may have given the young things the fright of their barely begun lives. Miss Hingis, Miss Kournikova and the Miss Williamses, not renowned for their respectful attitudes, may have regarded the wrinkles and pleats of their elders with little better than contempt. Now they will think again.

What else did we learn? That the Wimbledon crowd, unswervingly toff-to-middle class, provides a temporary antidote to those who imagine that the English, en masse, must revert to ripping off their shirts, revealing vulgar tattoos, brimful beer guts and violent streaks that terrorise the world. The Wimbledon crowd is violent only in its decorum. Small shouts of 'Come on, Jana' were all that it permitted itself on Saturday, although one radical, who was probably removed, did utter: *'Allez, Nathalie!'* Of course, every gathering of humans has its wickednesses, even here. The All-England Club had taken a phone call that very morning from a woman who announced plummily: 'I've been lucky in the wheelchair ballot for a ticket. Can you tell me where I can get a wheelchair from?'

Neither can we promise the environs were entirely tattoo free. There was Goran Ivanisevic's for a start (which he'd never have acquired had he known how much it would hurt) and a military policeman guarding an entrance near the Royal Box had a blatant 'Den' etched on his arm. I told you there was no escape from the World Cup. Anyone for Dennis?

6 JULY 1998
WIMBLEDON DIARY: FAMILIAR SIGHT OF ROSEWALL'S TOUCH

An honorary steward crept in to Centre Court late in the evening to watch Ken Rosewall and other veterans playing an over-45 doubles. It was a tight, competitive match, played in good spirit with wonderful rallies and touches. The steward commented to a woman next to him that it was a pleasure to see Rosewall had not lost his touch and asked if she recalled him in his prime. 'Yes,' came the reply. 'I remember him well. I'm his wife.'

– SE

22 JUNE 1999
LUSH GRASS, EAGER CROWD – PITY ABOUT THE TENNIS
Martin Johnson

It's a Wimbledon tradition to make mini celebrities out of people who spend the night sleeping on pavements for the chance to watch Henman or Sampras, but if we're honest, the real tennis fans are out there on Court 16. Shortly after midday, before Tim and Pete had even clambered into their chauffeured limos, the packed crowd settled into an expectant hush as the umpire leaned towards her microphone. 'Miss Papadaki to serve. Play.' What is it about Wimbledon, you wonder, that persuades people to sit glued to (and occasionally get excited about) a match which – were it taking place in their back garden – would not even induce them to draw back the curtains? 'Gee, honey, where shall we go first?' said an American tourist to his wife as he studied the order of play board. And you could see their problem. On the very next court to Miss C. Papadaki and Miss M. Saeki, was Miss M. Vento against Miss E. Gagliardi. Decisions, decisions.

This year, the show courts have had speed guns installed to measure the services, but no such device was available on No. 16, or indeed necessary. Miss Papadaki's opening serve, far from blurring off the turf and thudding into the backstop before Miss Saeki could blink, crossed the net like a wounded bumblebee. Miss Saeki's return was out. Miss Saeki is from Tokyo, which in itself guaranteed a crowd. Japanese players are always well supported at Wimbledon, and as a hundred camera clicks accompanied her every stroke, the thought occurred that Japanese tennis players must be – royalty and film stars included – the most photographed people in the world. I once saw a Japanese tourist in London taking pictures, from three different angles, of a parking meter with an out-of-order bag draped over it.

The match itself was only 20 minutes old when the line judges were all replaced en masse, as though Wimbledon's top brass had concluded that there was a real danger of officials nodding off in their chairs if exposed for too long to this kind of contest. Miss Saeki won in straight sets, but not a single rally prompted the audience to break into anything more animated than a polite ripple of applause. If only the spectators had been in possession of the official women's tour guide, they might have realised that this was something far more interesting than a match between two relatively anonymous tennis players. Miss Saeki, for instance, likes to ski, is 'outgoing and easy to get along with', and her favourite colour is red. Oh, and yellow. Her 'most memorable experience' is listed as watching a women's Federation Cup match in Tokyo, which may say something about the rich and varied life on the women's tennis tour. Miss Papadaki, from Athens, is (surprise, surprise) fond of Greek food, and her favourite actor is Kevin Costner. Interesting, or what?

One of the biggest crowds of the day was gathered around Court No. 5, which was hardly surprising as the first match on was a compelling clash between Miss S. Testud and Miss J. Pullin. In fact, it was such a crush around the outside courts that a spectator could conceivably have died at midday, spent the rest of the day being shuttled from court to court, and only have been discovered at close of play – by which time the crowd had dispersed just enough to allow someone enough room to keel over.

Meantime, over on Court No. 6, there was the umpire's nightmare of Delgado versus Delgado, which sounds a bit like a American movie courtroom drama, but was in fact a first-round men's singles between Ramon, of

Paraguay, and Jamie, of Maidenhead. Our boy won in straight sets, which was a bit of a surprise as his world ranking is 320 places lower, but was partly due to the fact that Ramon, a hard-court specialist, looked about as happy on grass as a baby giraffe on an oil slick. The 23-year-old Delgado is a near contemporary of Henman, and was once thought to have the brighter future of the two. In 1994, as a boy wonder, he reached the semis at Junior Wimbledon before losing to Mark Philippoussis. However, while Henman has gone on to amass career earnings of around £2.1 million, Jamie's five-year total of around £40,000 is the sort of figure Tim would be asking to open a supermarket.

30 JUNE 1999
CHORUS OF GOODBYE RAINY TUESDAY
GILES SMITH

Imagine: you set aside an entire day of your life for a visit to Wimbledon and then you don't get to see a single tennis ball struck. It could only mean one of two things: either it was raining, or you had a corporate hospitality ticket. More people entered the gates of the All-England Club yesterday than on any previous second Tuesday in the history of the Championships (it's been the same story all tournament: record attendances, day on day), and contrary to widely held belief, the vast majority of them were not merely passing through on their way to recline in troughs of salmon under the awnings of Astroturfed marquees. They were here for the action. And their reward was to get copiously rained on as the weather's ambition to take the finals into a third week began to be impressively clear.

According to some interpreters of Nostradamus, the world will end this Sunday morning. Obviously, it would be a big shame for Wimbledon if it did. If the weather produces a repeat performance today, we might not even be through the semi-finals by then. But no one who was in the grounds yester-day, as the floodwaters rose to ankle-height and all non-tennis-watching wildlife headed for the hills, could deny that the omens were there.

There were, to be accurate, breaks in the rain. But only short ones while the weather got its breath back before raining even harder. So thousands of people were left with nothing to do but play their dutiful part in the tradi-tional Wimbledon wash-out tableau, which essentially involves sitting mournfully in a court-side seat, wrapped in plastic like a service-station sandwich and staring out over acres of wet tarpaulin. It would have to be the most miserable sport-related experience this side of watching Tottenham.

Naturally, in these circumstances, after the terrifying events of two years ago, one's first reaction, at the merest hint of Wimbledon rain, is nervously to scan the list of the day's guests in the Royal Box, praying avidly that it doesn't include the names of any middle-of-the-road British pop entertainers who might seize this moment of downtime to revive flagging spirits (and their own careers) by running through an impromptu, karaoke-style selection of their best-loved hits. But there was no sign of Cliff's name on there yesterday. And, better news still, no sign of Vince Hill, nor Jayne MacDonald nor either of the O'Connors, Des and Sinead. The thought of Mick Jagger strutting and crouching in front of the posh seats with, perhaps, Ann Jones and Pam Shriver behind him, vainly trying to remember the words to 'Honky Tonk Woman', while a drenched Centre Court crowd clapped along (some of them in time) was an appetising one. But alas for us, if not for him, Jagger had been a guest on the Monday when his services were not required.

So, no redemption by rock; no despairingly cheerful Redcoat-style behaviour by stewards old enough to know better; just a hopeless, long-faced vigil. Even the big screen on the hill, which is as close as most customers get to the tennis on the show courts, was out of action. It was easy to criticise, but try throwing buckets of cold water over your television for seven hours on end and see how well it works. In fact, on a thoroughly miserable day, there was some slight consolation available in this breakdown: the television might have been bust, but at least there was nothing on.

30 JUNE 1999

WIMBLEDON DIARY: TONIC FOR THE TROOPS

How did Robinson's Barley Water come to be the official drink? Through Ken Woolcott, now 82, who started his career as a medical rep. In the 1950s Robinson's Barley Water was reputed as a tonic for invalids, but Woolcott persuaded the company to promote it as a sports drink. For 20 years he visited all British tennis tournaments, the Robinsons-sponsored Davis Cup fixtures in Vienna and Barcelona, and helped to train the British squad which included Sue Barker and Jo Durie.

– SE

WIMBLEDON DIARY: CAUGHT SHORT

An umpire escorted a player off court for a 'comfort' break and decided after several minutes that he seemed to be taking rather a while. Checking under the door, he discovered the player was no longer there. When he returned to the court the players were in the middle of a rally.

– SE

5 JULY 1999

WE MAY HAVE LOST GREATEST CHAMPION OF ALL
Chris Evert

It is the end of another era in women's tennis with the retirement from Wimbledon of Steffi Graf. We have lost a great champion – maybe the greatest of all time. That is always a shame when it happens. But people forget that she has been playing full time on the women's professional tour since the age of 13. And that means that she has been playing full-time tennis on the circuit for 17 years. I can tell you, it's a real grind out there. There's the competition, plus the travelling and injuries to contend with. Maybe it all took a toll on her after all this time. Clearly she feels that it is time to go on to something different.

The last great player to bow out was probably Martina Navratilova, and that was a few years ago, so this was an historic moment. No player is bigger than the game, though. You have to look at it that way. You can also look at all the players at the other end of their careers who have emerged during this Championship. There have been four talents who have emerged at this Wimbledon who have really stood out: Jelena Dokic, Mirjana Lucic, Alexandra Stevenson and Kim Clijsters. They may not have actually won it, but even to get to the semi-finals for the first time – like Lucic and Stevenson – is unbelievable at such an early stage of their careers.

When people die, there are also others born. But the sad part about a legend retiring is that you want all the elements in women's tennis: the young up-and-coming players, those just making a breakthrough, new champions, and veterans too. Retirement can be hard if there isn't anything to go on to. For me it was not difficult as I had a great husband and we wanted to start a family, plus there were one or two other projects that I was working on. It is only hard if you retire from tennis with nothing else in life to go on to, and no new goals. For Steffi, her future depends on what else in life she has apart from tennis.

I have to say that I was surprised Steffi lost the final. I picked her to win the tournament beforehand, and I still thought she was going to do it coming into the final. The way she beat Venus Williams was awesome and I thought no one could beat her on that form. That match was probably worthy of having been a final. In retrospect, Steffi played her best tennis in that match against Williams. In the last two matches she played well, but not at her best and definitely not at the high standard of the Williams match. I could tell her that when you get on in your career you can still have great days, but there are more bad days too, and Steffi being such a perfectionist, I can't see her playing if she's not in the top three or four. Her frustration may simply be pushing her into retirement.

However, Lindsay Davenport shocked everyone, including herself – possibly herself more than anyone else. Although she won the US Open once, I don't think that Wimbledon was even in her mind as her next win at a major. She would have thought that it was more likely to happen at the Australian Open or even the French Open. Lindsay's serving was the key to the match. Steffi just couldn't read it. Lindsay looked very comfortable in her movement, and that is saying something that she looked good moving on grass where she hasn't felt entirely at ease before. For someone who said they hated playing on grass, she was still not oozing with confidence, but this year we first heard her say, 'Oh, I can play on this stuff.' Lindsay dictated the points. She had Steffi on the run more than the other way round.

For me, because I am an American, the best moment of the fortnight was the look on Lindsay's face when she had clinched the title. She just put her hands over her face, half shocked, half crying. No one expected her to win, and I was the same. I would have picked five other players ahead of her, especially with her dislike of grass, and the fact that she is not a great athlete like Steffi. But she uses what she has to the maximum. Lindsay has been the No. 1 in America, and now she is No. 1 in the world again. With Andre Agassi also No. 1 in the world again, it is almost unbelievable to have two Americans once more at the top. It's a big thing for us as the sport has been lagging a bit over the last few years. Maybe this will give American tennis the boost that it needed.

Once again, Wimbledon has been magic. And it finished on time, which is amazing considering all the bad weather of the last week. It seems to be the same every year, and I don't know how they do it.

5 JULY 1999

SIX-GUN SALUTE TO SAMPRAS

Paul Hayward

Pete Sampras is entitled to be recognised as one of the great athletes of this vanishing 20th century. There will be those who question the right of a tennis player to be mentioned on the same page as Muhammad Ali or Pele. They are in urgent need of medication. Sampras's body was on Centre Court as he recorded his sixth Wimbledon victory in seven years yesterday but his spirit was far above. A straight-sets victory over Andre Agassi, 6–3, 6–4, 7–5, took Sampras level with Roy Emerson's record of 12 titles in Grand Slam events. Emerson will be an ex-record-holder very soon. Technically, Agassi is world No. 1 this morning. But the computer that came up with that calculation is off with the electronic fairies. In the first two sets especially, Sampras's game rose to a place where the rest of us will never go, except as dazzled voyeurs. It was sport as transcendence. And now many followers of the game will happily give up hope of ever seeing anything better on a tennis court.

There were 128 players in the men's singles a fortnight ago, and the other 126 must have shrivelled as they watched Sampras unravel his almost manically intense fellow American. For a fortnight Agassi had borne the look of a prize-fighter who had just burst out of a gym ready to wreak havoc. For six matches, he did. Then this. 'I ran into a bus today,' he said. 'This is probably the best I've played in many years,' Sampras said. 'Andre brings out the best in me. He elevates my tennis to a level that's phenomenal. I need to be at my best against him. If I'm not, it's a long day.'

It took Sampras only one hour 54 minutes to break Agassi. 'If he always plays that way against me, I'm going to win two out of every ten,' Agassi said. Two is stretching it a bit. In this form, Sampras is able to levitate like Michael Jordan. He can cut, slice, drive, lob and volley expertly. Most of all, he can summon a champion's will to play better than he has all fortnight, to do what's necessary and meet each threat.

Time is running out for sport's lavishly rewarded quasi pop stars to demand inclusion in the century's absolute and unchallengeable elite.

Sampras is definitely in. The only player to have won seven Wimbledon men's titles was a Corinthian called W.C. Renshaw in the 1880s. Sportsmen were so unheralded in those days that they had to make do with initials.

Agassi – who ought to know – thinks Sampras could win three or four more titles. Already, he has won 12 of the 14 Grand Slam finals he has contested. The man has everything: most obviously, yesterday, that sacred capacity to crank up his own excellence so that even the most accomplished opponent feels as if he is trying to light a barbecue in a typhoon. Agassi said it best: 'I went out there expecting him to be a big pain in the ass. I knew he would play big in the biggest situations. He played some impeccable tennis at the important times. You've got to weather his storm. When you do that he's vulnerable, but his storm was too strong today.'

The point is that Sampras's performance went way beyond what seems possible to the eye. If a measure of greatness is how many times one feels startled, astonished, bemused during a match, then the 24th meeting of Sampras and Agassi felt like a display of greatness in an event that has too often descended into an exposition of naked power. These were the world's two best players, no doubt about that. Tim Henman now knows the length of the voyage to the top.

The first majestic rally fizzed into being in the fourth game of the first set, when both players began striking the ball with the kind of crispness and range that confirms each to be in exemplary form. With his first break of serve, Sampras let out a yelp. Agassi had been bustling around the All-England Club as if he had been sticking his fingers in an unearthed socket. Towel, ball, towel, ball: he and the ballboy who kept him in weapons and wipedowns were starting to become best friends. But then Sampras's brilliance began to take hold, and Agassi's pigeon-toed swagger began to apply itself to the less glamorous business of retrieval.

Sampras won the first set 6–3 and broke his compatriot again in the first game of the second. 'He knows he can make great things happen in a minute and a half,' Agassi said. He saved another two break points in the second set but lost that one too, 6–4. 'Remember the French Open,' someone cried, but this was not Andrei Medvedev in the other half of the court (Agassi came back from two sets down to win in Paris). Nostradamus would have had to have been right for Agassi to get anything out of this match (even then it would have been a draw).

At 1–2 and 15–15 in the second set, he provided one of those images that will endure to the end of the next century as a portrait of psychic distress.

Agassi hit a fierce backhand cross-court shot that would have beaten any of those other 126 players in the original draw. But Sampras took off horizontally, met the ball in mid-air in the meat of the racket, and cushioned a return that fell like a raindrop on the other side of the net. Agassi looked as if he had been sprayed with liquid nitrogen. Frozen, disbelieving, he stared at the spot where Sampras had played the winner and finally looked to his corner for reassurance that he hadn't gone mad. It happened, all right. Sampras finished him off with two aces to take a 3–1 lead and start soaring towards the end of the match.

There was a time not long ago when Agassi was in danger of resembling his home town of Las Vegas: decadent, overfed, a mirage. This year, though, he has come roaring back: an artist and a warrior capable of destroying Patrick Rafter in straight sets. Agassi, only the fifth man to win all four Grand Slams, must have felt his own hyper-intensity was carrying him unstoppably through. But the greater the velocity, the harder the crash.

Agassi was more threatening in the third set but found himself trying to retrieve two break points again at 5–5. The game was lost with a timid backhand into the net, and from there Sampras had only to serve out for the match. He won it, typically, with a shot that has never been seen in the parks. An ace on his second serve. All this, remember, in a year when Sampras has played less tennis with less success than usual. When he pulled out of this year's Australian Open, citing fatigue, he had competed in 27 consecutive Grand Slams. Ah, the fire was dimming. Ha, ha. 'I'm still spinning a bit. I'm still a little overwhelmed by what I've done,' he said. It was not the sixth Wimbledon or the 12th Grand Slam that had him turning. It was the fresh, cold memory of how sublimely he had played.

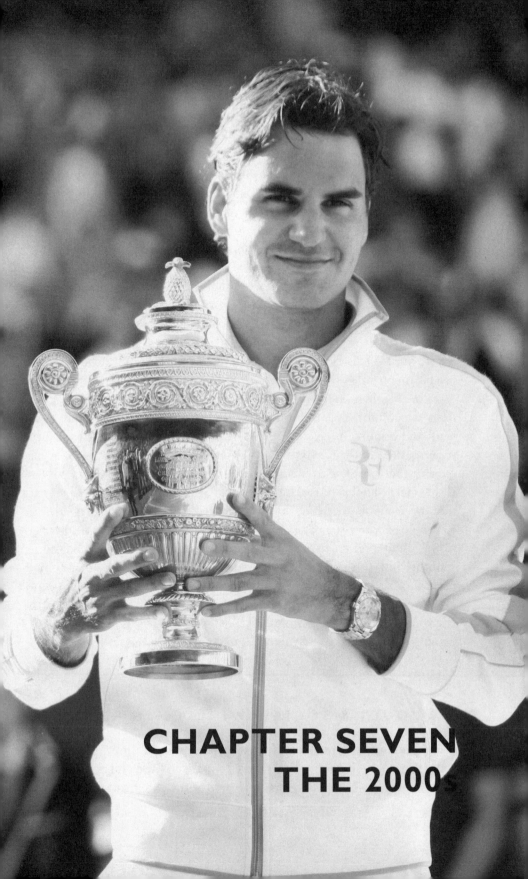

CHAPTER SEVEN
THE 2000s

FOOTNOTE COLUMN: WIMBLEDON'S ACE STRAWBERRIES

Alexander Chancellor

Wimbledon is famous not only for its tennis but also for the vast quantity of strawberries consumed there: 20 tonnes last year, according to the National Summer Fruits Association, or an average of 1.6 ounces for each of the 457,069 people who went through the gates. So, with Wimbledon fortnight starting again next week, it is appropriate that the English strawberry should have been chosen as the cover story for the new edition of *Country Life*. The magazine tells of an heroic English struggle to maintain market share against ruthless foreign strawberry importers with warm climates and cheap labour on their side. And this struggle, thank heavens, is reported to have ended in triumph for our gallant English strawberry growers, whose 'united efforts to keep this national favourite on our shelves are at last bearing fruit'.

Victory is theirs not only because the superiority of the English strawberry over all others could not be for ever gainsaid, but also because of the spirit and resourcefulness of the growers. They have finally convinced the supermarkets of their duty to buy home-grown fruit whenever it is available. But there is still a problem, and one which threatens to get worse. This is that, according to research by National Summer Fruits, strawberries are no longer popular with the young. In fact, the bulk of strawberry sales are to people over 40 years of age who cherish nostalgic memories of strawberries as childhood treats and buy them impulsively during the summer months. But the young have no such memories and are accustomed, because of foreign imports, to seeing them on the shelves all the year round. How are they to be won over? 'It is all about charisma,' William Pierce, the chairman of National Summer Fruits, told *Country Life*. 'Strawberries certainly have it – all we have to do is to get that message across.'

COURT & SOCIAL: WIMBLEDON RELISH

We might think Wimbledon is all strawberries and cream, but yesterday some Pimm's-swilling spectators were reminded of the global reach of the Championships. John Tautges, a reporter for the American CBS network, was overheard signing off his latest bulletin: 'Wimbledon coverage brought to you by Kansas City's Masterpiece Barbecue Sauce.'

– SE

2 JULY 2000

THE QUEEN, BORG AND I IN THE PALACE GARDEN

John McEnroe

Today, for the benefit of one of the finest charities in the world, the National Society for the Prevention of Cruelty to Children, I'll be playing Björn Borg in the Queen's backyard. I suppose you could say it is another example of the changing of the guard.

I've been one of those Americans you see outside Buckingham Palace, rattling the bars, shouting, 'Let me in'. I never thought for one minute they'd actually open the gates for me.

There have been discussions for the past few years about Björn and I playing a match here at Wimbledon but, sadly, it didn't work out and the fact that he's quitting the seniors tour at the end of the year meant it never would. Then I got a note from Björn saying a friend of his who knows Prince Andrew wanted to put on a match for charity at the Palace. That is rather amazing. I said: 'Listen, as long as the money is going to charity and we're not getting paid, it would be a fun thing to do.' So there we will be today, in the garden with the BBC cameras covering it, playing for maybe the last time.

The 1980 Wimbledon final will always be with us. It's great to be a part of history. I suppose that's why people want us to re-enact it all the time. I have conflicting thoughts on that. It's too bad in a sense that the closest we'll get to it is today, with 750 people paying an arm and a leg for a great cause, which is OK, and there's a level of pressure because you want to perform well. There's another part of me that doesn't want to play, you'd prefer to leave that match to your memory. I remember a guy from the *New Yorker* magazine asking me once if I'd watch the fourth-set tie-break with him and talk him through it. I had never really watched the whole thing before, only a few points here and there during Wimbledon rain delays. I didn't feel I wanted to watch it all, rather remember how great it was, what high-quality tennis it produced. I think it's better to leave these things as they were, to be careful that anything you do doesn't tarnish its memory.

The NSPCC hope to raise somewhere between £1 million and £2 million today so I shall go out and do the best I'm capable of doing.

As for Björn, we occasionally see each other at the seniors events. We'll call to check up on each other and he was the only player who came to my house during the recent New York seniors. I hope we keep in touch in the future, particularly now we're not going to see each other at tournaments from the end of the year, because he's the type of guy who would give you the shirt off his back. I shall want to make sure he's doing all right – you'd go the extra mile for Björn. To me, he is the greatest athlete we have ever seen in men's tennis and he brought an element to the game we had never seen before, with the girls screaming and crying over him. The way he looked, the way he was, he didn't need to say anything, but he had an aura. I don't think I've seen that since he retired.

I hope to have a couple of my own kids at the event today, my daughters, Emily, nine, and Anna, the redhead, who's four and a half. The little one is probably too young, and my other kids, my sons and my step-daughter, are at summer camp back home in the United States.

Once I had kids, my priorities changed. I wanted to get involved in charities that involved children and the environment. And then there's tennis, those are the three things I expect to be around for the rest of my life. Yes, I do some charity work but you don't like to toot your own horn. My main priority is my own children and it's right that they take up a lot of my time. I try to be the best father I can be and if more people were good fathers, there wouldn't be a need for so many charities.

The opportunity to go to Buckingham Palace comes along once in a life-time. I remember I was sitting behind your ex-Prime Minister, John Major, at a theatre one time and during the intermission he asked me if I'd like to come back and hang out for a while at Downing Street, which was pretty neat. I've had the opportunity to meet with Princess Diana and Sarah Fergu-son, the duchess, a couple of times but I don't think I really came to appreci-ate what royalty meant to you Brits until I came to Wimbledon, with all its pomp and circumstance. It is tradition, it is such an important factor here and you start thinking it's not bad when you see the effect it has on people. I suppose the monarchy is a bit like grass at Wimbledon. How long will it last? My guess is that they will both go on for many, many years to come.

I hope you think I've added something to the BBC's coverage of tennis this year. It's another step on the road to acceptance. It is a chance I'd wanted for years, and in 2000 the BBC reached an accommodation with my

American station, NBC, so there was time for me to work with both. I had a call from Dave Gordon, the executive editor, and he said they don't talk as much on the BBC as they do on NBC, and I said I'd heard that. But they hired me because I'm me. Pat Cash and I loved commentating together on the Sampras match the other day; we were like two kids at a candy store. I know there are those who might yearn for the days of Dan Maskell. I know he admired me as a player and I admired him as a commentator. But time moves on. Dan had an inimitable style, but it is a bit like wooden rackets. The past was great, but times have changed.

Who would ever have thought I'd be playing tennis at Buckingham Palace? The last time the Queen came to Wimbledon was 1977, wasn't it? That was my first year there, which I think caused quite a stir. That could be why she never came back.

5 JULY 2000

HENMAN'S HUNGER EXPLAINS
WHY RACKET HAD TO GO

Paul Hayward

A smashed racket, slack strings, the sole of his shoe hot from the blow of the Slazenger. This was how Tim Henman's seventh Wimbledon adventure ended: the air scorched from Mark Philippoussis's 34 aces, a flattened crowd wondering whether the glorious day will ever come. Outside Gate 11 yesterday, Sue Callaghan, one of Henman's most ardent fans, was enjoying a quiet lager and contemplating a temporary switch in nationality. The Union Flag, jester's hat and 'Go Tim!' badges suggested a life-long devotion to Henman's faltering cause. 'I always support my country,' she said defiantly. 'But tomorrow we're going to be Agassi's Angels. We're going all-American.'

There was little sign of lingering Henmania, which was always a bit too genteel to qualify as a medical condition. Hen-fondness, more like. On the news replays, Henman's tight face was scored with suburban rage; a look that has been deepening with five years of backyard frustration. Quarters, quarters, semis, semis, last 16: the litany of Henman's efforts got better and better and then suddenly got worse.

Bullied and blasted by an Aussie behemoth, Henman broke his weapon and with it the garden-party spell of nice mums in funny hats and ra-ra adulation. One spasm of understandable fury launched a drooling crowd into the skull of a ravenous 25-year-old athlete. There are no strawberries in there, no cute commentaries and come-on-Tims. Henman wants passionately to win the gentlemen's singles, so the racket, like Pete Townshend's guitar in the 1960s, simply had to go. The dip in Henman's eyes as he left Centre Court spoke of a certain mortification at what he had done to his expensive tool. But we can be certain that losing to Philippoussis hurt him more.

With cruel and metronomic consistency, the men's tour keeps throwing a shark into his waters. Todd Martin, Michael Stich, Pete Sampras (twice) and now Philippoussis have all popped up just as Britain's television sets were glowing with the annual dream of an all-the-way Henman pageant. Mangled racket, trashed summer. And as Henman traipsed off on Monday night, wondering how many iron conventions he had broken, there must have been an extra shudder from his coach and long-time mate, David Felgate, who knew that the cognoscenti would again question his credentials as a mentor to Britain's brightest talent.

On the BBC, John McEnroe came up with an ingenious solution which, he believed, would leave Felgate's dignity intact but improve Henman's prospects of crossing the grassy Rubicon. 'To get his career to reach the top of the mountain I think he needs someone with experience,' McEnroe said. 'I'm not saying he should dispose of Felgate. But if he wants to add something it's worth considering.' McEnroe thought Henman had been too tentative, 'got tight' when his serve malfunctioned and 'stayed back' too much. 'He knows deep down he could have won it.' An objective voice inside keeps saying that Henman is stuck for ever on the cusp of glory; that he is a good player but still no closer to being a great one. But the beauty of Britain's intermittent engagement with this wonderful sport is that there are 50 weeks in which optimism can be renewed.

The destruction of the racket which failed to make contact with so many of Philippoussis's serves is being treated not as a diplomatic incident but as a sign that Henman is serious about wanting to become the new Fred Perry. 'If Tim keeps injury-free he will have a lot more chances to win the Championship,' John Lloyd, Britain's former Davis Cup captain, said. 'He handles it very well. I like his attitude. Look at the serve-and-volley players like Pete Sampras, Andre Agassi, Goran Ivanisevic and Richard Krajicek. They are all coming to the end of their careers and there is no reason why Tim can't win it, along with people like Philippoussis and Greg Rusedski, if he gets his act together. I'm amazed how well Tim does here. He handles the pressure so well.'

Henman himself was not sighted. He had no desire to see others prosper in his absence. Despairing, a group of teenage girls asked a policeman if he knew where Henman might be. Try the players' entrance, he said. 'If he's not there,' said one cheekily, 'I'll come back and beat you up.' Such are the violent youthful passions which Henman has yet to quell.

7 JULY 2000

FAMILY POWER STRUGGLE WON BY THE SERENER WILLIAMS

Paul Hayward

Venus Williams used to 'make the decisions and be a role model' for her younger sister Serena. Then, one day on Centre Court, the filial cord was severed and Serena found out that she was all alone. Venus beat Aphrodite in straight sets. Their father, the creator of all this gleaming power, was elsewhere, precise location unknown. Burying a friend he had never met or attending to his businesses, or whatever. Those who assumed that Richard Williams must have knocked on Serena's dressing-room door before the match to deliver the immortal order – 'it's not your day today, kid' – will have to tailor their conspiracy theories to take account of the parental absence. Was there an in-house deal to secure this result? 'No, not that I'm aware of,' Venus said. The same to Serena: 'I can't answer that question for my family,' she replied. And then a firm 'no' to another inquiry about whether the Williams clan had regarded this semi-final as a chance for Venus to draw level in the hunt for Grand Slam titles. Serena has one: last year's US Open, as well as $3 million-plus in prize money to ease the discomfort of losing to her guardian angel.

All we can say for sure of the older Williams's 6–2, 7–6 victory is that it felt faintly wrong. Not because Serena obviously took a 'dive', but because clashes of this nature are the antithesis of what families are supposed to be about. Serena, the kid sister, was brutally cut away in a match which proved that power plus power often equals dour. The net ran between them like razor wire dividing a single Williams cell; a time-line showing the ultimate separateness of their lives.

There must have been summer days when the two sisters played each other for fun before being called in for tea. The bond between them took 18 years to build and 87 minutes to break, at least in the sense that Serena will probably never forget being skewered by her former protector so publicly. 'My mum said if you get opportunities you've got to take them,' Venus said coolly. 'I knew Serena would take the opportunity if I didn't.' Who says sibling relationships are not about power? With these Williams women, power is the essence and function of the game they mastered so improbably in Compton. Serena's power comes from the tight core of her densely muscled being. Venus's strength stretches the compass a little further. Taller, leaner and looser of limb, the currents flow all the way to her toes and fingers instead of humming inside her torso. They are two versions of a single, irrepressible force.

Venus had the better of four breaks of service in the first set and took it 6–2. Serena's counter-assault gave her a 3–1 lead in the second but still no real hold on the match. In the tie-break, Venus won six consecutive points to take the second set 7–6. There was a fervour, a developed kindergarten fury in Serena that Venus never once attempted to employ. She was serener than Serena. Venus, the goddess of love, performed as if a place in the final against Lindsay Davenport was always in her grasp.

'Serena is a little more emotional than I am,' Venus confided. 'It's really bitter, but somebody had to move on.' In her barely suppressed euphoria, she took us back to a childhood where yesterday's victim always skipped along behind four older sisters. 'You always get your way. Anyone who had a younger sibling knows that,' Venus said. 'When they don't get their way, mom and dad step in, "Give her the ice cream". As the older sister or brother, you roll with the punches. She's a real competitor, probably even more than I am. She hates to lose. That really hurts her deep. As a big sister, I was always able to get things first. Got my car first, went to school first. For the little sister — especially as there were four ahead of her — it's like always playing catch-up.'

Serena's mood was less than luminous. She struggled as badly to finish some sentences as she did the occasionally pulsating rallies which had the ball flashing into the deepest recesses of the court with sulphorous effect. She was sullen, shocked, almost resentful. Finally she managed to summon enough defiance to say: 'I'm only 18. Venus is 20. I have a lot of years ahead of me.'

Her father turned up in the end. Even gave a TV interview. But Serena's demeanour brought to mind something he had said earlier: 'She has a small weakness, in my opinion, because she wants to be perfect, and you can't be perfect on this earth.' The sisters are back in harness today in the women's doubles. Richard and Venus will doubtless want Serena to take the strain, to prove that she can rouse herself from a painful but ultimately harmless defeat.

Two soul sisters watched from Richard Williams's place: Dionne Warwick and Gladys Knight, who did the stewards at a packed Centre Court a favour by coming without the Pips. These two divas were heroines from another time, when black Americans were fighting for political rights rather than money and endorsement deals. The Williams sisters are the evolution of that struggle. Billie-Jean King, who coached the Williamses in Federation Cup matches, is not alone in comparing them to golf's Tiger Woods. If black players had found the magic door much earlier, tennis would probably already conform to the pattern in basketball, gridiron and, increasingly, football. The sisters have become *de facto* pioneers for a social group. For now, those who surged towards Centre Court yesterday will carry the memory of a more personal kind of history being made, and wonder how they themselves would have coped with having to slay their own kin on TV in the name of money and sport. When it was over, Venus put a long arm round Serena's shoulder at the net and said supportively: 'Let's get outta here.'

7 JULY 2000

LECONTE ELICITS BACKING FOR BAHRAMI ARMY

Giles Smith

'You would think they'd have put this on a bigger court.' Thus a crowd member yesterday, trying to get close to Court 14 and having to be content with stretching a neck at the entrance, amid a small but persistent throng doing the same. What they were straining to see was not some hot starlet from the women's tour, nor even a British hopeful tenaciously clinging on in the mixed doubles, but a 37-year-old Frenchman and his 44-year-old partner playing a man who reached a Wimbledon quarter-final 18 years ago and a friend of his from South Africa.

How did Henri Leconte (for the Frenchman was he) come by this degree of celebrity? Why is this man packing them in on the second Thursday of the Championships? Like one of his opponents yesterday, John Lloyd, he once reached a Wimbledon quarter-final. Like Lloyd again, he didn't win it or come any closer to the Championship again. Yet he seems to be on a kind of never-ending global farewell tour, perpetually wheeling out the old routine another time for a tearfully grateful public. Byron Black should be so lucky.

Last weekend Leconte was part of the Duke and Duchess of York's heritage tennis experience in the gardens of Buckingham Palace, doing the silly walks and the funny faces as a support act for John McEnroe, which was kind of how things were in the 1980s. The BBC love this fresh action so much, they have shown it again and again this week during rain breaks – our chance once more to feel the shock as Henri noisily protests a line call; then hoot with laughter anew as we realise that – guess what – he's only putting it on. The shrugs, the grimaces, the tumbles – they're all there. Still.

So you would have to reckon that *these* are particularly good times for the Leconte brand, though showbiz being showbiz, the revolution in his fortunes necessarily involves a certain amount of diminishment. Where people used to refer to him as 'the clown prince of tennis', these days they tend to leave out the 'prince of tennis' bit. What was once an accessory to his serious purpose as a player now appears to have become his reason for being.

Nevertheless, yesterday it took the Frenchman a good six minutes to get off the court as the autograph hunters pressed their programmes on him and fought to touch the hem of his shorts. Clearly he is right up there on the list of reliably hilarious things that happen at Wimbledon, just behind pigeons landing on the court, players kicking balls and line judges getting hit by stray serves.

He had given the crowd two sets of comedy, Henri-style. He fell over. He got up again. He fell over again. Sometimes he sat down. Then he stood up again. And so forth. At one point he had trouble with a bee, and you wouldn't have put it past Leconte to have freed the insect from a matchbox in his own pocket. With his partner, Mansour Bahrami (Wimbledon best: the second round of the doubles, 1988), he appears to have formed an alliance of hilarity. They are the Harlem Globetrotters of the senior tennis circuit, and Lloyd and his partner Christo van Rensburg were prepared to stooge it for laugh after laugh.

I'm not sure how well Leconte and Bahrami's material would stand up in another context, but this is Wimbledon, which is by no means a neutral testing ground for humour. It must be something to do with the silence – a variation on that irresistible urge to giggle which can overtake people in churches. The necessary restraint upon making noise calls out for relief, so the crowd catches whatever chance it can to laugh uncontrollably and free the tension. It could be a pigeon, or it could be Henri Leconte.

It is something of a surprise to learn that John Lloyd, 46 next month, is two years Mansour Bahrami's senior, though this may merely be something to do with Bahrami's moustache, a throw-back to the age of the crank-started car. Whatever, his is quite an act. Midway through a rally, he might produce a ball from his pocket and commence a second rally in tandem with the first. He has a routine where he lifts and lowers the net as the other players' shots pass over it. Like Leconte, he is extremely good at hitting a ball from between his legs – and extremely good at getting into a position where he has to do this, rather than hit it conventionally.

Personally, I don't see how any other player could last more than 20 minutes on the court with Bahrami without wishing to wrap a racket around his neck, but his performance prompted adoring smiles from his opponents yesterday and gales of helpless laughter from his followers – the Bahrami army. And it caused a spectator to reflect ruefully that 'people don't play to entertain the crowd any more'. True, I guess. But imagine if all tennis were like this. Surely we would all soon be casting around desperately for sharp objects.

8 JULY 2000

McENROE THE MAVERICK IS NOW MAKING WAVES IN THE COMMENTARY BOX

Andrew Baker

'Five minutes to on-air,' the floor manager says, and the tension in the BBC's Wimbledon studio ratchets up another notch. 'Any sign of John?' the producer asks no one in particular, trying to keep his voice calm. 'Any hint of John?' he adds. Outside the windows, beyond the reflections of the lights, the ghostly mass of Court No. 1 looms in the dusk. 'Three minutes to on-air,' the floor manager says. The make-up woman emerges from her little hutch by the studio door. 'Where's John McEnroe?' she innocently inquires. No one responds. She shrugs. 'I'll do him in situ,' she says, moving towards the empty chair intended for the American.

She has 'done' Pam Shriver, who is sitting behind the table next to John Inverdale. The latter, in his trademark open-neck shirt, is chatting to the director through his clip-on microphone like an actor performing an avant-garde soliloquy. Shriver interrupts him to inquire about her fellow pundit. 'What's his record?' she hisses. 'About a minute,' Inverdale smiles.

'One minute to on-air,' the floor manager says. 'He's on his way,' a voice calls from outside the studio door, and John McEnroe strolls swiftly in, plonks himself down in his chair, pops in his earpiece and waves away the make-up woman. 'I got some of that,' he says. 'I already got some of that at NBC.'

'Going on air,' the floor manager says. Inverdale grins at the camera. 'Welcome to *Today at Wimbledon*,' he says. 'We've got semi-final action for you and John's here to keep Pam in check.'

Well, what did you expect? That McEnroe the broadcaster should be significantly different from McEnroe the player? A conformist? A safety-first merchant? Get out of here. There is still an edge about everything John McEnroe does, an unpredictability which means that his colleagues and his fans can never take anything for granted. He will show up on time – just – but that is about all that you can count on. It makes for fun viewing, and a nervous producer. The British public love the results. The letters columns of respectable newspapers, which a generation ago were full of suggestions that the ill-mannered brat should be defaulted, or deported, or decapitated, are now publishing paeans of praise to the sober-suited pundit. Hacks who deplored his ultra-competitive antics now salute a consummate fellow professional. And the BBC, who have been frantic for a sporting success story, breathe a colossal corporate sigh of relief.

'The phrase that keeps cropping up in the emails from viewers,' according to Dave Gordon, BBC Sport's executive editor and the man behind the Wimbledon coverage, 'is "a breath of fresh air". You could almost say that John has dragged our coverage, kicking and screaming, into the 21st century.'

McEnroe does not look like a broadcasting radical. Nor does he look like the other former tennis stars who wander around Wimbledon in their tracksuits waiting for people to recognise them. He does not need the recognition. McEnroe scuttles from studio to court and back again in a smart suit, white shirt and properly knotted tie. Under the baseball cap, the greying hair is neatly cut. The earring and the sinister shades are the only concessions to personality. He looks like a maverick investment banker.

The contrast with the McEnroe who bestrode the show courts here like a bad-tempered colossus is exquisite. When, in the early 1980s, McEnroe broke the stranglehold that Björn Borg had exerted on the men's singles at Wimbledon, he did so in odd socks with a bush of hair barely restrained by a sweatband. He did so with a barely contained rage against those he considered his intellectual or physical inferiors. He swore at linesmen and photographers, assaulted floral displays, marmalised rackets. When an umpire objected to being called 'a ******* French faggot', McEnroe challenged him to a fight.

The crowds, particularly the crowds at Wimbledon, where proper behaviour had previously been as obligatory as all-white clothing, were scandalised and thrilled in roughly equal measure. The same people who longed for him to be thrown out of the tournament also yearned for him to win it.

And they adored the way he played tennis: the trademark, rocking preamble to a vicious serve; the volleys that were not so much hit as dismissed; his agility and determination; the bloody-minded will to win that was all of a piece with the rows and recriminations.

These days, on the seniors' tour, McEnroe keeps up the same standard of antics and almost the same standard of play. He will tell you that his serve is 10mph or so quicker with a modern racket than with the old Dunlop, but that it is also less accurate, less subtle. The arguments and protests also lack a certain something: sincerity, perhaps. There is an element of self-parody that was never present in the serious youth. This is probably why audiences love the televisual Mac. The British are famously fond of people with a sense of the absurd and the ability to be self-mocking; Americans are notoriously lacking in these attributes. Yet the man who coined the phrase 'You cannot be serious' (which is now in the *Oxford Dictionary of Quotations*) no longer has to be serious himself.

In the commentary box he combines wisdom and insight with one or two of the phrases that he helped to make famous. During Lleyton Hewitt's first-round exit, there was a disputed line-call. McEnroe, at the microphone, said: 'I know somebody said it in the past, but chalk flew up.' He has earned the right to be cheeky about the players. Arnaud Clément, he reckoned, was playing so lazily against Tim Henman that he would shortly ask for a chair and play sitting down. When a fellow commentator suggested that Steffi Graf had shown Andre Agassi a new forehand in training which he had disliked, McEnroe leered: 'That doesn't matter because I think he likes a few of the other things she's shown him as well.'

You might expect this kind of banter to go on non-stop in the *Today at Wimbledon* studio between video clips of the day's action, but you would be mistaken. Entertainers don't waste their best lines backstage. Inverdale mentions that he'd been filling in time on Radio 5 Live wondering who McEnroe might pick, as US Davis Cup captain, to play the doubles in the tie against Spain. 'Oh yeah?' McEnroe grinned, determined not to be drawn. 'Who'd ya come up with?'

On one topic, though, he loosened up a little. Venus Williams was talking on tape about how younger siblings always got what they wanted and the elders just had to put up with it. 'Hey, that's how I was,' McEnroe recalled. 'My kid brother Patrick always got the ice cream. That was OK, though. I got the title.'

McEnroe had a few words of caution for Vladimir Voltchkov, the first qualifier to reach the semi-finals of the men's singles at Wimbledon since Mac himself faced Jimmy Connors in 1977. 'Take a lot of deep breaths,' he counselled, 'and remember anything can happen. That's what sport is all about.' Maybe Voltchkov wasn't watching. Maybe he forgot the breathing. But hey, McEnroe lost to Connors.

'Off air,' the floor manager said. McEnroe stood up, unplugged his earpiece, signed a book and a cap for a production assistant, and disappeared into the darkness.

10 JULY 2000

SAMPRAS LORDS IT OVER CENTRE COURT DOMAIN

Paul Hayward

There is a line in Patrick Rafter's favourite film, *Jerry Maguire*, where a highly marketable American football star says to a beleaguered sports agent played by Tom Cruise: 'You are hanging by a very thin thread.' Rafter might have recalled that passage last night when the unthinkable happened on Centre Court and Pete Sampras looked vulnerable in a Wimbledon men's final. Rafter, the 'typical Aussie bloke', as his coach, Tony Roche, once described him, was 4–1 up in the second-set tie-break after taking the first 7–6. But then a double-fault and a poor stroke let the six-times Wimbledon champion back into a rain-interrupted match. Tension was mounting.

The only word which adequately describes Pete Sampras's hold on Centre Court over the last eight years is tyrannical. All of us sports addicts make mental lists of athletes we will still be droning on about when our teeth need soaking in Steradent. Sampras ought to be on everybody's list. He is now officially the greatest player to have grabbed hold of a racket. 'This is the best court in the world,' Sampras said through tears that fell in place of the spiteful rain, 'and I'd like to come back next year.'

However boldly the invader marches on to his lawn on Wimbledon's final Sunday, Sampras is able to send out whichever version of himself is needed to quell the hostile incursion. Against Vladimir Voltchkov on Friday, he dispatched the low-wattage semi-final cruiser, conserving energy for his first match at the 2000 Championships against a fellow seed. It was a strangely fragile and hesitant Sampras who re-emerged after the longest dreary downpour. The game itself was a mess of percussive spasms: serve-volley-serve. Neither player struck the ball with sufficient authority to suggest that the dry spells would yield a speedy winner. It was a sore shin against a dodgy shoulder. Yet this potentially ground-breaking encounter was kept on the emotional high-wire by the sense that Sampras was a faltering champion being held exasperatingly on history's cusp.

Proprietorial, vigilant, spikily defiant. Sampras is all these things when his dominion over the most sacred patch of turf in tennis is challenged. Even performing moderately, as he did for long phases through the fading evening light, he conveys the impression that he can shift into a higher dimension at any moment. His adversaries have to get past the aura before they start chipping away at the man.

Last year Andre Agassi burst out of the players' tunnel bug-eyed and intent on causing havoc with the champion's attempt to clinch a record-equalling 12th Grand Slam title. Sampras looked coldly across the net and unleashed a reign of terror. He was physically and psychologically dominant, punishing Agassi for his impertinence. Only Rafter can know whether the brutal subjugation of Agassi 12 months ago swirled in his thoughts as Sampras set off after a place in legend. Every last swinger and swiper on the men's tour knows that to defeat Sampras on grass you have to destroy the certain knowledge he carries that when he is on song he is invincible. Sampras's passivity on court, his preference for not making eye contact with his opponent, accentuates his almost callous power.

Seldom has so much history overlain a men's final here at the peak of the English anti-summer, which has forced the crowd back for a 14th session for the first time since 1988. The first Open-era final was won by an Aussie, Rod Laver, who beat Roche in 1968. Sampras had been chasing a 13th Grand Slam crown for a full year after joining Roy Emerson with 12 by crushing Agassi last year. Only injury could have stopped Sampras stepping into that exalted realm.

There would have been romance either way. The elimination of Agassi on Friday deprived this final of the most potent match-up in men's tennis: the fizzing baseline power of Agassi against the all-round might and athleticism of Sampras. But Rafter's story was a worthy addition to the book of Wimbledon epics. A lover of surf and ski, a rock-climber and skydiver, he worked his way into the elite by camping with his mother at junior tournaments and later sleeping on wooden floors. One of nine children, Rafter once kipped in one of those entrance halls where banks have started putting cash machines. Whether he was merely 'tired and emotional' is not recorded. 'He plays hard and parties hard,' Roche once said. Like Sampras, he has impressed with the quiet dignity he has brought to a sport where inflated incomes and the insular nature of the tour can distort perspective. On court, though, Sampras is no respecter of humility. The vocabulary he uses is one of ruthlessness and power.

It was the second-set tie-break before Sampras allowed signs of anguish to escape. A brief yelp was proof that for all his unwavering strength of concentration he needed Rafter's errors to help him back into the match. 'I thought I was on my way to losing,' he admitted. But Sampras is a towering champion, who has never been known to hand out second chances. Rafter, pottering nicely along, was still in a promising position with his one-set lead but was about to disappear in history's march. Sampras seized the next three sets in near-darkness and was then consumed by the magnitude of what he had achieved.

A short while back, he was asked why he shows so little of himself on court. He denied that he feels nothing, either in victory or defeat: 'If you just look at what I have to give up and sacrifice in my daily life to compete at this level, it would be very weird if, in my own way, I wasn't ecstatic about winning.' Last night, at 8.57p.m., he was euphoric and overcome, hugging his parents and mopping away tears. Hanging by a thin thread? For a while, yes, but it was only the golden twine of history.

10 JULY 2000

COURT & SOCIAL: BLOWING HOT AND COLD

Line of the day goes to Pat Cash. Interviewed by Iain Carter in an empty Royal Box to entertain the Centre Court crowd during the rain break, the Radio 5 Live commentator asked the 1987 Wimbledon champion what he would change about the Championships. 'How about moving it to the summer?' said Cash.

– SE

10 JULY 2000

SPORT ON TELEVISION: ALL ENGLAND ENJOYS AUNTIE'S HOSPITALITY

Giles Smith

It is probably fair to say that if the BBC ever lose the Wimbledon franchise, their whole game as a sports operation is up. The loss of Formula One and Test cricket, the FA Cup and Des Lynam and *Match of the Day* – that's one thing (OK, several things). But the loss of Wimbledon on top of all those would surely mean that the moment had come for everyone involved to walk out into the snow saying they might be some time.

So one would have to be understanding if the corporation's coverage of the Championships this year seemed more than a little anxious in a desire to keep on the right side of the All-England Club, or even to fill the club's executive members with a warm glow, which was partly what one felt when, during week one, Pam Shriver took us on a lengthy guided tour of the new women's changing-rooms. And which was partly what one felt again, early last week, when Gary Richardson went up on the roof of the main building with the handler of the falcon which the All-England Club employ to dissuade the pigeons from coming to mess about on Centre Court.

Reading between the lines (and sometimes in them), the substance of Shriver's report from backstage among the lockers was that the new changing-rooms were really nice, that the All-England Club had spent a lot of money on them, that sulky Russians from the men's circuit who complained that the club took inadequate care of them obviously didn't know what they were talking about, that the new facilities featured baths as well as showers and, by the way, did she mention how nice they were? Shriver was also able to enlighten us that, while Virginia Wade was very much the sort of person to have a bath after a match, Martina Navratilova preferred to take a shower. Which is the kind of information that only years in the professional game enables you to share.

Meanwhile, the substance of Richardson's report from up on the roof was that those pigeons had better watch out if they didn't want to get their heads ripped off by a highly trained bird of prey. And taken together, the import of both these inserts into the match coverage was that Wimbledon is far more than just a sports venue into which the tennis circus rolls for a fortnight every year: rather, it is an historic and infinitely intriguing place with great soap and a falcon.

'Is Wimbledon special like that?' Sue Barker further asked Peter Fleming. She was referring specifically to last Saturday's highly stirring Parade of Champions on Centre Court, but you could say that it has been the chief project of the coverage this year to ask that question wherever possible and to answer resoundingly: 'Yes, yes, oh yes, you bet your bottom dollar it is. And the only broadcaster that can reflect exactly how special it is, is the BBC.'

Incidentally, they showed the Parade of Champions again yesterday in the rain breaks. This was by popular demand, apparently, and it really was great, even a second time around – too good to be a filler. Indeed, it grew to be irritating the way that Sampras and Rafter kept coming out and disrupting it.

It will not have escaped the BBC's notice that tennis, which has lots of natural breaks suitable for commercials, is exactly the kind of sport a non-state-funded channel would love to have its wicked way with. Much of the new zest in this year's coverage will have been inspired by that thought, but the good thing was it had the viewer in mind, too, not least in the smart employment of John McEnroe to crisp things up in the commentary box. His nicely modulated irreverence (he poured some well-timed buckets of water on the flickering flames of Henmania and wondered at one point whether Britain, in its desperation to have a home-based Wimbledon winner, shouldn't simply adopt Alexander Popp) has gone down well amid the usual endless quests by the others to discover 'what's going through her mind now, John/Peter/Pam/Uncle Tom Cobbleigh?'

'It really is a privilege just to be part of these special occasions,' said John Barrett on Centre Court yesterday, during a rare burst of play. And, for the BBC, that's increasingly the case. You can bet they tidied up after themselves very carefully when they left.

25 JUNE 2001

COURT & SOCIAL:
FLOWER POWER GRACES THE CLUB

Stats corner: Horticultural – The All-England Club may be without their famous ivy this year, but they can boast 21,000 petunias, 13,000 geraniums and 3,500 hydrangeas. Meanwhile, the height of the grass on all the courts is exactly eight millimetres. Culinary – Last year 27,000kg of English strawberries were consumed with 7,000 litres of cream, washed down by 125,000 bottles of Champagne and 285,000 cups of tea.

– SE

COURT & SOCIAL: AGE CATCHES UP AT LAST

Had Ken Rosewall won the first and last of his four Wimbledon singles finals in 1954 and 1974, he would have had titles 20 years apart. That potentially remarkable feat is the statistic most often quoted to illustrate the durability of the 66-year-old Australian. As of Wimbledon 2001, we can add another. This is the first Championships since 1952 that the ageless Aussie has not entered either in singles, doubles, mixed doubles or veterans' events.

– SE

4 JULY 2001

LETTER TO THE EDITOR
SPOILING WIMBLEDON

Sir,

Watching Tim Henman play Todd Martin on television, I was appalled at the Wimbledon crowd's jingoistic behaviour. Martin wins three points in his second game in the third set – silence. He makes a mess of his return on the next point – applause. What has happened to our ideas concerning sport? I would not be at all surprised to find lager-inspired riots at Wimbledon within the next ten years.

Harold Sarsfield
Marlborough, Wiltshire

7 JULY 2001

RAIN HALTS HENMAN'S FINAL PUSH
Paul Hayward

The last time Britain had a player in the men's final at Wimbledon, Neville Chamberlain still thought that Hitler could be appeased. After 63 years, the country can wait another day. Tim Henman's semi-final against Goran Ivanisevic will resume on Centre Court at 1p.m. today before the women's final, with the British No. 1 clinging to a two-sets-to-one lead. As John Lennon once sang: 'How do you sleep?' Henman is on top, and playing sublimely, but a night-time's worth of reflection could yet change everything. This might not be the best time to point out that Roger Taylor twice surrendered a 2–1 lead in Wimbledon semi-finals. But psychologically, Henman has Ivanisevic on the run. He leads 2–1 in the fourth set with a man who has lost three finals desperately trying to restore his early advantage. What kind of irony would it be if Henman's quest was halted by A-grade English rain?

A powerful symmetry is pushing Henman towards tomorrow's men's final, in which the winner will meet Pat Rafter. A Henman–Rafter showdown would complete an unprecedented weekend of Anglo-Australian sport. First the second Lions Test in Melbourne, then the resumption of the first Ashes Test at Edgbaston, then Henman's attempt to win Wimbledon for Britain for the first time since Fred Perry in 1936. The original decision to delay the rest of Henman–Ivanisevic until 2p.m. aroused strong feelings last night before the order of play committee relented and moved it back to 1p.m. Rafter, who beat Andre Agassi in a five-set thriller, is already at a substantial advantage. Starting the men's game at noon would have narrowed the deficit, if only by one hour.

The frenzy was calmed, for one more clammy night. One newspaper has already wondered whether Henman winning Wimbledon would be the greatest British sporting achievement since the 1966 World Cup, forgetting Steve Redgrave's five Olympic golds, Seb Coe, Ian Botham and Bob Willis at Headingley in 1981, and Manchester United winning the European Cup two years ago, to mention only a few. Still, the fact that 65 years have passed since the last of Perry's three triumphs is easily British sport's biggest itch. Not that you would have known it when Henman and Ivanisevic strode on court with only 19 of the 100 or so Royal Box seats occupied and the auditorium around a third full. The All-England Club obviously offer exceedingly good cakes between matches, for five games had passed before VIP posteriors began to be lowered in significant numbers on cushioned seats. More tea, vicar? Maybe there was concentration fatigue throughout the arena after Rafter's thrilling five-set victory over Agassi. Whatever, the image of a depopulated Centre Court is hard to square with the idea that Henman's latest push was a national event for which pairs of tickets were changing hands at £3,000.

The new Goran who took to the court with at least half the audience still gossiping in corridors or performing ablutions was really the old Goran restored to life. He won the first set 7–5 with three stunning service returns, and his serve was in the groove that had produced 150 aces in five matches. Ominously, Henman was facing zingers of 130mph and more. And really, practising with Barry Cowan can not prepare you for that, even if he is a leftie like Ivanisevic. Both men started close to their optimum levels, so there was a sense that one would have to buckle psychologically before the other could seize control. At 5–5 in the first set, Henman did his new rabble-rousing routine, exhorting his followers to launch a kind of pitch invasion in Ivanisevic's head. But they were much more nervous than Perry's wannabe heir, which shows you how deep the fixation has grown. All the crowd had to do was sit there; Henman had Ivanisevic's hole-puncher of a serve to deal with.

Suffering is a Brit-watcher's favoured state, and having Henman crash into the umpire's chair in the fourth set hardly helps, particularly when the chair is built like something medieval infantrymen used to storm enemy castles. Henman had just won the second set courageously in a tie-break, and smashed through the third 6–0 in 14 and a half minutes while Ivanisevic's demons began staging a mental jail-break. The case for a Henman victory had been built around the fact that Ivanisevic had never conquered him. It was also reasonable to think that the Croatian's improbable run would end in a tangle of missed serves and mangled rackets if Henman could apply consistent pressure. But by the second game of the second set, Henman was already finding it tough, towelling himself down between points and blowing hard.

Ivanisevic remained stubbornly and inexplicably inspired. No wild card had ever reached the final of a Grand Slam event, but Croatia's finest was only ever slumming it at 125 in the world rankings. But the third set was mayhem, all of it in Ivanisevic's head. Then came the rescue-balm of soft, warm rain, and a break of almost two hours in which Ivanisevic was doubtless able to pull himself back from the edge. When play was finally called off at 8.10p.m., the imagination filled with the torments that both players must have endured last night. Henman – leading by two sets to one, but no longer with his boot on the opponent's head; Ivanisevic – in turmoil, but with a chance to regather himself for the final conflagration. Ladies and gentlemen, Britain's hopes of winning Wimbledon are suspended.

7 JULY 2001

COURT & SOCIAL: REMEMBERING BUNNY

Should Tim Henman become the first Englishman to reach a Wimbledon final since Bunny Austin in 1938, it will be a poignant match for honorary steward David Warwick. The 76-year-old, who mans staircase 7A on Centre Court, witnessed Austin's defeat at the hands of Don Budge. 'I was at Repton, the same school as Bunny Austin, and when he got to the final we were allowed up to Centre Court to watch him play,' he recalled. 'He was a baseline player with terrific court craft, very quick, never missed anything, but he lost quite easily that day as I recall – as he did against the American cannonball player, Ellsworth Vines, six years earlier. Finals day was sweltering hot, as this week has been, but people were much more dressed up, none of this casual wear. The ladies wore grand hats and flowers, the men suits. There wasn't any shouting or cheering, even to support an Englishman. Everyone was very laidback and polite.'

– SE

9 JULY 2001
GLOOM DESCENDS ON HENMAN
Paul Hayward

Readers of a sensitive disposition are warned that the following report contains material likely to upset or cause mass emigration. In cases of severe distress please contact the Australian embassy in London for information on how to join the winning side. Within 30 minutes on a grey Sunday yesterday, England lost to Australia at Edgbaston by an innings and 118 runs and Tim Henman was defeated in his third Wimbledon semi-final, this time by Goran Ivanisevic, who had already knocked out Britain's Greg Rusedski and was happy to appoint himself 'Public Enemy No. 1'. This followed Australia's 35–14 defeat of the British and Irish Lions on Saturday, and cemented Britain's reputation as the world headquarters of the anti-climax. The good news is there are still four Ashes Tests to play, a Lions–Wallabies decider to come in Sydney on Saturday and only 364 days to wait for the next Wimbledon men's final. Sport's primary beauty is its capacity for renewal, for revenge, though Australians in Britain will need to be forcibly gagged if Pat Rafter beats Ivanisevic in a men's final due to start on Centre Court at noon today.

Three days of rain-generated tension, which rendered the denouement excruciating to watch, took 15 minutes to resolve, with Ivanisevic breaking Henman in the third game and winning the set 6–3. 'I've just lost a match, but I only played four games today,' said Henman after what Martina

Navratilova called his 'brutal' defeat. Not content with wrecking a perfectly good Sunday and giving Henman a lesson in how to kill off a big match, Ivanisevic's post-match press conference was award-winningly lyrical, strange, God-fearing, funny and abusive towards John McEnroe: 'The way he's commentating, giving everybody s***, you know. "This guy is bad. This guy is going to choke." I mean, nobody is good for him.'

But then, poetry: 'If some angel comes tonight in my dreams and say, "OK, Goran, you going to win Wimbledon tomorrow, but you not able to touch the racket ever again", I say, "OK, I rather take that and then never play tennis again in my life".' This is assuming he slept at all. On Friday night, with Henman still leading two sets to one, Ivanisevic stirred 'every two hours' worrying whether his alarm clock would go off, until finally at 9.30a.m., he thought: 'OK, enough is enough, get up. *Teletubbies* starts at 10, so you have to watch.'

If there is one compensation for the violent deflation felt by the hundreds gathered on 'Henman Hill', which soon came to resemble the one Sisyphus pushed his boulder up, it is that Ivansevic will grace a final that would have had people queuing down to the M25, had Henman become the first British player to reach a men's final since Bunny Austin in 1938. On the subject of long waits, in the last century England won just a single Ashes Test at Lord's, the venue for round two against Steve Waugh's men.

Patience, queuing, stoicism, hope: the British are experts in them all, and before anyone starts vilifying Henman as a perpetual loser it's worth pointing out that there were plenty of experts willing to argue that the dream is still alive. 'He showed amazing mental strength,' Navratilova said. 'I didn't think he had it in him to win this thing. Now I do.' Ivanisevic himself said: 'He's a great player. In my opinion he can win Wimbledon next year. I don't see too many people beating him on the grass.' Conversely, there is no escaping the scale and potential significance of this latest wounding defeat at the end of Henman's eighth Wimbledon campaign. Ivanisevic is a wild-card holder – the first to reach the final of a Grand Slam event – with a serving shoulder that troubles him so much his nightly routine is 'five or six pain-killers and praying'. A popular conviction around the All-England Club is that Henman would be in tomorrow's final had Ivanisevic not been able to rise on Saturday, clutching a second chance, to watch La-La and Tinky Winky on his TV.

Academic, really, but Henman still felt he had been a victim of meteorological theft on that first dismal night. 'A rain break certainly helped me against Todd Martin, but having won ten of the 11 games at that stage, I think I was in the process of dismantling Goran's game,' he said. 'I certainly did my best. Unfortunately it wasn't good enough this year. I believe I'll win this tournament.' Friday, Saturday, Sunday: the British stomach performed its multiple somersaults before Ivanisevic delivered the final punch. With Henman's final service return of the fortnight soaring wide, the three Gorans lay on the court, saluted their fans, stood on a chair, jumped off and then disappeared down the tunnel. All this, 15 minutes after the first ball was hit. Italia 90, Euro 96, France 98: remember the decade of the England penalty shoot-out? It was like that, with Middle England on its knees as surely as Ivanisevic had been when he crashed that forehand drive past Henman on Saturday.

How Rafter must have enjoyed this chaos, the mental toll ticking up on his next opponent. 'Today when I serve for the match, my shoulder was 58 kilos heavy,' Ivanisevic told us. 'I went to toss the ball. I say, "Man, this is heavy, something's wrong. It's not easy."' On his first match point at 5–3 and 40–30, he crossed himself and shook his fist at the heavens, but hit a double-fault. 'OK, no problem, maybe God is at lunch, so he didn't see me. And then deuce. Again I hit a huge second serve on the line. Then I say, "OK, he has to be in." He just gave me another chance. He say, "Man, you were so annoying always asking for another chance, so I'll give him another chance."'

Which is what Henman has next year, when the bandwagon will roll again, fuelled by the wavering belief that he has never come so close to tracing Fred Perry's footsteps in the grass. It was sobering to think, last night, that he could yet be facing a lifetime of colossal regret, masquerading as a series of near misses, at a place where his great-grandmother and grandparents all played. The Henman family history is intricately bound up with Wimbledon, which is arguably the biggest invisible pressure on him to win. 'I tell you, three-day match, it looks like cricket, you know, except we didn't have a tea-break,' Ivanisevic said. Ashes cricket, maybe. The reward for Australia's Test squad is that all are expected to attend today's Rafter–Ivanisevic final. Insult to injury, of which, this weekend, there was plenty.

9 JULY 2001

COURT & SOCIAL:
GOLDEN EAGLE'S WINGS CLIPPED

Bill Clinton's entourage was brought down to size on arrival at the All-England Club on Saturday. The limo carrying the former US President, distinctive with its golden eagle insignia, arrived at gate five and swept up to the clubhouse. Unfortunately the cars behind, carrying more than 20 of his security guards (half Clinton's originally requested number), had been held up slightly in traffic and missed the opening of the gates. Stewards sent them on to gate four, where policemen and another steward directed them on to gate three, where they alighted, but not before the imposing group – armed with guns, gas canisters and truncheons – were made to get out their wallets and pay for ground passes. Clinton, judging it safe to attend following the uncontroversial defeat of Andre Agassi, had requested Royal Box tickets for his group bodyguard outing, but only three are said to have made it into the All-England Club's inner sanctum.

– SE

9 JULY 2001

VENUS NOT YET AMONG STARS OF WIMBLEDON

Chris Evert

I think it's premature to judge Venus Williams on the day of her second Wimbledon title to be somebody who can emulate Martina Navratilova's tremendous effort of nine victories here or Pete Sampras's magnificent seven in the men's game. Two things lead me to that view. Firstly, there are a lot of top players currently out there rivalling her for the big titles – her sister, Serena, for instance, Jennifer Capriati, Lindsay Davenport, Martina Hingis and now Justine Henin. It is going to come down to which of them is best on the day when it matters. Secondly, I don't believe she's going to be hanging around for the next ten years to become one of the truly great champions here. She might find other things becoming more important to her.

But in this year's final she proved herself to be the dominant player on grass. Once she settled in to the Championship, she looked really good out there. I don't know whether it is her favourite surface but it certainly suits her aggressive game. Grass rewards power and she definitely has the power. Against Henin, Williams had one important weapon that Capriati did not have in the semi-final – her big serve. I looked at the stats after the match and noticed that she got 35 out of her 56 first serves into play. That was an amazing percentage considering how hard she hits the ball. That serve hurt Justine, who likes to wind up on both sides to lash out at her big ground strokes. She couldn't do that against Venus and you have to give Venus credit for preventing her.

Venus looked as good in this match as she did in beating Lindsay Davenport in the final a year ago. With the exception of three or four games, her ground strokes have been consistently powerful. There has been a lot going on around Venus at this tournament and to her credit she has not let any of it bother her. Amid all the publicity surrounding Jennifer's hopes of a Grand Slam, Henin's exciting story, her own sister's emotional defeat by Capriati, she has presented a calm front. She has remained very focused and controlled throughout the tournament.

A big factor in deciding the outcome to the final was that Venus was the fresher player. She lost in the first round of the French Open, went home to relax, did not bother with any warm-up tournaments and had only one tough match before yesterday – her semi-final against Davenport. She had a lot in reserve and was in the process of peaking for the final. Henin, on the other hand, had used up a lot of emotions in getting so far. She had a very tough French Open – losing in that long semi-final to Kim Clijsters – she won the pre-Wimbledon tournament in Holland and four of her matches here have been close ones, three of them going to a deciding set. I just think that she had nothing left to give in that third set, having worked so hard to win the second set and get back in the match. All the tennis she has played over the last couple of months caught up with her and that contributed to the short and one-sided final set.

The rain break helped Henin win that second set. It kept her alive in the tournament when earlier it had killed off Tim Henman. That's how it is with stoppages. It works for some but not for others. When she got off court, her coach probably told her that she needed to start swatting the ball more, like she did in turning things round against Capriati, and for a while it worked for her. She has shown in the last two Grand Slams that she has the potential to win one. I think that she has good nerves, which is probably the most important thing, she is an excellent athlete, and I think she has an insatiable appetite to succeed.

10 JULY 2001

GRIPPING 'PEOPLE'S FINAL' OVERTHROWS SHACKLES OF POMPOSITY AND TURNS CENTRE COURT INTO FRENZIED CELEBRATION

Sue Mott

It wasn't just a match, it was a monument. The men's singles final, Wimbledon 2001, provides the definition of the beauty and terror of sport. The winner, the wild card, poised to reap the dream of a lifetime with tears falling down his face. The loser, reaping the whirlwind of another man's miracle, holding out his arms for brotherly embrace at the net when it was unbelievably, sensationally over. You could cry piteously, laugh uproariously. Both were the appropriate response.

Britain's contribution was the venue. But all sedateness had fled. The Centre Court, the cathedral, was a rock stadium, a bull ring, Madison Square Garden all rolled into one. The vicars had gone, the corsets ripped off; tennis has never, ever been like this. It was the time when the sport we in Britain have treated like a suburban, leaf-fringed, frilly-bottomed pastime rose to the heights of a Shakespearean drama. Tragedy or comedy, it was hard to tell.

It was an event that murdered the nerves, enthralled the spirit, numbed the backside and demonstrated, for once, man's humanity to man. Can you imagine a stadium so filled with passionate and intense partisanship where police cordons and barbed wire were not required to keep the two sides apart? Instead we had pure comradeship. Berserk but pure. The supporters of Patrick Rafter, with their inflatable kangeroos, and the fanatics of Goran Ivanisevic, with their insatiable yearning to see him fourth-time-lucky in a Wimbledon final, created the ambiance of a screamingly loud Olympus. 'I don't know if Wimbledon's seen anything like it. I don't know if it will again,' said Rafter in the aftermath, mysteriously not deprived of speech or sportsmanship by the searing occasion.

Maelstrom Monday, you wish it could be like this every year, when the gates are opened to real tennis fans who turned the celebration of every point into a penalty shoot-out. There was not one single soul there who would rather have been knitting. Never mind Tim Henman losing his third Wimbledon semi-final, credit-worthy though this was. Could not this be the moment when Britons actually realise that tennis is a game worth playing? Or will we go on swatting flies with more effort than forehands for as long as the British culture survives? This match could change lives. It ought to. A week ago the Sports Minister had turned up on the premises and declared himself 'not keen' on tennis. Maybe, had he bothered to watch this sustained tumultuous brilliance, he might realise that tennis is a glorious outlet for sporting expression in this country. For too long we have treated it as a social embarrassment. More to the point, the schoolchildren who continue to see their tennis courts vandalised, or dug up, or ill-maintained, might now see a reversal in the trend. They talked about Henman's assault on the Championship being the font of a British revival. But it was not to be. Death by meteorology. Instead we have an even greater gift. Simply, one of the greatest sporting dramas of all time.

'I shall remember this day for ever,' said Ivanisevic, who watched the *Teletubbies* by way of induction to his sporting heaven. It would be fitting if our children remembered the day they started to love tennis because of a (29-year-old) boy after their own heart. We have no choice but to go through the children. The adult tennis world in Britain remains a shambles. We must accept that the Lawn Tennis Association are desirous of improving and endorse the anger expressed by John Crowther, the chief executive of the Lawn Tennis Association, that British tennis has been allowed to rot towards slipshod nonentity. But that anger could also be directed towards a hierarchy at the All-England Club, who allowed the deep-cushioned seats alongside the Royal Box belonging to committee members to sit half-empty throughout this tirade of sporting thrills. You wonder about this. If members of the Australian cricket team could sit rapt for Rafter for three solid hours, and even Jack Nicholson, who has enjoyed a bit of entertainment in his life, could be consumed by the occasion, where was the commitment of our tennis lords and masters? Maybe out flying over the cuckoo's nest, some of them. Maybe asleep. Shaming, either way.

The lesson is that tennis is an extraordinary sport, as pugilistic as heavyweight boxing, as tear-jerking as Verdi, as intoxicating as ten pints of undiluted Pimm's. The atmosphere was nuclear-electric because both players attained a performance peak somewhere up there near K2. Rafter's wicked drop shots toppled over the net like happy drunks falling in the gutter in Earl's Court (element of premonition in those, you reckoned). Ivanisevic's returns ripped like a savage invasion down the lines. There were the lobs and the aces and vicious swings of momentum so that the crowd were left utterly wrung by emotion, little less than shellshocked.

You had to face the fact that the crowd went wild because the source of their dementia was competent. Both men could play. That has not always been the case in our British gladiators, the honourable exception being the departed Henman. His brief, brave, ashen-faced failure of Sunday was put in perspective by the angel-sponsored path of his semi-final rival all the way to the Championship. Dear old Goran (almost all Good Goran but for the furious racket-toss and net-kick that helped him lose the fourth set) stood on the sill of the players' box at the end like a warrior on the ramparts of a vanquished city. Now the truth dawned. He had been unstoppable all along. Not so British failure. It is a process, like a yob, that can and should be arrested. We have allowed both, violence and feebleness, to infiltrate British sporting culture but if this isn't a shining path to a better future, then nothing is. Watch this and aspire, we should tell every child in the country, and then fight to find the means to help them get there.

Australia did not produce Rafter by accident. He is the outcome of a continent that believes sport is a matter of celebration, passion and pure sweat. Of course, Croatia produced Ivanisevic by accident. He was probably born through spontaneous combustion. Either way, we could do with some followers in these lyrical footsteps and the first stop is admitting that for a lily-livered, white-clad, tiara-wearing sport, this had been pretty exciting.

22 JULY 2001
TV LICENCE DODGERS NETTED IN WIMBLEDON CRACKDOWN

As the men's singles final began at Wimbledon last month, an army of TV licence inspectors was mobilised all over Britain. By the time Goran Ivanisevic had beaten Pat Rafter they had bagged almost 2,000 licence dodgers and laid down the foundations of a new strategy. The Wimbledon operation caught more than double the expected number of licence evaders and was so successful that inspectors are now poring over programme schedules to establish when licence evaders are most likely to be watching television.

Doug Mullin, the regional manager for north-west Wales, said: 'When the Wimbledon final was on we thought it was worth having a go as we knew a lot of people would be taking time off work and watching television. When I knocked on doors most people just wanted to get rid of me and continue watching the tennis. It was funny: they would ask if they could carry on watching the final as I was recording their details. They didn't seem that shocked to see me. They were clearly aware they were watching television without a licence.'

24 JUNE 2002
NOSTALGIC SMELL OF GRASS PROVES LURE FOR USTINOV AFTER ALL THESE YEARS
Brendan Gallagher
Wimbledon 2002 Supplement

Wimbledon. The lure remains irresistible. Sir Peter Ustinov could be relaxing at his idyllic lakeside vineyard near Geneva over the next fortnight with wife

Helene, entertaining an agreeable and steady stream of friends and family. Heaven knows he deserves a rest after packing four or five separate lives into his 81 years. Instead, despite the inconvenience of dodgy legs and deteriorating eyesight – 'the twin curse of diabetes and old age'– he is yet again venturing forth to SW19. 'Just can't stay away from the place,' says Ustinov. 'Wimbledon is very special even though I have ranted and raved over the years at its elitism and apparent snobbery. The smell of freshly mown grass is so intoxicating and very nostalgic. It defines Wimbledon and reactivates schoolboy butterflies with memories of house cricket matches or school sports day.

'I am told it can also act as an aphrodisiac, it certainly gets the adrenalin pumping. Grass is beautiful in itself. Only the British with their horticultural fanaticism could contemplate holding such a massive tournament on grass in such an unreliable climate – the work involved in preparing 20 courts and maintaining them for a fortnight is quite staggering. The groundsmen are the real stars. In contrast, look at the ugly red clay courts of Roland Garros – as if the blood of some unfortunate bull has been spilled in the ring and coagulated under the blistering afternoon sun. Or perhaps somebody drank too much Champagne, urinated indiscreetly in the corner and then attempted to sweep away the evidence. A scruffy, unbecoming backdrop to a beautiful game.'

Tennis is Ustinov's joy and relaxation, the trivial sporting pastime that amuses and fascinates one of the world's most eclectic and discerning minds – playwright, actor, composer, conductor, author, commentator, UNICEF ambassador. He loves analysing the players of genius and character, as if casting his latest production. 'Genius sportsmen often lead quite difficult lives,' Ustinov observes, stroking a non-existent moustache, possibly a mannerism from his Poirot days. 'They have nothing to confirm their genius, nor anything to compare it against and must always trust their God-given talents. They are often not equipped to be alone in life and yet can be extremely difficult partners. Their personal lives can be erratic and turbulent. I notice Björn Borg, so calm and in total control on the court, has recently married for the third time. I wish him great joy. I found great happiness third time around.

'Emotionally, I identify most with players of delicate temperament. As an actor I know perfectly well that there comes a moment just before you forget your lines when you think, "To hell with this, what's the point, why am I attached to this text with chains?" Such vagrant thoughts stun the mind and you forget everything. Curiously, there is a fleeting sense of triumph and freedom before reality sets in. I see this time and time again with players like Marat Safin. Word-perfect one day, often against quality opposition, hopelessly fluffing their lines the next against journeymen players.

'When I last spoke with John McEnroe he was exasperated at being the captain of a Davis Cup team as wayward and financially conscious as the US squad. McEnroe, in contrast, played as if every game of his life was a cup decider. I often suspected that he wore Stars and Stripes boxer shorts. I forgave him all the histrionics because he is true to himself, utterly committed and would behave exactly the same had first prize merely been a slap-up meal at the Savoy Grill. It was not an act. Ilie Nastase, however, became "nasty" and premeditated. He became his own commercial, a caricature of himself. Gamesmanship became his game.

'Andre Agassi is a confusing mish-mash. Sometimes he resembles a thrusting young businessman who has hurriedly fetched his clothes from outside the shower and rushed to a meeting. He has extraordinary charisma, though. I'm sure that Jesus Christ – if He ever existed – looked like the modern-day Agassi, rather than the traditional figure of flowing curls. His habit of bowing to all four corners of the earth has a strangely Biblical, Middle-Eastern feel and somehow strengthens my curious and frankly rather bizarre view of a very singular man. He can be very endearing but also irritating.

'The crouching Jimmy Connors was like a demented ferret, an impression accentuated by his strange haircut and the fact that he hit everything with two hands; he often seemed to have six hands like a Buddha. Like McEnroe, he possessed a volcanic Irish temper. That, in my mind, is the safety valve on the English boiler. Alas, I fear Tim Henman will never win Wimbledon because I don't detect the flame of anger, delightful young man though he is. They say there are no characters any more but I don't know. Lleyton Hewitt is a busy, animated chap, full of energy and I love the way he convulsively picks at his racket strings when a shot goes awry, as if to transfer blame.

'The vigilance of the referees has become quite excessive. Why should a player be denied the sheer pleasure and release of smashing his own expensive racket into pieces occasionally? But no, we get this ridiculous schoolmasterly lecture and punishment from the umpires. Kipling's advice on treating the twin imposters – victory and defeat – equally is complete hokum. Britain is the only nation on earth that believes in the concept of the moral victory. Everybody else craves victory *per se* and either rejoices or despairs accordingly. A thousand curses on the British stiff upper lip.'

Ustinov's Oscars – for *Topkapi* and *Spartacus* – lay somewhere amid a mound of mementoes by the fireside, while thousands of books, manuscripts and song sheets compete for space in his living room and office. It is not exactly clear which room is which. 'Since the days of Hitler I find it repugnant to either burn or discard any book; freedom of speech is everything. I hoard everything. That's my excuse.' However, perhaps his most prized possession and trusty friend is a dusty old Dunlop Maxply tennis racket presented to him by Abe Segal. It was the height of technology at the time, though to the modern generation it predates the Ark. It is a link with another era and another set of heroes – Lew Hoad, Ken Rosewall, Roy Emerson, Rod Laver and John Newcombe.

'Australians, I love them,' says Ustinov. 'The most wonderfully uncomplicated, fun-loving nation on earth. They just get on with having a good time, playing sport and sinking a few schooners. I was honoured to keep their company and play with them. They taught me a lot about tennis, but more importantly life. I saw them in bad humour only once. I was at a drinks reception when Rosewall clearly turned his back on Hoad. "What is that all about?" I asked Lew, concerned that the great mates had clearly had a blue. "Well, it's like this, Pete," he said. "We were playing an exhibition match the other night and I was feeling right crook, temperature of 103, sore throat, headache, sick as a dog, I said to Muscles, 'Take it easy on me, mate, I'm right crook and should be in bed.' Muscles is a complete gentleman and promised to soft pedal. Well, blow me, come the match I was completely out of it, I just waved my racket around and everything came straight off the sweet spot. Unbelievable. Beat him love and two in 36 minutes flat. I've tried to explain to Muscles but he doesn't want to hear."'

Ustinov continues: 'As the years rush by I recall a scene from the film *The Way Ahead,* which I scripted with Eric Ambler back in 1944 – David Niven took the lead role. Two octogenarian Chelsea pensioners are yarning about the Boer War or some Afghan campaign in which they served and one suddenly turns knowingly to the other and says, "Of course, you are much too old to remember any of that." That's how I feel now. The tennis stories I could tell, but I'm getting much too old to remember any of that.'

24 JUNE 2002
STAGE IS SET FOR PERFECT TOURNAMENT
Sarah Edworthy
Wimbledon 2002 Supplement

At the Wimbledon Shop you can buy chocolate tennis balls, Championship towels, cushions, sweatbands, the bone-china wherewithal to replicate a

Championship cream tea, videos of epic matches and no end of goods discreetly adorned with strawberry and racket motifs. However, *Telegraph Sport* can reveal the one sensory dimension of Wimbledon fortnight that has long eluded those determined to take a bit of the All-England Club experience home with them: the specific colour of green paint which immaculately characterises the triangle between Church Road and Somerset Road in SW19. It is Permaglaze Spruce Green, code 14C39.

Journalists are entitled not to reveal their sources, especially of sensitive information, though this being the centenary of Slazenger's association with Wimbledon's Lawn Tennis Championships, it seems only fitting to introduce Les Denman — he who not only wields the Spruce Green paintbrushes over nearly 1,400 iron rods and poles that make up the skeletons of each court, but also heads up Slazenger's tournament equipment team.

His responsibility is to set up each court's canvas surround and mark out the intricate jigsaw of walkways around the normally open grass areas of the All-England Club. He is the set-builder for the theatrics performed by the world's top tennis stars on the 19 grass stages. Denman spends all year preparing for the three weeks it takes to conjure the public image of Wimbledon. His materials include 120 tonnes of wood, metal and canvas for the practice courts as well as the qualifying and main tournaments. The wood includes 40 pairs of posts, 22 umpires' chairs, 27 hand-operated scoreboards and 28 singles sticks.

The preparation for each year starts almost immediately after the equipment for one year has been dismantled and returned to storage. Denman then examines and repaints the iron. More than 70,000 square feet of canvas and 2,000 yards of stop netting are renewed each year, damaged not by the battering of a Rusedski or Ivanisevic serve, but by cigarette holes and smeared ice cream.

For all this effort it is a surprise to learn that Denman, a former postman and railwayman, does not like tennis. From 6.30a.m. to start of play, he checks the canvases, ropes, scoreboards and poles. 'But even if the canvas gets ripped I can't do anything until the end of play so I watch telly, read the paper, play cards and eat dates. I certainly wouldn't come out and sit and watch the tennis,' he said.

Nevertheless each year the club benefit from his innovations. It was his idea to put non-slip material on the steps of the umpires' chairs so they could climb up and down safely in wet weather. This year, on Court 11, he will be monitoring a prototype ratchet system he has devised to keep the canvas taut. 'If it works well, it will go out on all the courts,' he said. You cannot underestimate the knock-on work involved in each technical innovation. In 2001 the Centre Court surrounds had to be adjusted to accommodate a new television camera. Under Denman, a team of seven men worked for six weeks before the event to get everything ready.

25 JUNE 2002

KOURNIKOVA STARTING TO LOOK LIKE LAST YEAR'S MODEL

Martin Johnson

The first day at Wimbledon does strange things to people, especially if they've been wandering about without a hat in a sun as strong as yesterday's. 'Shall I take a picture of her?' said a girl to her boyfriend as an attractive blonde in a trouser suit was doing a television interview outside the players' entrance. 'What on earth for?' he replied. 'Well everyone else is,' she said. 'For God's sake,' he sighed. 'It's Sue Barker.' Sue Barker, Ronnie Barker, the Lord Chief Barker ... who cares? If it's famous, snap it. Anyone vaguely dressed like a tennis player yesterday sparked off an avalanche of whirrs and clicks, and however many millions the All-England Club make from their annual garden party, it's petty cash compared to the printing and developing department at Boots.

The most photographed tennis player at Wimbledon every year is, by some margin, Anna Kournikova, which is quite an achievement for someone who generally parts company with the tournament so quickly that her courtesy-car driver leaves the engine running. Anna was one of 11 'Ovas' in action on the opening day, losing her match to one, Tatiana Panova, and, according to a readers' poll in a tennis magazine, being relieved of her 'sexiest woman player' title by yet another one, Daniela Hantuchova. It's Ova for Anna, in more ways than one.

There was no split decision for the glamour title in Kournikova's match against her fellow Russian, Panova, and if this had been the James Bond version of *From Russia with Love,* it would have been the equivalent of Tatiana Romanova versus Rosa Klebb. There were more cameramen than anyone could remember seeing before on Court No. 2, and not many lenses were aimed at Miss Panova's side of the net.

The biggest cheer of the match, in fact, came before a ball had been struck in anger, when Miss Kournikova removed her tank top to reveal a bare midriff and a slit skirt that was more of a pelmet. After that, though, silence descended as Kournikova spent the first set giving a passable impression of someone who had mixed up her appointment book, and had turned up for a modelling engagement instead of a tennis match. Kournikova's determination not to shed any perspiration at all was a disappointment to everyone, not least her male admirers in the crowd, and her clear intention not to get involved in long points led to a mixture of blistering winners and shots that would have been called out in the court next door. It was a bit like watching Devon Malcolm in a Test match. A rapid middle-stump yorker, followed by a leg-side wide and a full toss over the wicketkeeper's head.

Panova may be ranked the 22nd-best woman player in the world, but this tells you more about women's tennis than anything else, and she actually lost to the 45-year-old Martina Navratilova at Eastbourne last week. She has approximately half the talent of Kournikova but twice the application, and while her opponent was the clear winner in the curves stakes, Panova certainly had a better grasp of angles. She ran for everything, while Anna's shoes were relevant only for the purpose of advertising Adidas. However, after losing the opening set 6–1, it all altered in the second when Kournikova, without ever changing tactics, started to hit more good shots than bad. She was broken to go 3–4 down with her opponent to serve, but then broke back twice to win the set 6–4, and actually appeared to be the stronger at 3–3 in the final set. However, Panova dug a bit deeper than Kournikova was prepared to do, and evidence of what this match meant to both of them came as they walked off. Panova was so emotionally drained she was close to blubbing, while Kournikova smiled (as she had done all match) and gave a cheery wave to the crowd.

The £6,300 she collected for losing pushed Kournikova's career earnings to more than $3 million, which, for someone who has not won a singles title of any description, tells you something about the obscene amounts of money sloshing around for players of modest ability. However, next to what she earns for modelling sports bras and adorning magazine covers, this is the kind of cash she probably keeps in a biscuit tin in the kitchen, and it makes you wonder whether she'll soon give up on tennis (it's only a hobby after all) and devote her full attention to the day job.

As a Russian with a deeper Florida accent than Chris Evert, Kournikova is entitled to feel a bit mixed up, and Evert has already advised her to give up the glamour work if she wants to make a serious go of her tennis. Kournikova, however, says that she doesn't get involved in half the modelling work people claim, and that she is still '100 per cent committed to tennis'. 'I didn't expect to do too great here this year, and my main goal was to enjoy myself and have a good time. I played much better than I have been doing, which is why I was smiling a lot on court. After all, I was close to winning against someone ranked 20-something in the world.'

However, the difference between the Kournikovas and the Panovas is the difference between a Centre Court debenture holder and one of those hardy souls who turn up every year, where finally getting hold of a ticket is a triumph for patience, humour, the ability to sleep on pavements and a strong bladder. It all depends whether you want it – or need it – badly enough.

28 JUNE 2002

COURT & SOCIAL: NEVER TRUST TO LUCK

Jelena Dokic goes on court with a full portfolio of superstitious rituals. She never steps on the white lines before and after a game. She blows on to her right hand while waiting for an opponent to serve. She has to bounce the ball five times before the first serve and twice before the second. 'The ball-boys and girls always have to pass me the ball with an underarm throw, which is luckier than an overarm throw,' said the 19-year-old No. 7 seed. But most important is where she sits in relation to the umpire. 'I have to sit on the left side of the umpire. I feel more confident from that position and it's served me well so far.'

– SE

29 JUNE 2002

COURT & SOCIAL: GETTING AHEAD ON COURT

Suzanne Strong celebrates her 20th year as Championships hairdresser by reclaiming her responsibility in grooming the ballgirls. Last year, for the first time, the girls had to do without professionally styled plaits as her salon, in the new Millennium Building, was too far away. 'This year we go to their changing-rooms between 11 and 12 every morning and braid like mad for what seems like hundreds of girls,' Strong said. There are 95 ball-girls, who request between one and six plaits each.

Her work is part hidden by this year's introduction of baseball caps, but Strong has another stage on which to release her creative talents — albeit risking the wrath of the groundsman. 'On the final Saturday and Sunday I go around snipping all the flowers to put in the flower girls' hair.'

— SE

4 JULY 2002

WHEN 'GIVE US A BREAK' HAS NEW MEANING

Giles Smith

The weather yesterday was playful — or, to put it another way, a complete pain in the backside. Not content with merely interrupting Serena Williams's quarter-final with Daniela Hantuchova, it found a way to drill it full of holes. So, just to recap: those rain breaks in full. First of all the players came out and warmed up, and then it rained. Then they came out again, warmed up and played five points, and then it rained. Then they came out again and warmed up, and then it rained. And then they came out again and played a set and four games. By which time there had not been a rain break for a full 52 minutes, so it was clearly high time we had one. Which we did. Later, the players found another brief gap in the clouds, long enough for Williams to widen the cracks that had appeared in Hantuchova's game at the close of the main session, and to finish things, 6–3, 6–2.

On, off, on, off, on, off ... it was like watching a pageant on the theme of Joan Collins's marital life. Cleverly maximising the spectators' frustration, the rain never even bothered to throw itself down with any force. For the most part, it restricted itself to a mild and intermittent drizzle — no more than if the wind had got under a lawn sprinkler somewhere in the Merton area, but still enough to make tennis a potentially hazardous occupation.

Mostly, the crowd, in no obvious danger of drowning, sat tight and suffered. Even Serena's mother, whose new caramel-coloured Carlos Valderama-style Afro almost commands a VIP enclosure of its own, stayed in her seat through the third of those delays, sensibly realising, perhaps, that by the time she had got her hair to the bottom of the stairs, the players would be coming out again and she would have to turn around and bring the whole unit back up again.

Some misrouted Henmaniacs (Timmy was due on another court at a slightly later hour) fought the boredom by trying to initiate a Mexican wave. The take-up for it was scant and restrained, as it so often is at Wimbledon, and what resulted was more of a Surbiton wave than a Mexican one. Meanwhile, back in the BBC studio, Boris Becker was smoothly insisting, with a slow smile on his face, that rain breaks were part of the package at Wimbledon and that players simply had to be easy about them when they came. All of which was spoken from a great height and with the effortless calm of someone who does not have to play any more.

The players seemed to come off extremely quickly each time, but this was almost certainly prudence rather than fussiness. After all, within approximately 0.8 seconds of the first drops reaching the ground, the court crew are getting ready to perform their Charge of the Light Brigade act with the court covers and to be caught hesitating on the grass in these circumstances is to risk burial under several hundredweight of tarpaulin. Opponents of Serena Williams these days tend to go on court expecting another kind of burial. At full tilt, she plays as though she is the car and the person over the net is the hedgehog. Her game tends to blend vitriolic serving with even more vitriolic ground strokes, and it has powered her to the top of the women's game in the wake of her sister Venus. If Serena reaches the final at this Wimbledon she will take over as women's No. 1, irrespective of the match's outcome.

The Williams sisters are seeded to meet at the tournament's sharp end and few would bet against them doing so on their current thunderous form. Williams family face-offs clearly unsettle some observers, who fear for the levels of competitiveness on these occasions and wonder whether they are witnessing some kind of pre-signalled division of the spoils: Michael Schumacher and Rubens Barrichello, as it were, only with added blood-ties.

Nobody watching yesterday, however, would have had any questions about levels of commitment. In a mood to close quickly, perhaps inspired by the weather, Williams chased down all that Hantuchova sent her and sent most of it right back to the baseline at speed. (There were, almost inevitably, a handful of debatable calls.) And then she skipped off to play doubles with her sister. The 19-year-old Slovakian looked a little bewildered by that point. The loss of the first set and her service game in the early stages of the second began a collapse which not even a rain-assisted spell back in the locker-room could enable her to arrest. Yet for the whole of a sometimes breathtaking first set, she fought fire with fire, holding break points on Williams's serve in the direct aftermath of losing her own. Her problem lay in getting the ball in play off the ferocity of Williams's serves, but she gave almost nothing away and in rallies frequently looked the match of her opponent in strength and speed.

Had you mentioned the name Hantuchova to a Wimbledon crowd before this tournament, most of them would have said 'bless you'. This year, whatever she may feel about it, she has been upgraded to the role of brightest starlet in the ascendant. She is credited with deposing Anna Kournikova in this area, though one suspects from her play that this would not be the limit of her ambitions. She'll be back.

30 APRIL 2003

WIMBLEDON ABANDONS THE ROYAL BOX CURTSEY

John Parsons and Caroline Davies

The long-standing tradition of Wimbledon's Centre Court players bowing or curtseying to the Royal Box has been scrapped. The order, which comes into immediate effect, was issued yesterday by the Duke of Kent, President of the All-England Lawn Tennis and Croquet Club since 1969, who has deemed it an anachronism in modern times. The only exception would be if the Queen or the Prince of Wales attended, which is about as likely as a British player winning a Wimbledon singles Championship. The Queen has visited on around four occasions, the last 26 years ago when Virginia Wade lifted the women's singles during the Silver Jubilee year. Prince Charles has inherited his mother's lack of interest in the sport.

Announcing the change, Tim Phillips, chairman of the All-England Club, said of the Duke: 'He feels the tradition of bowing and curtseying is pretty much on the way out, and he thinks it is time to stop it. We respect his views on that.' Wimbledon's association with royalty dates back to 1906, when King George V, then Prince of Wales, attended the final day's programme accompanied by Princess Mary at the old Worple Road ground. The couple became regular spectators. But the tradition of bowing or curtseying to the Royal Box was first documented on 26 June 1922, when King George and Queen Mary attended the opening day of the Championships on the present site in Church Road. When Leslie Godfree and Algie Kingscote walked on to the Centre Court to play the opening match in the new arena, they instinctively turned and bowed to the Royal Box, thus establishing a tradition that has existed ever since – although it has always been on a voluntary basis. 'One of the most difficult things I ever had to learn was that little bob,' Martina Navratilova, who won the ladies' singles a record nine times, once said. Indeed, in the heat of the moment, many top players simply forgot.

Miss Navratilova found the protocol very baffling during her early Wimbledon career, and, after being presented with a runners-up medal by the Duke of Kent, confided: 'I forgot to curtsey. I'd never been through something like that before. Usually at tournaments they give you a cheque, you thank everybody and leave.' Jennifer Capriati was in such a hurry to leave court when she was beaten in the 2001 semi-final by Justine Henin that she fled without so much as a glance at the Royal Box.

Crown Princess Stephanie of Austria is credited with being the first Royal visitor to the Championships in 1896. But by 1906 Wimbledon was a firm Royal favourite. Along with the Prince and Princess of Wales, later King George V and Queen Mary, the Grand Duchess Anastasie and Grand Duke Michael of Russia came to watch. The organisers were delighted when the Prince of Wales accepted the club's presidency in 1907. Queen Mary became a regular fixture, occupying the front row of the box and slowly retreating, row by row, during the afternoon to prevent the setting sun from shining in her eyes, thus forcing those behind gradually to renounce their seats. Protocol still prevents anybody sitting in front of the Royals in the box. In 1926 the then Prince of Wales, later King George VI, competed in the men's doubles, partnered by Sir Louis Greig. They were knocked out in the first round. The late Diana, Princess of Wales, was a regular spectator, as is Princess Michael of Kent and the Duchess of York.

23 JUNE 2003

SPECIAL AURA
OF WORLD'S BEST TOURNAMENT

Pam Shriver

Every Wimbledon is special but this one is more so — it is 25 years since I first came to the Championships as a raw, gangly teenager from Baltimore with no idea of what to expect, and I have been back every year since as a player or broadcaster. Unlike Europeans, not many Americans have the opportunity to see either Wimbledon or Roland Garros, except on television, until they go there to compete for the first time. For those of us from the States, the first time at Wimbledon as a player almost makes your eyes bulge. You get consumed by the culture, the tradition and the whole atmosphere. Wimbledon, the greatest tournament in the world, has an aura and you feel it. And when you're out there playing any of the great champions, it's a case of 'double aura'. That's when I had problems – against Steffi Graf, a couple of times in the semi-finals, and Martina Navratilova, my long-time doubles partner, and Chris Evert. Sometimes I fell short, but I was always soaking up the atmosphere.

You come from where you come from, and not all of the Wimbledon traditions immediately sit easily with you as a teenager. Now that I'm 40, I understand more about different cultures and traditions and realise it's not all done the way we do it in the States. Tennis is all the richer because the four biggest tournaments are played in Australia, France, England and the United States, where the cultures are so different. It struck home with me the other day when I was watching the US Open golf on television with my husband, George [former actor George Lazenby] and he mentioned how, of the four majors in golf, only one is played outside the US.

My first year at Wimbledon happened to be the start of Martina's dominance and I was also there through Steffi Graf's period of supremacy – they won 16 Wimbledon titles between them. Martina was the perfect example of someone who grew into playing on grass and dealing with the aura surrounding the Championships. Steffi achieved that from the very beginning – although I did beat her once at Wimbledon when she was very young.

Wimbledon manages to give the impression of staying the same when it is, in fact, always evolving. You need to find the right formula for keeping things intimate but also making changes, like the new Court No. 1, the Millennium building (which houses players, the media and All-England Club members) and phasing out the curtsey.

I don't think most of the players gave the curtsey or bow much thought. Their minds were on the match they were about to play or had just played. It was just something you did at Wimbledon, in the same way that your tennis clothing has to be predominately white: it's part of the tradition. Whether people curtsey or bow or not, it's still Wimbledon, although I wouldn't want them to tinker with the Centre Court or the Royal Box. I would love to do a mini feature for a television programme on players curtseying at Wimbledon – some were pretty good, others were horrible. Wimbledon stands apart from the other three majors in that it has always been able to operate as an independent entity.

COURT & SOCIAL: TAKE A BOW

In her post-match interview, Jennifer Capriati revealed the secret of the perfect curtsey. 'Just before I went out on court, there would be a guy showing you how to do it ... in the waiting room right before you go on to Centre Court,' she said. Question: 'Was the guy wearing a dress?' Answer: 'He was wearing pants.' Step forward the curtsey instructor.

— SE

COURT & SOCIAL: GREEN WITH WORRY

There are obvious stresses for competitors, but imagine being in charge of pernickety players' dietary requirements. Alan Hinkins, returning for his 49th consecutive Championships on the catering front, recalls how quickly the club have always responded to players' demands – for pasta, lighter salad dressings, the option of red meat, and green bananas.

'We always had requests to supply the dressing-room with green bananas, and I could never understand that, green ones. I was terrified by the responsibility. I kept fearing a player would appear in his post-match interview saying, "I lost because there wasn't a green banana there when I needed one",' he said.

— SE

COURT & SOCIAL:
LOOKING BETWEEN THE LINES

Never mind the hours of debate on whether the serve-and-volley game is in danger of extinction. Just ask the head groundsman to discuss the wear of grass on his prized courts. Whereas the courts today are notable for the brown worn areas along the baseline, yesterday's television replays of finals between Chris Evert and Martina Navratilova, or Pete Sampras and Jim Courier, during the rain breaks showed a notable sideways 'H' shape, with wear along the baseline and down the middle as players scurried in to patrol the net area. The later the date of the match, the less worn the service-box grass. It was a perfect illustration of Eddie Seaward's comment. 'There is very little wear in the service boxes this year,' he said. 'Everyone thinks it's a new phenomenon, but it's something that has been going on progressively for many, many years.'

– SE

SISTERS LAUGHING HARDEST AFTER LIMPEST OF FINALS

Giles Smith

This year the champion did not sink to her knees in exhausted ecstasy, nor leap and shriek at the moment of her 4–6, 6–4, 6–2 triumph and nor was any elated attempt made to enter the Centre Court guest box the difficult way. Instead Serena Williams lowered her head slightly and walked with humility to the net, as you would if you had just inflicted a defeat on someone who had been reduced to hobbling for much of the match, and if that hobbling someone was your sister.

There are people who maintain that any all-Williams affair – and this was the sixth time that Venus and Serena have locked up a Grand Slam final in two years – comes with its sting pre-drawn. It's too cosy; they like each other too much; there is not enough at stake. There are those who will further allege that you can no more trust the dramatic spontaneity of these occasions than you can trust the moment in a David Beckham launch when the shirtless orphan eludes security. What's certain is that any match involving anyone at all, related or otherwise, is going to struggle to burst into flames when one of the competitors is dragging her left leg behind her even as they enter the court, as Venus was this weekend. It's a good thing Wimbledon loans the players a bag carrier on these ceremonial occasions. You wouldn't have backed a burdened Venus to make it as far as her chair without a medical time-out.

Her problem was the stomach strain she sustained in Warsaw a while ago and which she aggravated at this Wimbledon, particularly during her semi-final against Kim Clijsters. The tournament has seen something of a return to grace and glory for Venus's game but it has happened despite sharp, abdominal pains which, according to Venus, restrict her ability to lower her body to the degree that she needs to and limit her reaching up to serve. Adapting to cope, she has strained other muscles, which is why she appeared on Saturday with her left thigh bound up. Asked afterwards whether she had been to all intents and purposes corseted under that strappy dress, Venus replied, 'I have a few wraps going on.' That she walked out at all on Saturday – and that she stayed out there until the end – had much to do with not wishing to rain on Serena's parade and Venus heavily implied that she would be more reluctant to risk herself had the other finalist been anyone other than a blood relation. Thus this was the first Wimbledon singles final in living memory in which one of the competitors played essentially as a favour to the other and the toll on the occasion's vitality as a contest was to prove steep.

Aside from a couple of exhibition-standard rallies, the match was principally engaging in two patches: in the second set where Venus pulled back from 5–1 down to 5–4 down to stand, extraordinarily, within three games of the title, but could not make up the second break; and at the conclusion of that first set, which Venus battled hard for and took. Yet even here there was food for the conspiracy theorists. With Venus on set point, Serena patted back into play a ball that was just begging to be destroyed. Afterwards, though, she denied that she was holding off in sympathy. 'Venus played really well in the first set and her ground strokes were just really kicking,' she said. 'I think, if anything, I fought harder.' In fairness, at other critical moments, Serena hardly seemed to be going easy. This was by no means a sunny day for her own game – long phases of this match went by in a dull haze of mis-hit ground strokes to a soundtrack of the crowd's near indifference, and Serena was frequently chattering in despair at her own racket head.

Yet at 4–2 in the final set, for instance, mercy took the form of a 107mph serve and a compilation of thunderous ground strokes carefully alternated between the back corners of the court to ensure they took the maximum toll on Venus's energy and will alike. If that was sisterly love, one dreads to think what Christmas with the Williamses must be like. Having limply surrendered her serve in the first game of the third set, Venus called out the trainer and took a medical time-out, which did little to crisp up the atmosphere, except in as much as it enabled one to anticipate a default. She briefly looked a little stronger on her return but soon yielded her serve again and, shortly after, the match. The afternoon ended with the sisters taking photographs of each other with their own camera, as if this were a family holiday.

Which, of course, to a large extent it was – and, despite Saturday's inescapable flatness, our amazement should be undiminished. One family has sewn up the circuit. Two sisters routinely compete for the major honours and twice at Wimbledon, in successive years, they have sent the rest of the field home and left last, laughing hardest. The day one ceases to be impressed by this is the day one ceases to be impressed by tennis.

As for the allegations of carefully calculated spoil-sharing ... well, if the fix is in, then Venus is truly owed some. After Saturday's defeat, she is now 5–1 down on the Grand Slam deal. Five times she has lost the biggest titles in the sport to her kid sister. Assuming it is a deal, then Venus is at the blunt end of it. Is she truly getting the parts she wants? She should have a word with her agent.

7 JULY 2003

FEDERER IS THE FUTURE, NOW
Paul Hayward

Boris Becker was surely right when he said last night: 'The future has come today.' Roger Federer has ushered in a new Age of Elegance in men's tennis. Power and grunting muscularity, the dominant currencies of our age, were locked in a trunk for the afternoon as this 21-year-old Swiss took over from Pete Sampras as the master of Centre Court. Make room on the list of modern sportsmen and women you would pay more than you could afford to watch. Mark Philippoussis, whose nickname, Scud, gives you an idea where his primary talent lies, was destroyed in straight sets yesterday by pure panache. In one hour 55 minutes he was sent back to the locker-room brooding on an especially demoralising defeat, 7–6, 6–2, 7–6. Federer dropped just one set throughout the fortnight on his way to the £575,000 first prize. The last Wimbledon champion to be so parsimonious was Richard Krajicek (1996), who broke a sequence of seven Sampras triumphs. Krajicek was an every-dog-has-his-day kind of champ. The people who really know this mentally exhausting game think Federer has opened a new imperial reign.

In football, players are running all day like dynamos; in golf new technology is giving the little white ball a fearful pounding; in rugby the new giants are smashing into each other like turbo-charged tanks. To win these days is usually enough. Winning beautifully is a dying art. Since the days of Becker and Stefan Edberg tennis has threatened to mutate into a kind of violence: a trial of forearm strength and racket tenacity. For almost a decade Sampras kept art's flame alive. But he, too, made his pact with the power game (remember that lethal serve?). It was the insurance policy that allowed him to play his more flamboyant strokes. Federer wisely resisted the comparison. 'This is one to his seven [Wimbledon titles],' he said once the tears he shed on court after his victory had dried. 'I'm just happy to be on the board with Borg and these people; to be a part of the history of Wimbledon.'

At the 117th Championships, in the fortnight of Britain's despair, Federer discovered just how good he is. We saw him learn, watched his self-assurance grow. A questionable record in the four Grand Slam events was tossed into an Alpine lake. Philippoussis managed to stay with him until the first-set tie-break, but then you could see the self-belief drain from his arms and legs. 'Too good,' complained Andy Roddick after Federer had treated him equally roughly in Friday's semi-final. The same haunting suspicion seemed to afflict Philippoussis as he twice dropped his serve early in the second set. In that middle phase of a lopsided contest Federer's best shots were exquisite and unanswerable. Philippoussis sucked in air. Ayers Rock would have had a better chance of getting the ball back than this giant and increasingly disconsolate Australian.

Federer won without having to perform as majestically as he did against Roddick two days earlier. By 2p.m. yesterday the hardest work was done – not just by him but Philippoussis, who knocked out Andre Agassi, the world No. 1, and Ivo Karlovic, who disposed of Lleyton Hewitt, the defending champion, in the fortnight's greatest shock. But Federer still woke knowing he had to make the daunting transition from purists' favourite to Centre Court governor. The pedigree was there. He was Wimbledon boys' champion in 1998 and impaled Sampras as a 19-year-old three English summers ago. Without his armour-piercing serve, Philippoussis would have been charcoal after an hour. Even here Federer had the cutting edge. His average first serve was 9mph slower than his opponent's but he still outscored him in aces 21–14. The experts are swooning because Federer can win any way he chooses: on any surface, with any array of strokes. He is not yet in the Sampras league of relentless concentrators. There are times when he becomes almost too relaxed: like the brilliant kid at school who no longer feels stretched. Yesterday put knowledge in his heart and teardrops in his eyes. The realisation was that he is the world's best tennis player. His first Grand Slam title was the oldest and best of all.

The age of Sampras ended in 2001. That year, Goran Ivanisevic, who came to the All-England Club on a wild card, laid on a festival of eccentricity. Last season Hewitt battered and hustled his way to the title. He was colossal at times. But it was always hard to imagine him summoning such manic, ball-belting intensity time after time. Federer and Roddick were close behind. It would be a crime against history not to say that Federer will have to reach this year's pitch a lot more than once for him to deserve the full comparison with Sampras, who is on a kind of gardening leave in Beverly Hills. Summer's breeze, though, has certainly flicked over the page.

In April, Sampras, who won a record 14 Grand Slam titles, was about to begin his two-month march on London. 'I've always had this little thing I do when I tie my shoes,' he said. 'I finish tying them, slap the ground and say to myself – here we go! But this time, it didn't feel good. And I stopped, right there and then.' Maybe he had a premonition of Federer planting flags in his old turf. The new champion's only cruelty yesterday was to render Sampras no longer missed. When the future arrived on Centre Court it emanated beauty and grace.

9 JULY 2003

SWISS MILK RETURN OF WIMBLEDON VICTOR FEDERER

Mark Hodgkinson in Gstaad

They gave Roger Federer a cow yesterday. Even better, the beast – with handle-bar horns and weighing 800 kilos – was dragged on to the clay court under what looked like several flower beds of effeminate, prissy headdress. Surely this wasn't a transvestite bull? Maybe, we thought, the Swiss do actually have a sense of humour. The men's Wimbledon champion, already wobbly after a 'welcome home' standing ovation from the 6,000 crowd, stood stunned, robotically patting the animal on the nose. Sadly, though, he didn't burst into tears.

Here at the Swiss Open was the country's first winner of a men's Grand Slam singles title. And they recognised Federer's achievement by getting a local farmer in traditional dress to proffer – very gingerly – a ceremonial milking stool. That ruined the gag slightly. The beast was clearly female. But Federer's expression had now turned from bemusement to childish excitement. 'I'm going to milk it,' he said. 'I'll do anything for it. I need to find a garage for it. It was a great idea, very funny. And a total surprise.' The farmer

– beaming next to the Simmental milking cow, the local breed around this Alpine ski resort, and wearing a just-for-the-tourists cow bell – bellowed: 'The cow weighs 800 kilos, but has half the power of one of Roger's serves.'

Although the cow had already celebrated its seventh birthday, Federer was then asked to name it. Put on the spot slightly, he paused for a few moments, stared at the court dust, and then replied: 'Juliette.' Quite why remained a mystery last night. There were suggestions that the name may have recalled a former girlfriend with whom he is no longer on speaking terms. But those who were shouting 'Martina! Martina!' as a suggestion, were just being unkind. Federer has a choice: he can either take Juliette home, or leave her in the Gstaad meadows – they will post him the cheese on a regular basis. The only condition is that the tennis player learns how to work her udders. They didn't teach him that in metropolitan Basle.

But there had been something of a giveaway for Federer in the Roy Emerson Arena (the man himself was there to offer his congratulations). Although preparations didn't stretch to a cattle grid along the baseline, the width of the red carpet had been tripled to five metres. 'Do you have any idea what your present is?' asked the MC. 'No,' replied the soon-to-be cowboy. Federer, though, must have expected Tina Turner's 'Simply the Best'. That was predictable enough for his entrance. Such is his relaxed style, he lounged into view in flip-flops and baggy white slacks, politely giving each of the four chalet-style stands a smile and a wave. There was already a belief at Wimbledon that Federer's fans were of the staid variety. But, no. High in the main stand yesterday, a rowdy pocket of twenty-somethings dared to interrupt the MC's interview with the Swiss version of 'Give us an R, give us an O ...' and then drowned out Federer in quite loud clapping. Still, this was hardly comparable to David Beckham/Japanese airport hysteria. There was no sodium flash photography, nor a sea of oestrogen-soaked banners. There was just one banner – and it showed a wonderful lack of imagination. 'Hello, Roger,' someone had scrawled in red felt-tip.

Any other tournament and Federer, 21, would now be somewhere hotter on a sun lounger, slurping lurid cocktails through a curly straw. He is only at 'the Wimbledon of the Alps' because he is still grateful to the event that handed him a wild card in 1998, allowing his circuit debut. Location is also key. 'A holiday tournament,' one player whispered. Gstaad does not really make sense – playing clay the week after Wimbledon and before a string of hard-court tournaments – but players dismissed in round one will stay on for chocolate-box mountains and Eurotrash nightclubs.

Yesterday's foil was Marc Lopez, a fresh Spanish qualifier who looks like he is still hanging on for puberty and should have been fetching the balls rather than dragging the top seed into three sets, 6–3, 6–7, 6–3. Federer, still acclimatising to serve-and-volleying on clay and shots that fly at 1,050 metres above sea level, could have sealed the deal in straight sets, but played some absent-minded tennis at the close of the second. He wafted at two match points at 5–4. The third set was nervy.

Yesterday's love-in was Federer's first interaction with his public. He had arrived at a local airport by private jet on Monday night, emerging with girlfriend Miroslava Vavrinec for Champagne, but there was no mobbing. The tournament director, who did not want Federer's head turned so as to keep him in the draw for as long as possible (he had won only one match in five previous visits), had deliberately not told anyone about the return. So, Jacques Hermenjat then thought: 'Let's give him a cow. That won't distract him.'

11 JANUARY 2004
GRAND PLAN WILL RAISE THE ROOF
John McEnroe

Wimbledon's capacity to surprise is astonishing – particularly for an old traditionalist like me! There was I last month, as guest speaker at the tennis writers' annual dinner at Wimbledon, gently chiding them for allowing sleeveless shirts at the Championships, and they go and sanction something much more remarkable and significant – a roof over the Centre Court. Incredible. Next, you'll be telling me, Mick Jagger's going to be knighted.

Having said that, it may surprise some people to learn that far from living in the past, Wimbledon have been the most forward-thinking of the four Grand Slam committees for some time. But I never expected this. Nor, I suspect, did the United States Tennis Association, who once more have been beaten to the punch by the English. Expect a hurried announcement from the USTA that they, too, propose to put a roof over their centre court, at Flushing Meadows. I cannot recall at any time a groundswell about a roof at Wimbledon. Even when the rain cost Tim Henman so dearly in that tortuous semi-final against Goran Ivanisevic in 2001 there was never a great hue and cry, as there was last year at the US Open when the rain made such a mockery of it. Somehow Wimbledon always manages to catch up and get the job done with a minimum of fuss.

There have probably been more discussions about a major championship still playing on grass than putting a roof over its Centre Court. Some people might say the money could have been better spent on another aspect of British tennis, but, since it's private money, it isn't really an issue. The manner in which the money is raised, though – from debenture holders who sell their tickets on for a profit – may leave a bad taste in some people's mouths.

The more I think about it, it was a pretty big decision to take but a good one. The only pity is that it's going to take so long to complete – five years probably – and that will be too late for Britain's best player. Hopefully, there will be more Henmans coming through in the future, which, if I have anything to do with it – and I now do – there will be.

Naturally, the purists will have their concerns, as I do. When you are dealing with the most beautiful tennis court in the world any change to it has to be a risk, but the architects seem confident in their ability to retain its integrity. Likewise, with their ability to deal with problems such as condensation beneath the roof and the grass, if anything, becoming too dry. The roof opens up a new vista for the Championships. Potentially, one could play there all year round. Maybe it's better to use grass a little more often. Britain could play all their Davis Cup ties there, although I would imagine the Wimbledon committee would draw the line at staging pop concerts.

I understand they have discounted the idea of holding evening sessions during the Championships, but it's early days. I am sure they could be persuaded to do so by TV, if the public demand is there. Now they've gone this far they might as well go the whole way. Personally, I used to like playing in the evenings. There are certain times when people's energy levels are up and for me they were in the evenings. It's no coincidence, either, that the majority of the greatest matches in history – outside of Wimbledon, of course – have taken place during what we Americans call prime time. The Younes El Aynaoui–Andy Roddick match in Melbourne last year is a perfect example of that. Certain situations, of course, may force them to play in the evenings. Let's say you're behind in the schedule on men's quarter-finals day and play on Court No. 1 is badly affected by rain. You're missing out on the opportunity to complete all the matches on the same day.

Doubtless there will be a few moans from players that fitness wasn't as much of an issue as it should have been, particularly if there is a dramatic change in temperature. If Andre Agassi is running Henman into the ground in the heat and the match suddenly has to move indoors, that's got to be to Henman's advantage. Sometimes, though, you just cannot tell how conditions will be indoors. I remember at my last Australian Open, in 1992, I had beaten Boris Becker and then won a gruelling five-setter in unbearable heat. I longed for a nice, cool indoor match, which I surprisingly received against Wayne Ferreira in the quarters. But I felt lifeless, and so did the ball, and I lost in straight sets. But that doesn't mean it's a bad thing.

There were times when the rain at Wimbledon could dampen your spirit, break your will. I've seen players melt in the locker-room. People don't realise that nervous energy can make you tired. And there were times for me as well when it was just too much, but that was more around the mid-1980s after I had missed a couple of Championships and I had problems with the media and all that 'superbrat' stuff. Usually, I came prepared for the worst in terms of weather.

Each of the Slams has its own characteristics and, as a result, poses its own particular problems. At the US Open it's the heat and the cold and the noise of the planes going overhead; at Roland Garros the clay courts can be physically debilitating; while at Wimbledon it was always more of a mental test. That may now change as far as the Championships are concerned. The great thing is that players will know they are definitely going to play, which will relieve them of the stress of waiting and not knowing. But ultimately, this is not about the players, it's about the spectators and television, who invest so much money. If the players don't like it, too bad.

28 APRIL 2004

JOHN PARSONS – A TRIBUTE

John Roberts, tennis correspondent of the *Independent*

It is reasonable to suggest that John Parsons was as well known in the tennis community as any of the players. Better known than some. J.P., to one and all, died in Miami on Monday, aged 66. He was the lawn tennis correspondent of *The Daily Telegraph.* At least that was his day job. Most of the time he was simply Mr Tennis, a wonderful busy-body in every sense, devoted to the sport he loved and generally aware of everything that happened, on the court and behind the scenes.

Such was his influence with everybody in tennis, from administrators to doormen, that many of his colleagues in the tennis media now wonder how they will be able to manage without him. He gave enormous help and encouragement to his fellow reporters as chairman and later secretary of the Lawn Tennis Writers' Association and as a member of the International Tennis Federation's Media Commission.

J.P. was a small man of immense courage, travelling the world to cover the game with a kind heart, a keen sense of justice and injustice, and an indomitable spirit that enabled him to overcome the debilitating side-effects of a kidney transplant. He was born with only one functioning kidney, which was later damaged by a blow from a rifle butt during an insurrection in Nigeria, where he was covering a tournament.

As a schoolboy he covered sport for his local paper, the *Oxford Mail*, graduating to a staff job. He participated in all sports and became a strict, but fair (he said) football referee. He wrote about Oxford United when they were still Headington United, and was the highest bidder in an auction to have Ron Atkinson clean his windows. J.P.'s grandmother was a staunch Oxford City fan whose feet would move in sympathy every time one of their players kicked the ball.

J.P. would love to have progressed as a tennis player, but, as he overheard Dan Maskell say, he was not going to go far with his patsy serve. He did, however, play a role in one of the great sporting moments in history: Roger Bannister's sub-four-minute mile in 1954. It was J.P. who dashed to the station from Iffley Road and handed the BBC film of the race to the guard, ensuring that it was safely on its way to be shown to the nation. A decade later, J.P. was writing on football and tennis for the *Daily Mail* before succeeding the eminent Lance Tingay at *The Daily Telegraph*.

He was made an honorary member of the All-England Club and wrote the popular *Official Wimbledon Annual*, usually having it half written before the Championships had finished. He also wrote an encyclopaedia of tennis and had a notion of compiling a book of anecdotes concerning the quirky things that have happened in tennis and to tennis journalists. We shall never know if he would have thought to include some of the stories about himself. Like the time he covered a 'Sport Goofy' junior event and revealed that the nine-year-old Monica Seles's father had first encouraged her to play by drawing Tom and Jerry on tennis balls. J.P. was ticked off by a humourless tournament official because Tom and Jerry were not Disney characters. Or the occasion a fatigued Todd Martin trudged into the interview room after a tough match at the US Open. 'You look done in, Todd,' said J.P., 'with all that strapping on your knees and elbows.' Martin, in a drawl reminiscent of Clint Eastwood, responded by saying: 'You're not looking so good yourself, John.'

Another time, J.P. found himself seated beside a young guest in the President's Box at the US Open, whereupon J.P. introduced himself and asked his companion if he was involved in tennis. 'No,' the young man replied. 'I'm an actor.' 'Theatre or film?' J.P. asked. 'I've done both, but right now I'm concentrating on films.' 'Anything I should watch out for?' 'I'm quite excited about a new release,' the young man said. Imagine J.P.'s embarrassment when he returned to London and saw posters advertising *Top Gun.* As J.P. said: 'He told me he was Tom Cruise and seemed very personable and modest, but I'd never heard of him.'

J.P. certainly had heard of Ken Dodd, who made him laugh until tears ran down his cheeks. He also loved musicals and *The Archers,* recounting that one of his former neighbours did not leave her house for a week after Grace Archer died. Two West Highland terriers in the Parsons's family also loved *The Archers,* but only because they relied on the signature tune at the end of the programme as a signal for their evening walk.

Charming and pompous in equal measure, J.P. was the scourge of interlopers in the press seats at Wimbledon, turfing out many a celebrity. His right index finger – known as 'The Dodgy Digit' – could be seen from a distance, wagging accusingly. Robert Maxwell and a minder once brushed past J.P. at a British Airways check-in at Heathrow, bellowing: 'Let me through.' J.P. gave the publisher a withering look and said: 'I see your manners haven't improved.'

J.P.'s judgment of tennis was excellent and his reportage was authoritative and comprehensive. Gerry Williams, the television commentator, encapsulated J.P.'s skills thus: 'Shakespeare he may not be, but if there's a story around he'll have it.' The Lawn Tennis Association suspected J.P. of hiding under the boardroom table during meetings, so often did he publish their news ahead of schedule. He was also a close friend of the late Philippe Chatrier, president of the French Tennis Federation and of the International Tennis Federation, who was instrumental in tennis's return to the Olympics.

The day before he was taken to hospital in Miami, J.P. was told he had won the ATP Tour's Ron Bookman Award for Media Excellence for the second time, on this occasion for his lifetime service to tennis. The Women's Tennis Association also honoured him. Tim Henman and Fred Perry's widow, Bobby, were among numerous visitors to J.P.'s hospital bedside.

A bachelor, J.P. is survived by his father, Les ('Nip'), 93, his mother, Marion, 92, and a younger sister, Heather Nason, who went to Miami from England to keep vigil. Shortly before the end, there was a characteristic J.P. moment. Although the television in his hospital room had multiple channels, it lacked the one that was showing the tennis. When a colleague paused while flicking the remote control, J.P. glanced at the screen and said, without malice: 'Basketball — what a silly game.' However, when the finals of the Nasdaq-100 Open, which J.P. had set out to cover, were broadcast by CBS on terrestrial television, one of the commentators, Cliff Drysdale, a former international player, paid tribute to J.P. in a moving get-well message.

19 JUNE 2004

BAD BOY NASTASE GETS ALL NOSTALGIC ABOUT GLORIOUS FAILURE AT WIMBLEDON

Robert Philip

You can tell a lot about a man by the memories he keeps. Asked to recall his favourite match, you might expect Ilie Nastase to nominate his defeat of Arthur Ashe in the 1972 US Open final, the 6–2, 6–2, 6–1 rout of Björn Borg in front of the Swede's adoring fans in Stockholm to win his fourth Masters title in 1975, or maybe one outstanding memory from 1973 when he was ranked No. 1 in the world, winning 16 tournaments including the French Open, the Italian Open, Monte Carlo and Queen's Club. Ah, but Nastase was an artist who used his racket to create delicate brushstrokes, a gossamer-soft drop shot here, an exquisitely curved lob there. His satisfaction came from covering the entire canvas in brilliant colours, not from winning trophies for his masterpieces.

'Maybe when I lost to Stan Smith at Wimbledon in 1972,' he says in his seductive Transylvanian version of English. 'People think I'm crazy but it's true. There were many matches I lost that I enjoyed because I still have a good time.' With Smith serving at 4–4, 0–30 in the fifth set of that now legendary final 32 summers ago, Nastase struck a seemingly unreturnable forehand down the line only for the lunging American to hit a flukey 'winner' off the very top of his wooden frame. To Smith went the title, to the Romanian went our hearts. 'So, how can I be upset I lost a great match by one or two points? That would be ridiculous. People say I was unlucky but, hey, to lose a final like that 7–5 in the fifth was a beautiful defeat.'

In the company of Ken Rosewall, Pancho Gonzales and Ivan Lendl, Nastase will forever be remembered as one of the best players never to win Wimbledon, his second appearance in the final against Borg in 1976 also ending in disappointment. 'I was 30 and I hadn't played many tournaments because I was banned for playing Team Tennis in America. Then, after '76, I was gone. Never winning Wimbledon is not a regret. I don't remind myself every day. I don't have to because people remind me. You think I don't sleep at night? Not that it makes me happy, but I'm not the only one. Becker and McEnroe are missing Roland Garros, Borg is missing the US Open. You can't live your life regretting such things.'

Despite the absence of a Centre Court triumph, there is just cause for regarding Nastase as the most naturally talented of them all, and one can only imagine how dominant this capricious genius might have become had he been permitted to travel abroad at an earlier age. 'That's my one regret,' he says. 'I give everyone four or five years' head start because I didn't leave Romania until I was 20. I didn't know what junior tournaments means, I didn't know what grass was, but the first time I was allowed to travel outside was to play in Davis Cup against France at Roland Garros. I was playing on the Centre Court against Pierre Darmon – and he was a good player, yes? – and though I lose in five sets René Lacoste [one of France's famous Four Musketeers] came into dressing-room and say, "I've never seen a player like you? Where you been?" I replied, "Romania". Thanks to Mr Lacoste I was invited to play French Open three weeks afterwards when I won the final of the doubles with [Ion] Tiriac.'

It is Tiriac's opinion that every tennis stadium should erect a statue in Nastase's honour, in recognition of the fact that though Bill Tilden, Lew Hoad and Rod Laver were towering figures within the game, the Romanian was the first player to transcend the sport as entertainer, sex symbol, serial carouser and trouble-maker. At the height of his bad-boy image, 'Nasty' could have started an argument on an empty court and even Muhammad Ali acknowledged him as his main rival in the art of making headlines. 'I met him in Caesar's Palace casino in Vegas one time when he come running over to me saying, "Hey, you the big mouth in tennis? You might have a bigger mouth than me but I'm prettier than you. Come here, I want to have picture taken with you." He put my fist on his chin, and his fist on mine then said, "See your fist in my face? It's because I want it to be there." I wish I had put this in my book but I forgot about it completely until now. Muhammad Ali is my greatest hero.'

Nastase's recent autobiography does not neglect many such incidents from a life that has taken him from an impoverished childhood in Bucharest to sporting superstar, friend of princes and princesses, through myriad affairs with actresses and models, two divorces and his recent marriage to Amalia, 30 years his junior at the age of 27, who made him a father for the fourth time ten months ago with the birth of daughter Alessia. 'It has been a wonderful life and it's great being a dad again though strangers think I am Alessia's grandfather. I always enjoyed being Ilie Nastase when I was playing tennis, and now I enjoy being the Nastase of 57 years old and that took me a long time. The first few years after I stop playing I was lost. Some players never get over that – one is Connors and one is McEnroe but I could give you more – who think they are the same. They want to play on the seniors and win and throw their rackets but, for me, that is gone. I want to be the person I am today because to look backwards doesn't do any good.'

Nastase played with laughter in his soul. I can still remember him competing with Tiriac in a senior doubles at Roland Garros where they infuriated their opponents by throwing up ten, 20, 30 successive lobs. Catching sight of a gorgeous blonde wearing a micro-skirt and very little else, Nastase left Tiriac to it, ambled over to chat, and returned with her telephone number on his wrist. 'Where the hell have you been?' demanded Tiriac. 'Talking to blonde.' 'Leaving me to do all the lobbing.' 'Ion, dear friend, there will be another lob along in a minute, there might not be another blonde ...'

'I am happy if spectators are happy but I do it all for me,' reveals Nastase. 'Just as I could not control my emotions, I could not control the desire to enjoy myself. The bigger the crowd, the more I wanted to perform. The result never really mattered.'

24 JUNE 2004
COURT & SOCIAL: HOLIDAY IN WIMBLEDON

Andre Agassi, who was forced to withdraw last week because of a hip injury, had already paid £8,000 up front for his accommodation near Wimbledon Common. He believed that he had little chance of a refund from the letting agency, so, rather than causing a scene, has invited some friends from the West Coast to come over for a holiday.

– MH

25 JUNE 2004
COURT & SOCIAL:
GUSSIE FLASHES DRAWERS AGAIN

The flash of her lace-frilled knickers was once debated in Parliament, and had the All-England Club seriously concerned about their effect on the sensibilities of the Royal Family. Now, though, there is a real poignancy about the undergarments of Gertrude 'Gussie' Moran. The 80-year-old is selling them on an auction website, eBay, to save herself from destitution. Last night, with a week to go, the bidding had reached £1,500. She is hoping for at least four times that, and deserves it. Whatever Anna Kournikova has done, she was only copying what Moran had already pioneered in the 1940s, when she caused outrage and a crush of desperate photographers on Centre Court, by being the first woman tennis player to deliberately show her pants.

Moran, who was accused of putting 'sin and vulgarity into tennis', had to be persuaded to sell her bloomers by her concerned circle of friends. She is trying to bring a little more comfort to a life measured out in social security cheques. She lives alone in Hollywood and refuses to accept charity from anyone but the state. It comes to something when the only way of keeping your dignity is to put a colour photograph of your smalls on the internet.

— MH

29 JUNE 2004
COURT & SOCIAL: SOAKED IN THE DRY

Even during the dry spells between the showers, the All-England Club members have been getting soaked. Several of the purple-and-green brigade were standing on the lawn of the members' enclosure just after 8p.m., enjoying a glass of Pimm's or two in a rare period of sunshine, when the sprinkler fired up, drenching those close by. The groundstaff had forgotten to change the pre-tournament timings.

— MH

5 JULY 2004
NAVRATILOVA HANDS OVER THE BATON
Sue Mott

The greatest women's tennis player of all time glanced around at Wimbledon yesterday and her gaze fell on the new superstar of the sport, all smiles and micro red mini-skirt, Maria Sharapova. 'Look at her,' said Martina Navratilova, indulgently. 'She's wearing her All-England Club badge already.' Tenderly, she touched her own circular badge, her mind flitting back over nine singles Championships, the first of them earned in 1978 long before Sharapova was born.

'Hey, Maria!' she called. The new champion looked up. 'Welcome to the club!' Navratilova said, gesturing to the badge. They smiled in mutual recognition.

Thirty years between them and yet they hold something rare and wonderful in common. The knowledge of how it feels to win Wimbledon. Now one is just beginning the adventure of a glorious career and the other is retiring from SW19 forever. Navratilova, having astounded the sporting world by competing in the singles, the mixed and women's doubles at the age of 47, will not be coming back next year. It's over. And Ova. The baton now passes to the younger generation. Is she regretful? A tinge. 'It's not about the last Wimbledon. It's about me not playing my best tennis. It wasn't good enough. But it doesn't always work out the way you want. The Czechs should have been in the final of the European Championship. But that's why we love sports so much. You never know the ending.' A wild giggle floated over from Sharapova's table. 'It's either a happy ending or a sad one.' The former champion looked wistful.

The perfect sentimentalist ending would have been for Navratilova to break Billie-Jean King's record of 20 Wimbledon titles. It will not happen now. They will be inseparably successful for ever. 'But it was never about records. It was about playing the game,' she insisted. Sentimentalism never gripped her as it did the onlookers. This time she did not pluck a few blades of grass from the court, as she had done, reverently and symbolically, in 1990 when she won her last singles title against Zina Garrison. 'It never occurred to me this time. Court 13! I wasn't going to take that with me,' she said with a grin. 'It was very anti-climactic. This has been the screwiest, windiest, most rain-interrupted Wimbledon I played. I never played on the Centre Court once. But this was not a trip down memory lane. It's been about playing the game. I wanted to play well so much that I got nervous. I didn't allow myself to think properly or my body to flow. It happens more when you get older. That's why the 17-year-old won. Did you see any nerves in her? I didn't have any nerves when I played Chris Evert 26 years ago. I was down 2–4 in the third and the young me just thought, "Oh, no problem". It's not the age thing. What am I supposed to have – dementia by now? What I am doing is meant to be inspiring people not making them say, "She shouldn't be doing that".

'You know, when I was playing Gisela Dulko in the second round of the singles on Court 3, one of my business associates overheard three club members talking about me, two men and one woman, all of them aged somewhere between 70 and death. Of course, the men were negative and the woman was positive. The men were saying, "Oh this is terrible for women's tennis", parroting Michael Stich's comments, so they weren't even able to think for themselves. They were being negative instead of celebrating what it is. How can anything that I do be negative? Did I stop being good? Yes, I am not as good as I was, but I still am pretty damn good.' Proof: 13 Grand Slam singles titles, 31 doubles, nine mixed doubles and a few sacred strands of shrivelled grass in her jewellery box. 'I know I have a talent. I owe it to the gods to explore that talent to the limit. It's a cross that I have to bear. A very pleasant cross. It's a legacy I have to live up to.'

Icons, like the rest of us, can achieve immortality by the simple expedient of having children. Navratilova, being gay, chose not to exercise that option. 'That would have been an ego thing. Just to pass on the genes. To get another male athlete and have an offspring. That would have been interesting to see. But that is ego talking. That is nothing to do with what's good in this world. So I don't regret that I don't have children. I have a bunch of children — with four legs.' She has 14 dogs, including a new baby Staffordshire bull terrier collected on this trip. 'That's plenty for me to look after.' Her face lit up with a smile. She also has a close family. Her sister lives in Stockholm and she regularly emails her relatives in Prague. She still, long after the Russian tanks have rolled away from Eastern Europe, finds it hard to believe in the freedom her home country enjoys. 'I am still amazed that Czechoslovakia is not a communist country. That's all I knew. Their freedom is one of the greatest delights of my life. I mean, Sharapova. She wouldn't have come out either. If the Communists were still going we would never have heard of her. They were sending people to Siberia. You didn't get out of Siberia. So I really appreciate where she came from. More so than anybody.' She thought a minute. 'Except, maybe, Solzhenitsyn.'

This, you are constantly reminded, is an athlete with a good deal more than tennis balls ricocheting around the brainpan. In the case of some sporting heroes, the grunt may be the most intelligent noise they utter. Navratilova always had an intellect to go with the game. 'That's why my perspective on life is rather unusual. That's why I appreciate everything I have and that's why I want to do everything I can for others. I am still amazed when I go to a grocery store that I can buy anything I want and that I don't have to wait in line. Really! You don't get rid of your childhood that easily. I was in Czechoslovakia until I was 18. I'd go get the bread and milk and butter every other day because we didn't have a refrigerator. Sometimes, on a lucky day, I'd go to the sweet shop. I never felt deprived, that was the norm.'

It has not been an easy life. Neither has Sharapova's in a different way. Martina's only advice to the younger star is 'Go with it! Go on the ride and enjoy it. She works harder than most, for sure. She is meticulous, very focused and determined. She is a great role model for kids. I didn't discover her back in Moscow. I just saw that she was good. Her father asked me what he should do and I said, "Go to Nick Bollettieri's in Florida. They will teach her a forehand and backhand. They hit a million balls there." Now she's got it all. She has the selfishness, the tunnel vision, you have to have. To tune out all the other distractions. Fame I don't think will be a problem for her. She's been groomed for it. I don't see her going off partying or wanting to be an actress. Boyfriends might be a problem but the biggest thing could be injuries. She being so long, she could be more prone to injuries. She has the body of an 800-metre runner. The ankles, the knees, even the hips could be more hard pressed because of the height. But Maria winning is the best thing for women's tennis. Those old farts were criticising women's tennis because I was beating somebody and can still compete. But her win proves there's good depth in women's tennis. I could see she was improving. I talked to her father a couple of times. He said, "Oh, she's not getting as good as she should be." I'm like, "Settle down, she's getting there." Now I think she's exceeded expectations. It will be tough for her. She'll be a good scalp to get for the others now. But she can handle it.

'Also it's good because a Williams didn't win. Not because they're not good but because they haven't given the game 100 per cent. It's almost been like a hobby. So OK, what's more important to Venus: design or tennis? What's more important to Serena: acting or tennis? The fact we are even asking the question is a tell-tale sign. Yes, absolutely, explore other things. But it must take some of their energy away from tennis. It would have been bad for women's tennis if Serena could still win and be No. 1 while talking about acting and reading scripts. So now we have a new star and Serena might start taking it seriously. Serena wants it, but she can't just want it during a match. As an American football coach once said, "Most athletes have the will to win but very few have the will to prepare." She's going to want to mount a comeback. She's got the attitude. She will want to be the queen again.'

It is disconcerting to hear the ease with which Navratilova talks about other, younger, players ascending to the throne that was her own. She wears a cap and shades but it might as well be the full ermine and tiara. For those who watched her revolutionary assault on the daintier aspects of women's tennis, there will only ever be one queen of Wimbledon. Perhaps she laments the ageing process, but in public there is absolutely no rage against the dying of the light and backhand. 'It's a natural progression, I only mind the wrinkles. I haven't had any work done, as you can see,' she said, ruefully pulling at the skin of her face. 'I always thought I would have these bags under my eyes taken out. But I'm too much of a wimp. My solution is just to go to a dimly lit place.'

So apart from having dimmer switches put into all her houses, her future is full and busy. She will compete at the Olympics in Athens, the US Open and the end-of-year women's championships. She will found a tennis academy in America, an animal shelter and probably ('I don't know if I have the temper for it') enter tennis politics. There are things to fix. 'The agents are an abomination for the most part. They milk the players and then throw you away like dirty laundry and look for the next great thing. That's going to be the trick for Maria. It's hard to know your friends.' Friends for Navratilova were hard won. She left the East at a time when it was called 'defection' not emigration. She became a gay icon and a politicised figure, whether she wanted to or not. She earned a multi-million-pound fortune and yet the most precious possession among her jewels are a few wizened blades of old grass. She represents the opposite of Oscar Wilde's weary cynicism. She knows the price of nothing and the value of everything. We will miss her.

21 JUNE 2005

COURT & SOCIAL: IT'S JUST NOT CRICKET

Wimbledon has come a long way since 1877, when 200 spectators paid a shilling each to watch the final and the dates were scheduled around the big fixture in the season's social calendar: the Eton v Harrow cricket match. The 200th anniversary of the schools cricket challenge last weekend – which used to attract crowds of 30,000 – prompted reminiscences of how Spencer Gore, champion of that first Wimbledon gentlemen's singles in 1877, and an Old Harrovian who came to lawn tennis via real tennis, failed to predict the explosion of interest in the lawn variety. 'This game won't catch on at all, there's not so much finesse,' he was reputed to have commented.

– SE

COURT & SOCIAL: DUKE ON THE BALL

Elena Baltacha, exasperated when she dropped her serve early in the second set during her first-round exit, struck a ball in pique towards the Royal Box. The dignitaries had just settled back into the front row after a break when the projectile came zooming straight towards ... HRH the Duke of Kent. The Duke – who lists flying and tennis as sporting interests – coolly caught it. It must be the first time the president of the All-England Club has been called into ball-retrieving action. Baltacha was unaware of the near diplomatic incident. 'I didn't care where it went. I didn't kill anyone, did I?'

– SE

24 JUNE 2005

HENMAN HANDS OVER TO A NEW HOPE

Andrew Baker

A popular T-shirt on Henman Hill yesterday afternoon bore the mildly blasphemous slogan: 'In Tim We Trust'. And so the Wimbledon fans have done down the years: trusted Tim to provide them with an annual fix of elation, tension, terror and the seemingly inevitable heartbreak. This year, the nation's favourite washing powder salesman has telescoped the whole agonising process into just two appearances, ten sets crammed with his trademark mixture of high achievement, deep disappointment, improbable escape acts and grim-faced capitulation. As usual, he has borne the hysteria of the media with stoicism, perhaps encouraged that with the emergence of Andrew Murray as a genuine force, he may never have to carry the hopes of the nation alone again.

There was little time for grief yesterday afternoon: the same fans who had willed Henman to save match points against Dmitry Tursunov were soon encamped on his eponymous hill, gripped by Murray's amazing defeat of the No. 14 seed, Radek Stepanek. But on the long walk to Southfields Station, or on the buses back to central London, many fans will surely have wondered if they had seen Henman's last stand on Centre Court. No doubt they will also have called to mind the highs and lows of Tiger Tim's long Wimbledon journey. The boy from Oxfordshire made his senior debut on the lawns of the All-England Club in 1994, stick-thin, tousle-haired and still in the painful process of evolving into a grown-up player. He lost in the first round, registering barely a flicker on the national consciousness. The next year he won his first Grand Slam match in the first round at Wimbledon, against Kenya's Paul Wekesa, only to make headlines for all the wrong reasons when he became uncharacteristically grumpy during a doubles match, and biffed a ball away which accidentally struck a ballgirl. Henman was disqualified, and made his first big splash in the national press: pictured rather awkwardly presenting an apologetic bouquet to the disgruntled girl.

But all of that was forgotten in 1996, when Henman became the first Briton since Roger Taylor in 1973 to reach the quarter-finals at Wimbledon. Des Lynam beamed, and the nation was hooked. It was clear that for the first time in nearly two decades, Britain had a player capable of winning Wimbledon. But when would he do it? Sadly, we are still waiting. He reached the quarter-finals again in 1997 — remember him beating the giant defending champion, Richard Krajicek? — then the first of what would become four agonising semi-finals, in 1998. Pete Sampras was in his way, and couldn't be shifted: it was the same story in 1999. That year Henman found a new way to toy with the fans' emotions, when he saved two match points to beat Jim Courier in five sets. The fans, the 'Henmaniacs', masochists all, lapped it up. But worse was to come: the ultimate nightmare of 2001, when Sampras was no longer around, and Henman came within two points of becoming the first Briton to reach the Wimbledon final since Bunny Austin in 1938. He had Goran Ivanisevic under a spell when — the irony of it — the British weather intervened. The players were driven from the court by the rain, and when they returned the next morning, the Croatian was inspired, and Henman was distraught.

There would be one more shot at a Grand Slam final, though Henman will tell you that there will yet be others. At the French Open last year, Oxfordshire's finest started a tournament on his least favourite surface ill and tired. But he decided to play as if he were not on clay but on grass, and his opponents were so disconcerted that they fell away from his path. To the incredulity of the locals, Henman scythed his way into the semi-finals, where he had the clay-court specialist Guillermo Coria on the rack. But a change of tactics — or perhaps a change in the mind — saw him slump to defeat. No matter. It wasn't Wimbledon, and that was always the dream that really counted, for Henman and his Henmaniacs and the millions of part-time tennis fans for whom this fortnight offers an interlude of delirious optimism and despair. Henman insists that he can still win it: but yesterday the custody of our dreams began to slip away from him and into a new pair of hands.

MURRAY MINTING A ROSY FUTURE

John McEnroe

It was the way Andrew Murray took his beating from the old man in that Superset event at Wembley last October that made me think he had a future in the sport. It was a 'I really enjoyed the experience, Mr McEnroe' type of thing. The last time anyone called me Mr McEnroe was when I beat Michael Chang in the third round at the French Open in 1988. The next year he won it. But before Murray jumps to the conclusion that he might do the same, or even win Wimbledon, he may first have to pay his dues. I thought to myself at the time that this young guy had something about him, that he had a really good head on his shoulders and would learn the game quickly. And so it has proved. I had heard the talk about him before he won the junior US Open, but there's nothing like coming face to face with someone on court to really get to know them.

Nor is he the only Murray I know. I was looking for a hitting partner the other day down at the Aorangi courts and someone said we've got Andrew Murray's brother for you. Jamie's a year older than Andrew. He's a lefty and real skinny, a couple of inches taller than his brother and needs to put on some weight, but I wouldn't discount his chances of making it as a player either. Like Rafael Nadal, he knows how to keep a little bit of the pressure off and is very respectful of his 'betters' while inwardly thinking, 'I'm going to beat this guy'. 'Hey, I can play good, yeah?' says the Spaniard, having just reached the final of the French Open. It's smart at that age.

The way both these young guys behave on the court is much more along the lines of what I like to see. It comes naturally to Murray, as it does to Nadal, to fire up the crowd. I remember at the end of the match against Radek Stepanek, the young Briton had a chance to put the match away at 5–3. I think he had a couple of match points but didn't win them. He could have tensed up and got all nervous, but he was still inviting the crowd to get behind him, so he was loving the moment. He's not going to love the moments obviously when there's really high expectations. He was disappointed probably not to win the junior French Open, but I expected him to have a couple of wins in the Stella Artois Championships, so when he came to Wimbledon I wasn't totally surprised he had a couple of wins. I thought Stepanek had more to offer. The Czech made the mistake of assuming because he had had a good year that he would just intimidate Murray and I don't think he's the intimidating type. He was completely outplayed, it wasn't even close.

I think he was surprised that Murray was there to win the match, he wasn't just there to show up. That's one of the things I like about the Scot. Often you feel that some of the guys who get wild cards are just there to experience the occasion; you sense Murray is there to win – and glean some knowledge. He has done very well on the grass but I think slow hard courts will see him at his best.

I would have to score him an 'A' for what he has achieved so far. It's not just the fact that he has won some matches but the way he has gone about it. He seems to be having some fun with it and he has surprised people. He's handling it as well as, if not better than, anyone could have expected. Plenty of guys out there hit shots, it's what goes on inside a player's head that makes the difference a lot of the time. He's going to be in the top 30 for sure and if he stays healthy then probably top 20. It's at that stage when it comes down to heart and desire and a little bit of luck whether or not you make the top ten. He's got a good chance, but it's not a shoe-in as it was for Andy Roddick when I first saw him, or Nadal. The American was so powerful he could just blow people off the court; Nadal just tries so much harder than his opponents. Murray is not at that level yet.

I think he's more or less done with Challengers and Satellites. He can go back to that level occasionally, but I don't see any reason why he should not spend a lot more time at ATP Tour level. Personally, I would wait and pick the right opportunities – they'll come. The endorsements will start coming in, if they haven't already. I understand his racket contract is up at the end of these Championships. I'm sure there are a lot of racket-makers who'd love to have a guy like Murray.

People may find it difficult to understand how Murray could have been losing matches at a lower level only a short time ago and then come to this elevated level and do what he's done, but you have to remember it's a learning process. I lost a couple of matches at college when I was 18 even though I was No. 20 in the world when I went there. Even when you're No. 1 in the world, you generally lose somewhere in the region of five to ten matches a year unless your name is Roger Federer. This is a process that you have to go through, one that toughens you up; it gives you a thicker skin. Tour-level tennis is not a fairytale where everyone automatically lives happily ever after. It's these wins at the higher level that make you want it more. I remember in 1977 when I played in qualifying at the French Open, I didn't sleep the entire night before I played the final round because I was jet-lagged and afraid I'd oversleep. I was frightened of going over my budget so I moved into a cheap hotel where no one spoke English and then I was worried that no one would wake me. I somehow qualified, moved back into the more expensive hotel where I caught up on my sleep and made it to the second round.

That same year I played Wimbledon and thought, 'This could be unbelievably addictive, this is a whole lot better than those other ones. If I can do something here ...' I made the semi-finals, moved from 230 to 70 in the world, and never played a qualifying tournament again. I remember thinking, 'Either I'm better than I thought I was or these guys are worse than I thought.' The same thought may have run through Murray's head these past two weeks. But it's not going to be easy for him with the burden of expectation he will soon inherit from Tim Henman. It was easier for me: I was the No. 1 junior in the world, but I can guarantee you that most people didn't know who I was and I was able to slip through almost unnoticed. They made up for it later, though.

27 JUNE 2005
COURT & SOCIAL: THE £10 CHAMPION

Wimbledon's oldest surviving champion, Phyllis King, will be 100 in August. As Miss Mudford, she won the women's doubles with Dorothy Shepherd-Brown in 1931. She took part in the tournament 16 times and her last appearance, at the age of 48, was in 1953. 'When we won, we received a £10 shopping voucher,' King recalled.

— SE

29 JUNE 2005
COURT & SOCIAL: STRAWBERRY WHIP

It would be 'Stop, thief!' anywhere else, but the dignified aura of the All-England Club extends even to petty crime. 'The strawberries in each bowl are pre-counted and priced accordingly. Therefore, please do not supplement this amount by taking strawberries from another bowl,' reads a notice in the restaurants.

— SE

2 JULY 2005

COURT & SOCIAL: FROM A MOLEHILL . . .

For the record, Andy Murray would prefer Henman Hill not to be known as Murray Field. He prefers Murray Mount or Mount Murray.

– SE

3 JULY 2005

DEPTH MAY PUT SAMPRAS RECORD BEYOND FEDERER

John McEnroe

This may not be the right time to say it, with Roger Federer on the verge of claiming his third Wimbledon title, but I think as time goes by we will see what a remarkable achievement it was by Pete Sampras to win here seven times. I don't think the Swiss, maybe even a better player than Sampras when compared on all surfaces, will surpass his record. I'm not saying it's impossible and I do believe that he will win, maybe, as many as five Wimbledon titles, I just think that there is more depth in the game today than there was in Sampras's era, guys who could step up on the grass, like Rafael Nadal and Marat Safin. The big Russian threatened to do so this time, but in the end, as usual, left the Championships prematurely. When Federer gets to five then we can start talking about his chances of overhauling Pete, but not before.

Power and physical strength will always be the greatest threat to Federer because he has just about everything else in his game and, of course, no little power himself. It's why Andy Roddick has a chance in today's final. A puncher will always have a chance. Power can be paralysing as I found to my cost towards the end of my career. It can shut you down. It would have been tough for me to beat Federer in my prime because while I had an all-round game like him it wasn't quite as good as his. I would have come at him, but I would have posed him less of a threat than someone like Sampras or Boris Becker. These guys had serious power. I remember playing Becker in an exhibition match in Atlanta in 1985 when he had just turned 18 and thinking, 'How does a guy serve this big at this age?' He had the biggest serve in the history of tennis. He would have played his game against Federer and come at him. I would love to have seen it. I know Sampras lost to Federer here in 2001 but he was a little past his best. He had, of course, a better serve than Federer – second serve particularly – and he would hit the lines with it, too. Even if you got the ball back it was not as if the point was won, you then probably had to deal with his volley. I know Boris shares the view with me that Sampras would still have had the edge over Federer on grass.

In my position nowadays as a commentator it can be difficult to comprehend how physically strong today's players are or how difficult conditions are when you're cocooned away in that air-conditioned booth. It's one of the reasons why I like to get out and feel things, walk the courts and have a hit with players. I had a hit with Safin before his third-round match against Feliciano Lopez. I was looking forward to seeing if I could return the ball when he rifled one at me. I wanted to fully understand what facing his kind of power was like. Unfortunately, he seemed to hold back a bit – perhaps he took pity on the old man. If you'd asked me afterwards I'd have said he wasn't ready to play which, as it turned out, was probably right. Yet I feel we were given a glimpse this summer of the kind of challenge he can offer Federer on grass. We know what threat he poses to him on hard courts from his semi-final victory over Federer in the Australian Open, but I think his narrow three-set defeat to Federer in the Gerry Weber Open in Halle told us he can be a danger on grass, too.

8 APRIL 2006

GARDENING SECTION: ACE OF BLADES

David White

Anyone after a perfect lawn would do well to observe the love, care and attention given to the perfect green oblongs at Wimbledon, which have been grown specifically to withstand the punishment meted out by two weeks of pounding feet playing 700 matches. 'Creating and maintaining courts for the only Grand Slam tournament still played on grass is the ultimate challenge for me,' says Wimbledon's head groundsman, Eddie Seaward, 63, who is preparing for his 17th Championships. 'They must not only look the part – weed-free, level, and perfectly mown – but also serve the practical purpose of meeting the needs of players and spectators in producing the highest levels of tennis. I want a surface that, irrespective of weather, allows the ball to come up hard and high with a consistent bounce, permitting good rallies, serves and returns.'

Given the intensity of use during the tournament, Wimbledon needs a hard-wearing grass grown on suitable soil (22 per cent clay added to sand and silt and resting on crushed rock or ash for good drainage) which produces identical playing characteristics for every court: one must not be 'quicker' or 'slower' than another or yield different bounces. Eddie works closely with the Sports Turf Research Institute at Bingley, West Yorkshire, to find a seed mix for the perfect grass for tennis: researchers test different types to destruction using a machine that mimics the slap, slide and scuff of tennis shoes. 'A 50-50 mix of the rye grass varieties Aberelf and Aberimp has been used at Wimbledon for the past few years,' he says. 'But we're always looking for improvement, such as drought-resistant strains.'

The yearly cycle of bringing 19 match and 22 practice courts to peak condition for Wimbledon fortnight begins in August, allowing Eddie and his 15 permanent groundstaff time to catch their breath before re-starting the process for the following summer. Repairing the ravages of 13 days' play makes re-seeding the main autumn task — usually completed by the second week in September. The courts are mown once or twice a month through the winter, weather permitting, to a height of 14mm (just above half an inch). From April, the cut is lowered by a millimetre every fortnight, until the tournament level of 8mm (0.3in) is reached. The courts are rolled and mowed more frequently as the tournament approaches, then daily during the Championships. 'Preparing the courts for the playing season starts in March, although it's crucial that a court is not so soft and wet that machinery damages the surface,' says Eddie. 'Firming the surface starts with a light roll, putting right any soil movement from winter frost heave. Fertilisers are applied from the end of April. Fungicides are used on an as-and-when basis.'

For a fast game of tennis, the grass should grow upright and strong to aid bounce. It should be aerated (to ensure oxygen reaches the roots), spiked and scarified, cutting through the grass 6mm (0.2in) into the soil. 'Grass has a habit of lateral growth which can weave and create a thatch effect, inhibiting bounce, so we use tried-and-tested techniques that produce a healthy, upright grass,' Eddie says.

Science is increasingly used to help produce the 'perfect' court. The irrigation system, for example, is computer-controlled, enabling water to be delivered in precise amounts. Radar tracks the approach of rain, Eddie's greatest challenge. 'Rain not only stops play, but can make the courts unplayable if we're slow getting the covers on,' he says. 'In the past, covers didn't allow much light on to the grass, keeping it dry but damaging it. They are now translucent, keeping grass healthier.'

Seventeen groundstaff can deploy the Centre Court cover (it weighs a ton) in just 22 seconds. 'I still hope for lots of sunshine before and during the tournament, but we now have the equipment to deal with rain,' says Eddie. His ground-maintenance staff doubles to 28 in the months running up to the tournament – three come each year from Myerscough College in Lancashire, which offers degrees in turf grass science, with other young greenkeepers drawn from a worldwide pool of applicants. 'Wimbledon is a magnet for groundsmen. Many have wide experience, but all approach working here with respect bordering on reverence. The first advice I always give is, "Forget your nerves – you know about grass, so just put your experience to work". New staff can hesitate about mowing their first court – to them it is sacred turf.' Eddie knows the feeling. 'I joined the Wimbledon staff having worked as a groundsman for schools and colleges, and with a lot of experience. But there is something special about the 42 acres of courts here that excited me then, and still does, every day of the year.'

Day one of the tournament is the peak of Eddie's annual cycle of excitement: will a year of preparation stand the test of play and the British summer? 'I'm here every day from before 8a.m. until past 10p.m., with a phone by my bed to be summoned in an emergency,' he says. So what has been the most memorable feedback? 'One Australian player told me, "Your courts, Eddie – they're just too ****ing good, no bad bounces at all." And an American spectator refused to believe grass was used at all. "These synthetic surfaces are better than the real thing," he told me. I took both comments as compliments.' And his thoughts about Wimbledon 2006? 'We're all working hard, preparations are going well, but ask me again after the winning ball has been played in the last match of the tournament.'

29 JUNE 2006

EQUAL PAY FOR WOMEN? YOU'RE HAVING A LAUGH

Martin Johnson

It wouldn't be Wimbledon without the annual debate on prize money, and the women banging on about equal pay, so it's high time the All-England Club got to grips with the modern world and started paying the girls precisely what they're worth. In which case, next year's ladies' singles winner will get a postal order for £2.95, a Zone One Travel Card for going on the tube, and a complimentary teddy bear (tea towel and apron set for the runner-up) from the Wimbledon Shop.

The All-England Club are not the kind of establishment who like to court controversy, which probably explains why their chief executive is forced into promoting the usual argument against equal pay, namely less money for less work. What he'd really like to say, but can't, is that the tickets for women's tennis matches in the first week of a Grand Slam should be subject to the same government regulations as a cigarette packet, and stamped: 'Warning. May Induce Irreversible Coma.'

If they want equal prize money, the answer's pretty simple. A single, mixed tournament. In which case they wouldn't be playing for this year's total prize fund of £3,112,140, but £1,006,080, which is the total paid out for the first-round men's losers. And if we're talking about equal workloads, at last year's Wimbledon there were 11,286 minutes of men's singles tennis, and 6,370 of women's. The men's tour generates twice as much income as the women's; demand dictates that Wimbledon corporate packages for the men's quarter- and semi-finals cost twice as much as the women's equivalent. At the Australian Open they've abandoned their traditional all-women days because television viewing figures were regularly eclipsed by *Skippy The Bush Kangaroo.*

With such a raw deal on the prize-money front (the winner gets just £625,000 this year) Amelie Mauresmo was grateful for requiring only 39 minutes to knock off her first-round opponent yesterday, thus avoiding the expense involved in sending her shirt to the laundry. Meantime, Venus Williams, champion both of Wimbledon and the equal-pay cause, must have been near exhaustion after a marathon against Bethanie Mattek, of the US. She squeezed through 6–1, 6–0 in 51 minutes.

This stage of the women's competition is more like a fashion show than serious sport, and while Mattek came a distant second in the tennis, she won the sartorial contest in, by common consent, the equivalent of straight sets. Mattek was determined to make an impression on this first, and probably last, appearance on Centre Court, and turned up in a halter top, Bette Midler headscarf, earrings like ship's anchors, shorts that couldn't have been shorter – and football socks. Mattek actually toned herself down for her first Wimbledon. She was fined for wearing a cowboy hat at the US Open.

Ranked 101 in the world, Mattek has averaged a modest £30,000 a year in a career that started in 1999, but yesterday's TV exposure led an advertising agency to offer her a £2,000 bonus for wearing two logos on her chest. They were pretty big (the logos that is) and, in allowing her to wear them, Wimbledon's dress code committee effectively made her £30 better off than a male first-round loser.

There are few sports other than a women's tennis match where a winner gets asked what she thought of her opponent and replies: 'Real cute.' Williams also said she loved Mattek's socks, then went wittering back to the equal-pay business, describing Tony Blair's endorsement of the cause as (and those of you with a stomach as delicate as David Beckham's should turn away now) 'giving credence to the free world'. What a load of old tosh. Carry on Wimbledon.

In fact, if the women want financial parity, let's go back to the last time there was equal prize money here, in 1967, when the men and women got nothing, and the men's singles finalist, Wilhelm Bungert, arrived for his game with John Newcombe on the No. 93 bus from Putney.

29 JUNE 2006
COURT & SOCIAL: WHAT A CHARMER

Andy Murray has caused a commotion among female followers of his official website. The general consensus is that the Scot must learn some etiquette. In his daily blog, he relates the hassle of being pursued by flirtatious girls: 'I put my bag down to sign some autographs and when I went to get some grips out of it later on, someone called Natalie had left a note with her phone number on it. So, Natalie, I'd appreciate a photo before I consider making a phone call because you could be a complete stinker!' Charming.

— SE

1 JULY 2006
COURT & SOCIAL: BACK TO BASICS

After 26 years at the All-England Club, former chief executive Chris Gorringe, who retired last summer, has been spotted odd-jobbing for the honorary stewards. Yesterday, wearing a yellow tabard, the former Voice of the Championships ('Ladies and gentlemen, may I have your attention please?') was spotted at St Mary's Church on car-parking duties, taking the money and directing operations. Parking has never been so precise. 'We are pleased to have one of our honorary life vice-presidents working so hard,' said chief steward, Andrew Gairdner. 'Yesterday he was selling hamburgers.'

— SE

5 JULY 2006
COURT & SOCIAL: BARE STATISTICS

The imperious Maria Sharapova was not amused; Elena Dementieva giggled. Wimbledon yesterday witnessed its fourth streaking incident, and he who was escorted off, decorously wrapped in an Army-issue blanket, merits a place in the Championships' statistics. For the record, yesterday's attention-seeker is the third to invade the hallowed turf of Centre Court, the second male to do so, and the first male to interrupt a women's singles match. (Court 14 makes up the count – in 2000, a male prankster invaded a doubles match involving Anna Kournikova.)

History-making Centre Court distractions started in 1996 with a female, clad in a mini-apron, who bounced across the grass before the start of the men's final between MaliVai Washington and Richard Krajicek. After a six-year gap, the next, a male, unleashed himself after Lleyton Hewitt and David Nalbandian had arrived back to resume their final after a rain delay. He won applause from the crowd for successfully hurdling the net twice.

— SE

6 JULY 2006
COURT & SOCIAL: IN TENTS QUESTIONING

A service steward, new to Wimbledon and Centre Court, saw the tent go up and was overheard asking: 'So, when it rains, do they carry on playing under it?'

— SE

I0 JULY 2006

REVENGE IS SWEET FOR COOL FEDERER
Sue Mott

You wouldn't think him capable of vengeance, Roger Federer. He has the calm, almost nonchalant, demeanour of James Bond, especially in that cream, bespoke jacket he wore on to court. But beneath those layers of woven fibre lurked a heart beating for one sole purpose: to avenge the hurt caused by his ferocious playmate, rival and year-long nemesis, Rafa Nadal, of Spain, who tore from him the chance to hold all four Grand Slam titles simultaneously by defeating him in Paris last month. This was payback time. From red to green. From clay to grass. Wimbledon is home to Federer, and a Swiss man's home is his castle. Nadal was looking out for boiling oil over the ramparts. It came. But he ploughed on through the barrage, the young Spaniard, and when it was all over, when Federer had his fourth title in succession, matching the feat of Pete Sampras and moving to within one of Björn Borg's quintet, they walked off the court together, champion and challenger, signing autographs side by side.

No one dies of shame who loses to Federer at Wimbledon. Such is his majesty, it is almost an honour. 'I like fight. I enjoy difficult challenge,' the 20-year-old French Open champion had announced before the final. That was good, then. Federer, who had not dropped a set in the tournament and had won 47 consecutive matches on grass, was as difficult a challenge as there could be. The Centre Court was primed for combat of a rare and superior order. One man almost down from Olympus, never mind an Alpine resort, against another man sprung from a Mediterranean island, fearless in battle and the winner of all four of their matches to date this year. Nice. A bogey man built like an electrified bull. Federer wouldn't have it all his own way. Except in the first set he did. Federer came out firing. The ultimate park warden, he was saying through his strokes: 'Keep off my grass.' Nadal, who had experienced having his serve broken only twice in the tournament, suddenly suffered three breaks in just one set. Once Federer held his serve to love and chalk flew up with his conclusive ace. 'Eat my dust,' the departing ball said.

Nadal, however, doesn't do surrender. What was he thinking after the first set? 'I was thinking, "Win one game",' he said afterwards. Uncompli- cated lad. He is trained to attack and he did, sometimes daring to out-rally and out-muscle the master, always with a clench of the fist and an audible Latin roar. The crowd loved him, cheering unrestrainedly when he broke

Federer's serve in the first game of the second set, to keep open the prospect of a five-set thriller. The only Spaniard to win this title, Manuel Santana, was in the Royal Box, casting his mind back 40 years to his victory in 1966. But even Santana thought Roger would win. Yet, with two straight tie-breaks, the match swung from one-sidedness to closeness. The contrast in styles was riveting. Federer played as though dancing a waltz, foot-perfect, well-timed, flowing to all four corners of the room and glorious on the eye. Nadal was in full tango mode, with explosions of power, extravagant passion and dark eyes that betrayed the level of his angst when outside forces threatened to thwart him. 'I love you, Nadal,' cried a male voice at the back of the cathedral, all overcome.

The boy was giving his all for the cause and no Wimbledon crowd, even one containing Jonny Wilkinson and vast amounts of royalty, can ask for more. He led by that break in the second set and served at 5–4 to level the match. Four errors then proceeded from his racket, under pressure, and there, probably, went the match. Lesser creatures against Federer would then pull out the deckchair and gently snooze to inevitable defeat while unanswerable shots pound the turf around them. Nadal was braver than that. He won the third-set tie-break, setting up the opportunity with a volley that was swiped with such assurance it must have rattled the teacups in Australia.

Now Federer was in new territory. Someone had claimed a set from him. Not just any someone, but the bullock-built nuisance who had been plaguing him all year. It required the spirit of a champion to rise to the occasion, to swat back the unquenchable upstart, and you wondered if their previous matches would come back to haunt him. Perhaps that trademark headband would need to double as a bandage around his troubled mind.

No fear. The champion made bunk of immediate history. Didn't he worry about losing that set? 'Not really. As long as I didn't lose three,' he said, the embodiment of after-match cool. He raced to a 5–1 lead in the fourth set, wavered for a couple of games and then swept away with game, set, match, championship and worldwide admiration. Nadal looked crestfallen as they met at the net, but their arms around one another spoke of intense mutual respect. So did that wonderful moment later when they slapped hands, crossing paths as they showed their respective trophies to an audience wild with appreciation.

There was another lovely moment. Sue Barker told Federer how much we loved the new rivalry, but she completely understood if he did not feel the same way. He grinned. 'Now I like it again.' Of course, his jacket is out of date now. It commemorates only three Wimbledon titles with that badge emblazoned on the pocket. Anyone for embroidery?

27 FEBRUARY 2007

NEARLY THERE
BUT OUR 34-YEAR FIGHT GOES ON

Billie-Jean King

The decision by the All-England Club to award equal prize money for women and men at this summer's Wimbledon Championships was a long time coming. But the news was not about the money, but about the message. Chairman Tim Phillips, chief executive Ian Ritchie and the other members of the committee of management did the right thing. It must have been difficult and I'm sure there were those who opposed the decision. But it is clear this was right for the tournament and the sport – and it sent a powerful message to the world. When Wimbledon first started paying prize money in 1968, my cheque for winning the ladies' Championship was £750, or 37.5 per cent of the £2,000 which Rod Laver won for capturing the gentlemen's title. By 1973 the women were getting 60 per cent of what the men made and by 1980 the women were edging closer, earning 90 per cent of what the men received. These facts demonstrate the lengthy process that led to last week's decision. It took almost 40 years for us to get there.

It was in 1973, at a pre-Wimbledon meeting of players at London's Gloucester Hotel, that the Women's Tennis Association was born. That day in June a room at the hotel was filled with women who would shape the future of tennis and set a path for the growth of women's sports around the globe. We wanted, and needed, one voice in women's tennis. In three short years we had come a long way since the original nine women players, including myself, had signed one-dollar contracts with Gladys Heldman to bring about the birth of women's professional tennis. There were 35 or so players there that day at the Gloucester Hotel. As we gathered, I asked Betty Stove to lock the doors so no one could leave until we made a decision. This moment had been nine years in the making and we emerged with one voice – the Women's Tennis Association. When we met at the hotel, one of our biggest goals was to secure equal prize money at the four majors.

We wanted more money at every event but we were especially focused on getting equal prize money at tournaments where the men and women shared the stage. The first major to step up and offer equal prize money was the US Open in 1973 and they have never looked back. The Australian Open was next. With those two tournaments on board we hoped Wimbledon and the French Open would step up as well. We were committed to making equal prize money a reality in 1973 and we remain passionate about our goal – and our promise to one another – in 2007. Just last year, the French Open awarded equal prize money to the men's and women's champions, but not to all women. There are still 127 players in the women's singles draw and countless others in the doubles who are not receiving equal pay. It is now time for the French to complete this process and award equal prize money for all women.

There was another important piece of tennis history in September 1973. Historians have frequently cited my match with Bobby Riggs, which became known as the 'Battle of the Sexes', as a turning point in women's sports. While it was a tennis match on the surface, it really was all about social change. After Bobby defeated Margaret Court, who finished 1973 as the No. 1 player in the world, I knew I had to play him. There was no doubt in my mind that if I was going to go through with this match, it was going to be about social change, and would be much bigger than tennis. I have always hoped that my match with Bobby would change the hearts and minds of women and men and bring us closer to gender equality on all fronts. In the end, that match became bigger than Bobby or me, it changed people. Women went to their bosses and asked for a pay rise. More men openly recognised the contributions women were making in society and fathers stood up and demanded equal opportunities for their daughters. In one of the last conversations I had with Bobby before he died in 1995, he said to me: 'Billie, we made a difference, didn't we?' We both knew we had made a difference and we were proud of what we had done.

We have worked to make huge progress over the last 34 years, and last week's announcement was yet another milestone for the gender equality movement. But, there is still work to be done. Every time we can reach a benchmark like this, it helps people ask in their daily life: 'Are we insisting on equality for our sons and daughters?' That makes the decision at Wimbledon a very important moment in history. Our friends at Wimbledon have done the right thing and they should be very proud of themselves. Because of their actions, others will follow. Wimbledon have now joined a new club, an important group of a select few. They have demonstrated they understand and appreciate the athletic ability, the entertainment value and the contributions women bring to their event. Wimbledon will be even more fun for us this summer, because prize money is now a non-issue. This summer's Championships will once again be a jewel on the Sony Ericsson WTA Tour and one of the finest events in all of sport. It will be a big day for everyone in women's tennis. And each of us who gathered at the Gloucester Hotel in 1973 with a simple dream will stand a little taller, smile a little wider and know that we made a difference. Rest assured, however, we will not stop until our mission to secure equal prize money at all four majors is complete.

25 APRIL 2007
HAWK-EYE GETS THE GREEN LIGHT
Mark Hodgkinson

Whoever thought there would come a time when Wimbledon's Centre Court would have giant video screens but no roof? The All-England Club announced yesterday that the iconic stadium, which will be open to the elements this year only because of work to construct a retractable roof for 2009, will almost certainly need the electronics to show Hawk-Eye replays. Although the line-calling system is plainly now much more 'in' than 'out', the statement was not quite 'game, set and match', as British inventor Paul Hawkins still has another fortnight or so of final grass-court testing before he gets the go-ahead to use it on the two leading show courts, Centre and No. 1.

These April news conferences have traditionally provoked a debate about why the All-England Club had continued to hold out against awarding equal prize money to men and women. But parity of pay was pretty much a non-subject yesterday, Wimbledon officials having already declared in February that they will end 123 years of inequality on the lawns of southwest London this summer. And so all that was left to say on that issue was that the club have received just 'two or three irate letters' of complaint. The 2007 Championships will be the richest tennis tournament in history, with an overall prize-pot of £11.3 million, an increase of 8.7 per cent from last year. The men's and women's champions will each receive a cheque for £700,000.

The testing of Hawk-Eye will not be over accuracy, but looking at how to calibrate the cameras for use on grass, as, unlike artificial surfaces, the courts will become roughed-up and change colour as the tournament continues. But chief executive Ian Ritchie sounded confident that the trials will be successful, and so Centre Court spectators this year should, for the first time, be able to see both all the way up the hill to Wimbledon Village and colourful computer graphics. The real test for the men in striped purple-and-green club ties, who want their Grand Slam to be seen as 'tennis in an English summer garden', is how to combine the traditions of the past with new developments. The two screens on Centre Court would sit on top of the roof-less stands this summer, but in future years they would be much lower, around the same level as the current scoreboard. Court No. 1 would have two screens this summer, just above the grass.

The introduction of Hawk-Eye on Centre Court and No. 1 Court would mean the removal of the Cyclops service machine, which has been bleeping since 1980, as Ritchie felt it would be 'inappropriate to have conflicting technologies'. However, Cyclops would not be blinded entirely, as it would be transferred to three other courts: 2, 14 and 18. All other tournaments have gone for two Hawk-Eye challenges per set, with an extra in a tie-break, and challenges retained if the player is correct. But as Wimbledon believe that the serve is more important on grass than on any other surface, and they would also be getting rid of the Cyclops bleep, they could increase the number of challenges, although probably not to an unlimited figure.

18 JUNE 2007

MAGIC SPELL OF THE WIZARD OF OZ

Brendan Gallagher

It was Sir Norman Everard Brookes, the son of a tough gold-mining baron from Bendigo and the epitome of a shrewd, no-nonsense, Australian sportsman, who started the rot exactly 100 years ago. Or opened the floodgates, depending on your perspective. Up to that point the previous 30 gentlemen's singles titles at Wimbledon had all been won by 'Brave Brits', but since Brookes's ground-breaking victory just two British players have triumphed – Fred Perry, of blessed memory, and the less heralded Arthur Gore. A century of frustration, false dawns, unrealistic expectation, occasional glimmers of light, even rarer moments of triumph and a grudging but growing admiration and even love for foreign interlopers has ensued for British tennis fans.

It was the enterprising Brookes, a man of independent means with the passion and ambition to travel halfway around the world at his own expense in pursuit of glory, who changed the face of Wimbledon, and arguably, tennis for ever. Brookes had already enjoyed one determined dart at the mother country back in 1905 when, as winner of the separate all-comers' competition, he then lost the traditional challenge match against the distinguished gentlemen's singles champion Lawrence Doherty, the Olympic champion and five-time Wimbledon winner.

Undeterred, Brookes vowed to return two years later – you had to plan well ahead in those days when the round trip to Britain alone involved nearly three months by boat. He opted for a fallow year in 1906 and played little competitive tennis, but then started practising assiduously on the family tennis court and planning for the 1907 campaign. He was on a mission, the Australian nation were behind him and joy was unconfined when, at the age of 30, he duly landed the overall title he coveted, defeating Gore comfortably in three sets. British supremacy was at an end and a tennis superpower had been born.

Brookes's triumph was a victory of its time. The assumption of effortless British superiority in all fields – sporting, political, military – was being questioned on all fronts at the start of the 20th century, whether it be in vicious guerrilla warfare on the high veld in South Africa or fending off booming Australian serves on Centre Court. British manhood was under siege. Not only was Brookes the first overseas player to win the Wimbledon title, he was also the first left-hander. Wearing a rather natty tweed cap borrowed from the golf links – he twice led his Melbourne club team to the Australian foursomes championship – Brookes was on the rampage in 1907. As well as smashing through convention to win the gentlemen's singles at Wimbledon, he marched off with the men's doubles with his great friend Tony Wilding, the dashing New Zealand barrister based in London who was to win four consecutive singles titles between 1910 and 1913. Wilding, who was engaged to marry Hollywood silent-screen star Maxine Elliot, was killed at the Battle of Aubers Ridge in May 1915 while serving with the Royal Marines.

Brookes and Wilding continued to flex their antipodean muscles in the summer of 1907. A month after their triumphs at Wimbledon they re-mustered as 'Australasia' and returned to Wimbledon and ended four years of British dominance to rout the home team and win the Davis Cup. Brookes delighted in representing Australia on the world scene and was involved in a further four Davis Cup triumphs during a long career and only stopped playing for his country at the age of 43. His last Wimbledon appearance came three years later in 1924.

A baseline player by inclination, Brookes quickly saw the need to perfect a serve-and-volley game to win at Wimbledon and ruthlessly worked at that aspect of his game. He also possessed a unique and confusing backhand, using the same racket face as for his forehand. Brookes achieved some strange and point-winning angles with his backhand volleys, however, and was the individual who established the long and noble tradition of difficult and mercurial left-handers. Unsurprisingly, if a little unimaginatively, the British press had dubbed him the 'Wizard' as a result of his sorcery.

To his chagrin, Brookes, who suffered from stomach ulcers, was rejected for active service for the First World War, though as he approached 38, age may also have been a factor. Instead he used his administrative expertise to become a commissioner for the Australian branch of the British Red Cross in Egypt from August 1915 to late 1916. He then resigned in January 1917 and in May became commissioner for the British Red Cross in Mesopotamia, rising to the rank of lieutenant-colonel. After the war, and as his playing career wound down, Brookes had one last, massive, contribution to make to Australian tennis, driving through the purchase of a 17-acre site for the Kooyong Club and the building of an 8,500-capacity centre court. For nearly 60 years Australian tennis based itself at the Melbourne club and held the Australian Open there before the move to Melbourne Park in 1988. Not only did Brookes kick-start Australian tennis as an international force, he secured its future as well. It spoke volumes that when he died in 1968, the Wimbledon final between Rod Laver and Tony Roche was the eighth all-Australian affair since 1956.

20 JUNE 2007
COURT & SOCIAL: RIGHT ROYAL HIDING

As an unknown, fresh out of the army, Tom Brown from San Francisco won the men's and mixed doubles in 1946. A year later he was beaten in 45 minutes flat by Jack Kramer. 'Kind of embarrassing with King George VI, Queen Elizabeth and Princess Margaret looking on, but I did get to chat with them in the Royal Box afterwards,' he recalls.

— SE

26 JUNE 2007
CAVADAY REFUSES TO FOLLOW THE SCRIPT
Martin Johnson

The simplest way of judging the health of British women's tennis is to nip into your local bookmakers. If you think that the Centre Court is about to be visited by little green men in a Martian spacecraft, they'll offer you 100–1, but if you were to plonk a fiver on one of our girls winning Wimbledon (and you'd have to have just arrived from Mars to even consider it) they'll add an extra nought on to the odds. It was, therefore, something of a surprise yesterday when the St John Ambulance people – hitherto busy with treating spectators for hypothermia – were informed that their entire fortnight's supply of smelling salts might well be required out on Court No. 2. There is not a single British woman who gets into this tournament by any means other than a wild-card invitation, but here was Naomi Cavaday, an 18-year-old from Kent, twice holding a match point against a former champion and world No. 1, Martina Hingis. She blew them, of course, and her third set 6–0 capitulation suggested that a small voice had suddenly gone off in her head. 'Get a grip of yourself, girl. Remember. You're British!'

It looked for a moment as if Cavaday had decided her task was hopeless on the evidence of the knock-up, dashing off the court with Hingis about to hit the first serve of the match. It seemed a bit early for a comfort break, but back she came to take the first three games, then save three set points, and finally win the first set by romping through the tie-break 7–1. Cavaday, who had her two match points on Hingis's serve at 5–4 in the second set, is by all accounts one of the most promising young British girls to come along for quite some time, though this in itself really isn't saying much. On top of which Hingis had been largely inactive for the previous five weeks with a thigh strain, but in view of the fact that Hingis would have been fancied to win in straight sets with one leg in plaster, it was still a decent performance by a youngster with a passing resemblance to Ann Jones.

This means that she'll have to get by on her tennis earnings as opposed to modelling contracts, but she's a powerful hitter, and certainly has the build for the modern power game, unlike Hingis, whose delicate brand of tennis belongs more to an era when the girls played in long dresses. Her first serve would barely break an egg, and her second wouldn't set off a speed camera on the Wimbledon bypass. She doesn't even hit her ground strokes with enough oomph to generate a decent grunt, and her only noise is the occasional girlish squeal after a bad shot. Hingis has not long returned to the game after three years devoted to riding her horses and going shopping, and a woman tennis player who hits a forehand without sounding like a sow about to give birth to triplets is truly an anachronism.

She said afterwards that her doctor had described her as only 60 to 70 per cent fit, but that she simply 'didn't want to miss out on Wimbledon'. Maybe it was because of the equal pay this year. Hingis has won $20 million in prize money, but have you seen the price of a Versace handbag recently? Added to which, the Wimbledon champion Amelie Mauresmo has just stumped up more than £6,000 for a bottle of wine, so no wonder the girls are forever pleading poverty. The equal pay argument, of course, blithely ignores the fact that the men play twice as much tennis in the course of a Grand Slam, and generate twice as much income through corporate packages. On top of which, most first-week women's matches should be subject to the same warning on a spectator's ticket as a chemist is obliged to put on to a bottle of pills. 'Warning, may induce drowsiness.' Last year, Mauresmo earned a derisory £625,000 for winning the women's title, while Roger Federer collected £30,000 more. A repeat this year and they'll both earn £700,000, so let's raise a glass to emancipation, and not concern ourselves with the fact that Federer would beat Mauresmo 6–0, 6–0, 6–0 wearing an Armani jacket, a pair of clogs and playing left-handed with a frying pan.

26 JUNE 2007

COURT & SOCIAL:
SOUR FINALE FOR PRIZE SWISS COW

Roger Federer's preparations for a possible record-equalling fifth successive title at the All-England Club have been disturbed by the news that his prize Wimbledon cow has been slaughtered. You would think that Federer's treasured cow would have special protection against being sent to the abattoir in the Swiss Alps, but the 800kg cow, which Federer was given by an adoring Swiss public after he won his first Wimbledon title in 2003, has been slaughtered for 'not producing enough milk'.

What a contrast to the happy scenes four summers ago. A few days after lifting the golden Challenge Cup for the first time on Centre Court, Federer appeared at a tournament in Gstaad, where he was presented with Juliette, a milking cow from the local Simmental breed. 'I'm going to learn how to milk it. I'll do anything for it,' Federer said, keen to embrace the great dairy traditions of his homeland.

Roy Emerson, the Australian legend who has a home in Gstaad, reports her demise. 'Juliette gave birth to a calf, and then she wasn't producing enough milk, so she was slaughtered. But her calf is still alive. So a descendent of the original Wimbledon cow is there for all to see.'

Emerson, the 1964 and 1965 Wimbledon champion, claimed his strength as a player came from milking cows as a boy on a Queensland farm. 'I am the only Wimbledon champion to have come from a dairy farm, and it would have been fun for me to have taught Federer how to properly milk his cow, but that's not going to happen now,' he said. When contacted about the sad news, Federer's girlfriend, Mirka Vavrinec, said she and the world No. 1 had been unaware of Juliette's fate.

— SE

3 JULY 2007
COURT & SOCIAL:
NOVOTNA DELIGHTS BLAZER BRIGADE

Nine years after she captured the women's singles and doubles title, and became the oldest first-time Grand Slam singles winner (at 29 years and nine months), Jana Novotna has won a legion of new admirers. Arriving in SW19 to find the owner of the house she had rented for the fortnight had swanned off to St Tropez taking all sets of keys, she agreed to be put up for a night in a house belonging to an honorary steward.

The steward had a gang of blazered colleagues around for a pint that evening. Novotna joined in, staying up to 1.30a.m. and regaled them with stories. 'She had such fun, she decided to give up on her rental property and stay there for the duration,' Joe West reports from the stewards' office.

— SE

3 JULY 2007
COURT & SOCIAL: CLASS ACTS

Patience is part of the Wimbledon champion's psychological make-up. Take Amelie Mauresmo. She has always ridden a bike from her rented SW19 home to the grounds, but when she hopped off her blue mountain bike at Gate 16 and waited in line for the bag check, she was admonished by a security guard for her bike. Having explained, to no avail, that she always travelled that way, the defending women's champion calmly rolled her eyes and wandered off without a hint of a 'do-you-know-who-I-am?' tantrum.

Ditto, Roger Federer. He may have won every match he's played at Wimbledon over the last four years, but he also went unrecognised at the gates. Asked to produce his pass, he rummaged at length around the bottom of his bag … with Andy Roddick chortling behind him.

– SE

5 JULY 2007

DOUBLES WIN TOOK 102 GAMES AND FOUR DAYS

Kaz Mochlinski

It was one of the most historic matches in the Championships' history, but the 5–7, 7–6 (7–4), 4–6, 7–6 (9–7), 28–26 win by Marcelo Melo and Andre Sa over Paul Hanley and Kevin Ullyett did not break as many records as it threatened to yesterday. It was still only the second time there had been more than 100 games in one match at Wimbledon, but at 102 it fell short of the record 112 played by Pancho Gonzales and Charlie Pasarell in their singles marathon in 1969.

The match began last month – on Saturday – and, after the break on Sunday, continued on each of the first three days of this week. At five hours 58 minutes, it was the second-longest match at Wimbledon, behind the six hours nine minutes Mark Knowles and Daniel Nestor took to defeat Simon Aspelin and Todd Perry last year. Fifty-four games, though, was a record for the fifth set in any match at Wimbledon.

6 JULY 2007

COURT & SOCIAL: WATER, WATER EVERYWHERE

You cannot be serious. It is the wettest Wimbledon since 1982. Reports that would usually analyse top spin and unforced-error ratios have instead alluded to Noah's Ark, underwater ball-tracking sonar devices and incidents of trench foot. So can those really have been sprinklers spraying water over the courts late at night? 'Yes! The courts are thirsty. The court coverers are so efficient, very little moisture gets to them,' head groundsman Eddie Seaward explained.

– SE

FEDERER'S FIFTH WIN
EQUALS 'LIVING LEGEND'

Mark Hodgkinson

Seated in the front row of the Royal Box yesterday was Björn Borg, so famously an emotional flat-liner. And so when Roger Federer put away a smash to win his fifth Wimbledon title in a row, so equalling the Swede's record, the Ice Man predictably allowed himself just a small smile. Federer, though, dropped on to his back on the Centre Court grass and began to blub. The Swiss, a five-set winner over the brilliant Rafael Nadal after a superb final of controlled violence, simply had no hold over his emotions and his tear ducts. He cried as he worked himself to his feet, wept as he hugged the Spaniard at the net, and wiped away tears after sitting down on his chair, and then carried on sobbing. After what has seemed like the wettest Wimbledon in living memory, Federer gave the All-England Club lawns yet another watering. 'It meant a lot to equal Bjorn's record,' Federer said. Surely even Borg felt a little emotional seeing Federer in that state? But, no. The 'Ice Borg' declined to melt.

Federer had cried after winning his first Wimbledon title, in 2003, but had controlled himself the three summers after that. Last night's wet-eyed reaction from Federer did not come from just his joy at winning a fifth Wimbledon, it was also that he had done it in front of the man he had described as 'a living legend', and had fended off the challenge of an opponent who, even deep into the fifth set, refused to wave a cheery *adios.* Twice in the fifth set, at 1–1 and then at 2–2, Federer found himself 15–40 down on his serve, and it seemed as though one man would be emulating Borg, but it would not be the Swiss. Nadal, also last year's runner-up, had been attempting to become the first man, since Borg, to win the French Open and Wimbledon in the same season. But Federer staved off the danger, and then upped his level in the Centre Court sunshine for a 7–6, 4–6, 7–6, 2–6, 6–2 victory. 'I told Rafa at the net that he deserved it as well,' Federer said.

After matching Borg's Wimbledon Big Five, which were achieved from 1976 to 1980, when Federer was still not born, the talk will now shift to whether Federer can win six Wimbledon titles in a row next summer, and whether he can pass American Pete Sampras's record of seven Wimbledon titles overall during his career. The 25-year-old also moved to 11 Grand Slam titles. That put him level with Borg and Australian Rod Laver on the list of most Grand Slams won, in equal third place, with Australian Roy Emerson on 12 and Sampras on 14.

Nadal's tennis was outrageously good, including, during the second set, sitting on his backside on his baseline when he struck a backhand pass beyond Federer at the net. This from a man who, though a triple French Open champion, was still meant to be relatively inexperienced on the lawns. Nadal was an altogether more dangerous player than he had been in last year's final. If Nadal makes a similar leap in improvement on grass during next year's Wimbledon, then he will beat Federer. Federer, the beaten finalist at the French Open for the last two summers, and Nadal are a couple of serial thrillers. Indeed, this was a contest which Borg and his great rival, John McEnroe, would happily have added to their canon of great matches.

Even before the tears at the end, it had been an emotional afternoon for Federer. In the build-up to the tournament, much had been made about the similar, cool on-court personalities of Federer and Borg. But Federer was probably as tetchy as he has ever been on Centre Court. Most of his anger was directed at the Hawk-Eye line-calling system. Such was his disgust that he asked for Hawk-Eye to be turned off. And there was also a four-letter word from Federer, which led to an on-air apology from the BBC. Federer, a tennis traditionalist, had always been against Hawk-Eye being installed for the first time this summer. But this was a proper rage against the machine in the fourth set from Federer, who did not believe that the computer was right, when it overturned an 'out' call on a shot from Nadal to give the second seed a break point. Nadal converted that for a 3–0 lead. Of course, umpire Carlos Ramos politely turned down the request to switch off Hawk-Eye. And it was a surprise that Federer did not also ask the umpire whether Nadal could be turned off as well. Federer continued to argue during the change-over. 'How in the world was that ball in? S***. Look at the score now. It's killing me, Hawk-Eye is killing me,' was the animated gripe from Federer, and he looked in trouble then and when facing those break points in the fifth set.

But, in the end, everything was golden for Federer. He had been wearing his walk-on outfit of white kit flecked with gold, had been playing in golden sunshine, and was hitting some golden strokes. The fifth golden Challenge Cup was his. He had emulated Borg, winning the bit of tennis bling he really wanted. 'Thanks for coming,' Federer said to Borg on Centre Court. Federer and Borg met afterwards, and had what the champion called 'a Swedish hug'.

9 JULY 2007
COURT & SOCIAL: SOUND DECISION

Rafael Nadal proved better than Roger Federer in having a foolproof radar when it came to shots in or out in the first two challenges during their final, but the introduction of the Hawk-Eye ball-tracking device suggests otherwise. Of a total of 194 challenges over line calls in the first 13 days of the tournament on Centre and No. 1 Courts, only 59 – just 30 per cent – were correct. The replay process, shown on a giant screen, has added a popular theatrical element. So much so that Radio Wimbledon is recording the 'whooooaarrr' of the crowd for Honor Godfrey, curator of the Wimbledon museum. Keen to capture the distinctive audio element of each Championship, she also has a Best Grunts and Shrieks collection on DVD.

– SE

24 JUNE 2008
LETTER TO THE EDITOR
SILVER SERVICE

Sir,

How sad that no beekeeper could be found to collect the swarm of bees at Wimbledon the other day. Have they not heard the old saying: 'A swarm of bees in June is worth a silver spoon'?

Alice Wakes-Miller
Thornham, Norfolk

2 JULY 2008
TROUBLE-FREE AT THE TENNIS
Celia Walden spends a decidedly un-recession day out at Wimbledon

'Credit crunch?' chortles waitress Sarah Scally in the Champagne tent at Wimbledon yesterday. 'Nope – we've seen no sign of that.' In fact, the only crunch to be heard from Centre Court was that of ice in cold glasses of Pimm's. 'Yesterday a bloke came in and ordered four Jeroboams of Veuve

Clicquot [at £95 each],' says Scally. 'The hotter the weather gets, the more money we make.' And that's not counting the rest: the luxury cushions to seat those ever-expanding corporate behinds (that'll be £15 please), the strawberries at £4.50 a punnet (40 pence a strawberry), ice-cream at £4.50 a scoop, £7 programmes and the useless but weirdly compelling giant tennis balls (£15, if you please). All in all, a decidedly un-recession day out.

But then Wimbledon has never attracted the likes of Ascot, has it? There's not a binge-drinker or a tattoo to be seen down in SW19. The women are kitted out in Jigsaw and Karen Millen, the men in Dunhill and Turnbull & Asser. Even the air seems more refined. 'In business terms, Wimbledon is just beneath the Chelsea Flower Show,' says Sir Victor Blank, the chairman of Lloyds TSB. 'It's immensely popular with the corporate *crème de la crème* and their partners. The food is very good here and it guarantees people a great day out.'

Up on Centre Court, Serena Williams's antics were proving a little too colourful for some. 'All that grunting should be banned,' commented one onlooker, prompting nods of disgusted approval from around about. 'It's intimidation, that's what it is – and men or women who make those kind of animalistic noises should be banned or given whopping great big fines.' That, however, was the only small break in the serenity. The wonder of Wimbledon is that it in no way represents the real Britain – just a wonderful, nostalgic vision of what our trouble-beset little isle should be like.

5 JULY 2008

ROBSON WINS WIMBLEDON GIRLS' TITLE, AGED 14

Laura Robson's Wimbledon debut came to a fairytale end as she defeated Thailand's Noppawan Lertcheewakarn 6–3, 3–6, 6–1 to claim the girls' singles title. A packed Court No. 1 saw the unseeded 14-year-old become the youngest winner of the title since Martina Hingis in 1994 – ironically the year Robson was born. Lertcheewakarn, the third seed, struggled to contain Robson's aggressive style in a one-sided opening set, but she capitalised when the south Londoner inexplicably fell apart in the second. Having done all the hard work with a break in the bank, Robson's authority suddenly deserted her and the tenacious Thai took control. But by the third Robson, the last home player standing at the Championships, had recovered her composure to become the first British winner of the girls' title since Annabel Croft in 1984. She will now be eligible for a wild card to the women's draw at SW19 next year and has dropped just one set during her march to Wimbledon glory.

VENUS WILLIAMS BEATS SERENA TO WIN FIFTH TITLE

Clive White

'It didn't work out as I planned,' said Serena Williams, an innocent post-match remark to the BBC's Sue Barker that could have been meant for the conspiracist, Elena Dementieva. If this result was pre-arranged, as the beaten Russian semi-finalist seemed to imply it would be, the Williams sisters should have received Oscars as well as the Venus Rosewater Dish and runners-up plate. That said, rarely has a Wimbledon final been contested more furiously yet watched with such total detachment by a Centre Court crowd, save perhaps when they last contested a final here five years ago. No doubt they enjoyed the spectacle and at one hour 51 minutes certainly got their money's worth, but no one, other than the two players on court, cared who won – and that probably included their mother Oracene and sisters Isha and Lynn. 'It's hard for all of 'em,' said the victor Venus Williams, adding mischievously, 'I like to think that they wanted me to win.'

It would have been nice if somebody did. Even Venus's celebrations – understandably – were muted. At least Serena's disappointment was tangible. The Centre Court crowd didn't seem to know who to support so they supported neither. For the most part it was an unusually hushed audience, even by Centre Court standards, which was a pity because some of the rallies and shot-making were of an exceptional quality and deserved rapturous applause. Some of their volleying was better than many men's.

It was a mystery how Venus managed to win because Serena seemed to be the one who was forcing the pace most of the time. She had a break point for a 4–1 lead in the first set and was a break up in the second but somehow managed to lose 7–5, 6–4. It was a result that confirmed Venus's position as one of the greatest grass-court players of modern times.

It was the defending champion's fifth Wimbledon title but she still has some way to catch Steffi Graf (seven) and Martina Navratilova (nine). It was her first Grand Slam success against her younger sister since their initial Grand Slam final meeting at the 2001 US Open. Serena leads 9–8 in all competitions.

The kid sister could hardly have got off to a better start, breaking Venus in the opening game. The weight of her shots then was too much for Venus, who took only one point from the first 11. Venus, for some reason, was particularly troubled by the wind during her service games, frequently aborting throw-ups. When she eventually held serve, she did so with a reaction volley that was hit so hard, roughly in the direction of her sister, that one was reminded of a specific piece of coaching advice from their father Richard, who once ordered Serena to 'take her eye out!' in a training session with her big sister. It seemed only a matter of time before Serena broke her sister again. Up until the 11th game she won at least two points on every Venus serve and then with Venus's first break point of the match she broke back for four all. When Venus passed her with a great running forehand in the next game the look of loathing on her sister's face should have been enough to ensure that Dementieva never again questioned the honesty of their matches – or, come to that, simply their honesty.

With Venus serving on game point, Serena hit a shot that appeared to be going wide. But as she shrieked out in disappointment the ball landed in. The umpire called a let, but after a short discussion at the chair Serena conceded the game. Venus was asked whether she could imagine other girls on the Sony Ericsson Tour conceding the point. 'No,' she answered. 'Serena is the ultimate sportsperson. We both are. We don't take injury time-outs. We just play. We don't question too many calls. And I would expect her to be the ultimate sportsperson.'

From a position of power, Serena now found herself serving to stay in the set and finally a backhand into the net gave Venus the set. Serena did not take the setback well and feinted, two or three times, to smash her racket into the turf. Venus needed to pull out her best to stay in front and in the first game of the second set that included a Wimbledon record serve of 129mph, which beat her previous record by two miles. When a 16-minute game eventually ended with Serena clinching her fifth break point of the game for a 2–1 lead it looked significant, but she promptly surrendered the break. Instead she again found herself serving to stay in contention at 4–5, this time facing two match points. 'Three sets, please,' someone yelled out, but it was not the general consensus and, anyway, Serena couldn't oblige.

7 JULY 2008

NADAL ENDS FEDERER REIGN
AFTER FIVE-SET EPIC

Mark Hodgkinson

In the near-darkness of Centre Court last night, Rafael Nadal lifted Wimbledon's glinting gold trophy for the first time after he defeated Roger Federer in a five-set, almost five-hour final that will live long in the memory. So Federer's domination of the All-England Club lawns, which had lasted for five summers, came to an end at 9.16p.m. yesterday, when Federer hit a forehand into the net. Spain's world No. 2 won 6–4, 6–4, 6–7, 6–7, 9–7, to become the first man since Björn Borg in 1980 to do the French Open and Wimbledon double in the same summer. He was also the first Spaniard to win Wimbledon since Manuel Santana in 1966.

Nadal had previously held two Championship points in the fourth-set tie-break. But Federer saved them both, on the second hitting a backhand pass down the line that will be replayed 10,000 times over on television screens and also in the cinema in his own head. A weaker man than Nadal could have folded after that, but the 22-year-old from Majorca steadied his nerve for the decider. This was almost five hours of drama-filled tennis. Chants of 'Roger, Roger' competed with 'Rafa, Rafa' on Centre Court. Up in Federer's VIP player box, his girlfriend Mirka Vavrinec, and the rock-star couple of Gavin Rossdale and Gwen Stefani, shook their fists in appreciation. Nadal's coach and uncle, Toni, looked as though he had gnawed his fingernails down to his elbows.

Nadal, although naturally right-handed, plays tennis with the racket in his left hand, and there were occasions when Federer must have felt as though he was facing an opponent with two forehands. Twice Federer had chances to break Nadal as the Spaniard served for the set, but both amounted to nothing. Most disappointing of all for Federer's supporters was when, after Nadal sent over a second serve at 91mph, all the defending champion could do was slice his return halfway up the net. Nadal closed out the set when Federer netted a backhand. That was the first set that Federer had dropped all tournament. Federer, though, came right back at Nadal in the second set, and established a 4–1 lead. But Nadal never allowed Federer to settle. Nadal's tennis was making the crowd coo and gasp; he struck one extraordinary retrieval shot from behind him as he performed the best pirouette you are ever going to see outside of London's Covent Garden. And Federer also had an idiot in the crowd to deal with. Federer could have had a break point for a 5–3 lead but as Nadal's shot looped towards him at deuce in the eighth game, and he waited at the net, someone chose that moment to shout out 'C'mon, Roger'. And that cry so distracted Federer that he both fired his forehand drive volley long over the baseline and then fired a nasty look in the direction of the rogue spectator.

But there was more controversy to come. Nadal was serving for a two-set lead, bouncing the ball behind the baseline as he prepared to send down a delivery at 5–4, 30–30, when umpire Pascal Maria warned the Spaniard for taking too much time between points. True, Nadal had been moving slowly between points, but was that really the time for the umpire to intervene? Surely a quiet word during the change-over would have been more intelligent officiating? But Nadal overcame that unnecessary drama, and a break point for Federer, to win the second set.

Such was the pre-thunderstorm gloom during the third set that almost the only things that you could make out on Centre Court were the numbers glowing on the electronic scoreboard, Boris Johnson's blond hair in the second row of the Royal Box, and a yellow ball flashing from side to side. It was a surprise that the umpire didn't offer night-vision goggles or miners' headlamps to the players. Break-point chances came and went for Federer. But Nadal also had an opportunity to break for a 4–3 lead when he had Federer at 0–40 on his serve, but the Swiss held on and let out a loud cry of 'C'mon'. Two more games passed in the near-darkness, so Federer was 5–4 up with the set on serve, when the rain started, and the green tarpaulin came across. They were off the court for 80 minutes, but on the resumption, Federer had the edge as the third set was completed with a tie-break. Federer served superbly in the shoot-out, hitting four aces through into the backstop, to take it 7–5.

The fourth set was also decided on a tie-break, and a switchback tie-break at that. Nadal led 5–2, but Federer came back to hold a set point at 6–5, only to fire a forehand into the tramlines. Nadal had his first Championship point at 7–6, only for Federer to produce an unreturnable serve that touched the line. At 7–7, Nadal was forced wide, but came up with the passing shot of the tournament, striking a forehand winner down the line with all the explosive power and precision of a laser-guided missile. So that gave Nadal his second match point. But Federer wasn't to be outdone, and he stayed in the final by threading a backhand winner down the line. It was even better than Nadal's shot. Extraordinary. And Federer won that tie-break 10–8 when Nadal struck a return long.

It was just before 8p.m., and 2–2, deuce on Federer's serve in the fifth set, when the rains came back to interrupt. After a break of around half an hour, they were back. A forehand winner from Federer gave him a break point for a possible 5–3 lead, but Nadal saved it with an overhead winner. And next it was Federer's turn to get himself out of trouble, as, at 5–5, 15–40, he saved a couple of break points. At 7–7, Federer saved three more break points. But, on the fourth, Federer hit a forehand long to give Nadal the break. Federer saved Nadal's third match point with a great return. On the fourth, though, Federer netted.

8 JULY 2008

OUTCOME WAS DECIDED BY THE DEGREE SPANIARD HAS RAISED GRASS GAME

Boris Becker

Rafael Nadal won the best final in Wimbledon history not just because of the drama but because of the stakes. At stake was Roger Federer becoming the first man in more than a century to win the tournament six years in succession. At stake was Nadal becoming the first Spanish men's champion in 42 years, and the first man since Björn Borg to claim the French Open and Wimbledon titles in the same season. For all those reasons this was the best final, across all the Grand Slams, that I have seen.

The outcome was decided not, ultimately, by any clear dip in form from Federer but by the degree to which Nadal improved on grass. Both players knew how close the outcome had been last year, when Nadal lost in five sets, and this time he came into Wimbledon with more skills and more shots. I had doubted, unlike many, whether he would be able to dethrone a five-time champion and yet on Sunday he still outperformed perhaps the best player the game has known. The margins were fine but there was a sense of a changing of the order because Nadal, at the age of 22, has time on his side.

Nadal fully deserved his moment of triumph and he showed, in his comments afterwards about Federer still being the best, what a humble man he could be. But beyond their mutual respect everyone on tour realises that they will head into the rest of the season with Nadal established as the official world No. 1, and Federer as No. 2. Nadal has finally shown, after four French Open victories, that his game is about far more than clay-court tennis and that he can beat his main rival on the surface where Federer has been supreme. The one concern is over Nadal's physical state. I am not at all surprised that he has pulled out of this week's event in Stuttgart on clay, because over the next month he has the Olympics and US Open for which to prepare. We saw how he constantly needed his knees strapping up at Wimbledon and so he has, for the sake of his body, to stop for a while. He has had a summer of non-stop tennis – three days after winning at Roland Garros he was at Queen's Club. Something you can always be sure of with Nadal is that he will never be lazy about his status.

Perhaps an even bigger question is where Federer goes from here, how he adapts to his new position as arguably the world's second best player. He will stay at No. 1 in the rankings for the time being, but this is fresh territory for him. It was never more in evidence than in the Wimbledon final that these two push each other to greater and greater extremes, and this will have to continue if Federer wants to stay at the top and to prolong this great rivalry. Still, I think, that as the defeated finalist we have to salute Roger. I must confess that I was a little disappointed in his performance in the first two sets, when his first serve seemed to desert him and Nadal looked as if he might win easily. But Federer never stopped fighting – not only did he come back from two sets down, he came back from three Championship points down.

But then I knew Federer would have to come out swinging after those first two sets, putting the pressure on Nadal's serve. But Nadal's first-serve percentage was very good throughout and he kept serving to Federer's backhand, the weaker side. For Federer the only option when he could not break the serve was to make Nadal play one more shot, to get himself into the rallies and eventually take his chances. He did that in the third and fourth sets, but Nadal is the marathon man; he loves the long matches. Both of them, playing for more than four hours, must have been feeling strain in their legs. With the rain delays there was the issue of moisture on the court, which tends to benefit the attacking player – and that, as we have seen so many times, is Federer. But Nadal was equal to him, even when he had just lost two tie-breaks narrowly. It did not surprise me that he had the mental strength to gather himself for the fifth, but this was still an incredible match to win. We have a new king of tennis.

8 JULY 2008

NORRIS, OLD SPORT, I WAS FULFILLING MY CIVIC DUTY AT CENTRE COURT

Boris Johnson

It was round about halfway through the second set and things were hotting up on Centre Court when I noticed the mobile starting to flash silently in my breast pocket. Furtively I fished it out. There was no choice. You have to be on call. Even in the throes of the greatest tennis match ever played, you have to be ready to respond to events. I saw that someone had sent me a text. Was it news of a burst main on the Marylebone Road? Had the police made some breakthrough? It was my old mucker Steve Norris, and here was the message he had the effrontery to send me. 'Shouldn't you be attending to civic duties,' texted Nozza, 'rather than swanning around in the Royal Box at Wimbledon?'

I am afraid I was simply too engrossed in the game to reply, and so here – belatedly – is the reason, Steve, old horse, why I spent the bulk of Sunday watching tennis. I was there because I had never been to Wimbledon before, and I discovered that it is just about the sublimest thing this country has to offer. Oh, it wasn't just the flummery of the Royal Box, though I must say that the quality of the entertainment was stratospheric. It was the game that was the thing. It was the theatre. It was a pageant that told you all you needed to know about the human condition. In the four-hour, 48-minute struggle between Roger Federer and Rafael Nadal we saw the eternal conflict between time and talent. Any human activity – sport, art, literature, politics, even journalism – will produce its dominating exponent. There always seems to be someone who possesses a God-gifted ability to command the stage; until the years go by, and nature starts to take her course, and the sap runs more thickly in the veins of the master, and the younger talents start to snap at his heels. And slowly experience becomes no substitute for energy, and genius finally loses out to sheer hunger – and that is what happened on Centre Court on Sunday.

When I think of the great Wimbledon champions of my lifetime, I think of the pathetic moment when they were eventually tipped off the pedestal. Borg was mighty in his time, wielding his wooden racket two-fisted like a Viking Berserker; and yet even in the moment when he snogged that trophy for the fifth time, his tendons were becoming invisibly less full of snap, and his fabled monocular vision was getting imperceptibly foggier, and he was ripe to be displaced by the genius of McEnroe; and then McEnroe's magic was gone and everyone idolised Becker until Becker made his last leap and the era of Sampras was ushered in, Sampras who served like a bullet to win seven times until he was himself usurped by some gigantic Croat with a gigantic serve.

Now the amazing Federer, who had won five times in a row, has both depressed and consoled us with the fact of his professional mortality. Of course I was on the side of Federer, especially since his opponent had a peculiar habit of bending forward before every point and tugging from behind at the gusset of his shorts. It was very rum indeed. There we were in the Royal Box, with the President of Switzerland and assorted dukes, duchesses and the heir to the Spanish throne, and Rafael Nadal seemed to be unable to sort out what is known as a serious wedgie. I pointed this out delicately to one of the tennis supremos, and he said that it was a well-known Nadal phenomenon. This pant-twanging was a ritual, he said, like saying a Hail Mary, and the challenger had been doing it since he was eight. I suppose I might have forgiven him for that, because we all suffer from some sort of obsessive-compulsive disorder, but sometimes there was also frankly too much Nadal soundtrack to the rally.

The Swiss champion was silent, and almost impassive, while Nadal would yelp with each shot like a loose fan-belt. And while both men played shots of extraordinary creativity, and while I found myself rubbing my palms and jiggling up and down at the suspense of the rallies, it struck me that Federer was the true merchant of style. Nadal certainly carved huge quantities of top spin from the ball, and yet there was a rasping clunking noise as he hit it. Federer seemed to serve faster and more smoothly, with less effort, and, though he made a few unforced errors, there were some shots which seemed to approach the Platonic ideal. The Greek philosopher said there were these things out there called the Forms, eternal perfect examples of worldly things. Well, we don't need to look for the Form of the cross-court forehand zinger – it was forged on Sunday afternoon by the racket of Roger. And yet, somehow, we all knew that Nadal had the edge. Every time the rally went beyond five or six shots, you felt the Spaniard was the more dangerous, and so the crowd did that wonderful British thing: they got behind the underdog. Ro-ger! clap, clap, clap, they went, and as the evening wore on, the passions rose.

The crowd started to gasp at every point like a huge vacuum cleaner. Roger recovered his energy, and the shades lengthened, and the pigeons started to swoop across the court as though they had no idea of the titanic battle taking place. It was just magic, and it struck me that it could not happen anywhere else but the Centre Court at Wimbledon. I feel grateful beyond words to have been there and, if you really want to know, the last incumbent of my present office didn't go once in eight years – and refused to visit this wonderful adornment of London, even when the tournament was not in progress. How can we hope to produce a champion of our own, when some politicians are still so idiotic as to pretend it is an elitist sport? So that's why I felt it necessary to watch the tennis on Sunday, Steve. It was not only a joy to take the hospitality of the Royal Box. It was a civic duty.

MURRAY MADE TO FIGHT TOOTH AND NAIL

Mark Hodgkinson

Welcome to Wimbledon after dark and after hours. A daytime outdoor tournament suddenly became a night-time indoor event last night. And with Andy Murray needing five sets to beat Switzerland's Stanislas Wawrinka under Centre Court's closed roof and artificial lights, it was after 10.30p.m. when he moved into the quarter-finals on the Wimbledon grass for the second summer in succession. This was comfortably the latest finish in the history of the Championships, Murray even pushing back the *Ten o'Clock News* on BBC One. And we used to think that Tim Henman's teatime thrillers were late.

These sort of late-night matches are commonplace under the lights of the Australian Open's Melbourne Park and the US Open's Flushing Meadows, but not at the All-England Club. Murray was not always at his best at the late-night Wimbledon Championships. The 15,000 spectators on Centre Court were still adjusting to the brave new world at the All-England Club of indoor tennis on the grass, when they were also asked to deal with the sight of Murray making a slow start against Switzerland's No. 2. 'Come on, Andy, bloody hell,' someone blurted out early on in the match. And there were a few more 'bloody hell' moments to come before Murray made the last eight once more, setting up tomorrow's match with Spain's Juan Carlos Ferrero, a former world No. 1. Murray had been on court for almost four hours when he completed a 2–6, 6–3, 6–3, 5–7, 6–3 win.

When Murray joined Wimbledon's Last Eight Club last season, he did so by coming back from two sets down to beat France's Richard Gasquet. That had been tense and late, but not as tense and as late as this. If a roof and lights had not been available yesterday, the match would have been halted because of poor light. Just as he had done against Gasquet, Murray used the energy of the crowd against Wawrinka. Murray used so much emotional energy during last year's win over Gasquet that he ended up putting in a flat performance on his next appearance, losing in straight sets to the eventual champion, Spain's Rafael Nadal. A year on, Murray should be able to handle the situation a little better against Ferrero.

One theory that has been doing the rounds at the grass-court slam has been that the Centre Court roof would help Murray's chances of becoming the first British man to win Wimbledon since Fred Perry 73 years ago. Murray has won seven of his 12 career titles under a roof and learned to play indoors. The weather was so poor when Murray was growing up in Dunblane that, between the ages of eight and 15, the majority of his tennis was played with a roof over his head, at an indoor centre down the road in Stirling. Playing indoors supposedly helps Murray to establish a rhythm on his serve, as he does not have to worry about the wind or the glare from the sun as he tosses up the ball. That was the theory, anyway. The reality was that Murray was not hitting the ball cleanly in the opening stages of his first grass-court meeting with Wawrinka, the world No. 18 and Switzerland's best player after Roger Federer. Early on, Murray was desperately searching for his touch, like someone trying to locate a piece of bread at the bottom of a fondue. In the first set, Wawrinka was hitting almost everything off the honey-spot of his strings, and Murray plainly was not. Under a closed roof, the sound of a ball coming off the strings is always going to sound a bit different to how it would in an open-air stadium. But Murray's tennis did not sound right. Or look right.

The roof had been closed for the end of Dinara Safina's win over Amelie Mauresmo. And the decision was made to keep it closed for Murray's appearance. If he was not involved in the first match that featured the roof, he was at least playing in the first match to start indoors. An outdoor tournament had suddenly become an indoor one. And Murray's form was not quite the same as it had been for the three outdoor matches that had preceded this. Murray started poorly, losing the first set. But he gathered himself, winning the second and third sets. Wawrinka refused to go away, taking the match into a decider. Murray broke early in the fifth set, only to lose his advantage. Still, he broke for 5–3, and then served it out.

I JULY 2009

FLOODLIT WIMBLEDON – HOW WAS IT FOR YOU?

FOR – CASSANDRA JARDINE

I don't know which was more exciting: Andy Murray and Stanislas Wawrinka slugging it out in those long rallies, or Monday night's battle for

BBC airtime. As the players notched up two sets each in the first three hours, one by one discreet little pop-ups announced that the old stalwarts of programming were being knocked into the tramlines. First *EastEnders* moved to BBC2, then *Crimewatch,* and finally the *Ten o'Clock News* team were sent to kick their heels in the locker-room for a full 45 minutes while the final set was played. Since, by the end, no fewer than 11.8 million of us were glued to our screens, the first outing of the new, all-weather, any-hours Centre Court roof must be judged a resounding success. And didn't it look thrilling when the camera panned backwards during banana-breaks to show the giant light-box that seemed to have landed, like ET's spaceship, in the dark of London SW19? The biggest drawback was the difficulty of getting my ten-year-old to go to bed.

The roof, and its lights, are the best new developments in British tennis since women emerged from long skirts. But that won't stop those who hate change moaning about the good old days. The sun, the shadows, the wind: if they go, strawberries and Pimm's must surely follow. And, oh, what fun it was flipping channels to Wimbledon every half-hour to be greeted with yet another picture of the covers on and rain coming down in stair rods. I shall not miss those melancholy moments when the camera panned over empty seats, Cliff Richard sang, and commentators filibustered about the prospects of the tournament going into a third week. Farewell, too, to all those tedious old cracks about Swimbledon and Wimbleduck, the subtext of which was that this country wallows in its reputation as the home of the stoical loser.

It was bad enough for Brits to find rain had stopped play just as they hit the after-work sofa, but how much drearier was it for fans on the other side of the world who set their alarms for 3a.m. only to find they could take their cup of tea back to bed? Since the advent of the cover they will be saying 'thank you', just as often as the umpire on Monday politely ticked off noisy spectators waving Union Flags. Vulgar, glitzy, gladiatorial: yes, yes, yes. This is tennis for the time-poor, buzz-craving denizens of the 21st century. So, hooray for CBS and the other networks who put pressure on Wimbledon's organisers to cover over. Those who pay to broadcast the matches to 1.8 billion people in 131 countries aren't the only ones who don't enjoy a fortnight of uncertainty. Football fans don't have to tolerate damp teams trailing off the pitch, so why should tennis lovers? It may be tiring for the players, but I would rather watch a great match through to the end. Far better that than the bathos of sitting in the office next day to hear, mid-afternoon, that last night's cliffhanger had been concluded and, guess what, Henman had lost after all.

But it's just not cricket, mutter those who would rather see the tournament die than evolve. Talking of which, the same forces of commercialism have vastly improved that game, too. With Twenty20 competitions – where the emphasis is on scoring runs rather than killing time – and new drainage systems, cricket has ceased to be a sport only for those who choose to enter a coma. Until a couple of years ago, I had never willingly watched a match, let alone bought a ticket for one. Now I love every last pompom-waving, screen-flashing moment.

Covered matches will inevitably change tennis. A good thing too. After tedious years watching serve-and-volley games packed with all the drama of clay-pigeon shooting, soggy balls are making for slower, longer rallies. And, amplified under cover, the resounding pings that accompany each hit add to the fun. Wimbledon has not lost its specialness. No one has suggested swapping the grass for concrete. And for those who really hate uninterrupted play, there are still 18 other courts. There, the diehards can enjoy a great day out, cradling a cup of tea, contemplating their wasted money, waiting for the action to start.

AGAINST – PHILIP JOHNSTON

It was when Garry Richardson walked on to the Centre Court shortly after 10.30p.m. on Monday to interview an exhausted Andy Murray before he had even made it to the locker-room that you began to wonder whether Wimbledon was changing for ever. And not for the better, either. Of course it was a great spectacle. Anyone coming home after work at 8p.m. or so and expecting to see the usual diet of mixed doubles from Court 14 involving a quartet of anonymous eastern Europeans was treated to a gladiatorial clash of epic proportions. But it did seem odd to someone who lives in Wimbledon and can, therefore, testify to what a beautiful sunny evening it was that the match was being played after dark at all. The decision to use the All-England Club's £80 million roof for the first time had been taken in the previous match when there had been a spot or two of rain; but it need not have been kept on for the Murray match – and, since this is meant to be an outdoor sporting event, nor should it have been. The roof ensured the game could be finished in prime television time, an additional bonus for the BBC, which cleared its schedules to continue coverage at the expense of the *Ten o'Clock News* and was rewarded with a record audience for what was not even a quarter-final.

Presumably, the urgent need to get on with the rest of its programmes led to the bizarre spectacle of Richardson wandering on to the Centre Court to bombard a bewildered Murray with his familiar litany of fatuous 'how do you feel' questions. Cannot a sporting triumph be enjoyed for its own sake any more without being filtered through a protopsychological interrogation? What is happening to Wimbledon? On Monday night, John McEnroe, who was among the commentators, said he never thought he would live to see the day when the venerable club would host a match played under covers and with an electronic monitor to sort out disputed line calls.

Floodlit, covered tennis late into the night is terrific entertainment but it is not what the tournament is about, otherwise why not simply keep the roof on the showcase court all the time? As Murray said, it means playing in more humid conditions, the ball slows down and, over time, the grass would wear out more quickly. Soon, there could be suggestions that Wimbledon would be better without grass; after all, the other three major championships – the US, French and Australian – used to be played on grass but are no longer. Of course Wimbledon has changed over the years: unnoticed by most, the scoreboards for women's matches have this year dropped 'Miss' or 'Mrs' before players' names; players don't wear long white trousers any more (they still wear white, mind you, though for how much longer?); improved racket technology enables modern players to make shots about which past champions could only have dreamed; and men and women are paid the same prize money.

But there used to be an old-fashioned gentility about Wimbledon that is rapidly disappearing. Until relatively recently, it was possible for those without show-court tickets to get in to see matches on the outside courts and enjoy the atmosphere without having to queue for hours, something youngsters are prepared to do but their parents aren't. The younger age profile has contributed to greater boisterousness. To see crowds routinely breaking into a Mexican wave while matches are still in progress is unnerving: it may be a way of keeping up spirits during a rain break, but isn't the tennis itself entertainment enough? The dreaded wave has also intruded into Test cricket at Lord's, though it is invariably brought up short when it reaches the Pavilion, since the members steadfastly refuse to join in. Nevertheless, cricket has already succumbed to the demotic (and financial) pressures of our times with the onset of Twenty20 and its razzmatazz, colour and nail-biting finishes. How long before a Test match is played under floodlights with a white ball, with all that entails for the conditions and the wicket? When you see Garry Richardson standing in the slips, microphone in hand, then we will know the game is up.

2 JULY 2009

LETTER TO THE EDITOR

THE GOOD, THE BAD AND THE UGLY AT WIMBLEDON

Sir,

On Monday, we were one of the lucky spectators to enjoy watching Andy Murray under the new roof, and what a match it was. Without the roof, we would have been lucky to see two or three sets. However, there were empty seats on Centre Court because of concern about getting home at such a late hour. There were no Wimbledon buses to take people back to the tube and railway stations and only a small line of taxis waiting. Now the roof is working so well, please could officials sort out the transportation?

Veronica Bliss
Compton, Hampshire

4 JULY 2009

MURRAY HAS TALENT TO RISE AGAIN

Mark Hodgkinson

With Andy Roddick hitting the ball beautifully in the Centre Court sunshine, Andy Murray resorted to hitting his fists against his strings in frustration at how the match was playing out as his Wimbledon ended in the semi-finals. So Bunny Austin, a finalist in 1938, remains the last British man to have featured in a title match on the grass of the All-England Club. Murray joined Mike Sangster, Roger Taylor and Tim Henman on the list of British players to have reached the semi-finals here, but to have gone no further. British men in Wimbledon semi-finals are now on a nine-match losing streak.

The expected mistakes from Roddick's racket never came. For the British tennis public, the wrong Andy went through into the final. Roddick's strings had one use out there on the grass; to play excellent tennis. Murray occasionally biffed and bashed his hand against his strings when events turned against him. Nothing much worked out for him on his first appearance in a Wimbledon semi-final — he was falsely accused of swearing by the umpire, and received a warning for 'an audible obscenity', even though the 22-year-old's language was as clean as the dialogue from *Little House on the Prairie.*

The semi-final should be remembered for a smart, controlled, powerful performance from Roddick, which included some of the best tennis he has played on the lawns of London. So, instead of Murray going through to a first Wimbledon final, to play Roger Federer for the Challenge Cup, it was Roddick who made the second Sunday at the grass-court Grand Slam for the third time, as he won 6–4, 4–6, 7–6, 7–6. Roddick was the runner-up to Federer on Centre Court in 2004 and 2005, and he has lost 18 of their 20 career meetings. Even so, if he can play as well against Federer as he did against Murray, there is still a possibility that he can win the second slam title of his career, six years after his first at the 2003 US Open. This plainly is not the end of Murray's Wimbledon story: he is going to be back at this stage again, deep in the draw.

5 JULY 2009

SERENA FLAUNTS HER ASSETS

Mark Hodgkinson

'Are you looking at my titles?' was the provocative slogan on the front of the T-shirt that Serena Williams was wearing at the All-England Club, a couple of hours after the women's final. No one could ever accuse Serena of suddenly coming over all coy. And, yes, everyone at Wimbledon yesterday couldn't help but obsess over Serena's 'titles'. If you've got it, flaunt it. By beating her older sister Venus in an all-American, all-Williams final that was played on the Fourth of July, Serena won her third Venus Rosewater Dish and the 11th Grand Slam title of her career. So Serena now has three of the four Grand Slam titles in her possession, since she was also the champion at last season's US Open and at this year's Australian Open. But, as Serena doesn't also hold the French Open trophy, you could say that the Californian doesn't quite have a perfect set of 'titles'.

Serena is the world No. 2. Dinara Safina, a Russian, has never won a slam, and she's the world No. 1. Work that one out. Venus had been hoping to win Wimbledon for the third summer in succession, and for the sixth time in her career, and she is regarded as one of the all-time grass-court greats. But yesterday on Centre Court she wasn't even the best grass-court player in her own family.

There can be little doubt over who is the extrovert of the two sisters. It wasn't a T-shirt that you could ever imagine Venus wearing. 'This T-shirt is available in stores, if you guys want to go get one,' said Serena, who had also worn the top when out jogging in Wimbledon Village during the fortnight. 'Everyone can have one. I've been wearing it a little bit during the tournament. I thought last night when I was getting my stuff together, "Well, if I win, I'll wear the T-shirt because then I'll have 11 titles and I wouldn't know if everyone was looking at my titles or",' and she paused for effect, '"at my Gatorade bottle".' On the entertainment scale of one to classic, this final was about a three or a four, with Serena winning 7–6, 6–2.

The Williams girls are now 3–1 in Wimbledon finals, as Serena defeated Venus in the 2002 and 2003 title matches, and Venus beat Serena last year. All of Serena's three Wimbledon titles have come from beating Venus in the final. Serena has won six of her eight slam finals against her older sister. The power of Serena's shots gave her the Dish. When Venus lost the tie-break, it was the first set she had dropped on these grass courts since a third-round match at the 2006 tournament. Serena didn't have a break-point chance in that opening set. Venus had a couple, and yet she couldn't convert either. Venus, who had been hoping to become the first woman to win three successive titles here since Steffi Graf in the early 1990s, has been wearing strapping around her left knee for most of the tournament, and her movement certainly appeared to be a little restricted yesterday. In the second set, Venus didn't hit the ball with as much pace as she had done in the first set, and she was broken twice, the second time for the match. On the fourth match point, Venus put a backhand into the net, and Serena dropped to her knees. 'She was too good. She had an answer for everything,' said Venus, who, sportingly, didn't want to make too much of 'a fuss' about her knee. So Serena's most difficult contest of the Championships was in the semi-finals against Elena Dementieva, Russia's Olympic champion, when she had to stave off a match point, and not in the final against her sister. Yesterday was all about Serena flaunting her 'titles'.

6 JULY 2009

'LEGEND' FEDERER REWRITES HISTORY BOOK
Mark Hodgkinson

This was the day when Andy Roddick's serve was broken just the once, in the 77th game of a 77-game Wimbledon men's final. That one break of Roddick's delivery, after more than four and a quarter hours of play on

Centre Court, was all that Roger Federer needed to take the fifth set 16–14, to become the first man to win 15 Grand Slams, and to regain the world No. 1 ranking. 'Roger is a legend, an icon and a stud,' said Pete Sampras, who had flown in from California to sit in the front row of the Royal Box to see his 14 slams being superseded. It would seem that winning the men's Wimbledon singles final in straight sets, or in anything approaching a straightforward manner, has gone out of tennis fashion. Federer's 5–7, 7–6, 7–6, 3–6, 16–14 victory meant that, going on the number of games that had been played on Centre Court, this was the longest Wimbledon final of all time, plus the longest final played at any of the four majors, and the 30-game fifth set was the longest played in a title match at the majors.

Just a year ago we had the longest Wimbledon men's final, if you measure a match with the clock, as Rafael Nadal required four hours 48 minutes to beat Federer 9–7 in the fifth set, when the stadium was so dark that the umpire should have provided night-vision goggles. This was half an hour shorter than last year's final, and last summer's Nadal–Federer match remains at the top of the leaderboard of greatest finals contested on these lawns. Though Federer started slowly yesterday, he won a sixth Wimbledon trophy, putting him just one short of Sampras's record seven titles – something to aim for next summer.

Roddick turned in one of the sharpest performances of his tennis life, and yet when he returned to the locker-room he had pink-tinged eyes, and he was holding the silver runners-up plate, and not the champion's golden, pineapple-shaped trophy. This was the third time that Roddick had lost a Wimbledon final, after defeats to Federer in 2004 and 2005, but this was the most difficult for the American to accept. 'Tennis is cruel,' said Federer, who was in Roddick's position last summer: emotionally battered. Now Federer is the happiest that tennis has seen him. This month, he and his wife Mirka will become parents for the first time. If Federer had not broken Roddick in the 30th game of the fifth set, they might have ended up playing through the night and into this morning. The fifth set was extraordinary. Serving at 8–8, Federer found himself at 15–40, but he produced a couple of big serves to get back to deuce, and he held. When Roddick came out to serve at 14–15, it was the 11th time that he had got up off his chair to serve to stay in the match. Roddick had won his previous 37 service games. A forehand error from Roddick's racket brought up match point for Federer. Another forehand mistake from Roddick, and the match was over. Federer had served 50 aces in the match, just one fewer than Ivo Karlovic's Wimbledon record.

Federer's reaction to victory was to leap into the air. Roddick's reaction, after an embrace with Federer at the net, was to fling his racket on to the grass, and to then sit down on his change-over chair, and to put his head in his hands as he waited for the prize-giving ceremony. Meanwhile, Federer put on a white tracksuit with a golden '15' embroidered on the back.

It was not just the closeness of the fifth set that would have been so upsetting for the American, it was also the fact that he had held four points in the second-set tie-break to go two sets up, and on the fourth of those, when he had most of the court to play with, he could not keep his backhand volley inside the lines.

Sampras had jumped on a plane to watch Federer, a close friend. It was the American's first visit to Wimbledon since he lost early in the 2002 Championships to a Swiss sub-journeyman player, George Bastl. This was not about Federer confirming his place as the greatest player to have picked up a racket and swished it at a tennis ball, as he had already done that by winning his first French Open last month. This was about the accumulation of Grand Slam titles, about Federer becoming the most successful player in history.

6 JULY 2009

RODDICK STOPPED BELIEVING

Boris Becker

Roger Federer got lucky yesterday. He was playing for the world record of tennis, and the occasion got to him. Andy Roddick had the best chance of his career to win Wimbledon: the American's four squandered set points in the second-set tie-break were actually four virtual match points. Federer would not have come back from two sets down. But at that crucial moment, Roddick stopped believing. It is the few grains of doubt, or just not being comfortable in that situation, which make all of the difference.

The same can be said of the fifth set. The decider in a Grand Slam final is not about what your coach has told you, but about instinct and emotion. Both men put themselves on the line, but when you are so close to what you have worked your whole life towards, you can get second thoughts – almost like cold feet. Roddick was one point away from serving for his first Wimbledon title in that last set, but he couldn't take it. Federer needed only one Championship point, which tells you everything. He broke Roddick's serve only in the last game of the match. That is percentage tennis. Roddick had played exceptionally well. It was not only his serve — that's where it starts, of course, but once the ball was in play he was the aggressor, controlling the points from the baseline, coming to the net, going for the lines. It was Roddick who dictated the tempo, and I was surprised — as I believe Federer was — that he could keep it up so consistently.

As it was, Federer won because of who he is. Because he is the greatest tennis player of all time, because he is the six-times Wimbledon champion, a 15-times Grand Slam winner. He has been so dominant over the past six years that he had the experience and character to stand there as Roddick came forward and attacked, and even though he was not having his best day, Federer knew he would make it hard for Roddick to win. That is the quality that he has. I hear that after he had showered up he changed into a T-shirt claiming that there is no finishing line. It is a good message, because the danger for Roger is running out of motivation. He is not just part of history; he is driven by history. He needs a new goal, but I don't know what that might be. At this point, 16 Grand Slams is the same as 15. He has to think about what is next. That, for me, is the slam, even if it is not in the calendar year. He will surely be thinking about winning the US Open and the Australian so that he has all four in a row, all four trophies in his possession at one time. It is something very few people have achieved.